A Concise History of
Architectural Styles

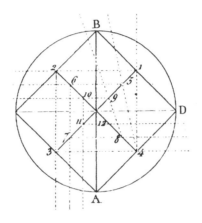

A Concise History of
Architectural Styles

Emily Cole General Editor

A & C BLACK · LONDON

LIST OF CONTRIBUTORS

PHILIPPA BAKER (Early Christian and Byzantine/ Domes) studied History of Art and Architecture at the University of Manchester and is a freelance editor specialising in art and architectural books.

SUSIE BARSON (Babylon, Assyria, Persia/Islamic/ Arches and Arcades) gained an MA in Architectural History at the Bartlett School of Architecture, University of London. She now works as an historian at English Heritage.

EMILY COLE (Pre-classical/Early and Classical India/Ancient Greece/Roofs/Towers) gained an MA at the Courtauld Institute, University of London, where she studied Architectural History; she now works as an historian for English Heritage.

MARIA FLEMINGTON (Neo-classical) has an MA in Architectural History from the Courtauld Institute, University of London. She now works as Collections Manager for the National Trust at Ham House, Surrey.

EMILY GEE (Classical Japan) has an MA in Architectural History from the University of Virginia, and works as an Inspector of Historic Buildings at English Heritage.

TESSA GIBSON (Romanesque/Windows) gained an MA in Architectural History at the Courtauld Institute, University of London, and now works for the National Trust.

EMMA LAUZE (Ancient Rome/Columns) has an Architectural History MA in Roman Urban Planning from the Courtauld Institute, University of London. Since completing her studies in 1994, she has worked at the Paul Mellon Centre for Studies in British Art on a variety of publishing and research projects.

MARY PESKETT-SMITH (Renaissance/ Pediments and Gables) has an MA in the Architectural History of Renaissance Rome from the Courtauld Institute, University of London. She is currently engaged in a research project at the Paul Mellon Centre for Studies in British Art.

EMILY RAWLINSON (Pre-Columbian/Baroque and Rococo/Palladianism/Doorways/Stairways) gained an MA in Architectural History at the Courtauld Institute, University of London, and now works for Pevsner Architectural Guides.

JAMES ROTHWELL (Gothic/Vaulting) gained an MA in Architectural History at the Courtauld Institute, University of London, and now works for the National Trust.

SARAH VIDLER (Ancient Egypt) obtained a BA (Hons) degree in Archaeology of the Eastern Mediterranean, University of Liverpool. She works for English Heritage.

ALICE YATES (Picturesque) read Architectural History at the University of Edinburgh and gained an MSc in Historic Conservation from Oxford Brookes University. She is currently Projects Assistant at the World Monuments Fund in Britain.

XU YINONG (Early and Dynastic China) has a PhD in Architectural and Urban History from the University of Edinburgh. He is Senior Lecturer in Architecture at the Faculty of the Built Environment, University of New South Wales, Australia.

First published in Great Britain 2003 by
A&C BLACK PUBLISHERS LTD
38 Soho Square, London W1D 3HB
www.acblack.com

Reprinted 2006

ISBN-10: 0 7136 6744 3
ISBN-13: 978 0 7136 6744 8

A CIP catalogue record for this book is available from the British Library

Cover design by Dorothy Moir.

Printed in China

This book was created by
THE IVY PRESS LTD
The Old Candlemakers, Lewes, East Sussex
BN7 2NZ

CREATIVE DIRECTOR Peter Bridgewater

PUBLISHER Sophie Collins

EDITORIAL DIRECTOR Steve Luck

DESIGN MANAGER Tony Seddon

DESIGNER Jane Lanaway

PROJECT EDITOR Caroline Earle

COPY EDITOR Mandy Greenfield

DTP DESIGNER Chris Lanaway

Contents

Introduction

A Concise History of Architectural Styles *renders accessible, to students and non-students alike, the vast range of architectural terminology used to describe buildings throughout the world and throughout history. The title achieves this not through the conventional method – an alphabetical glossary – but through a sequence of chronologically arranged chapters, each featuring a collection of fine line engravings accompanied by authoritative text.*

The chronological arrangement of this book allows the reader to place elements, forms, techniques and styles firmly within their context. Introductory passages provide a framework, covering the relevant religious, social, political, or economic background, and alluding to aspects such as siting, function, material and the role of the architect.

In addition, there is an illustrated chapter, covering ten elements common to the architecture of almost all periods and countries – columns, towers, arches and arcades, doorways, windows, pediments and gables, roofs, vaulting and stairways. The volume also features a glossary of terms that offers a quick reference point, giving succinct definitions of features raised and discussed within the main text.

The chronology of architectural styles begins with Egyptian architecture, and follows the major styles in use throughout history. Each style is broken down into headings, governed variously by building type, country or historical development. Where buildings are seen to be especially representative of a particular style – for example, the Parthenon for Greek architecture or Hagia Sophia for Byzantine – they are covered in some detail. The range of architectural vocabulary is reflected by the length of each chapter. For those styles that have long been studied in detail, in particular classical (Greek and Roman) and Gothic forms, complicated architectural terminology was developed early on, and they are discussed at length. Other styles – such as Pre-classical or Pre-Columbian – have been allowed less, because there is not as much non-specialist information available.

In every chapter, illustrations are used to display the elements and features that make a style characteristic, from ground plan to roof top. Special emphasis is given to ornament where it is integral to architectural effect.

The latest style covered in the chronology is the Picturesque movement of the late eighteenth and early nineteenth centuries. The architectural language that followed, in the later 1800s and early 1900s was, even more than that of the preceding generations, one of recurring motifs. Terminology remained for the most part traditional and set, and attention was given instead to building materials and methods of construction. One only need understand, for example, Gothic architectural terms in order to be able to codify and describe the buildings of the Gothic Revival, or Egyptian architectural terms to understand the details of the Egyptian Revival. Such omissions in coverage mean that this book cannot claim to give a complete overview of the history of world architecture, something already done, most notably, by Sir Banister Fletcher in his History of Architecture (first published in 1896 and still outstandingly valuable and relevant today). And yet this volume surpasses the boundaries of a conventional glossary. The addition of historical context to architectural vocabulary, which remains the book's primary focus, helps our understanding of buildings at a basic and fundamental level, avoiding the complex architectural analyses given in many histories. Such an approach makes the book accessible to those new to architecture, while also providing the information necessary for those keen to learn more.

A major feature of this volume is its illustrative material, derived from various eighteenth- and nineteenth-century architectural treatises, dictionaries and archaeological and topographical studies. The use of these illustrations – in the main, copper- and steel-plate engravings – is appropriate for many reasons. Their level of detail and accuracy is perfectly suited to this book's aims and subject matter. In a more general sense, the illustrations recall the era when a widespread interest in world architecture first emerged. With developments in printing and artistic technique from the early 1800s onward, illustrated books became commonplace, and were sought after by a new, larger and more varied reading public. In an age when foreign travel was far more difficult and expensive than today, topographical works provided a rare opportunity to learn about the scenery and buildings of distant lands. Many of the illustrations reproduced in this book derive from such works, which were themselves arranged in a similar way, with a text almost wholly made up of captions. The illustrations bring to mind the fascination that buildings must have inspired among architects, enthusiasts, scholars and patrons, and hint at the ever-present Victorian ideal of striving for knowledge in both art and science. Last, but by no means least, the illustrations of A Concise History of Architectural Styles make it aesthetically pleasing and a beautiful object to possess.

Architectural Styles

Ancient Egypt *3200–30 BC*

Mastabas

The architecture of ancient Egypt first flourished with the unification of Upper and Lower Egypt under the rule of the first pharaoh, Menes. During the course of the Old Kingdom (3200-2680 BC), the earliest evidence of Egyptian monumental architecture began to appear in the form of mastabas. Egyptian religion taught that the physical life was only temporary, while the spiritual life was eternal, and thus those monuments to eternity needed to endure. The tomb and the temple became the focus of this belief: the tomb providing the gateway to the afterlife and temples housing the gods. This ensured their careful planning, design and decoration, which combined the aesthetic with the utilitarian. Ancient Egyptian cities and palaces have collapsed back into the soil, but their spiritual homes still inspire modern architecture.

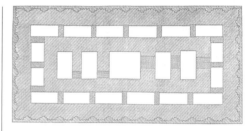

Mastaba
The mastaba ('bench' tomb) was designed to simulate the plan of an ancient Egyptian residence. It consisted of a regulated mound containing several small rooms covering a broad pit, allowing both space for the deceased and provisions for the afterlife. The structure was formed from wooden or crude mud-brick pillars covered in rubble and then walled in mud-brick.

Palace façade
The royal *mastaba* was often constructed using a façade of alternate projections and recesses. This is thought to derive from the timber panelling of early palaces, for the tomb was the residence of the king's spirit on earth. Formed from mud-brick, its origin may lie in the influence of Mesopotamian architecture. It was often brightly painted, and traces of highly coloured decoration survive.

Burial chamber
During the course of the 3rd and 4th Dynasties (2780–2565 BC) attention turned to the security of the tomb, and architectural innovations were concentrated inside the mastaba. The exterior became simpler, while the burial chamber itself – the owner's final resting place – was sunk deep into the rock, and protective measures, such as stone portcullises, were incorporated.

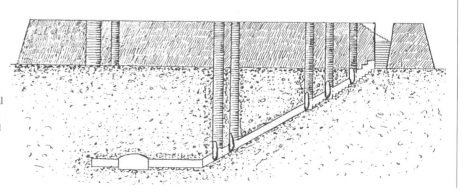

The 4th Dynasty (2680–2565 BC) saw the development of non-royal *mastaba* cemeteries in association with royal tombs. The occupants were high officials – the tomb was probably an honour bestowed by the pharaoh – and the tombs incorporated a small chapel: often a simple niche containing an offering table for dedications to the deceased.

False door

The tomb housed the deceased for eternity. A false door (a mud-brick or stone imitation of a wooden door included in the façade) allowed the occupant's spirit, or *ka*, to enter and leave the tomb at will. The 'door', usually on the eastern side of the tomb, faced the Nile, enabling the spirit to travel upon the river.

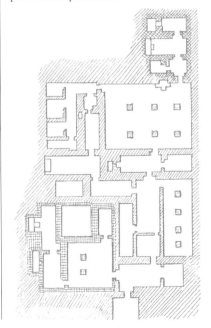

Plan form

The most sophisticated tombs contained many chambers, creating a full-scale residence for the deceased, as well as a gateway to eternity. The rooms were decorated in vivid relief with scenes of daily life and natural motifs, depicting the afterlife as an idealized parallel to Egypt. They included storerooms, a chapel, resting places and dining areas.

Mud-brick mastaba

Mud-brick, formed from a mixture of mud and straw, was the standard domestic building material in ancient Egypt. It lent itself readily to the arid climate and had been used on a monumental scale by the Mesopotamians in the construction of ziggurats (stepped temples). The use of mud-brick permitted the application of everyday techniques to monumental architecture.

Ancient Egypt

Pyramids

The architectural feature most strongly associated with ancient Egypt is the pyramid, commonly known through the Great Pyramid of Cheops at Giza, the only survivor of the seven wonders of the ancient world. The pyramids first appeared as tombs for royalty during the 3rd Dynasty (2780–2680 BC) and were perfected during the 4th, before being abandoned as the preferred royal necropolis during the Middle Kingdom (2134–1786 BC), when they were incorporated into the architecture of private tombs. Highly decorated inside with funerary spells (known as Pyramid Texts), the royal pyramid provided guidance for the dead pharaoh as well as shelter. The superstructure was believed to bring him closer to the sun god Re, with whom he traversed the sky, accompanied by his high officials, who were buried in mastabas alongside.

Step Pyramid of Saqqara (c. 2778 BC)
On the desert edge at Saqqara, the first pyramid enclosure of the 3rd-Dynasty king Djoser also contained a dummy palace, jubilee celebration buildings and temples. The step pyramid proved to be the most significant architectural innovation of the Old Kingdom. Its architect, Imhotep, was later deified.

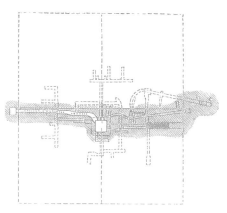

Rubble filling, Step Pyramid of Saqqara
With a superstructure of six mastabas creating the steps, the pyramid was built from earth and rubble, with a burial chamber cut into the bedrock. It was faced with stone carved to imitate timber and reed structures: the earliest experimentation with stone as a building material in monumental architecture.

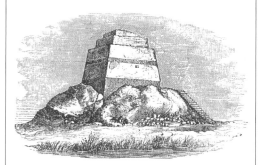

Pyramid of Meidum (3rd Dynasty)
Originally constructed as a seven-stepped pyramid, the surviving structure of Meidum consists of thick layers of masonry. The construction of this pyramid probably began under the reign of Huni and was completed as a true pyramid with angled sides during the reign of Snofru.

Cross-section, Meidum Pyramid
The transformation from step to true pyramid (although now lost) was enabled by facing the stepped infrastructure with limestone blocks cut on an angle to create a smooth surface. A total of eight layers of masonry stood above the burial chamber.

Pyramid of Unas, Saqqara (6th Dynasty)
This pyramid, a royal tomb situated adjacent to the step pyramid, is simple and poorly built. Its most notable feature is the decoration of hieroglyphs and imagery (Pyramid Texts) that was found here, providing instructions for the deceased's journey into the afterlife.

Abu Sir Pyramid complex (5th Dynasty)
The pyramid complex north of Saqqara included the pyramids of the three pharaohs, valley temples for reception of the deceased after transportation by river, and causeways leading to the mortuary temples, where the final offerings were made prior to burial within the pyramid.

Bent Pyramid, Dashur (c. 2723 BC)
Built during the reign of Snofru, this pyramid was never actually used. The sudden change in angle from 54 to 43 degrees gives it a 'bent' appearance, which was presumably necessary to support the superstructure. It contains a corbelled chamber and was faced with limestone.

Portcullis, Pyramid of Unas
Set into the passage leading to the burial chamber, portcullises demonstrated the need to protect the deceased from tomb robbers. Wooden props supported granite slabs until the mummy was *in situ*; removal of the props on exiting enabled the slabs to drop and seal the tomb.

Private pyramid, Abydos
From the Middle Kingdom onwards the pyramid became a feature of non-royal funerary architecture. Simple structures containing the fundamental elements found in royal tombs – a chapel and chamber capped by a brick pyramid – became a popular burial motif, even fronting rock-cut tombs.

Ancient Egypt

The Great Pyramid, Giza

The 4th-Dynasty pyramid complex at Giza marked the apex of the pyramid in ancient Egyptian architecture. Constructed during the reign of three generations of pharaohs – Cheops (grandfather), Chephren (father) and Mycerenus (son) – the complex contained all the architectural features associated with a royal tomb on a grand scale. Thousands of blocks of stone were transported by river and then dragged to the desert's edge by sled in order to build the pyramid. In due course the huge scale of the pyramids and their complex buildings led to tales of tyrannical cruelty under the Egyptian kings of the period, although the true nature of their construction remains unclear. The Great Pyramid of Cheops demonstrates the purest form of geometrical architecture and still inspires modern architecture, with contemporary buildings such as the Louvre Pyramid in Paris directly reflecting its form.

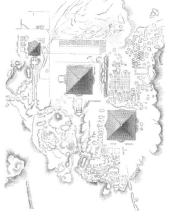

Giza necropolis
The three main elements of the necropolis – the pyramids of Cheops, Chephren and Mycerenus – lie on a near-diagonal axis. Their attendant mortuary temples and causeways face towards the Nile, while a western *mastaba* cemetery was built for high officials.

Sphinx
Built in association with the pyramid of Chephren, the Sphinx is carved from a single outcrop of limestone. It is the earliest-surviving example of this form, depicting a lion with a pharaoh's head, headdress and false beard. It acted as guardian of the royal tombs.

Corridors, Great Pyramid of Cheops
The pyramid chambers of the king and queen and a subterranean chamber, built within the superstructure of the pyramid, were accessed via three stone-lined corridors (both descending and ascending), the longest of which measured over 100 m (328 ft). These undecorated corridors created a solemn passage for the deceased.

Great Pyramid of Cheops (2680–2565 BC)
The largest of the three pyramids, this reaches a height of 146 m (479 ft) and measures 231 sq m (2,485 sq ft), covering an area of about 5.2 ha (13 acres). The stone used in its construction includes imported limestone. On each side was a pit with a royal boat, allowing the pharaoh's spirit to travel freely.

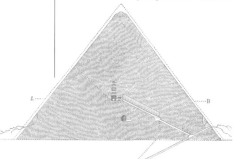

Outer casing, Great Pyramid of Cheops

The pyramids were originally cased in limestone, creating a smooth white surface, and were capped by a pyramidion, a gilded pyramid-shaped stone inscribed with prayers. The reflection of sunlight from the pyramid may have been intended to associate the dead king with the sun god Re, and would have given the necropolis a dazzling appearance.

Core, Great Pyramid of Cheops

The core of the pyramid consisted of thousands of locally quarried blocks. These blocks, weighing an average of 2.5 tons, were transported to the site under human power, necessitating an enormous workforce, and were then manoeuvred into position with the aid of a thin lime mortar lubricant.

Relieving stone, Great Pyramid of Cheops

Four relieving stones, supporting much of the superincumbent weight, surmount the entrance to the pyramid. The entrance was sealed and covered by the limestone casing, rendering it invisible from the exterior and increasing security. The use of these stones shows the ancient Egyptian understanding of the application of physics to monumental architecture.

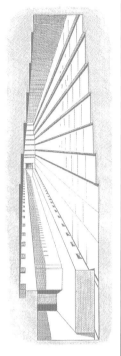

Corbelled gallery, Great Pyramid of Cheops

Leading to two levels of chambers, the granite-lined King's Chamber and the Queen's Chamber, the great gallery consists of seven projecting courses, each supporting the one above. An unadorned ascending gallery, it reflected the restrained monumentalism of the pyramid with the continued use of large-scale masonry.

Burial chamber, Great Pyramid of Cheops

Separated from the gallery by a portcullis-protected antechamber, the burial chamber was roofed with five tiers, each built of nine stone slabs, one above the other. A vault of two relieving stones surmounted this. Two narrow shafts ran from the chamber to the exterior, although their exact purpose is unknown.

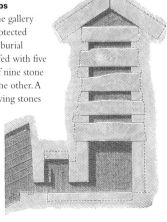

Ancient Egypt

Rock-cut Tombs

While the pyramids provided the basis of royal funerary architecture in the Old Kingdom, during the Middle Kingdom (2134–1786 BC) private tombs moved away from the mastaba model to rock-cut tombs hewn directly from the hills alongside the Nile. Soon the pharaohs also adopted this practice, in an attempt to protect their tombs from violation by the ever-attendant tomb robbers, culminating in the spectacular tombs of the New Kingdom (1570– 1085 BC), created by craftsmen supported by the king. The choice of the west bank of Thebes as the site of the Valley of the Kings may have been prompted by the natural pyramid shape of the Western Mountain. These tombs continued the earlier practice of imitating domestic architecture, providing multiple chambers for the storage of funerary goods as well as for the interment of the deceased. The brightly coloured decoration covered subjects ranging from daily life to high ritual, the mythology of the gods and even funerals themselves.

Portico tomb entrance, Beni Hasan (2130–1785 BC)
Constructed during the 11th and 12th Dynasties, these tombs for provincial officials were wholly rock-hewn. The entrance faced the rising sun and simulated the portico found in models of Middle Kingdom domestic houses that were included among funerary goods.

Plan and elevation of tomb, Beni Hasan
A simple floor plan shows an entrance flanked by two pillars, leading to a rectangular chamber supported by four columns, with a niche cut into the rear wall. The ceiling was either flat or slightly vaulted and the entrance provided the only light source.

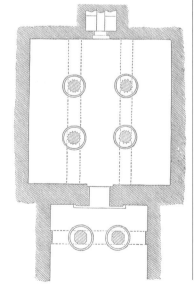

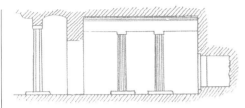

Column bases, Beni Hasan
The columns stood upon large, flat, circular base stones, which, with slight modification, became the standard form of column base throughout subsequent Egyptian architecture.

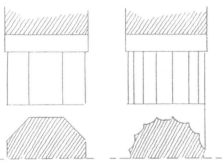

◁ **Tomb entrance, Valley of the Kings (1570–1085 BC)**
Capped by the natural pyramid form of the Western Mountain, the tombs of the pharaohs were cut into the bedrock of the Valley of the Kings in an attempt to hide them from tomb robbers – in total contrast to the high visibility of the pyramids. The construction of a later tomb buried Tutankhamun's tomb, preserving it until it was discovered in the 20th century.

Sarcophagus
The highly decorated burial chamber housed the sarcophagus, a large stone coffin in which the mummy was interred. Often carved from solid blocks of granite, the sarcophagus was elaborately decorated with hieroglyphs, which provide some of the finest examples of Egyptian art.

Columns, Beni Hasan
The columns were cut to either a flat octagonal or fluted sixteen-sided form. It has been suggested that this was purely aesthetic, in order to soften the appearance of the traditional square structure. The columns narrow slightly from base to top and have no capital, except a square slab or abacus.

Plan, New Kingdom royal tomb, Thebes
Rock-cut royal tombs began as a relatively simple form, but by the Rameside era of the 19th Dynasty had developed into a sophisticated series of chambers, with raised relief decoration, linked by corridors and stairways built by specialised teams of workmen from the village of Deir el-Medina.

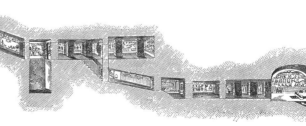

False floor, Beni Hasan
Further elements – including pits, false floors and dummy chambers – were introduced to protect the tomb from violation. A false floor led any trespasser to an empty dummy chamber, while the true burial chamber was concealed beneath them.

Ancient Egypt

Temples

Like tombs, temples were intended to last for eternity and were therefore built from stone. The house of a god or of the spirit of the deceased, the temple continued the traditional practice of monumental architecture mimicking domestic dwellings, which derived from the belief that the spiritual world ran parallel to the physical. Little evidence of early temples survives, due to the construction of later temples on the same site; however, later New Kingdom and Greco-Roman temples still dominate the modern towns that surround them. The temple publicly declared the power of the pharaoh and his relationship with the gods – its public spaces being decorated with imagery of the king's victories and of his piety. Temples were also important social and political centres; in the New Kingdom the priesthood exerted great power and temples were economically independent, serving the gods alone.

Mortuary temple
Mortuary temples were built adjacent to the tomb and provided a place for offerings to be made to the deceased and a resting place for the *ka*. They had the same fundamental elements as most temples: entrance hall, courtyard, sanctuary and niche.

Sphinx temple, Giza
The temple situated adjacent to the Sphinx is a valley temple associated with the pyramid of Chephren. The valley temple was a landing and reception point for the mummy, which was transported there by river, prior to the funerary offerings and burial ceremony.

Sun temple, Abu Gurob
Dedicated to the sun god Re, the finest sun temples were built during the 5th Dynasty. The temple complex consisted of two buildings – the valley building and the upper temple – connected by a causeway. At Abu Gurob, an enclosure wall contained the upper temple, where an open courtyard housed a massive obelisk and a large alabaster altar.

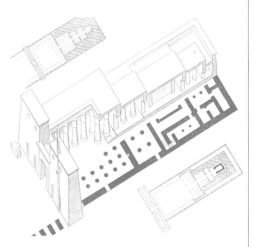

The Rameseum (c. 1279 BC)
The mortuary temple of Rameses II displays a return to the traditional form of pylon, courtyard, hypostyle (*see page 23*) and sanctuary. It focused its attention on worship of the dead king.

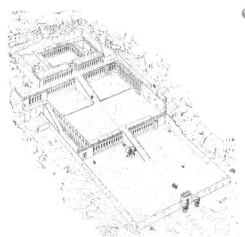

Temple of Hatshepsut, Deir el-Bahri (18th Dynasty)
This was primarily a mortuary temple, but also a sanctuary dedicated to Amun (the chief deity), with shrines to Hathor (guardian of western Thebes) and Anubis (guardian of the necropolis). It combined influences from the adjacent, earlier mortuary temple of Mentuhotep II with a unique terrace design. The construction incorporates free-standing and rock-cut elements at the base of the Western Mountain.

Colossi
Colossi were monolithic (cut from a single stone block) statues of the pharaoh as deity – shown either standing or seated, and wearing the crowns of Upper and Lower Egypt or a royal headdress. They commonly fronted New Kingdom temples and could weigh up to 1,000 tons.

Cult temple (New Kingdom)
The temple was the architectural interpretation of the mythological origin of Egypt. The enclosure wall denoted the edges of the waters of chaos, while the sanctuary was built on a raised floor symbolic of the primeval mound upon which Egypt was founded.

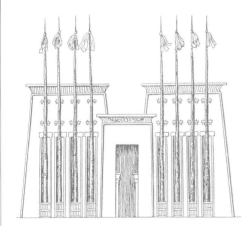

Pylons
The temple gateway of was flanked by high trapezoidal stone towers, or pylons, sloping gently inwards and topped with a cornice. They were elaborately decorated with relief: usually political propaganda on the front and ritual on the rear. They were often fronted by colossi and niches for flagpoles and banners.

Ancient Egypt

Temple of Karnak, Thebes

Built on the east bank of the Nile at
Thebes, Karnak was the centre of the
cult of Amun, chief of all the gods.
As such, it became the religious focus
of Egypt during the New Kingdom,
possibly linked to the choice of the
Theban west bank as a royal necropolis.
The largest religious complex of the
ancient world, Karnak was added
to by pharaohs over a long period,
contributing to its magnificence and
power in return for the god's favour.
During the Amarna Period (1570–
1314 BC), attempts were made to
reduce the power of the priests by
removing the capital to Middle Egypt
and establishing a new religion. But
with the death of the pharaoh Akhenaten,
the old order was quickly re-established
and Karnak flourished again. The
New Kingdom saw temples increase in
scale and grandeur – now much less
accessible to the populace as a whole.

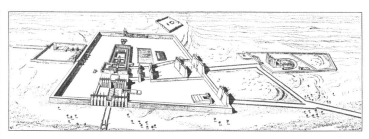

Temple complex
With its enclosure
incorporating the main
temple, a sacred lake,
subsidiary temples,
housing, educational
centres and ancillary
buildings, the temple
complex provided a
religious and social focus
for the city of Thebes.
Temples had now replaced
pyramids as the focus of
monumental work
programmes, and Karnak –
house of the sacred triad
of Amun, Mut and
Khonsu – dominated.

Temple plan
Karnak's immense scale
included six pylons,
a first courtyard large
enough to withstand the
encroachment of a smaller
temple on the south,
the largest-known
hypostyle, and a sanctuary
dating back to the
Middle Kingdom. It was
constructed mainly from
sandstone and limestone.
Granite and quartzite were
used to embellish the
temple with statues
and obelisks.

Mud ramp
Surviving behind the right flank of the first
pylon are the remains of a mud ramp used in its
construction and decoration. The ramp was raised
to accommodate the erection of the pylon, then
was gradually demolished, allowing artists to
decorate the stone from the top downwards.

Crio-sphinx
A ceremonial processional
of stone crio-sphinxes led to
the entrance of the temple,
providing a symbolic escort
to those entering, and allowing
a transition to the spiritual
realm. This sphinx depicted
the pharaoh protected between
the paws of a ram-headed
lion – the ram being
a manifestation
of Amun.

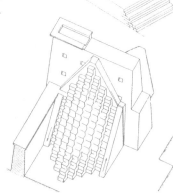

Obelisk

The obelisk demon-
strates the technological
achievements of the New
Kingdom. A monolithic
square stone pillar ending
in a point, often of
granite and weighing
up to 350 tons, it was
transported to the temple
and decorated *in situ*. The
finest 18th-Dynasty
examples were inlaid
with gold hieroglyphs
honouring Re.

Capitals

Column capitals imitating natural
plant forms – papyrus, lotus and
palm – appeared throughout
monumental architecture.
Their form was thought to
derive from archaic reed-built
shrines. Now carved from stone,
the columns were highly
decorated with carved and
painted hieroglyphic texts, ritual
imagery and natural motifs.

Hypostyle hall

The hypostyle (meaning
'ceiling supported by
pillars') hall at Karnak
consists of 134 columns
supporting a roof of
enormous stone slabs.
Built during the reign of
Rameses II (1279–1213
BC), the hall contains a
central aisle of tall
papyriform columns
flanked by shorter
lotus-form columns,
enabling the ceiling to be
raised and allowing
windows to be introduced
between the two
roof levels.

Temple of Khonsu (*c.* 1198 BC)

Dedicated to Khonsu (child of Amun and Mut), this
temple follows the New Kingdom cult-temple form. The
floor level rises in a series of steps, and the ceiling lowers,
until the sanctuary is reached. The increased intimacy
thus created reflects the temple's restricted access, for only
the priest and pharaoh were allowed into the sanctuary.

Ancient Egypt

Nubian Border

Egypt's southern border with Nubia, or Kush, was of great importance to the state's wealth and power. Nubia was a rich source of stone and gold, and Egypt's control of these resources made it a major force in the ancient world. The city of Aswan, site of an important granite quarry, lay in the border country, and expeditions south brought exotic minerals, flora and fauna back to the pharaoh. Ancient Egyptian temples and estates were established in Nubia and there is evidence that Egyptian by-laws were respected. During the Middle Kingdom, frontier posts or 'forts' were established to protect these imports, and in turn supported entire communities. The New Kingdom saw Nubia finally become a province of the Egyptian Empire, and tomb decoration began to depict dark-skinned Nubians.

Temple of Abu Simbel, Lower Nubia (c. 1260 BC)
Built during the reign of Rameses II, this memorial temple was cut from a pink sandstone bluff at Abu Simbel. Fronted by four colossal statues of benevolent, enthroned kings, its pylon-type façade faced east. It had a central statue of the falcon-headed sun god Re, and was surmounted by a row of baboons hailing the sunrise.

Cross-section, Abu Simbel
The temple penetrates deep into the sandstone cliff, following the traditional Theban temple form, and in its scale and coarse construction is designed for impact rather than practicality. Its decoration focuses on the northern battle of Qadesh and the king's proximity to the gods. All these elements are a physical demonstration of the pharaoh's military might, divinity and dominance over nature.

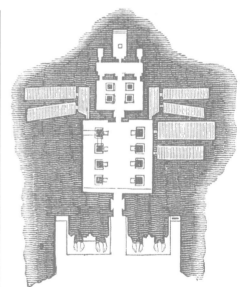

Plan, Abu Simbel
A narrow entrance between the two central colossi leads to a wider hypostyle hall, succeeded by a niche holding statues depicting the three national deities of Egypt and the king on an equal level. Oriented so that on Rameses' birth date the sun rested on the statues of Amun and Rameses, the hypostyle is abutted by narrow chambers thought to have provided storage areas.

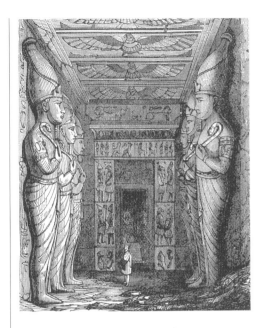

Osiride pillars, Abu Simbel

Eight square-cut stone pillars support statues depicting Rameses II as Osiris, bringer of civilization to primeval Egypt and king of the dead. The Osiris cult underwent a revival during the New Kingdom and the statues are seen sporting straight beards (a symbol of life), not the curled beard of the dead god. The representation of Osiris's distinctive *atif* crown shows the king depicting himself as an immortal worshipped in his own lifetime.

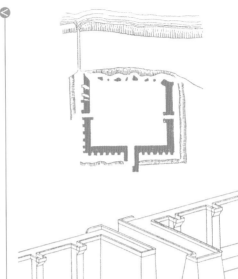

Fort gateway, Buhen

A western gateway, allowing access to the central fort within the enclosure wall, was uncovered at Buhen. A spur at the head of the projecting gateway enabled effective monitoring of traffic and security, by allowing increased manning of the parapet. The narrow access to the fort itself prevented any large-scale assault.

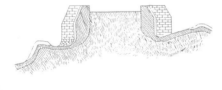

Fort, Semna (12th Dynasty)

At least eight mud-brick and stone forts were constructed along a 60-km (37-mile) stretch of the Nile running from Buhen, near the Second Cataract, to Semna. At the southern end two forts, built from a mud-brick core faced with stone, stood on either side of the Nile guarding the boundary of Egyptian occupation. An enclosure wall afforded some protection to the town serving the garrison.

Crenellation

Both the fort and enclosure wall display features anticipating later European castles. Crenellation (battlements) surmounting the walls provided alternating indentations for archers, while moats and parapets added to an already intimidating structure. The forts protected those who were exploiting Nubia's mineral resources, and reinforced the pharaonic presence in the south during the Middle Kingdom.

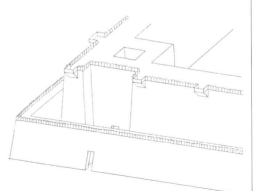

Ancient Egypt

Greco-Roman Temples

Greco-Roman building in Egypt culminated under the Ptolemies (305–30 BC). Foreign rule saw a revival of Egyptian forms and traditionalism, although a fundamental change had occurred. Darkened Egyptian temples were now shrouded in mystery, in comparison to the public majesty of the New Kingdom temples. But large-scale building projects were initiated, temples rebuilt or enlarged, and Egyptian religious beliefs were preserved by the invader kings alongside their own. The basic elements of construction and room arrangement remained, augmented by the *pronaos* and a free-standing central sanctuary. Under the later kings, the temple still fulfilled a strong social function, thereby providing a focus for the town and giving it administrative and economic (as well as sacred) value.

Plan, Edfu Temple
Built from sandstone, the temple followed a streamlined and yet intricate plan. The pylons enclosed stairways giving access to its roof, while a large courtyard led to the *pronaos*, hypostyle, antechamber and, finally, a free-standing sanctuary surrounded by a corridor. Decorative texts state that the temple was built according to the ancient ideal, which re-emphasised its dedication to the cult.

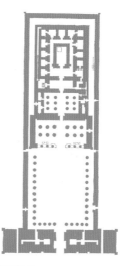

Courtyard
Entering via the first pylon, under a winged sun disc representing the god Behdet (creator and protector of the world), the visitor reached a courtyard flanked by colonnaded porticoes. With its elaborate and brightly painted capitals, and its large statue of the god Horus as falcon, the courtyard provided an impressive public aspect to the temple.

Cross-section, Edfu Temple (c. 130 BC)
The most complete of the Greco-Roman temples, Edfu was dedicated to the falcon god, Horus. Constructed over a period of 180 years, it displays all the typical major elements: broken-lintel doorway, elaborate column capitals, a screen wall across the hypostyle hall, and use of the roof for ritual.

Pronaos, Edfu

The *pronaos*, or 'Hall before the Great Seat', was the columnar fore-hall of the temple and the entrance to the god's abode. At Edfu it contained three rows of six columns arranged behind a screen wall. The only light entered via a roof aperture, emphasising the transition between the outer physical world and the inner spiritual world.

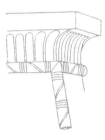

Hathor-headed columns, Dendera (1st century BC)

Identified by the Greeks with Aphrodite, Hathor was the supreme god of love. Columns crowned with four-sided, Hathor-headed capitals supported the hypostyle hall of her temple, clearly identifying it. The capital's upper part depicted the *mammisi*, or birth house, a building linked with divine descent.

Cornices

The cornice, a projecting ornamental moulding along the top of temple walls and pylons, was a standard element of Egyptian decoration. Designs ranged from the earliest, simple mud-brick and reed through to detailed cult symbolism (the striking cobra and sun disc), and lent elegance to monumental structures.

Screen wall

Designed to restrict the level of light entering the *pronaos*, thus creating an environment for cleansing prior to approaching the sanctuary, the screen wall was made of thin stone and ran between the first row of columns. Highly decorated with images of the king and queen, with cult themes and mythological motifs, the screen wall further emphasised the cult role of the pharaoh.

Babylon, Assyria, Persia *c. 2000–333 BC*

Babylonian Architecture

Babylonian or Chaldean architecture is the ancient architecture of former Mesopotamia (modern-day Iran). The scant remains are mostly to be found in the land between the rivers Euphrates and Tigris. Those excavated at Ur and Wurka are the remains of temples, ziggurats (stepped temples) and tombs, ranging in date from 2235 to 1520 BC. From the Assyrian period of the 9th to 7th centuries BC there are substantial remains of palaces and temples around the ancient cities of Nineveh, Nimrud, Koyunjik and Khorsabad. The ancient Persian period ranges from 538 BC to the conquest of the Persians by Alexander the Great in 333 BC. Surviving monuments include those at Pasargadae, Susa and – most spectacularly – at Persepolis. The architecture of the whole period was influenced by Egyptian, Babylonian and Greek cultures, intermixing their styles.

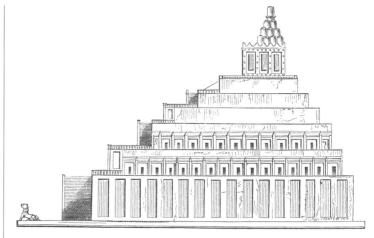

Temple of the Seven Spheres, Birs Nimrud (c. 2000 BC)
One of the few remaining monuments built of sun-dried brick and wood, this temple comprised seven storeys connected by staircases. The lower storey was square, with six storeys above – not placed centrally above each other. On the upper storey was the *cella,* or sanctuary, of the temple.

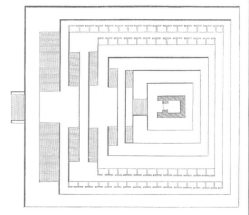

Dedication, Temple of the Seven Spheres
The temple was dedicated to the seven planets, and each storey was faced with glazed tiles of a different colour. The lowest storey was black (Saturn), the next orange (Jupiter), then red (Mars), yellow-gold (Sun), green (Venus), blue (Mercury) and finally white or silver (Moon).

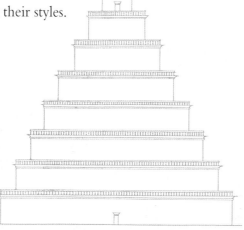

Ziggurat, Birs Nimrud
The word 'ziggurat' means 'uprising finial', and describes a rectangular mound built in stepped-back stages and crowned by a temple. It was the means by which the Babylonians aspired to reach the heavens. This one has a square plan, with access by means of stairs.

Elevation and plan, Temple at Borsippa (c. 2000 BC)
This terraced pyramid has a small temple at the summit. The sides of the terraces are directed towards the cardinal points of the compass, with steps located on the same side on each terrace.

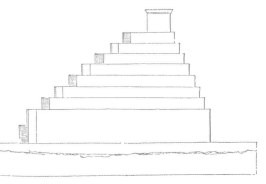

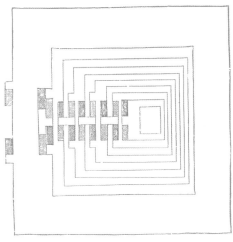

Ziggurat
Early Mesopotamian temples were raised on a mud-brick platform, and topped by a ziggurat, an artificial mountain made up of tiered rectangular stages. A variety of treatments for decoration was used on the wall surfaces of ziggurats: cone mosaics laid into wet plaster, and coloured and glazed brick.

Hanging Gardens, Semiramis (c. 7th century BC)
The celebrated Hanging Gardens of Semiramis in Babylon, one of the seven wonders of the ancient world, dated from the late Chaldo-Babylonian kingdom. They may have comprised terraces disposed in stages, one above the other, so that each stage formed a separate garden.

Bas-relief, Koyunjik
This is a representation on a bas-relief (low-relief carving) found at Koyunjik of a four-storeyed temple flanked by a gateway, similar to the ancient Egyptian pylons. The entrance was on the ground floor, the second terrace was buttressed and the top storey (missing) was reserved for the *cella*.

Babylon, Assyria, Persia

Assyrian Architecture

Assyrian architecture is one of palaces and fortifications, built to demonstrate strength and power, but often with a veneer of decoration in the form of polychromatic brickwork. Built of clay brick, the only evidence of their form and arrangement are the ruined remains, which show the position of key structures, and the stone-carved relief panels featuring buildings, animals and people. The palace of Khorsabad (720 BC) represents an important and complete Assyrian palace plan, with examples of stonework (vaulting, columns, jambs and lintels) and architectural sculpture, such as monumental winged bulls and griffins.

City gateway, Khorsabad
On climbing the stairs to the palace, one would have faced one of many arched gateways flanked by winged stone bulls with human heads, with the arches springing from their backs. The arch was decorated with blue enamelled bricks, with a pattern of figures and stars.

Gateway, King Sargon's Palace
The gateways to King Sargon's Palace at Khorsabad were built into the thick walls. The two small dark areas in the middle of the plan represent the position of the sculpted stone bulls flanking the central portal, which led to the large open outer court.

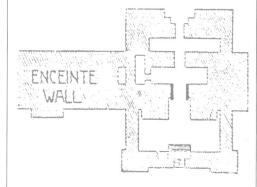

ENCEINTE WALL

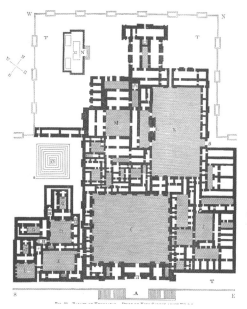

Plan of King Sargon's Palace, Khorsabad (720 BC)
The palace was situated on a mound raised above the plain, close to the fortified city. It was reached via a flight of steps (*bottom*). Three great portals led to an outer court, within which were six or seven smaller courts, with stables and cellars. Residential and state apartments were located deep within the complex. The planning was not axial or symmetrical, but on the diagonal.

Tunnel vault
This was an early method of vaulting used by the Assyrians. The vaulting here has been constructed without centring (a temporary structure), setting rings out of the perpendicular. This method was certainly used for subterranean drains, and probably also to vault the roofs of the narrow palace rooms.

Observatory, Khorsabad (720 BC)

Like earlier temples, the one at Khorsabad had seven storeys, but each was placed centrally above the other, not to one side. It had terraces that formed ramps wrapping around the tower, like those around the tower of Belus, or Babel, at Babylon. They were coloured following the same code as the temple at Birs Nimrud.

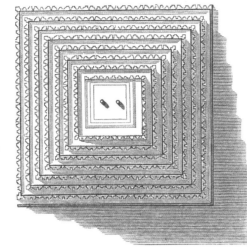

Gateway, King Sargon's Palace

The main gateway to King Sargon's Palace had an arched entrance and distinctively Assyrian stepped cresting on the battlements, meant to symbolise a sacred mountain.

Palace court, Khorsabad

This shows a conjectural restoration of one of the corners of the palace. The walls of the staterooms were lined with sculptured alabaster slabs showing portraits of kings, historical events and naturalistic human figures and animals. Above, the walls were of painted stucco. External walls had reeded pilasters and panels.

Palace room, Khorsabad

This conjectural restoration of one of the principal rooms at Khorsabad shows how the lower walls were lined with alabaster slabs, while light was admitted by the open upper part of the walls. Many narrower rooms and passages in the palace were vaulted, but the royal rooms probably had a decorated timber ceiling.

Pedestrian gateway, Khorsabad

The gateways for travellers on foot were ornamented by awesome winged bulls with human heads. Between these stood the figure of a giant seen in the process of strangling a lion.

Babylon, Assyria, Persia

Assyrian Palaces at Nineveh, Nimrud and Koyunjik

Temples were built in Assyria both with and without ziggurats, but by the late Assyrian period palaces were much more numerous and important, emphasising the central role of the monarchy. The city of Nimrud was restored and enlarged in the 9th century BC with a palace built within the walls of the citadel. It had a large public court with a suite of apartments on the east side and a series of large banqueting halls on the south side. This was to become the traditional plan of Assyrian palaces, built and adorned for the glorification of the king. The remains of the palaces at Nineveh, Nimrud and Koyunjik (from the 8th to 7th centuries BC) have similar plan forms, being built on elevated platforms surrounded by terraces.

Assyrian ornament, Nineveh

A sculptured ornamental border from the ruins of Nineveh shows winged bulls and a stylised plant form, thought to represent a sacred tree. Borders of flowers and animals could also be painted on the beams of ceilings, sometimes with gilding and inlaid precious stones to add richness and contrast.

Sculptured griffin, Nineveh

Assyrian bas-reliefs featured powerful and life-like representations of men and animals, revealing an observation of anatomy and movement, and at the same time stylising the subject for architectural ornament. Large stone panels, or orthostats, were arranged in tiers on high walls, or as friezes on long walls. Common subjects were fierce beasts, bulls, lions or griffins (half-lion, half-bird), sometimes with the king shown slaying them to demonstrate his bravery, and symbolising the triumph of good over evil.

Pavement slab, Central Palace, Koyunjik (704 BC)

The outer border of this ornamented pavement is a pattern based on the leaves of the lotus flower (and is similar to ancient Egyptian ornament), with another stylised flower within, separated by narrower bands of rosettes.

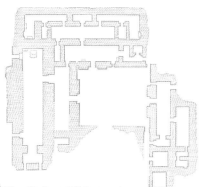

Assyrian capital forms

Among the ruins of the Palace of Nineveh antiquarians found sculptured panels reflecting some of the architectural details made by the Assyrian (or possibly Greek) builders. These voluted capitals show an affinity with the Greek Ionic and Corinthian forms.

Plan, North-west Palace, Nimrud (884 BC)

One of the earliest buildings on the site of the mound of Nimrud, this palace had at its heart a square court reached by the main entrance. This stood at the head of a flight of steps guarded by winged stone bulls, and led to a great hall. On the east side private apartments, including the women's quarters (harem), were located, and on the south side were banqueting halls.

Conjectural restoration of an Assyrian palace

Antiquarians speculated on the complete forms of Assyrian palaces. James Fergusson's reconstruction presents their main features, including an elevated, buttressed terrace; a handsome flight of steps lined with carved figures paying homage to the king; an open upper storey to admit light; and a crenellated roof ridge.

Lamussu

Lamussu (colossal stone beast) guarded the royal gates from the intrusion of evil, with the fierceness of a lion, the far-sightedness of an eagle, the strength of a bull, and the wisdom and intelligence of a human being.

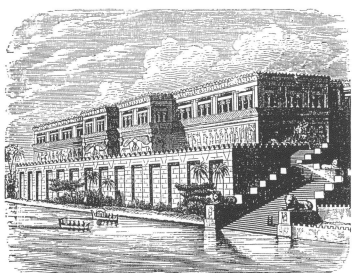

Obelisk of Divanubara (c. 800 BC)

Built with sun-baked and kiln-burned bricks, this obelisk was a tall, tapered block surmounted by stepped layers, with carvings and inscriptions that reveal a sepulchral function.

Babylon, Assyria, Persia

Persian Architecture:
The Palaces of Persepolis

Knowledge of Persian architecture from the 6th to 4th centuries BC is derived chiefly from the remains of palace-temples at Pasargadae, Susa and Persepolis, which show a mixture of Egyptian and Greek influences as well as certain unique features. The continuation of Assyrian building traditions can be seen in the habit of building on mounds or platforms (now reached by even more magnificent stone staircases, lined with carved images of animals and attendants on the king) and by the use of large-scale relief decoration and brightly coloured glazed brickwork. What is different at Persepolis is the sheer scale of the palaces, which are dominated by great square audience halls (*apadana*) with many pillars, involving more complex planning and a greater use of stone.

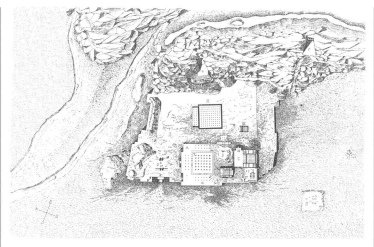

Plan of Persepolis (521–465 BC)
The whole site is surrounded by a wall, which encloses three great terraces: a high central terrace flanked by lower platforms. On these are the remains of the great palaces of the Persian kings Darius and his son Xerxes. The northern terrace contains the Propylaea (gateway) of Xerxes; the rest of the buildings are located on the central terrace.

Palace of Darius (521 BC)
This conjectural restoration shows a double flight of steps reaching an open loggia, through which one progressed to the central hall. On the top of the building was a raised platform, or *talar,* on which the king (who was also the high priest) performed religious ceremonies. This restoration was based on the carving of the palace on Darius's tomb.

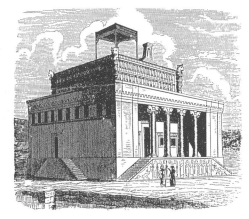

Winged bulls, Hall of 100 Columns
In front of the Hall of 100 Columns are the remains of a portal with winged stone bulls with human heads, similar to the Assyrian winged bulls (lamussu) at Nineveh and Nimrud. These colossal creatures flanked a gatehouse made of mud-brick walls faced with glazed polychromatic bricks.

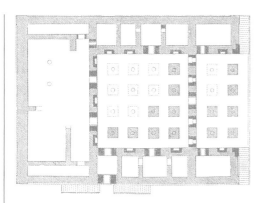

Plan, Palace of Darius
A central hall, or *apadana*, contained sixteen columns and was surrounded by smaller cells. Towers at the four corners may have contained guardrooms and stairs. From the western portico there would have been a view of open countryside.

Façade, Palace of Darius
The palace was reached by a flight of steps on either side of a terrace, leading through a portico to a doorway. This doorway had a curved and reeded cornice, similar to those seen over the doorways to Egyptian temples.

View from the top of the Great Stairs
On the left is the Propylaea of Xerxes, and behind that (*to the right*) stand the pillars of the Apadana of Xerxes. In the distance are the remains of the smaller halls of Darius and Xerxes.

Stairs with stone parapet
The steps leading up to the Apadana of Xerxes were lined with stone-carved panels of marching soldiers: two spear-carriers are shown in this detail. The depiction of human figures is combined with architectural ornament: stylised plant forms and foliated rosettes, or lotus petals.

Central doorway, Palace of Darius
Another view of the Egyptian-style cornice shows, in the door jamb, a stone slab with a carving depicting the king being escorted from outside by a servant carrying a sunshade.

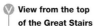

Babylon, Assyria, Persia

Persepolis: Palace of Xerxes

The palaces of Darius (ruled 522-486 BC) and his son Xerxes (ruled 486-465 BC) functioned both as royal dwellings and as temples. The complex of halls and palace apartments combined the functions of residential quarters for the king and his entourage, and a place to conduct ceremonies and government administration. The king played an essential and principal role in all forms of government, but he was also the chief priest of his people, so the palace was a symbol of the union of temporal and spiritual power. The temple – probably comprising a wooden stage and a canopy – was situated on the roof of the palace, where the Persian kings worshipped the planets and were also highly visible to their worshipping subjects.

Stone columns, south hall, Apadana of Xerxes
The Apadana of Xerxes consisted of a square columned hall with towers at the corners and porticoes on three sides, reached by a double stone staircase. The tall, fluted columns supported double bull capitals, which in turn supported a flat timber roof. The beams of cedar and cypress wood would have been richly ornamented on the underside.

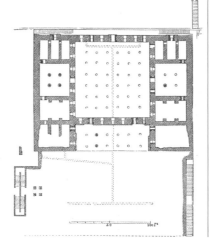

Plan, Apadana of Xerxes and palace apartments (c. 485 BC)
The palace was built on a platform approached by a double flight of steps. An open portico of twelve columns had two doorways on the inner wall leading to an *apadana*, or audience hall, flanked by two ranges of apartments. The central room in these ranges was square with four pillars, with three small chambers on one side and guards' chambers on the other. The hall had thirty-six columns each equidistant from one another, and was lit by six windows. At the back a doorway opened on to a narrow terrace leading to the lower terrace.

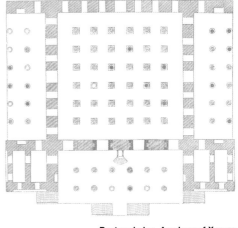

Restored plan, Apadana of Xerxes
Stairs ascended to one of the three open loggias, from which one progressed to the Apadana of Xerxes, a large central room supported by thirty-six columns with porticoes on three sides.

Pillar of the western portico

This pillar, unique to Persepolis, has a tapering, finely fluted shaft resting on a torus and fillet at its junction with the circular base. At the top rests the fantastic, stone-carved capital in the shape of a double horse's head and neck.

Double staircase

A double flight of steps led up to the Palace of Xerxes, with carved panels of soldiers and spear-carriers in procession, and images of wild beasts fighting, at the top and bottom. The outer walls were lined with slabs carved with stylised plant forms.

Hall of 100 Columns

This vast, square hall was the great architectural creation of the Persian Empire. It was lit by seven windows, set in stone surrounds on the entrance wall. This restored view shows how it might have looked inside: a huge space filled with pillars, plastered and painted in bright colours, with double bull bracket capitals. The pillars helped support the flat roof for a stage known as the *talar*.

Pillar of the northern portico

The bell-shaped base of this column has a similar finely fluted shaft to that on the western portico, but a very different capital (again, unique to Persepolis). The capital is composed of a base, featuring the lotus motif and with a convex profile on the upper surface, and an I-shaped top section. The central shaft is fluted, and the bars of the 'I' are carved into double scrolls or volutes.

Hall of Xerxes

This restoration gives some idea of the appearance of the hall, with its handsome staircase, portico, walls built of mud-bricks, then covered with glazed and enamelled tiles. The *talar* has conjectural *acroteria* at the corners, in the shape of bulls or griffins.

37

Babylon, Assyria, Persia

Persian Architectural Craftsmanship

At Persepolis many skilled craftsmen from all corners of the Persian Empire were employed. Throughout the buildings the finish was meticulous, as befitted a site of royal and sacred significance. Some of the walls were polished to a high degree of reflectivity, and the sculptural details in the stonework often seem to have been executed with jeweler's tools, the edges are so sharp and pristine. At the same time, the stonework could be massive, with whole window and door surrounds (as well as several steps in a staircase) cut from a solid block of stone. Woodcarving could be intricate, with fine moulding on the great beams. Sometimes timbers were covered with thick sheets of precious metals – some plated with gold and inlaid with ivory, green serpentine and red haematite. The carved friezes were painted in turquoise, red and yellow, as was the plaster covering the thick brick walls.

Column

Tall columns with bull's head capitals were used for porticoes and to support the roof of the hypostyle hall, partly inspired by the ancient Egyptian precedent. Since the columns carried timber beams rather than stone, they could be taller, slimmer and more widely spaced than Egyptian ones.

Persian carpentry

This drawing shows, from an oblique angle, part of the construction of a hall at Persepolis: the mud-brick wall, the flat timber roof supported by a moulded beam of cedar wood, the double bull capitals and the slender fluted columns.

Volute and rosette

Greek craftsmen from Ionia are known to have worked at Persepolis and may have brought with them the scrolled volute shown in detail here. The rosette in the centre was a symbol of the sun and fertility.

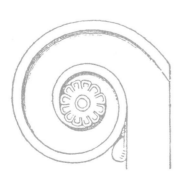

Capital

This shows a palm-leaf design on a convex base, which tapers in and then expands outwards to support a rectangular fluted shaft, with a pair of scrolled volutes at the top and bottom.

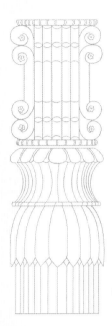

Tomb of Darius, Naksh-I-Rustam (485 BC)
The cross-shaped façade of this tomb was cut directly into the cliff face. The central part represents the portico of a palace (probably Darius's own palace at Persepolis) with columns and bull capitals. A door in the centre gives access to the interior of the tomb. At the top of the façade two rows of bearers support a dais on which the king worships before a fire altar. The figure in the winged disc may be the god Ashur, or the spirit of the dead king.

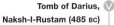

Fine detail
The different sections of the Persian capital are shown with great clarity in this line drawing. The fluted upper section, with four volutes on each face, is a rectangular block; the lower parts are circular. These two sections measured more than 5 m (16 ft) in height.

Range and variety
Here, a variety of sculptural treatments for walls, column bases and capitals are shown: the lamussu derived from Assyrian sculpture, the foliage designs and bell-shaped bases from Egypt, and the fluted shafts and volutes from Greece. Only the double-headed bull (or horse) capital was unique to Persepolis.

Rock tomb
As well as free-standing tombs, the Persians built rock tombs for their kings, cut into the cliffs and featuring carvings of architectural façades and figures. High up in the face of a cliff in a ridge of hills a few kilometres north of Persepolis are four rock-hewn sepulchres built for Darius and three of his successors.

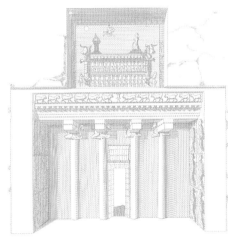

Early and Classical India *c. 300 BC–c. 1750s*

Stupas and Stambhas

The earliest architecture to survive in India today was built by the Buddhists, a religious sect founded in the 7th century BC. Chief among Buddhist works were the stupas, also known as topes or *dagabas*. These originated as burial mounds but, after the cremated remains of Buddha (d. 483 BC) and his disciples were placed within them, became relic shrines, commemorating Buddha and his teachings. Until the emergence of the Buddha idol, they served as the principal focus for worship. Stupas were also built to honour sacred sites or events. An associated architectural form was the *stambha* or *lath*, a free-standing monumental column. One, or even two of these stood close to every great stupa and in front of important *chaitya* halls.

Decoration
Although most early stupas were unadorned, there is evidence that later examples were elaborately decorated, especially from the 2nd to 3rd centuries AD. This, the great stupa at Amaravati in the Deccan, was covered with stucco and ornamented with medallions, wreaths and scenes from the life of Buddha.

Toranas
The railings around a stupa were often broken at the cardinal directions by gateways, known as *toranas*. These were simple in form, consisting of two posts linked by architraves, but were richly sculpted, as here at Sanchi. By contemplating the imagery on *toranas*, worshippers entered the state of mind necessary for *pradakshina*.

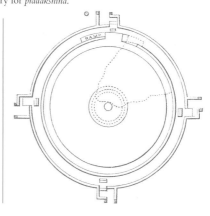

Elements of a stupa
The essential feature of a stupa was its hemispherical dome, known as an *anda* (literally, 'egg'). At its pinnacle, stood a feature called a *tee*, often surrounded by railings. Above the *tee* rose the *yasti* or pole, which gave support to umbrella-shaped tiers (*chhattras*), varying in number. This image depicts a relic casket, which has been modelled after the stupa in which it was housed.

Pradakshina
Worship would be performed by walking around (circumambulating) the stupa in a clockwise direction, a rite known as *pradakshina*. This took place on a paved pathway, enclosed by railings (*vedika*).

Railings

The railings *(vedika)* that surrounded stupas were important elements in their own right. They demarcated the boundary of the sacred area and were often richly decorated, predominantly with medallions carved with birds, flowers, animals and mythological figures.

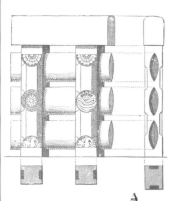

Manastambha

Stambhas continued to be built into the 17th and 18th centuries, and were particularly popular with the Jains, who erected them in front of their temples. This Jain example is known as a *manastambha*, and carries a small pavilion on its capital. *Stambhas* were also used by the Hindus, as *dipdans* (lamp-bearing pillars).

Decorated capital

Above the ornamental necking rose the *stambha*'s capital. Many of these were of the Persian – or, more precisely, Persepolitan type. This example, dating from the 1st century AD, is carved with horses and elephants bearing human figures.

Early stambha

The earliest *stambhas* to survive were erected by King Asoka (c. 269–232 BC). These may have been based on lost wooden models, and were inscribed with religious doctrines and historical information. The necking of this *stambha* bears honeysuckle ornament, a sign of Persian and Assyrian influence.

Early and Classical India

Chaitya Halls

The most sacred of Buddhist architectural works in India were *chaitya* halls. These served as temples for congregational worship, and are comparable – in plan and function – with Romanesque and Gothic churches. Unlike churches, however, *chaitya* halls are predominantly caves, cut directly out of the rock using mallets and iron chisels. The earliest halls to survive date from the 2nd century BC, and may have been inspired partly by the caves of Persia and Asia Minor. They continued to be built for nearly 500 years. *Chaitya* halls consist of a main space divided into a nave and aisles by two rows of columns. A rock–cut votive stupa, also known as a *chaitya*, provides the principal religious focus. The form of the stupa, with the passageway around it for *pradakshina*, gave *chaitya* halls a part-circular termination that is known – as in Christian churches – as an apse.

Screen, Bhaja
Originally, rock-cut *chaitya* halls were fronted by timber screens. These included one or more doorways at the lower level, and had a great window admitting the light above. Although the screen has vanished from this early *chaitya* hall at Bhaja in the Deccan, the socket holes remain. Screens continued to be built, but stone was used in place of timber.

Free-standing chaitya hall, Chezarla
The first *chaitya* halls appear to have been free-standing buildings, constructed of timber. Though none survive, they are known through brick and stone copies, such as this rare example near Chennai. A similar structure, dating from the 2nd to 3rd centuries AD, exists at Ter in the Deccan.

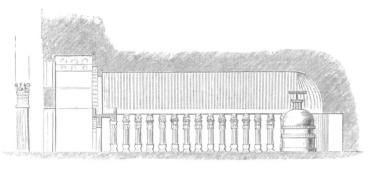

Chaitya hall, Karli (1st century AD)
One of the largest and best-preserved early *chaitya* halls is that at Karli, in the Deccan. Its plan follows the set pattern – a hall divided by two rows of columns, with a stupa as its focus. The interiors of *chaitya* halls were relatively simple, though this example has richly carved pillars.

Chaitya window
The great *chaitya* window was an integral element of the hall's architecture, and allowed sunlight to reach its interior. Its horseshoe-like shape, also known as *gavaksha* design, became a recurring motif on the façades of *chaitya* halls, and continued to be used on temples for many hundreds of years.

Stupa, Karli
Rock-cut stupas were often richly adorned. The light entering the hall through the great window would have fallen directly on to the stupa, leaving the rest of the interior in relative darkness. This stupa, at Karli, has a two-storey drum, set off with rail ornaments, and carries a *tee* and elaborate wooden umbrella.

Chaitya roofs, Ajanta
Typically, the main space of a *chaitya* hall was barrel-vaulted, and the aisles carried half-vaults. Both bore ribs, either of timber or of stone, cut to imitate timber forms. This hall at Ajanta in the Deccan has an exceptionally tall triforium, which was originally plastered and elaborately painted.

Early and Classical India

Viharas

Another significant early type of Buddhist building was the *vihara*, or monastery. Examples date from the 2nd century BC. Most were simple rock-cut caves, where monks met, prayed and slept. The essential elements were the object of worship (a Buddha figure or stupa), the monks' cells (containing stone platforms for beds) and the shrines for images. *Viharas* were often built in groups as monastic complexes. The most famous collection of such caves survives at Ajanta in the Deccan; the *viharas* range in date from the 2nd century BC to the late 5th century AD. Many of the later examples were richly ornamented and are unparalleled in the history of Indian art. *Viharas* were also erected by the Jains, a sect that grew up at the same time as the Buddhists.

Cells

Typically, a horseshoe arch, echoing the design of the great *chaitya* windows, was placed above the doorway of the cells in which the monks slept. In later times, when design developed and became more elaborate, cells were given domed roofs and carved façades.

Early free-standing vihara

Although the oldest surviving *viharas* are rock-cut, they seem – like *chaitya* halls – to have originally been free-standing structures. According to contemporary descriptions, these were pyramidal in form and consisted of halls raised one above the other on wooden posts.

Vihara and chaitya hall

The earliest rock-cut *viharas* were built next to, though detached from, *chaitya* halls. They consisted simply of a rectangular court, with small cells opening off this main space. Initially, there was no need for a chapel, as worship was performed in the adjacent *chaitya*.

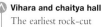

Sanctuary and chapels

By the 5th century AD, *viharas* included chapels and a sanctuary, so that worship could be performed independently of the *chaitya* halls. The sanctuary was placed immediately opposite the entrance, and typically contained a stupa or image of Buddha.

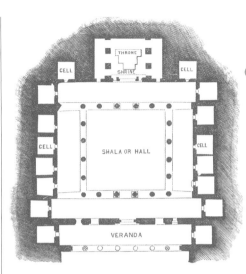

Verandahs

The majority of *viharas* were fronted by verandahs (large porches). These served as a transition between the outside world and the semi-darkness of the rock-cut hall, and often provided the principal focus for ornament. Columns were carved, and sometimes walls and ceilings were painted with frescoes.

Sala, Bagh (5th century AD)

Some later *viharas* had rooms that were known as *salas* attached to them. *Salas* served principally as school rooms, but may also have been used as refectories *(dharmasalas)* or for religious worship. This example, at Bagh in central India, was accessed from the main hall via a long, twenty-pillared verandah. The internal walls of the verandah would have been richly decorated.

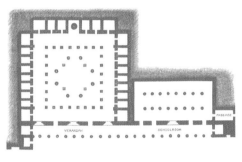

Structural vihara, Takht-i-Bahi (3rd century AD)

In Gandhara, now northern Pakistan, *viharas* were invariably free-standing structures, built of stone. This, the monastery at Takht-i-Bahi, includes a square court with a stupa at its centre (A), a court with image niches (B), a residential court or *sangharama* (C), and a meeting hall or *upasthanasala* (D).

Pillared hall, Ajanta (5th century AD)

As *viharas* grew larger and more splendid, pillars began to be placed within the hall's interior, in order to support the increasing roof spans. At first four pillars were used, then twelve, and later twenty or more. The pillars as well as the roof and walls of this hall at Ajanta in the Deccan, which dates from the late 5th century AD, are covered with coloured decoration.

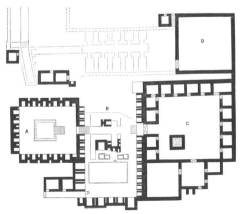

Early and Classical India

Rock-cut Temples

From the 6th century AD, Buddhism experienced a period of decline and there was a resurgence of Hindu dynasties throughout India. Under the Hindus, the temple was developed as a characteristic architectural form, revered as the abode of a deity. All Indian temple architecture is essentially similar, whether built by the Hindus or the Jains. The Indian classical works on architecture (the *Shastras*) divided temples into three styles, differentiated not by religion but by geographical area. The two main styles were the Dravida or Dravidian style belonging to southern India, and the Nagara or Indo-Aryan style of northern India. The third style, the Vesara or Chalukyan, was a mix of both and was focused on central India (the Deccan). Some of the most accomplished early temples to survive are Dravidian.

Dravidian tower form
All *rathas* bear prominent towers *(vimanas)*, made up of distinct, stepped tiers *(talas)*. The towers are topped by dome-like ornaments known as *sikharas* (not to be confused with the same term as used to refer to Nagara towers). This tower form was to become the most characteristic feature of the Dravidian style.

Ratha
The Dravidian style appeared in its purest early form at Mamallapuram in the 7th century AD, in a series of remarkable monolithic temples that were known as *rathas* or *raths* (literally, 'chariots of a warrior' or 'processional cars'). These were cut from blocks of granite, and were left unfinished. The *rathas* were sculpted imitations of structural buildings, possibly the early free-standing *viharas*.

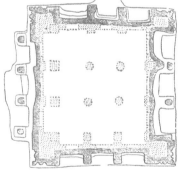

Dravidian temple plan
In plan, the Dravidian temples remained largely undeveloped, consisting of a single space, which was sometimes pillared.

Indra Sabha cave, Ellora (9th century AD)
At Ellora there are temples built not only by the Hindus, but also by the Jains. These are closely comparable to the Dravidian examples, such as the Kailasa temple. The finest is the early 9th-century Indra Sabha cave, shown here. The columns are carved with rich foliate motifs, reminiscent of the Greek acanthus.

Lion pillar, Mamallapuram (7th century AD)
This carved pillar is representative of the Dravidian style and typifies those found at Mamallapuram. It has a base with a seated lion *(vyalis)* – a device of the Pallavas, the ruling dynasty – and a curved, cushion capital *(kumbhas)*. Above the *kumbha* is a flared, lotus-like element called an *idal*, and a broad, thin abacus known as a *palagai*.

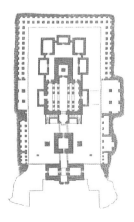

Vishnu sculpture, Badami cave (6th century AD)
A common sight in the sculptural schemes of Hindu temples is Vishnu, one of the religion's most sacred deities. Here, at one of the earliest temples in the Dravidian style, the 6th-century cave at Badami, Vishnu is shown seated on the five-headed serpent Ananta.

Kailasa temple, Ellora (8th century AD)
In this temple, constructed in the mid-8th century, the rock-cut phase reached its climax and the Dravidian temple plan made its first fully developed appearance. The Kailasa is a free-standing structure, from which the rock has been cut away externally and internally.

Early and Classical India

Temples: Layout and Interiors

The plans of Indian temples were carefully regulated. It was thought that a correctly proportioned building was in harmony with the universe and could bring order to the community. Geometric diagrams known as mandalas were used, as were the cardinal directions; temples were built on an east–west axis, aligned with the rising and setting sun. Initially, all temples consisted of a simple sanctuary, often with a separate pillared portico. Over time, the sanctuary (*garbhagriha*) grew more ornate, its tower more prominent and the portico became a hall, joined to the sanctuary. Temples in the north, south and centre of India diverged in style from the 5th to 7th centuries, giving rise to the Dravidian, Nagara and Vesara styles, though architectural traditions varied from place to place.

Column

The columns or pillars used in the interiors of Indian temples, principally in their *mandapas*, evolved gradually over hundreds of years. This example dates from the 17th century, by which time carving had become incredibly rich and varied. The heavy, drop-like corbel pendant, favoured by the Dravidians, is called a *puspobodigai*.

Garbhagriha and mandapa

The most sacred part of an Indian temple was its sanctuary, a small, dark room known as the *garbhagriha* (womb chamber), where the deity was placed. The sanctuary was surrounded by a pathway for *pradakshina*, and was approached via a *mandapa*, an assembly hall for worshippers. The short vestibule between *mandapa* and *garbhagriha* was known as an *antarala*.

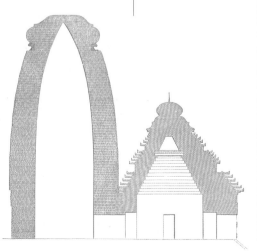

Tower and roof

The position of the *garbhagriha* was marked externally by a tower or spire, while *mandapa* roofs were lower and usually pyramidal. The *mandapa* shown in this example has a *pida* roof, a characteristic Orissan form of diminishing tiers.

Orissan style

At Orissa in eastern India there survives a distinctive group of temples, which reached the peak of their development in the 10th and 11th centuries. In plan, these followed the northern style, being based on squares and, as was typical, consisted of two spaces: a sanctuary, known in local terminology as a *deul*, and a *mandapa*, known as a *jagamohan*.

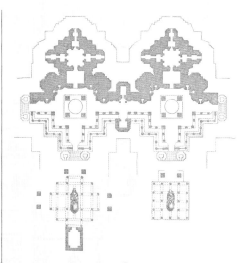

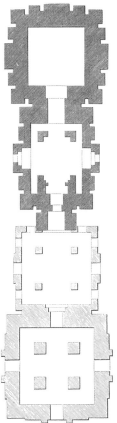

Hoysala style

Although the three Indian temple styles – Dravidian, Nagara and Vesara – remained dominant, there were regional variants, often named after a ruling dynasty. Such was the Hoysala style, a subdivision of Vesara, which was characterised by its stellate (star-shaped) sanctuary and double temple plans.

Multiple mandapas

In more complex temple plans, multiple *mandapas* were aligned on the principal axis. Each of these halls was used for a special purpose, such as dancing, eating or making offerings.

Decoration of porches and mandapas

In contrast to the plain and simple *garbhagrihas*, the temple's porches and *mandapas* were very richly decorated. Pillars were carved with reliefs of gods, demi-gods and celestial beings, as here at Chidambaram in south India.

Mandapa dome

The open, central area of *mandapas* were often carried up as corbelled domes, which were then richly carved. The example from the Jain temple at Abu (1032 and later), in western India *(far right)*, incorporates sixteen *vidyadevis* (goddesses of knowledge) and has a central pendant.

Early and Classical India

Temples: Exteriors

A great deal of thought went into the siting of Indian temples and the precise timing of each stage of their construction, reflecting the belief that temples were directly related to cosmic patterns. Typically, stone courses were not bonded with mortar, but were made stable by the burden of weight pressing downwards. Stones were placed using earth ramps, and in some cases a whole building was filled with sand or earth during construction, which was later removed through doorways. Building projects were overseen by a chief architect *(sutradhara)* and a superintendent of works, but were viewed as the combined effort of a number of people. Temples were commonly built through the patronage of powerful kings, resulting in dynastic labels being applied to particular styles.

Amalaka

This elevation epitomises the Orissan variant of the Nagara style. The tower *(sikhara)*, of a curvilinear form on a square base, is divided into *bhumi* (horizontal mouldings), and is topped by a feature called an *amalaka*. This was based on a gourd or melon, and was usually surmounted by a *kalasha*, an ornamental vase or waterpot.

Sikhara and vimana

The easiest way to differentiate between India's two main temple styles is to study their towers. Nagara (northern) temples carry curved beehive-shaped towers known as *sikharas*, while Dravidian (southern) temples have multi-storey pyramidal towers called *vimanas*. The word *sikhara* means peak or crest; temples were conceived as mountains, the sacred place of the gods.

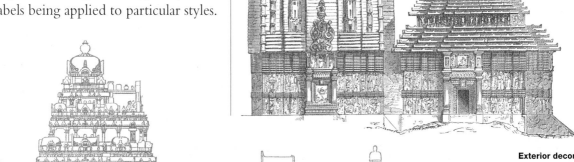

Exterior decoration

Decoration *(alankara)* of temples was viewed as a requirement. This mid-8th-century temple at Pattadakai was one of the richest buildings of its day, and was adorned with Dravidian motifs: tall pilasters, sculptured niches and *gavakshas* (horseshoe arches).

Towers of Vesara temples

The towers of temples built in the Vesara (or Chalukyan) style follow the Dravidian form in being stepped or terraced. However, the storeys *(talas)* are less emphatically expressed than in Dravidian examples, and are often more richly sculpted.

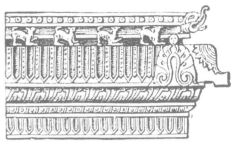

Entablature

In Indian terminology, the entablature was known as the *prastara*. All Indian sculpture was conceived dynamically, and was deeply cut so as to make changes of plane more obvious.

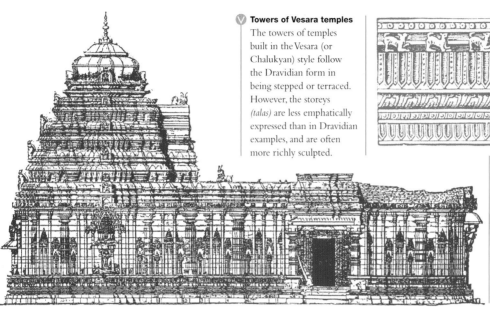

Pilaster

Pilasters, as used in Indian architecture, were very similar to those used in the buildings of Greece and Rome – that is, shallow pillars or columns projecting only slightly from the wall. Indian pilasters were complete with capital and bracket.

Basement

Indian temples were often raised on a high plinth *(adhisthana)*, which brought external sculpture up to eye level. This was especially the case with Vesara (or Chalukyan) temples.

Temple porch

Porches were lavished with ornament and, like Buddhist railings, marked the boundary between the outside world and the sacred space. This porch is typical of the Dravidian style in having a bold cornice, groups of colonnettes, sculpted beasts and a rich plinth or basement.

Development of sikharas

In later *sikharas* of the Nagara or northern style, the tower was often ornamented with smaller representations of itself, known as *urusringas*.

Early and Classical India

Temples: Complexes

The last major development of north Indian Nagara temples occurred in the 10th century, but the southern Dravidian style continued to develop for several hundred years. It entered its period of greatest expansion *c.* 1250 under the Chola kings. There were *mandapas* (assembly halls) for a variety of purposes, and massive gateways – sometimes reaching as high as 52 m (170 ft) – punctuated courtyards (*prakaras*) enclosing the ever less conspicuous sanctuary. These splendid gate towers displayed the wealth and power of a temple, and increased the visual impact of the approach to the holy shrine. In many cases, additions to temple complexes continued until the 18th century. The Hindu style thus significantly overlaps that of the Muslims, who had begun their great Indian works of architecture in the 1100s.

Prakara

In southern India, the original temple confines often became inadequate. Courtyards (*prakaras*) were built around the original building, enclosing shrines, *mandapas* and other structures.

Gopuram

Gopurams, monumental towered gateways, are among the most magnificent of Indian buildings. They led devotees into the sacred temple complex, and consisted of a stone basement carrying levels of brick, wood and plaster. The upper level was often topped with *stupikas* (diminutive stupas).

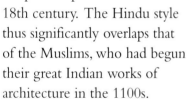

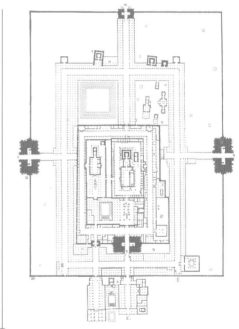

Tank, Rameshwaram (17th/18th century)

An important feature of temple complexes was the tank (*talar*), which was used for bathing and for sacred purposes. The tank was fed by rainwater, springs or channels, and often had stepped sides. The one shown in this plan (*top left*), of the temple complex at Rameshwaram, is surrounded by a colonnade on three sides.

Chaultri, Pudu Mandapa, Madurai (17th century)

Chaultris, or pillared halls, were often built as part of later Dravidian temple complexes, and served a number of uses, from porches to halls of ceremony. This hall was built for the reception of a local deity. It has a total of 128 pillars, each carved in a different form, arranged in four rows.

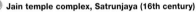

Shrine, Belur (12th century)

Shrines to minor divinities were placed within temple complexes from early on. This, one of several at the temple at Belur, is adorned with a roof imitating that of the temple itself.

Temple complex, Bhubaneshwar (late 11th century)

In the Nagara-style temple complexes of northern India, unlike the south, the main temple with its *sikhara* remained the most prominent feature. Gateways were low and usually modest, as here at the Great or Lingaraja Temple of Bhubaneshwar in Orissa.

Jain temple complex, Satrunjaya (16th century)

The Jains, unlike the Hindus, often grouped their temples together in vast numbers. Here, at the sacred hill of Satrunjaya in western India, more than 500 temples and shrines are contained within fortified enclosures, known as *tuks*. These *tuks* boasted ornate gateways and corner bastions.

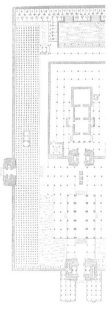

Thousand-pillared hall

Dravidian temple complexes built in the 17th and 18th centuries had pillared corridors and thousand-pillared halls, which were comparable with Egyptian hypostyle halls.

Early and Dynastic China *1500 BC–C.19th*

Timber Halls: Form and Structure

The vast majority of buildings in pre-modern China were timber structures, which had always been considered proper dwelling places for the living or places in which to worship the gods. The most typical Chinese building was a rectangular hall on an elevated platform. Its wooden columns were joined together by means of tenon and mortice in a complex trabeated (beamed) system, and it had curtain walls, rather than walls that supported the structure. Probably by the 7th century AD sophisticated modular techniques were fully developed and universally employed, standardising planning and construction. This resulted in the adaptability of timber halls to diverse uses, large spans affording maximal unobstructed space, complete freedom in placing doors and windows, and the possibility of expanding the basic ground plan in all directions.

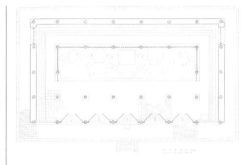

Floor plan, Foguang Monastery
This hall is one of the earliest existing wooden buildings in China. Its floor plan is typical in taking the long side as its main façade with a marked axis. The width of its intercolumnar space or bay (*jian*) – a basic structural unit of the building – diminishes slightly from the centre to the sides.

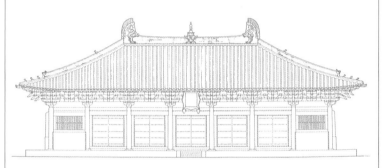

Elevation, Foguang Monastery
The roof is emphasised by its construction in sweeping curves and by its tremendous overhang. Also visually prominent are the bracket sets (*dougong*) under the eaves of the roof – structural members directly supported by the columns. The columns themselves, each showing some extent of entasis, or convex curving (*juansha*), all lean slightly towards the centre (*cejiao*) and are progressively longer, the further they stand from the central bay (*shengqi*).

Structure of the main hall, Foguang Monastery, Mt Wutai (AD 857)
The columns, resting on plinths, are here fixed together by tie beams at various heights above the floor. The bracket clusters serve to strengthen the column–roof relationship, reinforce the bearing capacity of beams and rafters, balance the weight on both sides of the columns, hold the longitudinal elements together and create a large overhang of eaves. The roof is supported by beams of diminishing length, placed vertically over one another across the plan and separated by struts. This column-beam-and-strut, or *tailiang* structure facilitates the curving of the roof.

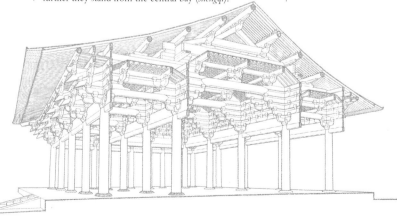

Plan, Hall of Supreme Harmony, Forbidden City, Beijing
First built in 1420, this hall is the largest existing timber structure in China. It is very common for a timber hall to contain colonnaded open galleries on its outer sides and (in this case) a gallery to the front.

Elevation, Hall of Supreme Harmony
Throughout the centuries important changes occurred in both the form and style of timber halls. By the 15th century the roof had become higher and steeper, whereas the ridge and eave lines became straighter and more mechanical. The columns, no longer demonstrating entasis, became equal in height. The overhang of the eaves was considerably reduced.

Plan, Hall of Prayer for a Harvest Year, Temple of Heaven, Beijing
The same structural principles could be applied to diverse plans. First built in 1540, this building is laden with symbolism. The circular plan symbolises Heaven (the Chinese believed that Heaven was round and the Earth was square). The roofs of the hall are supported by three circles of columns, the four larger central columns representing the seasons, the middle twelve the months, and the outermost twelve the divisions of the traditional Chinese days.

Structure, Hall of Supreme Harmony
With the use of columns and beams of huge size, bracket sets lost much of their structural function and were reduced to a more delicate scale and an even size. Having become principally ornamental elements, they spread continuously over columns and tie beams, separating rather than joining roof and columns.

Plan, Forbidden City
An individual building did not usually stand alone as a self-contained structure, but was considered part of a building compound designated for a certain social establishment. Hence the ubiquity of courtyards, around which individual buildings were formally grouped, with marked axes. It would be ideal for the main buildings of a compound to face south.

Elevation, Temple of Heaven
Raised on top of a three-level white marble terrace, the hall has three roofs, which are covered with bright-blue glazed tiles and surmounted by a gilded ball.

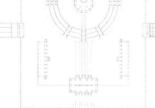

Early and Dynastic China

Timber Halls: Exterior Ornament

Chinese timber buildings are noted for their structural frankness and for the close association of ornament with structure – ornaments in general not being created for their own sake, but for structural purposes. Paint, for instance, is applied to the structural members of the building in order to prevent the wood from decaying, but at the same time assumes a decorative function. The exterior of a hall may be divided into four parts where different modes of ornament are used: the roof, with a prominent overhang to protect the building from rain; the painted bracket sets, which are structural as well as ornamental; the building proper, which comprises painted columns, walls, doors and windows; and the platform or terrace on which the building stands, so that the timber structure can be moisture-proof. In each dynastic period, specific sumptuary law was enacted to regulate the scale, form and ornament of individual buildings.

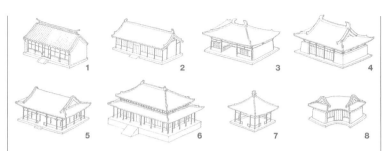

Roof forms

The visual emphasis on the roof is evident from the sheer variety of its forms. There are four basic types, from which a plethora of combinations derive: gabled (1, 2), hipped (3, 6), half-gabled and half-hipped (4, 5, 8) and the pyramidal (7). Of these, the hipped roof was considered of the highest rank.

Northern and southern styles

Considerable differences in style exist between buildings in south China and those in the north. The northern construction style *(above right)* is usually more robust and its ornament less delicate. But the most visually conspicuous difference is the southern tendency to a more dramatic upturn of the corners of the eaves *(above left)*.

Finials

An earthenware finial, or *chiwen*, stands at each of the two ends of the ridgepole to cover the joint of the roof slopes. By the 14th century it had already developed into a range of fantastic animal images that carried with them the symbolism of fire-fighting power. This dragon-like animal was said to be so elusive that it had to be fixed to the ridge with a sword.

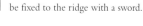

Acroteria

Acroteria, each in the form of a certain fantastic animal (hence the Chinese name *xiaoshou*, meaning 'small animals'), were placed in line on the sloping ridge at the corner of the roof. Their initial function was to shield the bolts that kept the ridge tiles in place.

Decorative painting

Polychrome painting, or *caihua*, is applied to all the exterior wooden members of the building. From around the late 14th century, warm colours (especially red) were used in the north on columns, doors and windows, while cold colours were painted into designs on architraves, brackets and other members that appear in the shadow of the eaves. Illustrated here are two major styles of painting: *hexi (above)* and *Suzhou (top)*.

Baluster heads

Particular attention was paid to the decoration of baluster heads. The two immediately below have motifs of a dragon or phoenix flying amid clouds and were used for important palace buildings. Other balusters, with motifs ranging from lotus flower to pomegranate, were incorporated in gardens.

Balustrade

Platforms or terraces of timber buildings are often demarcated by balustrades. By the 10th century, wooden balustrades could be found in private gardens, although marble ones appear to be more common. The one shown here, with water spouts, forms part of the terraces on which the Hall of Supreme Harmony stands.

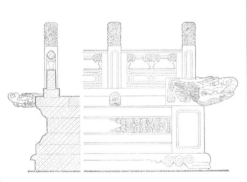

Early and Dynastic China

Cities

Cities in dynastic China functioned primarily as administrative centres of the imperial government. They were not corporate entities of their own, but political nuclei of the (largely rural) areas in which they were located. To be properly regarded as 'cities', they had to be walled – a fact signified by the Chinese word *cheng,* which means simultaneously 'city', 'city wall' and 'to wall a city'. From the 14th century on, the significance of city walls transcended their pragmatic function, symbolising the presence of government and social order. A large number of cities were planned in advance and thus achieved regularity of form. But there were also cases where some degree of planning was superimposed on the unplanned settlements – but too late to be thoroughgoing.

Canonical plan, Imperial City
This diagram represents the notion of the ideal city as systematised around 100 BC: square in plan, with three gates on each side; oriented to the four cardinal points, with an emphasis on the north–south axis; and demonstrating the centrality of the palace in the city. Prescriptive rather than historical though it is, it proved to be most influential for city planning throughout the succeeding two millennia.

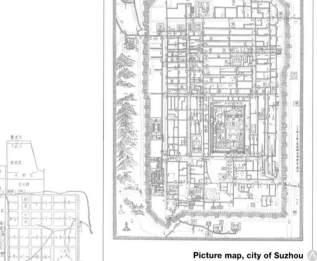

Picture map, city of Suzhou
This map of the time-honoured city was carved on stone in 1229. From the 8th to the 10th centuries, cities in economically advanced regions experienced profound change in their internal structure, marked by the gradual collapse of the walled-ward system and the emergence of a much freer street network for trade and commerce. The prefectural offices occupied the inner walled enclosure, and a dual system of water and road transport prevailed.

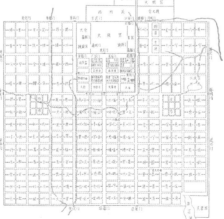

Plan, Tang Dynasty capital of Chang'an
Built in the late 6th century AD, this was the largest city in the world at the time. The palace enceinte (main area of a fortress, surrounded by a wall or ditch) is positioned in the north centre of the city, and due south is the imperial enclosure for government offices. The rest of the city is divided into 108 walled, strictly supervised residential wards and two walled markets located symmetrically in the east and west.

Plan, city of Shaoxing

The preference for a city plan of square or rectangular shape found expression in favourable conditions mainly on the North China Plain; cities in the south, where topographical configurations were complex, were often more irregular in form. This plan was produced in 1893. The prefectural city of Shaoxing is famed for its canals and bridges.

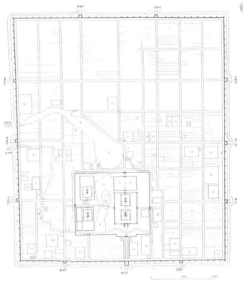

Plan, Yuan Dynasty capital of Dadu

Built between 1267 and 1284 in, Dadu (or 'The Great Capital') on the site of present-day Beijing was a triple-walled city of a nearly perfect geometric form, with the palace enclosure situated on the main axis of the city, surrounded by the imperial enclosure. The outer city wall had three gates on each face, except the northern one, which had only two.

Plan, Ming and Qing Dynasties capital of Beijing

Built on the ruins of the Yuan Dynasty capital of Dadu, this city was designated the imperial capital in 1403 and remained so throughout the last centuries of the dynastic era. An outer city wall was built in 1553 to protect the prosperous south suburb, thus creating an axis 8 km (5 miles) long, running from the south central gate of the outer city to the Drum and Bell Towers in the north.

Plan, city of Datong

Included in this northern city were local government offices and granaries, the local military headquarters and barracks, a Confucian temple, Buddhist and Taoist temples, and a bell tower and drum tower. This city was also typical in having within its walls empty spaces for growing grain and vegetables. Additional walls were later built to protect the prosperous areas outside the city gates.

Early and Dynastic China

Pagodas

There are two principal sources of the Chinese pagoda: the native multi-storeyed timber tower created prior to the arrival of Buddhism in the 1st century AD (forming the main body) and the Buddhist stupa from India (functioning as its spire or finial). Preferences concerning the base plan varied in different dynastic periods; the square plan was dominant before the 10th century AD, but thereafter polygonal plans prevailed. Similarly, pagoda form and style continued to change, partly due to the influence of new stupa forms in the West and to alterations in faith, and partly due to stylistic evolution. Most often built of wood or brick, or a combination of the two, the pagoda was not always confined to Buddhist sites, but was sometimes built as a solitary scenic structure, and occasionally used for feng shui interpretations.

Plan, Shaka Pagoda, Fogong Monastery, Yingxian (1056)
Hexagonal in plan, this timber pagoda occupies the central point on the main north–south axis of the monastery, a choice of location that was prevalent in China before the 8th century.

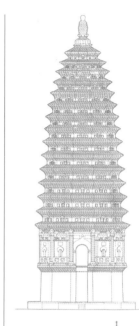

Pagoda, Songyue Monastery, Mt Song (523)
This is the earliest surviving brick pagoda in China and the only one with a dodecagonal (twelve-sided) base plan. The interior is a hollow octagonal well, whereas the exterior has a high double-plinth storey, above which are fifteen successive repetitions of the basic storey unit, each with its own roof. The whole structure diminishes with height, and is crowned with a mast and discs.

Sarira Pagoda, Qixia Monastery, Nanjing (937–75)
This small, solid stone pagoda has a five-storey appearance and an octagonal plan. Particularly noteworthy is the lavish application of lotus motifs to the base and finial: the lotus being part of the imagery of the 'Pure Land' school of Buddhism.

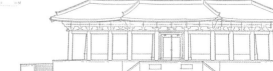

Elevation, Shaka Pagoda
Towering to 67.3 m (221 ft), this pagoda is the tallest timber structure in China. There are fifty-four different types of bracket set supporting the eaves, but the large number of bracket clusters is unexpected when viewing the pagoda from a distance, because of its supreme harmony and structural unity.

Cross-section, Shaka Pagoda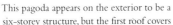
This pagoda appears on the exterior to be a six-storey structure, but the first roof covers only the skirting verandah. However, there are four additional mezzanine storeys that provide space for large structural members. Thus the pagoda is, in fact, a nine-storey building.

Pagoda, Miaoying Monastery, Beijing (1271)
Designed by a Nepalese architect for Mongol emperors, this white-washed, brick pagoda was built in 1271 in Dadu (present-day Beijing). It clearly shows its *dagaba* (stupa) origin with the Tibetan *chaitya*.

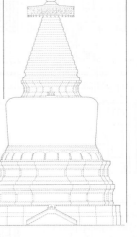

Anatomical perspective, Pagoda of Bao'en Buddhist Temple, Suzhou
Built in 1153, but largely reconstructed in 1898, this nine-storey pagoda is an example of building in a combination of wood and brick. The brick core is wrapped with wooden cladding so that the exterior looks as if it is a timber structure.

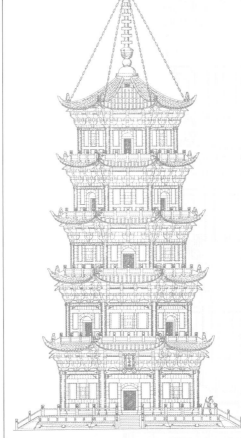

Renshou Pagoda, Kaiyuan Monastery, Quanzhou (1228–37)
This is one of the twin pagodas of Kaiyuan Monastery (the other being the Zhenguo Pagoda). Executed in stone in 1237 and 1250 respectively, both are octagonal in plan and have elaborate bracket sets that are imitative of woodwork, and the southern style of markedly upward-curving eave corners.

Early and Dynastic China

Houses

Owing to the vastness of China, regional and local environmental, historical, cultural and ethnic conditions have produced striking diversity in house forms and styles. Such diversity is in contrast to the universality of the 'governmental style'; in any given area, the higher the social rank of an institution, the less distinctive was the regional style shown in its buildings. On the other hand, houses of different regions evince a remarkable degree of integration, in that some common elements prevail that characterise Chinese vernacular architecture: they share not only basic structural principles, but also characteristics of orientation, symmetry, axiality and layout.

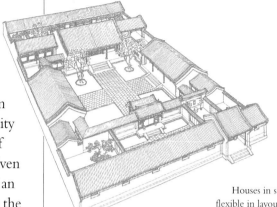

Perspective of a house, Zhejiang Province
Apart from the dramatic upturn of its eave corners, also characteristic of the southern house is the employment of the column-and-tie, or *chuandou*, structure. This differs from the more official *tailiang* structure in that the weight of the roof is borne directly by columns rising successively towards the ridge of the roof and receiving the purlins.

Typical courtyard house, Beijing
This house has its main entrance at the south-east corner of the compound. Each gate symbolises to the visitor coming from the outside the threshold of yet another domain, because the passing of each gateway represents a penetration into a new depth of the family's privacy. This group privacy is more valued in its relation to the outside world than the privacy of each individual within the family.

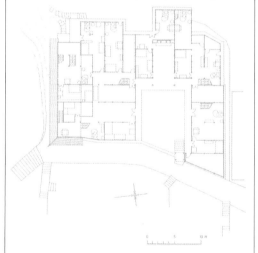

House plan, Zhejiang Province
Houses in southern rural areas could be fairly flexible in layout, adapting themselves to the local topographical conditions. Housing an expanded family of parents and married children, this compound integrates quarters for small family units, each symbolised by a stove.

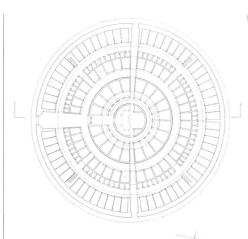

Anatomical perspective, communal residence, Fujian Province

Occupying the centre of the compound is the ancestral hall. The two inner rings consist of guest rooms and areas for wells and domestic animals. The ground floor of the outer ring contains kitchens, washrooms and rooms for miscellaneous use; the first floor is used for grain storage; and the second and third floors are dwelling quarters.

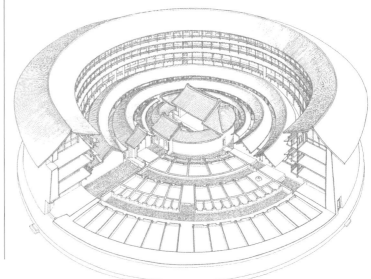

Plan, communal residence, Fujian Province

From the 3rd century BC on, the Kejia (also known as Hakka, meaning 'guest families') people migrated at various times to the southern provinces of Fujian, Guangdong and Guangxi from central China. Their hostile reception by the locals led to the development of the tradition of living collectively as a clan in large, walled, multi-storey communal buildings of circular or rectangular form.

Cross-section, communal residence, Fujian Province

The outer wall of this four-storey building, over 1 m (3 ft) in thickness, is built of rammed earth and is joined to the inner timber framework. Small windows opening to the outside are set in the wall only above the first floor, while the apartments with balconies face inward.

Seal-form house, Yunnan Province

Like the houses in southern Anhui and some other areas of the south, this square-planned, two-storey house carries inward-facing character and privacy to the extreme. Its chambers are tightly connected to each other, and the court through which daylight and ventilation are obtained is reduced to a tiny vertical opening called a 'sky well'. The whole building resembles the Chinese seal in shape, hence its name.

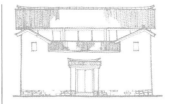

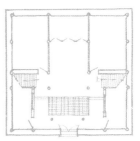

Early and Dynastic China

Gardens

In their physical form, nearly all the classical gardens existing in China at present date from no earlier than the 19th century. Yet the culture that produced them developed over 3,000 years. The distinction between the two major traditions of imperial parks of the royal families and private gardens of the classically educated may already have been conspicuous by the end of the 3rd century AD; they were to influence each other over the ensuing one and half millennia. Like landscape painting, gardens were meant to abstract the essence of idealised nature and thus reproduce the conceived spirit of the landscape. Literature was another crucial dimension, with gardens providing both subjects and settings for composition, and with allusive names rendering the gardens meaningful.

Plan, Summer Palace, Beijing
Initially built in 1750, this was one of five imperial gardens in the west suburbs of Beijing. The whole composition follows the West Lake at Hangzhou, but at the same time commands views beyond the immediate surrounding landscape, including the western hills. This technique, known as 'borrowing views', was frequently used in garden design.

Plan, West Garden, Beijing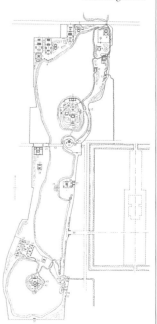
The layout of this imperial garden started in the 1450s–60s. Lying to the west of the Forbidden City, but within the Imperial Walled Enclosure, it consists of three lakes. Like the lakes at the Summer Palace, these ones have islets in them, representing the mythical islands of the immortals, believed to lie off the coast of Shandong province. Again echoing the Summer Palace, small gardens with their own walls are encapsulated within it, forming the so-called 'gardens within a garden'.

Bird's-eye view, Garden of the Master of the Fishing Net, Suzhou
The garden is a place for the visitor to move around: 'the views change with each step' – around the pond, for instance. There are also primary vantage points, such as a pavilion, a gallery and a kiosk, from which particularly desired views are presented. This principle was derived from theories of landscape painting.

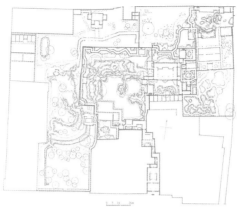

Plan, Lingering Garden, Suzhou
This private garden, expanded in the late 19th century, uses a common method for creating richness and variety of views: it divides the garden into smaller parts of different size, each with its own distinctive theme and character. Walls, fences, verandahs, buildings, rockeries, groves and bridges are used for this purpose.

Bird's-eye view, Mountain Villa of Embracing the Emerald Green
Here, a series of terraces follow the contours of the slope, on which stand individual buildings. The whole garden complex merges well with the surrounding landscape, and an air of unadorned simplicity is apparent among its buildings.

Plan, Garden of the Master of the Fishing Net
The present layout of this city garden is the result of reconstruction in 1795. It is a classic example of the private garden built as an extension of the house. But although house construction was largely an impersonal art in the hands of craftsmen, the layout of a garden was as much the proper work of a scholar as were poetry and painting.

Plan, Mountain Villa of Embracing the Emerald Green, Suzhou
This mountain villa was built in 1884 on the southern slope of Tiger Hill, 3 km (1¾ miles) northwest of the city. It is a good example of adapting the garden to the topographical conditions of the site, thus making full use of them.

Cross-section, Lingering Garden
The use of elements of mutually contrasting and yet complementary attributes – the pairing of yin and yang concepts – to emphasise salient points or imply infinite change (as well as ultimate harmony) is common in Chinese gardens. Similar attributes include the small and the large, the dark and the bright, the void and the solid, and so on.

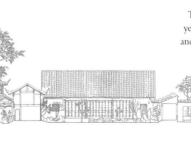

Classical Japan *pre-C.6th BC–C.19th*

Shinto Shrines

Shinto, meaning 'way of the gods', was the traditional religion of early Japan, before Buddhism arrived in the 6th century AD. It was initially practised in places of great natural beauty demarcated by piles of stones and other organic boundaries. Natural materials – primarily wood for the frame and grass for coverings – were later used for constructing simple forms, such as gateways, or *torii*, and small shrines. While the formalisation of Shinto, with these raised-floor shrines and gable roofs (based on the agricultural model of the storehouse), grounded the religion in the Japanese landscape, Shinto was essentially a vernacular religion without a large architectural repertoire. As an extension of the careful use of natural elements to create a place for worship, the spatial organisation informed the pattern of worship, and the site arrangement was as important as the set pieces themselves.

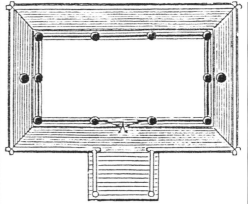

Plan
A staircase to the central doorway, which is the only opening in the plank walls, reaches the elevated inner shrine, and verandahs follow the perimeter of the main room. A free-standing column supports the ridge at the centre of each gable end.

Construction
At Ise Jingu, the shrine buildings are framed in Japanese cypress. They are supported by columns inserted directly into the ground, rather than raised on foundation stones, which was the practice at other, earlier shrines.

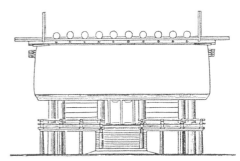

Torii
The principal element, and one of the earliest architectural forms, of a Shinto shrine is the *torii*, or gateway. It is of post-and-lintel construction, with upright wooden posts, usually inserted directly into the earth, supporting two horizontal beams. The arrangement of this form is believed to allow the passage of prayer through the *torii* gate.

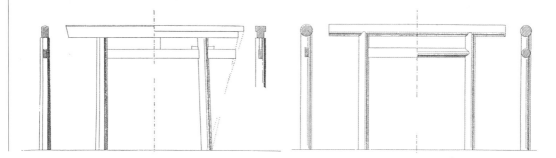

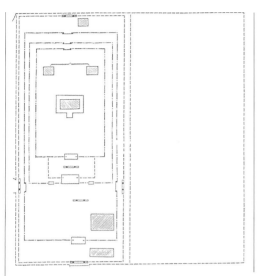

Tamagaki
A key architectural element of an early Shinto shrine is the surrounding *tamagaki*, a wooden fence of horizontal boards attached to upright posts.

Setting
Ise Jingu on the eastern coast of Japan was first built in the 4th century, on a site of great natural beauty that had been used for Shinto worship for centuries.

Site plan
From the 8th century on, festivals were organised nationally and any group of several shrines was known as an Ise shrine. The inner shrine, or *naiku*, is for the ancestral god of the imperial family and the outer shrine, or *geku*, is for the local god.

Ise shrine
The shrine at Ise Jingu was both the ancestral shrine of the imperial family and the national shrine. It is identified by a deep-pile, reed-thatched gable roof with bargeboards that continue up through the ridge to form two pairs of forked finials, or *chigi*, and ten billets, or *katsuogi*, that together produce a distinctive profile to the building.

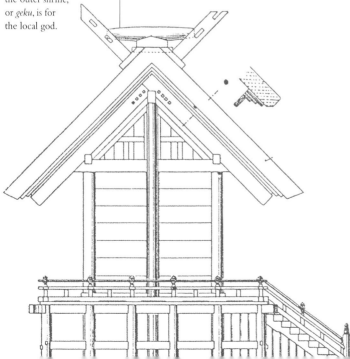

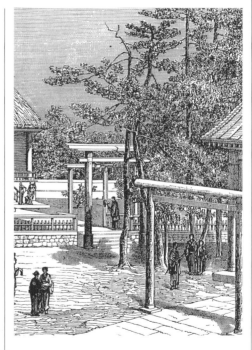

The building tradition
A practice known as *shikinen-sengu* ensures that knowledge of the building tradition is perpetuated down the generations by rebuilding the shrines every twenty years in exactly the same way.

Classical Japan

Buddhist Temples

The importation of Buddhism from Korea and China in the 6th century AD brought intensified doctrines, ritual and architectural form. The degree of architectural decoration increased dramatically and surfaces were carved, painted, lacquered and gilded; details such as elaborate brackets at the roof soffit (underside), painted surfaces, thatched roofs with carved profiles, and decorated columns were introduced.

The first Japanese Buddhist temple, at Hokoji in Nara, was built in 588. While ancient Shinto temples had a strict configuration of buildings, early Buddhist temples in Japan did not follow a prescribed layout, but usually included a *hondo*, or image hall, a pagoda to hold sacred objects, and other structures such as a belfry, lecture hall and domestic buildings for the monastery.

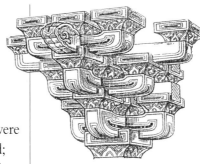

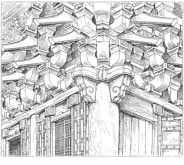

Brackets

An important component of the roof of a Japanese Buddhist shrine is the bracket, an exposed element that decorates the soffits of the verandah and supports the overhanging eaves. Brackets are often a cluster of wood pieces, or struts curving upwards to a decorative block cap.

Column details

The base of this column and the arrangement of column to tie beam show how internal temple pillars were lacquered and decorated with organic patterns reproduced from embroideries. At the innermost sanctuary, the patterns on the columns and tie beams were gilded.

Pagoda plan, Horiuji (7th century AD)

This pagoda is an example of the type initially introduced to Japan from China and often used as part of a temple site to hold images and shrines at the lower storeys and bronze bells above. The pagoda plan is usually square, with central steps to each side and a perimeter verandah under the overhanging roof.

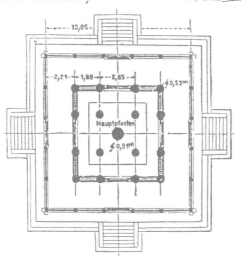

Yokohama temple complex (19th century)

This scene at a temple at Yokohama includes a *torii* (gateway) and a pair of monuments marking the entrance to the thatched shrine in a wooded site. It is a good example of the use of these complexes, where outside rooms are as important as the shrines themselves.

Hondo, Horiuji (7th century)

The main shrine (or *hondo*) at Horiuji is one of the oldest surviving timber-framed buildings in the world. The *hondo* is assembled by a mortice and tenon technique and consists of a floor 1.2–1.8 m (4–6 ft) above the ground raised on stone piers and reached by steps. The building is nine bays long and seven wide and has an inner room framed with columns that are much taller than those supporting the verandah, giving the appearance of a second storey.

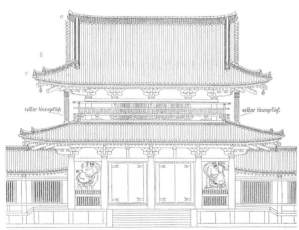

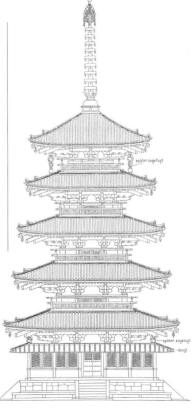

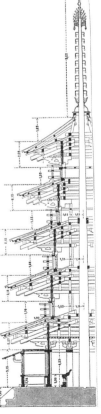

Pagoda elevation and section

Pagodas are generally three to five storeys high, tapering in slightly to each floor to produce the distinctive profile with staggered overhanging roof. The daringly tall buildings on the Japanese islands, where there is an ever-present threat of earthquakes, are of light and flexible timber construction.

Classical Japan

More Buddhist Temples

The development of Buddhist temple architecture in Japan is divided into several periods following its arrival in the 6th century. The first period is known as the 'early historic' period of temple architecture and includes the Asuka, Nara and Heian phases. Medieval Buddhist Japan, from the 12th century on, is divided into the Kamakura phase and the Nambokucho and Muromachi periods. From the 16th century, the Momoyama and Edo periods continued until the 19th century. Whereas Shinto shrines and early Buddhist temples relied upon integrity of material and construction, later Buddhist architecture often exhibited ostentatious decoration to all surfaces and structural members. For example, the bracket ends in the gateway of the 17th-century temple at Nikko are carved with dragon heads and unicorns, instead of a 'truthful' arrangement of a projecting tenon from the horizontal beams.

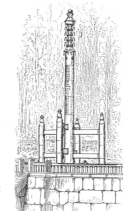

Bronze column, Nikko
This bronze column, sited on a raised stone platform, stores copies of the Buddhist scriptures whose titles are inscribed in gold at the top.

Bell
The bell is an architectural element that guides the religious practice of Buddhism on both an aural and visual level. Buddhism brought chanting, drums, gongs and bells to the Japanese religious ritual.

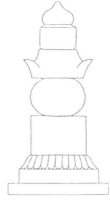

Monument
Sculptural objects play an important role in Buddhist architecture. Carved wood and stone lanterns, or *ishi-doro*, occupy the outdoor rooms on the approach to the shrine and are found in domestic gardens. This stone monument stands with thousands of other monuments in a sacred grove. The monuments are all 3–6 m (10–20 ft) high and consist of individually shaped stones, such as a lotus moulding on the base and an onion dome on the top.

Pagoda, Nikko (17th century)
The five-storey pagoda at Nikko is capped with a slender column that further increases its height and relates to the surrounding trees. Roofed walls with intricately carved wooden panels and stone bases enclose the pagoda and the associated buildings in the complex.

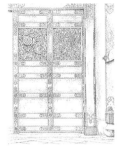

Ceiling

The ceilings of Buddhist temples are often elaborately decorated. This ceiling in a 17th-century shrine is coffered with a series of square panels divided by hammered metal casings, then gilded and carved with patterns.

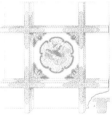

Gateway, Nishi-Honwan-Gi

Elaborate gateways resembling temples guard and announce Buddhist sites. This example, the east gateway at the temple of Nishi-Honwan-Gi, Kyoto, shows the gateway and a gate within it – both elaborately decorated, suggesting the wealth and importance of the site and giving an indication of the rich offerings to the gods.

Gateway, Nikko (17th century)

The temple gateway at Nikko has a heavy roof and surrounding gallery and is covered in imagery of dragons, water, clouds and drapery, in hammered metalwork, carved wood, laquerwork, gilding and painted relief. This makes a statement about the status of the Shogun family who commissioned it.

Temple interior

From the 12th century, the *hondo* became a temple to enter and pray in, not just an image hall, and the size of its interior was enlarged to accommodate worshippers. This rare glimpse into the interior of a temple shows its imposing scale. The roof is framed by a series of tie beams assembled in a decorative way.

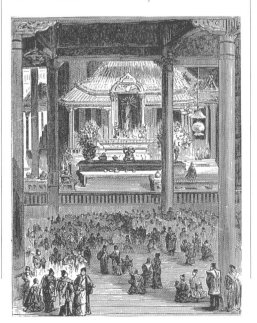

Classical Japan

Domestic Architecture

The climate and geology of this country of islands have had an influence on the design of its traditional domestic architecture. Houses are often built to face south and have deeply projecting eaves, high courtyard walls, movable windows and partitions to maximise the benefits of sea breezes and ocean currents. Flexible, one-storey timber construction makes use of the rich forests, and protects against the constant threat of earthquakes. Houses that survived in the late 19th century, which were described by European architects as being three centuries old, were similar in description to those they recorded as new. This shows the long-standing traditions of domestic architecture in Japan.

Thatched roof

The most common form of domestic roof in rural Japan is a gable with deep-pile thatch, as used in temple architecture. There are regional varieties in the design of the ridge. This example of a 19th-century merchant's house outside Tokyo shows an additional gable with a triangular window, and emphasises the careful attention to the symmetrical trimming of the thatch at the eaves and gable end.

Verandah

An important room in the Japanese house is the covered porch or verandah, which acts as a transitional space between indoors and out. A short supplementary roof, or *hisashi*, often projects from below the eaves of the main roof and is made of wide, thin boards supported either by posts or brackets.

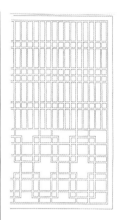

Tokyo streetscape

Urban residences from the late 19th century range from rows of tenements under a common tiled roof, with individual entrances that lead directly on to the street, to houses of the wealthy with elaborate thatched roofs with smoke outlets, and a verandah and broad windows overlooking the street.

Entrance

Just as the entrance to the Shinto shrine is marked with the *torii*, and the Buddhist temple is entered through an elaborate gateway, so the traditional Japanese house has a verandah or vestibule that brings the ritual of entrance and progression from religious sites into everyday life. *Shoji* are the sliding screens that divide the vestibule from the inside rooms.

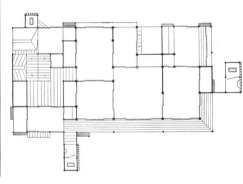

Entrance plan

This plan shows the entrance to the house of a *samurai* (member of the military caste), with steps up to the *shoji* that lead into the hall. This hall is defined as a three-mat room and the only furniture is a free-standing low screen, called a *tsui-tate*.

Windows

Windows are not made of glass in traditional Japanese architecture, but of an opaque white paper that allows muted light into the house. This is framed for security and support by wood or bamboo mullions. Interior screens are more elaborately ornamented with a lattice of thin wood strips.

Tokyo house plan

This traditional Japanese house is composed of a series of interconnected rooms divided by sliding screens and with some circulation spaces. The rooms are not encumbered with furniture, indicating a flexible division of room function.

Classical Japan

Government and Business Buildings

From the 7th century, urban Japanese architecture was informed by Chinese design practice, both in the arrangement of cities and the siting of important buildings within them. Like Chinese models such as Beijing, the 8th-century cities of Nara and Kyoto were arranged within a rectangular grid of streets, with the imperial palace at the centre, and houses of the nobility, other palaces and government buildings organised symmetrically along a north–south axis. While temple and domestic architecture is noted for its lack of monumentality, the buildings of the nobility and government made a more dramatic impact on the landscape. Elaborate castles, such as the early 17th-century example at Himeji, used traditional roof forms to create a commanding ensemble on a prominent high site.

Palace wall
The wall surrounding this palace is flared at the base and of monumental construction (sometimes partnered with a perimeter moat), suggesting the importance of defence from attack and earthquakes. The end wall with black ragstone plinth is plastered in yellow, with five parallel white lines, which indicate that a person of royalty owns the palace.

Palace, Tokyo
From the late 16th century, the architecture of the ruling class made a dominant addition to the Japanese landscape, with fortified structures of one storey or some built on to small cliffs. This small palace in Tokyo shows the relationship of the building to the surrounding gardens.

Government building
This scene shows the reception of an ambassador at the Japanese court. The placement of furniture and trees is as integral to this building as its structure. The emperor sits at the highest point under the verandah of the thatched roof.

Tea manufactory
This complex of buildings is similar in form to domestic and shrine architecture, with its gabled overhanging tile roofs supported by exposed brackets and capped with a pronounced ridge.

Weavery
This silk weavery does not differ greatly from domestic design, with latticed windows, units of reed *tatami* on the floor and no furniture beyond the weaving apparatus. Urban building plots were often long, with a narrow street frontage serving as shop space.

City view, Tokyo (19th century)
The engineering prowess emphasised in this series of timber bridges shows the local response to the prevalence of both water and earthquakes in Japan. The roofs and low buildings also fit the hilly terrain.

Mikado's court (19th century)
The interior of this court shows how progression through a series of levels – as well as the contrasts in scale and openness of the main hall to the emperor's (or *mikado's*) raised room – stresses his status and controls the vistor's experience.

Tea-house
From the 16th century, the consumption of tea in Japan, as a ritual and as an art form in traditional life, began to result in its own architecture (which in turn informed house design). The tea-house was often rustic, with rough finishes, and was approached by a series of peaceful paths to a space defined by its number of mats. This example shows how shuttered louvred openings and deep verandahs engage the tea drinker with the outside environment in an urban setting.

Pre-Columbian *900 BC–AD 1532*

Early Sites

Entire cities with hundreds of stone monuments, some of them half-buried in the tropical forest, survive as witnesses to the complex civilisations that inhabited the Mesoamerican region, comprising the whole of Mexico, parts of Guatemala, Belize and Honduras, from as early as 900 BC until the Spanish conquest in 1519. Monumental pyramids, platforms, temples, squares, ball-courts, processional roads and sacrificial altars were used as stages for the performance of religious rituals, on which daily life depended. The strict social hierarchy of the different cities was reflected in large palace compounds, as rulers increasingly used architecture to promote themselves and ensure their immortality. While the majority of surviving buildings belong to the Maya civilisation, which flourished between AD 300 and 900, a number of other Mesoamerican groups, such as the Olmec and the Toltec (as well as individual cities such as Teotihuacan) were responsible for several important architectural innovations.

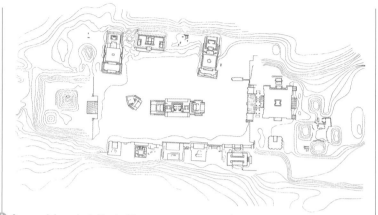

Ceremonial precinct, Monte Alban
The Zapotec site of Monte Alban in the valley of Oaxaca was inhabited in four phases stretching from 500 BC to AD 700. It was planned around a characteristic ceremonial precinct. Two stone platforms, the northern and southern acropolises, enclose a large plaza around which other temples, pyramids, funerary mounds and a ball-court are arranged. All the buildings are raised above the level of the plaza and accessed by large stairways.

Pyramid of the Niches, El Tajín
The Pyramid of the Niches belongs to the Totonac site of El Tajín (*c.* AD 200-900). The small structure rises in six tiers to an upper sanctuary by means of a wide, balustraded staircase on the eastern side, decorated with a step-and-fret motif that is very common at El Tajín. The pyramid is carved on all sides with 365 square niches – the solar year being a recurring theme of Mesoamerican architecture.

Talud-tablero profile, Teotihuacan

The *talud-tablero* or 'slope-and-panel' profile first appeared on the buildings of Teotihuacan. The feature consists of an outward sloping section, or *talud*, supporting a rectangular, vertical stucco panel, or *tablero*. This is treated as a frieze and often framed, sculpted and brightly painted.

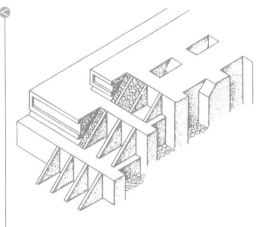

Talud-tablero terracing, Teotihuacan

The *talud-tablero* profile could be repeated all the way up the pyramid, as in several structures at Teotihuacan. This form of façade terracing is found with regional variations throughout Mesoamerica. It was both visually effective and economic, as the elegant framing members were held together by thin slabs tied into a rubble core.

Grid plan, Teotihuacan (c. AD 150–650)

The city of Teotihuacan was laid out on a grid plan, with the Pyramid of the Sun in the centre and the Avenue of the Dead as its main axis stretching 3.2 km (2 miles) from the Pyramid of the Moon and intersecting with a second axis at the citadel. The city was therefore divided into quarters, a plan later imitated by the later Aztecs.

Pyramid of the Moon, Teotihuacan (c. AD 200)

The pyramid dedicated to the moon deity is a giant structure at the northern end of Teotihuacan's major axis. A stone stairway cutting through a four-tiered *talud-tablero* platform at the base led to a wood and thatch sanctuary on the summit.

Stelae, Teotihuacan

The early free-standing votive stones found at Teotihuacan served a purely religious function. They were carved with semi-abstract representations of gods, including the famous Quetzalcoatl or feathered serpent. Later Maya *stelae* (upright stone slabs) were sculpted with realistic representations of kings and functioned more as secular monuments than as votive stones.

Pre-Columbian

Classic Maya

The Maya civilisation produced some of the most important monuments of pre-Columbian Mesoamerica and its 'Classic' golden age was between AD 500 and 900. The recent deciphering of Maya hieroglyphs sculpted on steps, friezes, columns, free-standing *stelae* and altars has provided a breakthrough in the understanding of Maya architecture, in the dating of structures and in the naming of rulers. Pyramids were often built over existing older ones, a tradition that conveyed ancestral authority to the new structure while also allowing for greater heights. The search for height was fundamental to Maya religious architecture, manifested in vertiginous staircases reaching up to the gods. Other essential traits were the innovative use of the corbel vault and elaborate sculptural schemes.

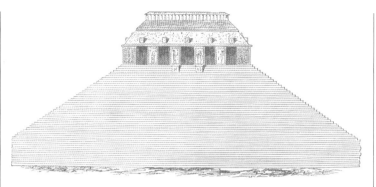

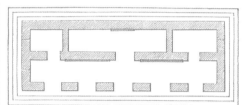

Temple of the Inscriptions, Palenque (AD 675)
A steep staircase leads up nine levels, symbolic of the levels of the Mesoamerican underworld, to a sanctuary with a concrete mansard-type roof, characteristic of the buildings at Palenque. A hidden vaulted staircase descends from the temple to a crypt at the base of the pyramid, where King Pacal (616–83) was buried. A stone tube built alongside the inner stairway allowed the dead king to communicate with the living.

Sanctuary plan, Palenque
In the Temple of the Inscriptions, the inner sanctum is protected by a five-bay vaulted entrance portico, decorated with stucco figures and the famous 'inscriptions': 620 hieroglyphs telling the story of Palenque's rulers.

Roof combs
Roof combs, or *cresteria*, crowned the summit of most Classic Maya pyramids. They consisted of two pierced framework walls leaning against each other with attached stucco relief sculpture depicting gods and rulers.

Sacrificial captives, Palenque
Sculpted monolithic limestone slabs, representing captured chiefs kneeling with vivid expressions of fear, decorate the galleries of the east courtyard of the palace at Palenque. The galleries were used for court ceremonies – the sculptures acting as reminders of homage due to the ruler.

Corbel vaulting

One of the chief engineering achievements of the Classic Maya was the invention of the corbel vault. Initially, narrow chambers were spanned with rows of stone projecting gradually over each other. In later vaults, the Maya turned the stepped profile of the ceiling into the thickness of the wall, holding it with mortar and rubble. This made the surface of the chamber smooth for plastering and painting.

Double corbel vaulting, Palenque

At Palenque, the Maya overcame the limitations of vaulting narrow chambers. By building two corbel vaults side by side, sharing a central stabilised load-bearing wall, the weight on the side-walls was diminished, making it possible to span wider rooms.

Stela, Copan

The Classic Maya site of Copan (*c.* 540–760), Honduras, is famous for its fine three-dimensional sculptures, including a number of monolithic *stelae* in the plaza. In the Classic period, these large outsized standing stones were sculpted and painted with representations of the ruler in ceremonial garb, with an elaborate headdress, feet turned outwards and hieroglyphs narrating his victories.

Altar, Copan

Altars were low cylindrical monolithic stones consistently placed at Copan in front of *stelae* and often depicting the sacrificial victims surrendering to the ruler of the *stela*. This subject increasingly replaced the more strictly devout subjects of earlier altars, which sometimes took the form of godly monsters or deities.

Pre-Columbian

Maya Puuc Style

Towards the end of the Classic Maya era, in the 8th and 9th centuries, the emphasis shifted from cities dominated by imposing religious structures to cities in which the ruler's palace became the architectural focus. Set on high platforms, palaces were increasingly complex with multiple rooms and several vast quadrangles. A number of regional styles are distinguishable, owing to geographical differences, as well as conquests and alliances between the autonomous kingdoms. A group of cities in the region of Yucatan share a 'Puuc' style of architecture, characterised by a more geometric approach to sculptural decoration, by the repetitive (almost obsessive) use of the same motif over large expanses of wall surface and by the use of symbolic ornamentation drawn from Maya cosmology.

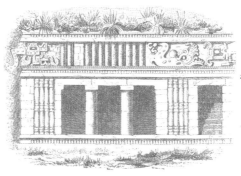

Palace, Sayil (c. 700–900)
The second storey of the palace at Sayil in Yucatan is an open porticoed façade with monolithic columns and stone abacus. The frieze is sculpted in typical Puuc style, with effigies of gods and serpents, separated by clusters of ringed balusters. These are stone representations of the wooden primitive hut, establishing a symbolic relationship between the ruler and his people.

Façade, Pyramid of the Magician, Uxmal (569)
The sanctuary at the summit of the Pyramid of the Magician is sculpted with the outsized mask of a godly cosmic monster. Entry is made through its jaws, symbolising the passage to the underworld. This type of cosmological 'entrance' is typical of the neighbouring Chenes region.

Nunnery, Uxmal (c. 700–900)
The quadrangle in the Puuc city of Uxmal, which the Spanish later called the 'Nunnery', is composed of four long, free-standing palaces around a patio. The northern block is raised on a high platform. The side-palaces are also raised above the level of the southern entrance block, itself accessed by a stairway from the plaza outside the quadrangle. The palace was therefore conceived as a continuous ascending experience.

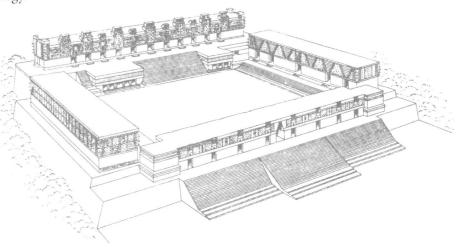

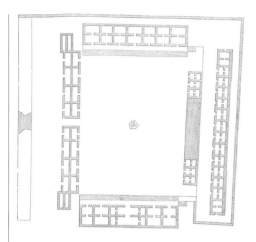

Nunnery plan, Uxmal
Late Classic palaces were complex. The Nunnery has more than forty double-chambers and a six-room ceremonial apartment. Its size was facilitated by Puuc construction methods using cut stone only as a veneer over a rubble core.

Mosaic frieze, Uxmal
The Governor's Palace at Uxmal is adorned with a long mosaic frieze. Fret motifs and masks of Chac (symbolic of the sun and the rain respectively) are geometrically distributed all along the façade around a central effigy of the ruler.

Palace of Masks, Kabah (c. 700–900)
The mask of the god of rain, Chac, repeated obsessively on the Palace of Masks at Kabah, constitutes one of the chief leitmotifs of Puuc architecture. The god is consistently depicted with a projecting trunk-like nose and a deeply carved eye on either side. Maya agrarian societies naturally worshipped the rain and sun gods above all others.

Step-and-fret motif, Mitla
The Zapotec site of Mitla, in the valley of Oaxaca, belongs to the post-Classic era, but is an example of the development of the mosaic frieze of the Puuc region. Every palace at Mitla is ornamented with juxtaposed panels of intricate geometric patterns, derivatives of the step-and-fret motif.

Pre-Columbian

Post-Classic Sites

By the 10th century, or the beginning of the post-Classic era, the majority of Maya cities were in decline and the centre of building activity shifted to central Mexico, where Maya influences infiltrated the Toltec civilisation, leading to the creation of two important Toltec-Maya cities: Tula and Chichen Itza. Post-Classic cities were increasingly engrossed in the activities of war, and this is reflected in austere structures, such as the warrior temples of Tula and Chichen Itza. The stone ball-court and *chacmools* (stone figures) of Chichen Itza testify to the importance of human sacrifice in the post-Classic era. Such customs were taken further by the Aztecs, whose capital, Tenochtitlan, featured some of the most outstanding examples of Mesoamerican architecture.

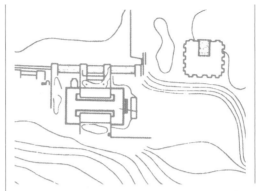

Ball-court, Chichen Itza
Usually I-shaped, ball-courts were surrounded by high walls with seating for spectators. The elaborate bas-relief on the inner walls of the court at Chichen Itza shows the losing team being sacrificed to the gods. Their heads were deposited on the adjoining *tzompantli* (skull rack).

Ball-court ring, Tula
The sacred game was played with a hard ball, which the teams attempted to pass through two large sculpted stone rings, attached to the sides of the court. The rings at Tula, with rattlesnake ornamentation, were dedicated to the plumed serpent Quetzalcoatl.

Atlantes, Tula
At the summit of 'Pyramid B' at Tula, four giant atlantean figures representing Toltec warriors supported the roof of the entrance vestibule of the sanctuary. Bas-relief sculpture inside the temple and in the colonnaded hall at the base of the pyramid reiterated the warrior theme.

Column, Tula
Columns were generally more common in post-Classic sites. The largest columns at Tula were made of four or more blocks of stone with carved tenons fitted together with mortar. Other columns at the site were built of rubble around a wooden core.

Sculpted abacus, Chichen Itza

The upper sanctuary of the 'Castillo' or Great Pyramid points to new roofing techniques, using pillars, columns and wooden lintels as supports. The two columns of the entrance vestibule depict the plumed serpent coiled around the shaft, with a rare sculpted abacus.

Chacmool sculpture, Tula and Chichen Itza

Statues of reclining human figures, or *chacmool,* appear in both religious and secular edifices at Tula and Chichen Itza. With their heads at a ninety-degree angle and holding disc-shaped receptacles on their bellies, *chacmools* were altars for sacrificial offerings, often of human hearts.

Stone of Tizoc, Tenochtitlan

The Aztec civilisation produced skilled sculptors, responsible for deep and sometimes terrifying figures carved on buildings. This altar, or Stone of Tizoc, was carved with fifteen scenes of the emperor dragging a captive. The upper surface is carved with a solar disc.

Puuc style, Chichen Itza

The small buildings forming the Nunnery at the southern end of the site are accessed by a *sacbé* or white, levelled processional road. The buildings are decorated in the Classic Maya Puuc style, with masks of the rain god Chac, large mosaic friezes and fret motifs. The density and aggression of the carving are typical of the post-Classic period.

Pre-Columbian

Inca Architecture

The pre-Columbian Inca civilisation of
Peru, Bolivia and Ecuador developed a
monumental architecture from *c.* 1100
until the Spanish conquest in 1532.
Most of their ceremonial buildings
served to worship the sun god and the
'Inca', his earthly representative. The
Inca were ingenious in turning the
rugged land of the Andes to their
advantage by perching their cities in
strategic sites, using elaborate systems
of terracing and founding religious
and sacrificial structures, such as *ushnu*
(sacred tables), around natural springs
and rock formations. Diplomats rather
than warriors, they developed a complex
network of roads in and out of their
capital, Cuzco. The art of masonry
combined with the use of
gold reached its climax
in 15th-century Inca
palaces and temples.

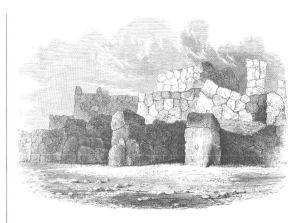

Inca masonry
Walls of prestigious Inca
edifices were built without
mortar, with roughly hewn
polygonal blocks of stone
fitted together by grinding
each one until it locked
into place. This technique
was used both in fine brick
buildings and in large
constructions, such as the
fortress of Sacsayhuaman.

Tambo
Tambos were relay
houses, built on the
Inca road as resting
places for messengers.
The *tambo* is typically
Incan in being a low,
windowless, rectangular
chamber with an
elegant trapezoidal
door as the only source
of light. Rows of
trapezoidal niches
constitute the most
important form
of ornamentation
on interior and
exterior walls.

Chullpas, Lake Titicaca
The pre-Inca sepulchral
towers, or *chullpas*, found
around Lake Titicaca were
built to bury the dead with
all their possessions. These
windowless houses had
circular plans and several
chambers for the eternal
cohabitation of the members
of a family. The association
of circular towers with the
sacred was taken further by
the Inca, as in the Torreon
at Machu Picchu.

Machu Picchu (15th century)
The city of Machu Picchu, perched 2,430 m (7,972 ft) on a mountain peak, is the best example of the adaptation of Inca architecture to the landscape. Fertile terraces overhang the precipices. Three temples of fine masonry, built on slopes using the natural granite as walls, form the ceremonial precinct.

Houses of the Virgins of the Sun, Lake Titicaca
These large houses, also called 'Houses of the Chosen Women', were a type of educational convent for a select group of women – often concubines of the ruler. They were seen as the wives of the sun and their house was appropriately sheathed with gold. Trapezoidal entrances with double-jambs were reserved for such prestigious buildings.

House of Manco Capac, Lake Titicaca
Manco Capac was the legendary 12th-century founder of the Inca dynasty. His house, constructed on an island in Lake Titicaca, is one of the oldest surviving Inca buildings. Individual upper chambers stand out like towers above the solid masonry of the first storey, an Inca solution to the engineering of two-storey structures.

Torreon, Machu Picchu
The Torreon (tower) is a small sanctuary in the centre of the ruined Inca city of Machu Picchu. It has a semi-circular wall – a form reserved for sacred edifices – of the finest mortarless masonry, adorned with trapezoidal niches. It encloses a cave with an *ushnu*, a natural rock formation used as a sacrificial table, sculpted to receive the neck of a llama.

Pre-classical *C.7th–C.1st* BC

Mycenaean: Citadels

Aegean art reached its peak
c. 1650–1450 BC and was at first
dominated by the Minoans, based in
Crete. However, at the height of its
influence, the Minoan civilisation fell,
and its position was quickly inherited
by the Mycenaeans, a race of warriors
who flourished in Greece from 1600 to
1200 BC. This has been termed the
'Heroic' or 'Homeric Age', as the life
and buildings of the Mycenaeans match
perfectly the descriptions in Homer's
epic poems, the *Iliad* and the *Odyssey*.
Although Cretan artisans may have
been employed on the reworking of
Mycenaean citadels, the two styles
remained distinct. Mycenaean buildings
were carefully planned and focused on
the megaron (central unit), while the
Minoans favoured complex,
labyrinthine forms.

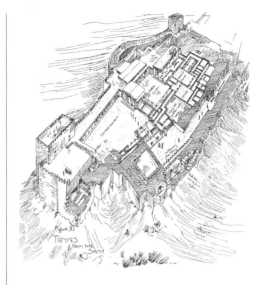

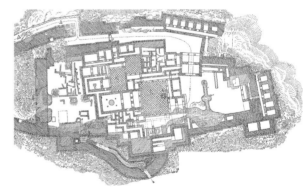

Arrangement of palaces
Palaces, like the citadels
that contained them,
were well defended.
At Tiryns Palace (late
13th century BC), near
Mycenae, visitors had to
pass through a series of
enclosed courts and
through two H-shaped
gates *(propylaea)*, before
reaching the porch of the
principal suite (megaron).
Around the megaron were
a complex of chambers,
including bedrooms
and bathrooms.

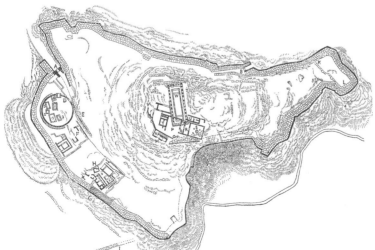

Citadel of Mycenae (c. 1340 BC)
Citadels were built on strategic, often impregnable
hills, and were enclosed by strong curtain walling.
At the upper end of the site was the palace, where
the ruler and his family lived. The dwellings of
important figures, such as military leaders, were also
found within the enceinte, but most of the
population lived outside the citadel's walls.

Lion Gate, Mycenae (*c.* 1250 BC)

Citadels were entered via monumental gateways, such as the Lion Gate at Mycenae, which consists of two vertical stones carrying a vast lintel. In the relieving triangle (*see page 88*) above is a limestone slab carved with a relief of two lions. The curtain wall to the left and a rectangular bastion to the right (*see plan, left*) provided cover for those guarding the entrance.

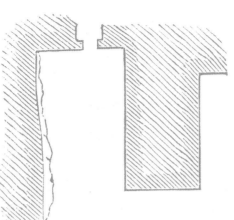

Cyclopean stonework

The Mycenaeans' imposing walls – which were composed of massive irregularly cut blocks of stone – were attributed by the classical Greeks to the mythic Cyclopes, a race of giants. These walls have thus been termed Cyclopean. They served to defend citadels and were sometimes topped with palisades (protective fencing).

Triglyph frieze

A common form of ornamentation in both Minoan and Mycenaean palaces was the so-called triglyph frieze or motif. This was formed of half-rosettes divided by vertical bands, and was used as a continuous series. It has been asserted that it formed the inspiration for the Greek Doric frieze of metopes and triglyphs, but there is no proof of this.

Megaron

The megaron formed the central complex of a palace and the main domestic unit. It was a long, narrow suite composed of a columned porch (termed the *aithousa* by Homer), an antechamber *(prodomus)* and the megaron proper. This illustration shows a reconstruction of the megaron at Tiryns, dating from the late 13th century BC. The *aithousa* was entered from an inner court and faced south.

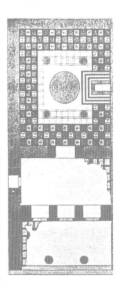

Circular hearth

The megaron proper contained a raised throne and was centred around a fixed circular hearth, framed by four wooden columns supporting the roof. The floor of this megaron was painted with a chequered pattern, while the walls were adorned with frescoes.

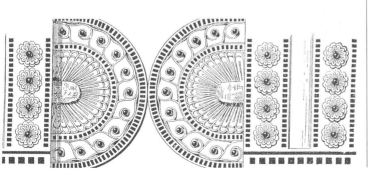

Pre-classical

Mycenaean: Tombs

Some of the most splendid Mycenaean monuments are the tholos or 'beehive' tombs, developed gradually from *c.* 1510 to *c.* 1220 BC. They were almost certainly built to house the remains of kings and their relations, as distinct from rock-cut chamber tombs, which served the people in general. Both were underground structures, tholoi being set into hillsides. The two major tholoi – the so-called Treasuries of Atreus or Agamemnon (*c.* 1250 BC) and Clytemnestra (*c.* 1220 BC) at Mycenae – were discovered by Heinrich Schliemann in 1876 and were deemed 'treasuries' by the Dorians of central Greece because of their rich grave goods. The corbelled dome is their most impressive feature. That of the Treasury of Atreus, rising to 13.2 m (43 ft), is said to have been the largest-known pre-Roman vaulted construction.

Relieving triangle
A 'relieving triangle' was a distinctive feature of Mycenaean architecture, and was sometimes filled with a sculptured panel. The triangle served to absorb the thrust above the door and therefore relieve the lintel. The entrances to tholoi were surmounted by a lintel and a relieving triangle.

Plan elements
There are three elements of a tholos: the *dromos*, a horizontal passageway (1); the *stomion*, a deep entrance fronted by a doorway (2); and the tholos itself, the principal round chamber (3). In two known cases, an additional burial chamber (4) opens off the tholos.

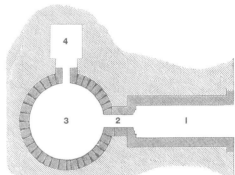

Corbelled dome
The corbelled dome of a tholos resembles an old-fashioned beehive, and was formed of horizontal tiers of ashlar (square-hewn) masonry. These were corbelled, meaning that each tier was built out beyond the one below, until the top was reached. As the dome was built, earth was placed around it, providing stability. The whole was finally covered with a tumulus (earth mound).

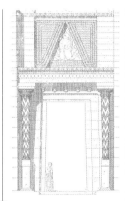

Main entrance
A number of tholoi had decorated, coloured façades. That of the Treasury of Atreus (*c.* 1250 BC) was perhaps the most elaborate of all. The entrance, which was closed with double doors, was flanked by attached columns, and above was a frieze of red porphyry.

Decoration of the dome
Originally, it seems that some – if not all – of the interiors of tholos domes were richly decorated. Traces of bronze nails have been found within the tiers of the domes, and these probably bore bronze rosettes or stars. The tholos thus imitated the dome of heaven. There were also metallic friezes decorating the lower courses of the dome.

Dromos
The tomb was approached via a horizontal passage *(dromos)* lined with stone blocks, as here at the Treasury of Clytemnestra (*c.* 1220 BC). The existence of a wall at the entrance to this *dromos*, as well as blocking within the *stomion*, proves that the tomb was sealed up after use, and the *dromos* filled in. This was the case with all tholos and chamber tombs.

Column
Mycenaean columns, (like Minoan examples), were slender and tapered sharply downwards. Those that adorned the entrance to the Treasury of Atreus had shafts of green alabaster, carved with spirals and chevrons in relief.

Surface decoration
The walls and ceiling of the side-chamber at the Treasury of Minyas, Orchomenos (*c.* 1220 BC), were covered with slabs, decorated with spirals, rosettes and other popular motifs, and show traces of colour.

Pre-classical

Etruscan: Tombs

Just as Mycenaean architecture seems to have influenced the classical Greeks, so the structures raised by the Etruscans are important in the evolution of Roman architecture. The Etruscans probably originated in Asia Minor and settled in west-central Italy (Etruria), between the rivers Arno and Tiber. From the late 7th century BC their power grew, and for a while Rome itself was ruled by Etruscan kings. But with the establishment of a republic in 509 BC, Etruscan civilisation began to decline and its various city-states were conquered. Nonetheless, the Etruscans did not cease their architectural activity, which retained its distinct character until the 1st century BC. Few Etruscan buildings survive, but those that do are extremely fine, especially the tombs, which were located mainly in specific necropolis sites. The earliest were covered by tumuli, but from around 400 BC chambers with ornamented façades, entered directly from the outside, were built.

Tumuli
From early times, the Etruscans marked the resting places of the dead by tumuli (earth mounds). They were built together in vast numbers and were arranged in rows, as at Cerveteri (Caere).

Regolini Galassi, Cerveteri (Caere)
One of the most magnificent Etruscan sepulchral monuments is the Regolini Galassi tomb at Cerveteri. The original (probably royal) tomb dates from *c.* 650 BC and consists of a tumulus with two stone chambers.

House tomb
The Etruscans thought that the dead should dwell as they had in life. Many tombs were built in imitation of houses, and were even arranged along paved streets. They were cut from rock, and on their façades were carved doorcases and sometimes windows. Such tombs often contained rock-cut furniture, including beds (on which the bodies rested), bedsteads and pillows. The plastered, painted walls were hung with household utensils.

Corbelled chambers, Regolini Galassi
The burial chamber of Regolini Galassi is rectangular and has an unusual roof, built like the dome of a Mycenaean tholos, being corbelled. It was reached via a long passageway (*dromos*) with side-chambers.

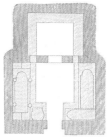

Tomb of Porsenna, Chiusi (Clusium)

One extraordinary funerary monument was the tomb of Porsenna, a renowned Etruscan king of the 6th century BC. This was described by the Roman scholar Varro as having a rectangular podium (platform) carrying five cones – one in each corner, and one in the centre – which, in their turn, carried two similar storeys. The lower cones bore a circular canopy, to which bells were attached by chains.

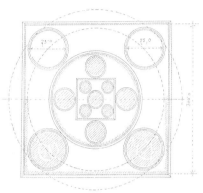

Cube tomb

Some tombs were free-standing, cut directly out of the rock. These – which have been termed cube tombs – appear originally to have carried roofs. The one shown here is reconstructed in the form of a pyramid, although most may have been curvilinear in form. Rich mouldings are particularly characteristic of cube tombs. Entrances were typically surrounded by an elegant frame, with tapering door posts and lintels projecting right and left.

Pre-classical

Etruscan: Other Buildings

The Etruscans, as we know from the writings of Vitruvius, a Roman architect and engineer of the 1st century BC, developed a style of temple building which, though inspired by Greek and oriental examples, was quite distinctive in its own right. It conformed to specific rules, referred to as '*tuscanicae dispositiones*' by Vitruvius. Temples were usually of mud-brick and timber, though stone was used later, and seem to have been built to face south. They were placed at the centre of towns and fronted on to squares, in which altars were placed. The Etruscans were also capable engineers and built numerous bridges and aqueducts. With the increased need for defence from the 4th century onwards, monumental city walls were erected. These were punctuated with fine gateways, the most famous surviving examples being those at Perugia (*c.* 300 BC), Volterra (*c.* 300 BC) and Falerium Novum (*c.* 250 BC).

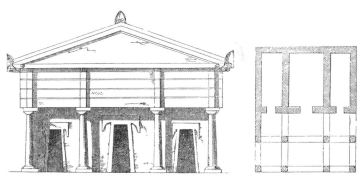

Three-cella plan

Many Etruscan temples were divided into three *cellas* (sanctuaries), the central one being the most important and sometimes the largest. This reflected the worship of a triad, the three divinities usually being Tinia (Jupiter), Uni (Juno) and Minvra (Minerva). In front of the *cellas* was placed a spacious colonnaded *pronaos* (vestibule with portico). There were no side or rear entrances, so the emphasis was strongly frontal. The wooden architraves shown here are typically Etruscan, and were placed one above the other to form the entablature.

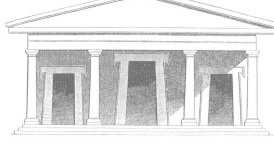

 Alae

There were variations on the three-*cella* plan. The two outer *cellas* could be left open as wings *(alae)*, and the columns ranged along the sides. The *alae* could also be enclosed by walls along the sides of the temple, forming lateral corridors. In the well-known case of the Temple of Jupiter Capitolinus, Rome (dedicated 509 BC, rebuilt and rededicated 69 BC), there were three *cellas* flanked by *alae*.

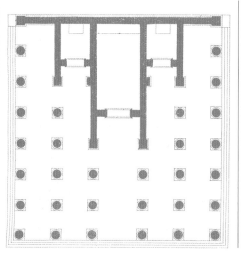

Temple elevation

Temples were always set on high podia (platforms), constructed of ashlar masonry. Stairs at the front rose to the level of the *pronaos*, which could be used by religious figures to address the masses. The pediment was low-pitched and projected beyond the columns, as did the eaves. Etruscan columns seem to have been a simplified version of the Greek Doric; they were unfluted, with base and plain capital. This form was inherited by the Romans as the Tuscan order.

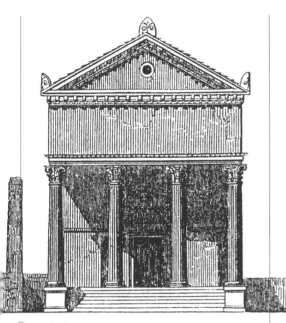

Temple decoration
Temples were lavishly decorated with painted terracotta, which served partly to protect the wooden elements of the structure. For example, the sides of the roof bore *antefixae* (slabs used to close the end of a row of tiles), and there were statues over the pediment and within the *pronaos*. This is a Roman Corinthian temple believed to imitate Etruscan examples.

Pointed arch
The Etruscans were able to construct pointed arches by the same method used to construct corbelled chambers for tombs. This involved building up stone courses horizontally, and corbelling the inner edges to form an arch.

Voussoir arches
The Etruscans, unlike the Greeks, favoured the use of the arch in their domestic buildings as well as in city gates, bridges and other public monuments. It is possible they were the first people in Italy to adopt the arch, though it may have been developed by the Romans contemporaneously. The basic form is composed of voussoirs wedge-shaped stones.

Ancient Greece *mid-C.7th–C.1st BC*

Early Architecture

A period of decline, often referred to as Greece's 'Dark Age', followed the destruction of the Mycenaean civilisation in the 12th century BC, and it was not until the 8th and 7th centuries BC that the arts began to revive. From these early times, one specific building type predominated: the temple. A temple was conceived as the abode of a god, the specific deity varying with local preferences and traditions. Initially, the temple took the form of a single room or hut, walled with sun-dried bricks. Outside was the altar, which was used for animal sacrifices. Gradually columns appeared in the interiors of these buildings, and then took their place on the façades. Finally, in the late 7th century BC, the main body of the sanctuary was entirely surrounded by a single row of columns, known as the peristyle. The peristyle was unique to Greek architecture and was to remain one of its most characteristic features.

Xoanon/early temple

It is probable that Greek temples originated as primitive huts, built to provide cover for a crude wooden statue of a deity, known as a *xoanon*. The vast majority of temples were orientated east–west, so that the rising sun would illuminate the *xoanon*.

Roof construction

In Greek architecture, timber lintels (horizontal beams) supported heavy cross-beams, which in turn carried struts and sloping rafters. Spans could not be large unless internal columns were provided. Later, elements of this timber construction would be translated into stone.

Trabeated system

The fundamental principle of Greek architecture is the post-and-lintel system, also known as trabeated, or columnar and trabeated. In this system, horizontal beams (lintels) are borne up by columns (posts). The arcuated system – that involving the use of arches – was not used by the Greeks.

Triglyphs

A great many of the characteristic details of classical architecture originated in timber forms. The triglyph, which is distinctive of the Doric order, is a good example. In early times, the ends of beams that projected beyond walls were cut off and ornamented, according to Vitruvius, with boards painted with blue wax.

Intercolumniation

The term intercolumniation refers to the open space between two columns. Vitruvius – a Roman writer of the 1st century BC – established five main variants: pycnostyle, in which columns are placed closely together (1½ diameters); systyle, with the columns a little wider (2 diameters); eustyle, a little wider still (2¼ diameters); diastyle, wider again (3 diameters); and araeostyle, in which the columns were placed 'further apart than they ought to be' (4 diameters).

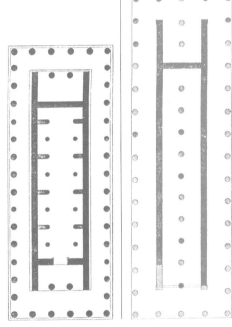

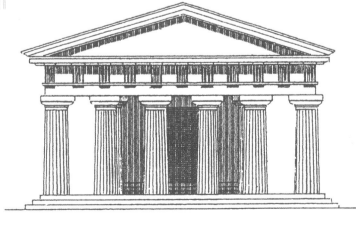

Internal colonnade

Early temples are often recognisable by the existence of an internal row of columns (colonnade). These supported the ceiling and roof, when walls were too far apart to permit the use of a simple transverse beam. Other significant features that define an early temple are a wide intercolumniation (architraves were of wood and were able to bridge large gaps) and long proportions. This, the 7th-century Temple of Apollo at Thermum, was one of the first buildings to boast a peristyle (surrounding colonnade).

Crepidoma

Temples were built on a stone platform known as a *crepidoma*. This most commonly had three steps. The top step, on which the columns rested directly, was known as the *stylobate*. The sub-structure of a temple was termed the *stereobate*.

Ancient Greece

The Temple: Forms and Elements

Once the basic temple plan had evolved, by the late 7th century BC, its forms and elements remained much the same from then on. The aim of the Greeks was to perfect their buildings in every way possible, but they did this slowly and without changing the essential ingredients – peristyle, portico, *pronaos, naos* and *opisthodomus* (rear porch). Greek architecture was a mathematically based art, and was indebted to the findings of the Ionian philosopher Pythagoras (*c.* 580–500 BC), for whom numbers were an expression of the fundamental language that linked humans and gods. The Greeks felt that when ratios and proportions were properly applied to both ground plans and elevations, the result would be beauty, perfection and '*symmetria*' (not symmetry as we understand it, but a perfect balance of parts). The standard unit of measurement used to achieve *symmetria* was the module, which was traditionally equal to the diameter or half the diameter of a column at the base of its shaft.

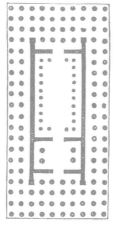

Dipteral plan
Dipteral is the term applied to a temple surrounded on all sides by two rows of columns – a double peristyle.

Pediment
A pediment is the low-pitched, gable end of a roof, most often placed above a portico. The triangular surface of the wall, enclosed by the horizontal cornices of the entablature beneath and by the sloping sides (raking cornices), is known as the tympanum.

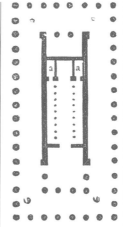

Pseudodipteral plan
Pseudodipteral refers to a later development of the dipteral plan, in which the inner row of columns was omitted. This form became particularly popular in the later phase of Greek architecture, around the 2nd century BC, and, according to the Roman architect and military engineer Vitruvius, was pioneered by the architect Hermogenes.

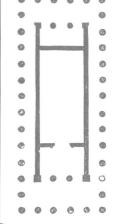

Basic temple plan
Greek temples were almost always rectangular in form, and were made up of certain set elements. The building was surrounded by a peristyle, also known as a peripteral colonnade or a *pteron*. Set within the columns, and divided from them by a passageway *(pteroma)*, was the main sanctuary itself. This usually consisted of three parts: the vestibule or porch *(pronaos)*, the shrine proper *(cella* or *naos)*, and the rear cell or porch *(opisthodomus)*.

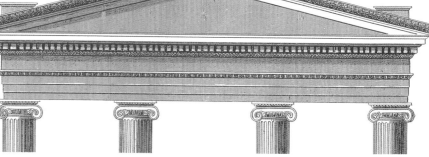

Portico

A portico was the principal porch or entrance to a temple, and was roofed and usually open at the sides. The number of columns that made up a portico determined its architectural name. For example, tetrastyle (four columns), hexastyle (six columns, a particularly common form) and decastyle (ten columns).

Temple interior

The temple interior would have been far plainer than the exterior, a fact that reflected the building's innate role. Temples were not designed to hold congregations of worshippers. It seems that only the clergy or privileged persons would have been permitted access, while the worshippers would have gathered before and around the building.

Cella

The *cella*, or *naos*, at the centre of the temple contained the statue of the deity. It would have been heaped with offerings, as would the vestibule *(pronaos)*. The rear porch *(opisthodomus)* was sometimes enclosed with bronze gates and often served as a treasury.

In antis

Where a portico recedes into a building, with the columns ranging along the front wall, it is known as *in antis* ('between the *antae*'). The *antae* are the pilasters or corner posts, which project slightly and form the outer edges of the portico.

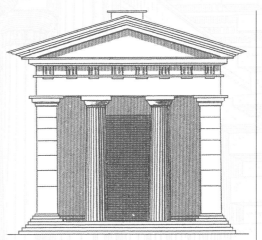

Prostyle and amphiprostyle

Prostyle, the opposite of *in antis*, describes a portico that projects before the front of a building. Where a second, similar portico is placed at the opposite end, and no columns appear along the sides, it is termed *amphiprostyle*.

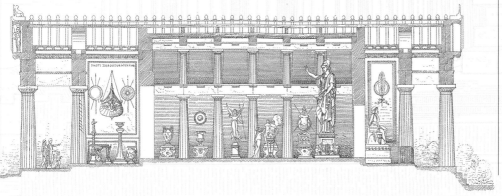

Ancient Greece

The Orders: Doric

The orders, structural systems for organising component parts, played a crucial role in the Greeks' search for perfection of ratio and proportion. Column, shaft, capital and entablature were measured and decorated according to one of the three accepted modes – Doric, Ionic and Corinthian. The Doric order was developed in the lands occupied by the Dorians, one of the two principal divisions of the Greek race. It became the preferred style of the Greek mainland and the western colonies (southern Italy and Sicily), known as Magna Graecia. Doric reached its peak in the mid-5th century BC, and was one of the orders accepted by the Romans. Its characteristics are masculinity, strength and solidity.

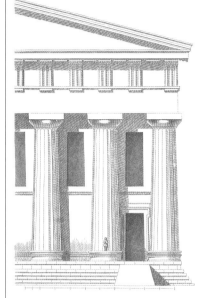

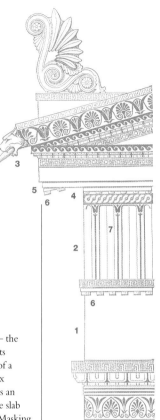

Characteristic features

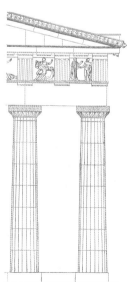

Doric columns are always without a base, are usually fluted and topped by a simple, squat capital. Their height, including the capital, varies from four to six times the diameter at the base of the shaft. The Doric entablature consists of a plain architrave, a frieze of alternating triglyphs and metopes, and a plain crowning cornice.

Triglyphs and metopes
One of the most distinctive features of the Doric order is its frieze, made up of triglyphs and metopes. Triglyphs are vertical blocks, usually aligned over each column and each intercolumniation. They consist of two vertical grooves (glyphs), bordered by two hemi- or half-glyphs (hence the triglyph or three-glyph). Metopes are the square panels between the triglyphs, and were often richly decorated.

Doric capital
The Doric capital – the upper member of its column – consists of a cushion-like convex moulding known as an *echinus*, and a square slab termed an abacus. Masking the joint of *echinus* and the column's shaft are horizontal mouldings called annulets. A similar moulded band – known as the *hypotrachelium* – appears lower down.

Entablature
The entablature is the upper part of an order, placed above the column and capital, and is made up of three horizontal elements. These are architrave (1), frieze (2) and cornice (3). The soffit (underside – 4) of the Doric cornice inclined, and bore projecting square blocks known as mutules (5). Originally, these formed the ends of sloping rafters. Mutules are usually decorated by drops (*guttae* – 6), and are centred over triglyphs (7). *Guttae* also appear beneath triglyphs.

Antefixae

The tile-ends at the edges of a roof were concealed by ornamental blocks known as *antefixae*, vertical elements often carved with an anthemion (honeysuckle) motif (*below right*). Unlike their Doric counterparts, Ionic temples do not normally bear *antefixae* on their flanks. The image below also shows a carved *sima* moulding and *acroterion* (*see page 107*) in the form of a griffin.

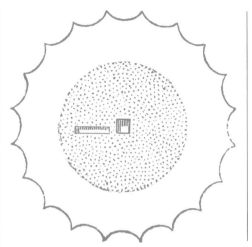

Flutes and arrises

Doric columns are generally carved with vertical, parallel channels known as flutes (as shown on this cross-section of a column), which should – properly speaking – number twenty. Doric flutes meet in sharp ridges called arrises.

Sima

Sima, or *cymatium*, is the term applied to roof gutters placed along the gables and flanks of buildings. Those of both Doric and Ionic temples often had outlets for rainwater, modelled in the form of lions' heads.

Key pattern

A common form of ornamentation used on Doric temples is the fretwork known as key pattern, Greek key design, meander or, as in this case, labyrinth motif.

Ancient Greece

The Orders: Ionic

The Ionic order appears to have been developed contemporaneously with the Doric, though it did not come into common usage and take its final shape until the mid-5th century BC. The style prevailed in Ionian lands, centred on the coast of Asia Minor and the Aegean islands. The order's form was far less set than the Doric, with local variations persisting for many decades. Even when it became more coherent, there were accepted alternatives. At first Doric and Ionic were confined to their respective areas of origin, but gradually the two styles intermingled on single buildings such as the Propylaea, Athens (437–431 BC). A century or so later, Ionic really came into its own, with masterpieces such as the temple of Athena Polias at Priene (c. 340 BC). According to the Roman architect Vitruvius, the Ionic order's main characteristics were beauty, femininity, and slenderness, derived from its basis on the proportions of a woman.

Egg-and-dart
The Ionic order, in particular, is often ornamented with carved mouldings. One of the most common was egg-and-dart, also known as egg-and-tongue or egg-and-anchor.

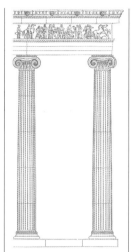

Characteristic features
Ionic columns, unlike their Doric counterparts, are always set on a base (the part between the shaft and the *crepidoma*). The order's capital – its most distinctive trademark – bears two spirals (volutes) and supports the entablature, which is much lighter than that of the Doric order.

Bead-and-reel
Another common carved moulding associated with this order is bead-and-reel, or bead-and-fillet. This often ornamented the astragal, a semi-circular band that separated shaft from capital.

Entablature
The Ionic entablature evolved in various stages, but in its most characteristic form (4th century BC onwards) consisted of an architrave divided into three broad bands known as *fasciae*, a continuous frieze (either plain or sculpted) and an often elaborate cornice bearing dentils, or tooth-like blocks.

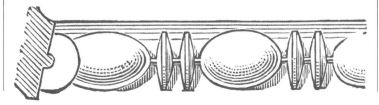

Capital

The volutes of an Ionic capital rest on an *echinus*, almost invariably carved with egg-and-dart. Above the scrolls was an abacus, more shallow than that in Doric examples, and again ornamented with egg-and-dart.

Anthemion and palmette

Ornament carved with palmette, a stylised palm leaf, and anthemion (honeysuckle) was frequently placed around the necking of Ionic columns. Anthemion was in itself an extremely well-used motif, and was commonly seen on Greek temples.

Attic base

The Attic base – so-called because it was perfected in Attica – was widely used in the 5th and 6th centuries BC. It consists of two tori (convex mouldings) the lower of greater diameter than the upper, joined by a concave element known as the *scotia*.

Flutes and fillets

Ionic columns were fluted, the typical number of flutes being twenty-four. These were deeper than Doric channels, and were divided by narrow, flat-faced bands known as fillets.

Volute

The volute, also known as the helix, is a spiral scroll that adorns the Ionic capital. It appears to derive from naturalistic forms such as the nautilus shell or fern, and made an early appearance in so-called Aeolic capitals. The circular, central part of a volute is called the eye.

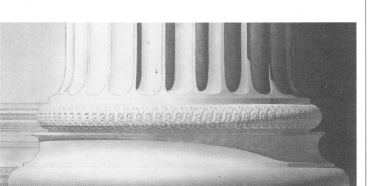

Ancient Greece

The Orders: Corinthian

The third of the Greek orders was also the last to be developed. The earliest documented examples of the use of Corinthian are (internally) at the Temple of Apollo Epicurius, Bassae (429–390 BC) and (externally) at the Choragic Monument of Lysicrates, Athens (335–334 BC). Corinthian was not, like the Doric and Ionic orders, a structural system. It was purely decorative, its effect due almost wholly to its elaborate floral capital. This, according to Vitruvius, was designed by the Athenian sculptor Callimachus, and may originally have been worked in bronze. Apart from this capital, all the constituent parts were borrowed from the Ionic order. Gradually, in Hellenistic times (after the death of Alexander in 323 BC), Corinthian did begin to develop, but it was left to the Romans to blend the elements together and make it perfect. Vitruvius stated that the Corinthian order imitated the 'slenderness of a maiden'; its overall effect is one of elegance and beauty.

Origins of Corinthian capital design
According to Vitruvius, Callimachus designed the Corinthian capital after seeing a basket overgrown with acanthus leaves. This had supposedly been placed on a young woman's grave by her former nurse, and contained a few of her most treasured belongings. In springtime, the acanthus sprouted and grew up around it. A tile, placed over the top of the basket, forced the leaves to curl into spirals at the outer edges.

Characteristic features
As with the Ionic order, Corinthian can best be recognised by its capital. As the order's other features are taken from Ionic, one would expect to find a base to the column, fluting, an architrave divided into *fasciae*, a carved frieze and a dentilled cornice.

Capital

The Corinthian capital has, in its perfected form, two tiers of eight acanthus leaves. From the uppermost of these rise stalks *(caulicoli)*, which terminate in volutes or helices. These support the abacus (top slab), which typically has four concave faces. At the centre of each side is a carved anthemion (honeysuckle motif).

Early form of capital

This was the form in which the Corinthian capital made its first external appearance, at the 4th-century Choragic Monument of Lysicrates. There is only a single row of acanthus leaves, the place of the lower row being taken by water leaves (a type of lotus leaf or ivy). The capital is unusually high: it amounts to 1½ diameters of the column, rather than the later accepted height of 1⅙ diameters.

Acanthus

The main decorative element of the Corinthian capital is the leaf of the acanthus, a tough, herbaceous plant native to the shores of the Mediterranean. The Greeks took their inspiration from the pointed-leaf variety *Acanthus spinosus*, while the Romans preferred the broad profiles of *Acanthus mollis*.

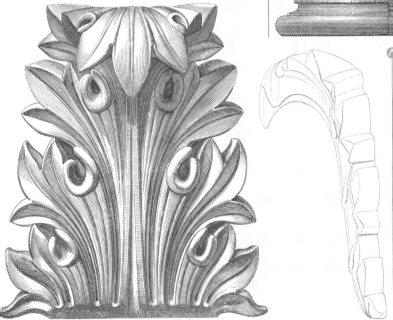

Base

The base of a Corinthian capital followed that of the Ionic order. It was usually of the Attic style, having two tori mouldings separated by a *scotia*. The divisions between these elements were marked by narrow bands called fillets. Another common form – the Asiatic base – had two *scotias* with separating astragals, and a torus above carved with horizontal reeding.

Ancient Greece

The Rise of the Doric

During the 6th and early 5th centuries BC – termed the 'Archaic' and 'Early Classical' periods – Greek architectural forms steadily developed, with Doric being the paramount order. Wood was substituted with stone – a process known as 'petrification' – and forms conceived in timber were conserved in the new material. The majority of buildings to survive from this period are to be found in Magna Graecia (southern Italy and Sicily), which largely escaped the wholesale destruction caused by the Persian Wars of 490–480 BC and thus retains some of the earliest, most interesting and most intact of Greek temples. Today, these seem severe and plain, but originally – as with all Greek buildings – they would have been richly coloured and elaborately sculpted. It was during this period that the Doric order and the form of Greek temples were finally developed, there being no major improvements after *c.* 500 BC.

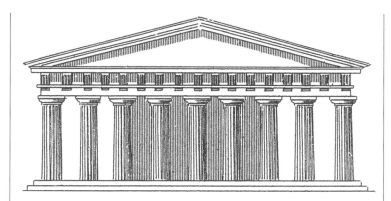

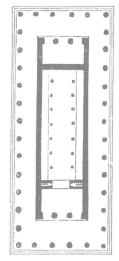

Paestum, southern Italy (6th/5th centuries BC)
At Paestum – known in Greek times as Poseidonia – there survives a remarkable group of temples. The earliest of these is known as the 'Basilica' and was built *c.* 540 BC *(top)*. The temple is unusual in being enneastyle (its portico has nine columns), an odd number that suggests the presence of an axial colonnade. The hexastyle Temple of Poseidon (*c.* 460–440 BC) (*above and right*) also has an internal colonnade, though here it is of two rows, a more developed arrangement that allowed an uninterrupted view of the deity.

Entasis
From early times the Greeks incorporated intentional distortions – known as 'refinements' – into their temples. One of the most basic of these was entasis, a slight curving of the outline of the shaft of the column so that it was wider at its middle. This was particularly pronounced in the 6th century BC. Entasis was seen as corrective of an optical illusion; columns with perfectly straight sides were believed to appear concave.

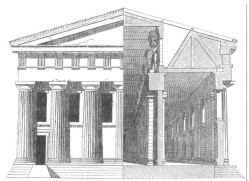

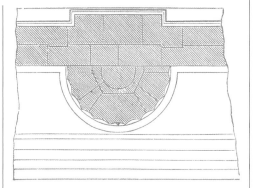

Engaged column

A column projecting directly from a wall-face is known as attached, engaged or applied. If between half and three-quarters of its curved shaft is exposed, it can also be termed a half-column.

Atlantes

Atlantes, known as *telamones* by the Romans, are architectural supports carved in the shape of male figures. These are often shown straining against a weight, as at the Temple of Zeus Olympius (*c.* 510–409 BC), Agrigentum, where they are believed to have borne up the external entablature and relieved the masonry behind them. It has been speculated that they were used internally. The female counterparts of atlantes are known as caryatids.

Superimposed order

A superimposed, or superposed order refers to the placement of one row of columns upon another, creating a double tier or storey. Superimposed orders – Doric on Doric – were frequently used in temples of this period as a means of supporting the roof. Later, especially in Roman times, orders followed a particular sequence; Doric, Ionic and then Corinthian.

Pseudoperipteral temple

One of the largest Doric temples was that built at Acragas (now Agrigentum) in Sicily, dedicated to Zeus Olympius (from 480 BC). It was also one of the most innovative; the temple was pseudoperipteral, meaning that its peripteral columns were attached to the walls, rather than free-standing. These columns were of a colossal or giant order (that is, they rose beyond a single storey in height) and were unconventional in having bases.

Ancient Greece

The Age of Pericles

Greek architecture reached its height in the mid-5th century BC, a period often termed the 'High Classical' age. During these years some of the most magnificent buildings in the world were produced, largely due to the sound political and economic background of the time. The Greeks had finally vanquished the invading Persians, who left massive destruction in their wake. There was exultation at the Greek victory, and a renewed sense of pride and patriotism. The spoils of war were used to build glorious new sanctuaries, and the fervour for building reached its peak under Pericles, the great Athenian statesman who ruled *c.* 444–429 BC and gave his name to the whole age.

Characteristics

Doric temples of the 5th century BC often demonstrate recognisable characteristics; columns appear taller and more slender than in 'archaic' examples, friezes are more lavishly decorated, and intercolumniations are wider. All of these changes reflect the influence of the Ionic style.

Hecatompedon

Hecatompedon refers to a temple measuring 100 Greek feet in length. One example is the Hephaesteum (or Theseum) in Athens, built in 449–444 BC.

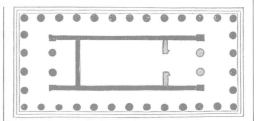

Hephaesteum

At this period, construction seems to have moved from the inside out – that is, the sanctuary proper was built first, and the peristyle was then added around it. The Hephaesteum is in a remarkable state of preservation, due to the fact it was converted into a church by the Byzantine Greeks.

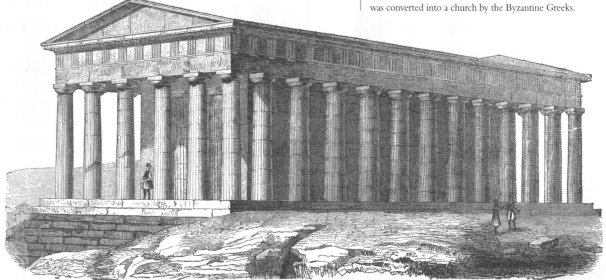

Temple on the Illisus, Athens (449 BC)

During the 5th century BC, Ionic temples began to make their first fully developed appearance. This temple in Athens clearly demonstrates the main characteristics of the style: slenderness and elegance. It is tetrastyle (has a portico of four columns).

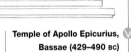

Acroteria

The word '*acroteria*' properly refers to the plinths or pedestals at the apex and corners of a pediment. *Acroteria* has also been taken to refer to the statues or ornaments placed on the pediment. The *acroteria* of this Temple of Zeus at Olympia (c. 470 BC) were made of bronze. Others were more modest in form, but were elaborately carved.

Temple of Apollo Epicurius, Bassae (429–490 BC)

The unusual plan of this temple can be explained by its orientation. It is aligned north–south, rather than east–west, and so a special side-door was inserted in the east wall. The statue of the deity would have been placed opposite in a space known as an *adytum, naiskos* or *sekos*.

The three orders

Architecture in the 5th century BC remained conservative and traditional. However, there were exceptions, one of the most notable being the Temple of Apollo Epicurius at Bassae in Arcadia, designed by Ictinus, who was also responsible for the Parthenon. Here, for the first time in Greek architecture, the three orders appeared in one building: Doric in the peristyle, Ionic in the interior and a single axial column in the Corinthian style.

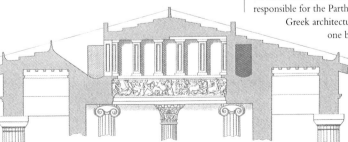

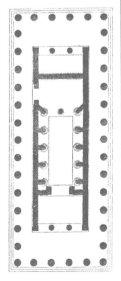

Ancient Greece

The Age of Pericles: The Acropolis

The Acropolis of Athens was left in a state of chaos after the defeated Persians withdrew in 480 BC. The first or 'pre-Parthenon', as well as all the other buildings on the site, had been completely destroyed. There were plans to rebuild Athens's sacred centre, but nothing happened until 447 BC, when Pericles took the lead. Anxious to express the glory of his country and the increasing dominance of Athens, he decided upon an ambitious scheme. In 438 BC Ictinus and Callicrates were brought in as architects of the principal temple – dedicated to the city's patron goddess, Athena Polias, and known as the Parthenon – and Phidias was employed as head sculptor. The two Periclean buildings of the Acropolis (the Parthenon and the Propylaea) represent Doric architecture at its zenith, the architects having achieved a perfection of proportion realised neither before nor since.

Acropolis
Acropolis refers to the citadel or 'upper town' of any Greek city. The majority of Greek cities were built on hills and the acropolis, at the summit, was the centre of religious and political life.

Panathenaean festival
The Parthenon – like all Greek temples – not only functioned as the abode of a god, but also had a social and ritual role. Once a year, the Athenians held a Panathenaean festival in honour of Athena's birthday. The entire city would take part in a procession, which reached its climax with the offering of an ornate tunic (*peplos*) to the goddess.

Chryselephantine
In the inner sanctum (*cella*) of the Parthenon stood a statue of Athena, carved by the famous sculptor Phidias. This massive statue, along with similar works, is described as *chryselephantine*, meaning that it had a wooden core overlaid with ivory and gold.

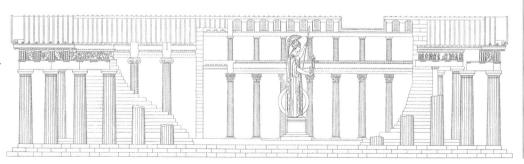

Sculpture, Parthenon

The Parthenon boasted a wealth of outstanding sculpture, including two elaborate pediments carved between 438 and 432 BC. The west pediment, shown here, told of the confrontation between Athena and Poseidon.

Propylaea (437–432 BC) ⋁

Monumental entrance gateways, known as *propylaea*, marked the approach to sacred precincts or enclosures. The Propylaea of Athens was reached via a steep ascent from the plain below the Acropolis. The building has hexastyle porticoes to front and rear, but only one of its wings was completed, as construction was stopped by the outbreak of the Peloponnesian Wars.

⋀ Polychromy

All of the buildings on the Acropolis were built of white Pentelic marble, which was then ornamented with polychromy (coloured decoration). At the Parthenon, elements such as capitals, metopes and pedimental tympana would have been brightly painted.

Ionic columns, Propylaea ⋁

At the centre of the Propylaea was a road for carts and sacrificial beasts. It was lined to the west by Ionic columns, a typical choice of this period. It was also practical; their greater height masked the change in floor level, while their small diameter took up minimal floor space.

Plan, Parthenon ⋀

The present Parthenon occupies the same site as its predecessor, and follows its plan. Although the early temple was hexastyle, while the present one is octastyle, the structure remained the same. The rear chamber (*opisthodomus*) contained four Ionic columns and was originally termed the Parthenon (Hall of the Virgin), a word later taken to refer to the whole building.

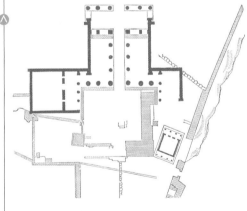

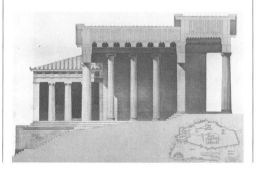

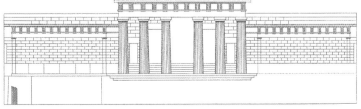

Ancient Greece

The Age of Pericles: The Acropolis II

The ambitious plans that Pericles had for the Acropolis were brought to an abrupt halt in 431 BC. In that year the Spartans rose up in defiance of Athens, which had grown increasingly in power and prestige, and the Peloponnesian Wars began. These were to last until 404 BC, though there was a brief interlude between 421 and 413 BC. This provided the opportunity to finish some of the monuments of the Acropolis, and work was duly started on Athens's two great Ionic temples, the Erechtheum (421–406 BC) and the Temple of Athena Nike or Nike Apteros (421 BC). The architect of the latter was Callicrates, who had worked on the Parthenon, while the Erechtheum has been attributed to Mnesicles, designer of the Propylaea. The architects may have remained the same, but the style was very different. There was a shift in favour of the flexible forms of the Ionic style; the Doric was never again to reach the perfection embodied in the Parthenon.

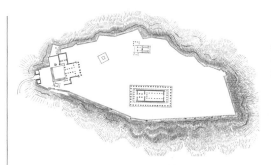

Temenos, Acropolis
The sacred precinct – the area surrounding a temple – was known as a *temenos*. Here the enclosure of the Athenian Acropolis is shown, with its four buildings dating from the 5th century BC.

Caryatid
A caryatid is a carved female figure, used instead of a column to support an entablature. Vitruvius states that the word caryatid derives from the women of Caryae, who were taken into slavery as punishment for having sided with the Persians. Similar figures with baskets on their heads are known as *canephorae*.

Caryatids, Erechtheum
The most famous examples of caryatids are those of the south porch at the Erechtheum. This fine structure is not so much a porch as a tribune (raised platform), as it is inaccessible from the outside.

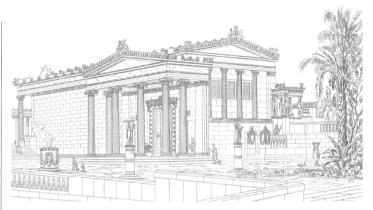

Erechtheum (421–406 BC)

The Erechtheum is a temple dedicated to various gods, including Athena Polias and Erechtheus. It was built on two levels – possibly in response to a building already on the site – and has three porches or porticoes, one (the west) attached. It bears no resemblance to the classic, rectangular temple plan, and this unconventionality is a mark of the period.

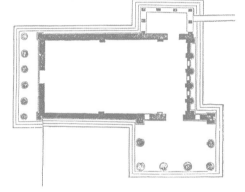

Temple of Athena Nike (421 BC)

This small Ionic temple, which was planned before the Propylaea but not actually begun until 421 BC, was built on a natural promontory or bastion of the Acropolis. In plan, it is *amphiprostyle* tetrastyle (that is, it has two porticoes, east and west, each comprising four columns). Like the Erechtheum, the Temple of Athena Nike (Wingless Victory) represents Ionic at its best. The continuous frieze, which depicts Athena and the gods, as well as battle scenes, is particularly characteristic.

Console, Erechtheum

The Erechtheum has a beautiful and well-preserved doorway within its north portico. On either side are two carved consoles, S-shaped brackets that support the cornice. Consoles are usually of greater height than projection. The mouldings around the doorway, in the form of architraves, are known as *antepagmenta*.

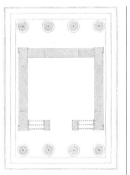

Decoration, Erechtheum

The Erechtheum displays the Ionic order at its most elaborate. In this detail of the building's entablature can be seen the classic Ionic motifs – egg-and-dart, bead-and-reel and anthemion (honeysuckle). The frieze was of black limestone, to which figures of white marble were attached by clamps.

Ancient Greece

The Beginning of Decadence

The ascendancy of Athens was fruitful but short-lived. In 404 BC the Peloponnesian Wars ended with the fall of the city. From this time, there was a gradual degeneracy of Greek architecture, as less cultivated states – Sparta, Thebes and then Macedonia – rose to the fore. In this period, which is often termed 'Late Classical', continual warfare prevented the initiation of ambitious architectural projects. On the mainland, energy was devoted to buildings other than temples, and the three orders began to coalesce on individual buildings. Asia Minor was less affected by war, and the Ionic style experienced a comeback, thanks to the patronage of the Persian *satraps* (governors) and the encouragement of Alexander the Great, who conquered Asia Minor in 334–333 BC.

Finial, Choragic Monument
Finial refers to an ornament placed at the crowning point of a roof or prominent terminal, such as a pediment. The finial placed at the apex of the Choragic Monument of Lysicrates was lavish, being designed to carry the tripod. It is decorated with acanthus leaves and helices (scrolls).

Choragic Monument of Lysicrates, Athens (335–334 BC)
Circular structures, called tholoi, became popular in Greece during this period. Their purpose is not clear, though they often imitated temples and some housed statues. Perhaps the most famous tholos is the Choragic Monument of Lysicrates, built at the foot of the Acropolis. This was a small, hollow shrine, designed to carry a bronze tripod (a bowl with three legs) won by Lysicrates during a choral contest in the theatre. It was very elaborate and, most significantly, used the Corinthian order externally for the first time.

Dentils, Choragic Monument

The cornice of the Ionic order, as developed in Asia Minor, bore dentils, small rectangular projections that appear as a series, with gaps (interdentils) between. Dentils were also used, in a slightly reduced form, in the cornice of the Corinthian order, as on the Choragic Monument of Lysicrates. Traditionally, in Asia Minor, the frieze of the Ionic order was omitted, though it appears here.

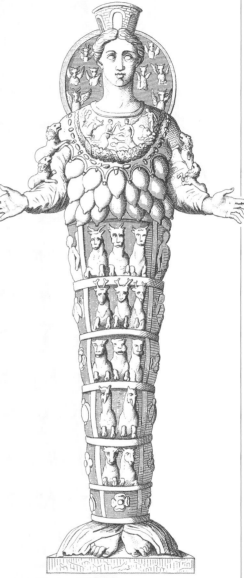

Temple of Artemis, Ephesus (begun 330 BC)

The Ionic Artemision of Ephesus, properly the Temple of Artemis, was the most important sacred building of Asia Minor and, along with the Parthenon, was one of the seven wonders of the

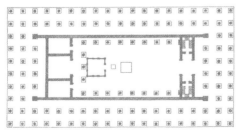

ancient world. Several temples had existed on its site before its 6th-century predecessor burned down in 356 BC. The scanty remains of the temple have led to uncertainties about its plan – it seems now that it was octastyle, rather than decastyle, as shown here. It was, however, certainly dipteral (two rows of columns on each side) and was famous for its sculpted decoration, most notably its *columnae caelatae* (carved columns).

Artemis

The great temple of Ephesus was dedicated to Artemis, known as Diana by the Romans, the goddess of chastity, the moon and the hunt. Traditionally, the temple is said to have contained a statue of Artemis in her polymastic form – that is, with many breasts. This image may relate to the goddess's role as mother figure and bringer of fertility.

Ancient Greece

The Hellenistic Phase

The death of Alexander the Great in 323 BC is widely regarded as the end of the Hellenic period (which had begun c. 650 BC) and the beginning of the Hellenistic phase. Under Alexander, the Greek Empire had spread as far as India and Nubia, but the traditional Hellenic influence had remained strong. With Alexander's death, this vast territory was broken up into independent kingdoms, the lifestyle and arts of which have been termed Hellenistic, for they imitated true Hellenic principles. There was a general move away from earlier forms; the Ionic and Corinthian orders were regularly used in preference to the Doric, which almost fell out of use, and attention was paid to an array of architectural types. This last phase of Greek architecture was to have a vital impact on the Romans, who finally conquered Greece in 30 BC.

Tower of the Winds, Athens (mid-1st century BC)
The so-called Tower of the Winds in Athens was built as a *horologium* (clock-tower). Time was measured internally by means of a *clepsydra* or water clock, and externally by a sundial. Each of the eight sides of the building bore a carved relief representing a wind (the west wind Zephyrus, for example) and a weather-vane pointed to the direction from which the wind was blowing.

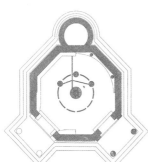

Corinthian capital, variant form
In the Hellenistic phase, the orders lost their previous rigidity and forms became experimental. At the Tower of the Winds, for example, a variant form of the Corinthian capital appeared. It has only a single row of acanthus leaves, no volutes and a square abacus.

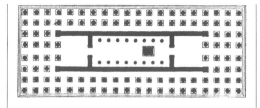

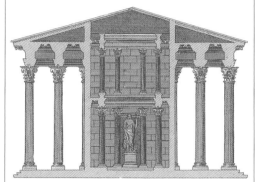

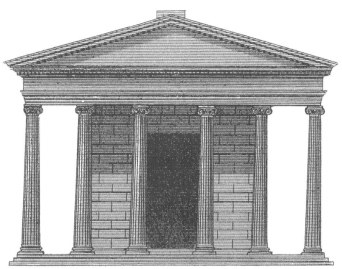

Dipteral temple

Temples surrounded by a double row of columns (dipteral) became popular from the 4th century BC onwards. Their chief virtue was grandeur, which was often heightened (as in this case) by extra lines of columns at the front and rear (tripteral). Shown here is the magnificent Athenian Temple of Zeus Olympius (begun 174 BC).

Ionic order, Temple of Dionysus, Teos (mid-2nd century BC)

The popularity of the Ionic temple continued in the Hellenistic phase although, typically, new forms were developed. Hermogenes, a renowned architect of the 2nd century BC, invented a new set of rules for the order, which he set down in writing. The Temple of Dionysus at Teos is an Ionic building of his design.

Corinthian order, Temple of Zeus Olympius

Few purely Corinthian temples were built by the Greeks; it was a form left for the Romans to develop. However, the Temple of Zeus Olympius (Olympicion) is a notable example. The order has become heavily proportioned and, with an increase in the height of the entablature, excessively tall.

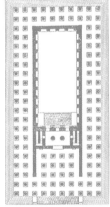

Hypaethral, Temple of Apollo Didyma, Miletus

A building with its central space open wholly or partly to the sky was known as *hypaethral*. One example was the Temple of Apollo Didyma, near Miletus, a vast building constructed over 300 years (313 BC–AD 41). Its open courtyard contained a shrine and laurel bushes, and its enclosing wall was faced with pilasters.

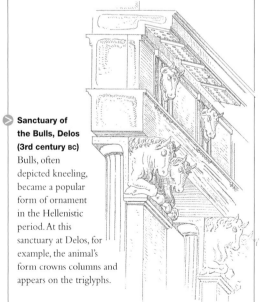

Sanctuary of the Bulls, Delos (3rd century BC)

Bulls, often depicted kneeling, became a popular form of ornament in the Hellenistic period. At this sanctuary at Delos, for example, the animal's form crowns columns and appears on the triglyphs.

Ancient Greece

Tombs

Death and the burial of the dead were subjects of great importance to the Greeks. The most common indicator of a place of burial was a tombstone known as a stele. However, in Hellenistic times there was an upsurge in tomb building on a grand scale, especially in Asia Minor, where foreign rulers employed Greek architects and craftsmen. Such tombs often imitated temples in plan and design, having pediments and a peristyle. The *pièce de résistance* of tomb architecture, and one of the seven wonders of the ancient world, was the Mausoleum at Halicarnassus, begun around 353 BC by King Mausolus of Caria and his wife and sister Artemisia.

Lion Tomb, Cnidus (4th century BC)
The Lion Tomb at Cnidus, near Halicarnassus, seems to commemorate men who died in battle, most probably a naval encounter. Its name derives from its crowning feature, a massive lion, symbol of valour, pride, strength and victory. The tomb has engaged Doric columns and a stepped pyramid above.

Mausoleum, Halicarnassus (begun 353 BC)
Mausoleum – now taken to mean a magnificent, large-scale sepulchral monument – derives from the tomb of King Mausolus at Halicarnassus, built to designs by Pythius and Satyrus. As nothing was left standing of the Mausoleum after its destruction in the 16th century AD, the building's form and decoration have been a source of constant and heated debate. Here, the podium of the tomb is depicted as excessively tall.

Design and plan, Halicarnassus
There have been numerous attempts to reconstruct the Mausoleum at Halicarnassus, some more acclaimed than others. According to Pliny, the building had a peristyle of thirty-six Ionic columns, probably enclosing the burial chamber, above which rose a vast pyramid of twenty-four steps. The height of the whole building was a colossal 41 m (135 ft), including the podium. The plan has been shown variously as rectangular, square and cruciform.

Podium, Nereid Monument, Xanthus (c. 420 BC)
A podium is a low wall, continuous base or pedestal, on which columns are carried. Sometimes, as here, entire structures stand on a podium, which can be ornamented. The Nereid Monument at Xanthus was built in the form of an Ionic temple.

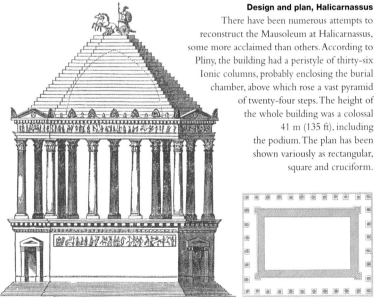

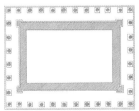

Decoration, Halicarnassus

The most admired feature of the Mausoleum of Halicarnassus – and the principal reason for its being considered a wonder of the world – was its decoration. The building was adorned with statues of men, lions, horses and other animals (both internally and externally), by four sculptors: Bryaxis, Leochares, Scopas and Timotheus.

Coffering, Halicarnassus

The flat ceilings of Greek buildings were decorated with coffers, sunken square or polygonal panels. Their form appears to imitate joinery patterns of timber predecessors. This is a restoration of the coffering within the peristyle of the Mausoleum at Halicarnassus.

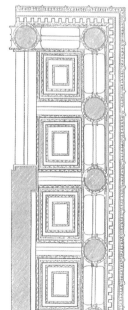

Quadriga, Halicarnassus

At the very pinnacle of the Mausoleum of Halicarnassus was placed a *quadriga*, a sculptured group consisting of a chariot drawn by four horses, with driver (*auriga* or charioteer). Fragments of this particular group survive in the British Museum.

Ancient Greece

Theatres and Odea

Theatres are said to have originated in the 6th or 5th centuries BC and were originally designed for the performance of choral dances relating to festivals of Dionysus. Later, they were used for the staging of tragedy and comedy, the two divisions of Greek drama, which reached its height under Pericles. Theatres were usually sited on a hill and tiers of seats – wooden at first, but later stone – were built on the slopes, while the hollow provided a focus for the action. All theatres were open-air, the Theatre of Dionysus at Athens (*c.* 500 BC) and the Theatre at Epidaurus (*c.* 350 BC) being among the best known. Often built in close proximity were *odea*, or music halls. An odeon (or *odeum*) was smaller than a theatre, and developed slightly later; the earliest known example was built by Pericles *c.* 435 BC at Athens.

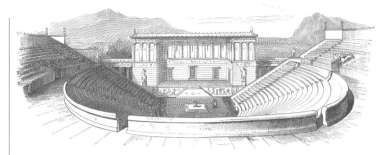

Proscenium

In Hellenistic times, the action was transferred from the orchestra to the roof of a proscenium or *proskenion*, a colonnaded structure placed along the front of the scene building (*see opposite page*). The roof formed a raised stage or *logeion* (speaking place), and made it easier for spectators to view performers. In time, the scene building behind grew to two storeys in height, the upper façade forming a background (*episcenium*) to the stage. Under the Romans, the stage became very low and the *episcenium* more elaborate than before.

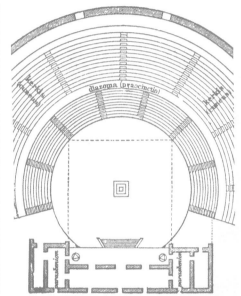

Orchestra

The flat, circular space at the base of the *cavea* was termed the orchestra, literally 'dancing place'. As its name suggests, the orchestra was the space where the performers danced and sang, and an altar to Dionysus was sometimes placed at its centre. The actors reached the orchestra via passages known as *parodoi*.

Cavea

The large semi-circular seating area of a theatre was called the *cavea* or auditorium. This contained tiers of seats, those nearest to the orchestra being reserved for priests, officials and other dignitaries. The seats were divided by radial stairways into wedge-shaped groups known as *cunei*, with horizontal walkways providing access.

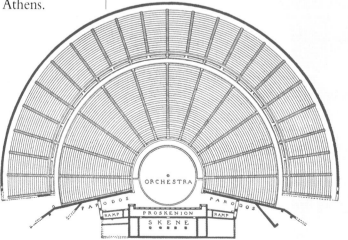

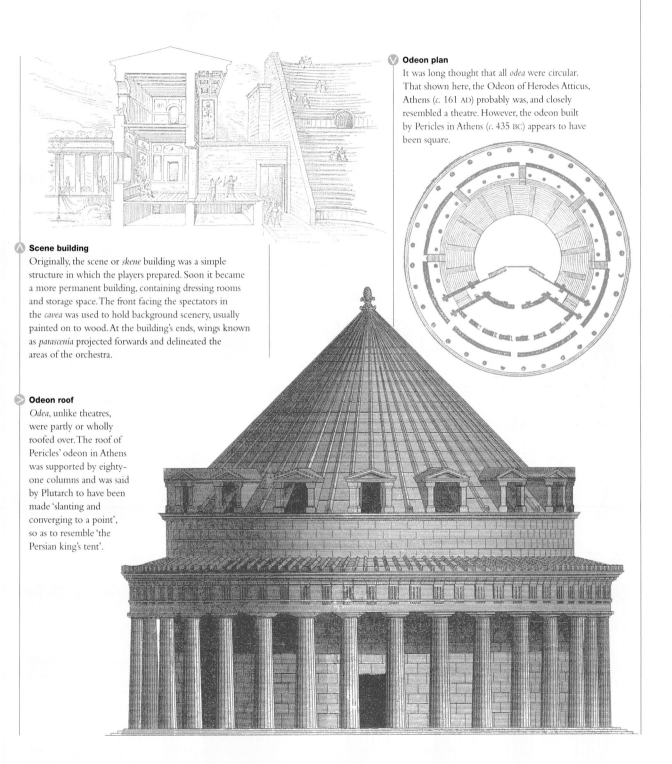

Odeon plan

It was long thought that all *odea* were circular. That shown here, the Odeon of Herodes Atticus, Athens (*c.* 161 AD) probably was, and closely resembled a theatre. However, the odeon built by Pericles in Athens (*c.* 435 BC) appears to have been square.

Scene building

Originally, the scene or *skene* building was a simple structure in which the players prepared. Soon it became a more permanent building, containing dressing rooms and storage space. The front facing the spectators in the *cavea* was used to hold background scenery, usually painted on to wood. At the building's ends, wings known as *parascenia* projected forwards and delineated the areas of the orchestra.

Odeon roof

Odea, unlike theatres, were partly or wholly roofed over. The roof of Pericles' odeon in Athens was supported by eighty-one columns and was said by Plutarch to have been made 'slanting and converging to a point', so as to resemble 'the Persian king's tent'.

Ancient Greece

Other Secular Structures

There was, as we have seen, less emphasis on religious architecture in Hellenistic times, and an increase in the range of secular structures. The *agora*, an open market place within the city, formed the focus for social and business life, and contained buildings such as *stoas* (colonnaded shelters), *bouleuterions* (council assembly rooms), *prytaneions* (administrative offices) and *balaneia* (baths). Outside the *agora*, cities were purely residential, though houses remained, on the whole, unpretentious – people spent much of their time outside or in places of public assembly. Buildings related to sports (gymnasia, stadia and so forth) were of particular prominence. Athletic contests often formed part of religious festivals, and special Panhellenic Games or Festivals – comprising the Olympic, Pythian, Isthmian and Nemean Games – were held in four-year cycles, known as Olympiads. Women were generally not allowed to take part and even spectators were solely male.

Double-storeyed stoa

A *stoa* was a roofed, colonnaded structure, which offered shelter from wind and rain and provided a place to walk and talk. *Stoas* were built to be architecturally magnificent and in many cases bore superimposed colonnades. In this case, the Stoa of Attalus II at Athens (*c*. 150 BC), the lower order is Doric and the upper order Ionic.

Stoa roof

The ridged roof of a *stoa* was usually borne by a row of Ionic columns, placed along the centre of the building. *Stoas* were frequently placed around the sides of an *agora*, or in a *temenos*.

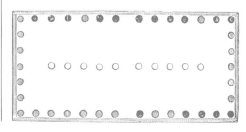

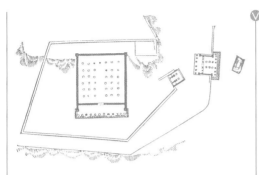

Stadium

The stadium or *stadion* was a running track for races on foot. The track itself was straight and levelled, and averaged around 183 m (600 ft) in length. Athletes would usually turn sharply at a pillar or post at each end. The sides were embanked, while one end – in later times – bore seating for spectators.

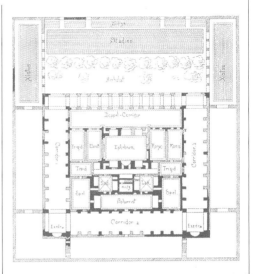

Meeting hall

The Greeks had square meeting halls – akin to Egyptian hypostyle halls – which were roofed, edged with seats and contained a great number of columns. The best-known example is the Telesterion or Hall of Mysteries at Eleusis, built mainly in the 5th and 4th centuries BC.

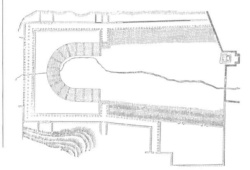

Gymnasium

A gymnasium proper was a large open space used by boys and men for exercise of all kinds. It was often surrounded by colonnades *(stoas)*. However, the word is also used to refer to the court, as well as the buildings around it, which included baths, dressing rooms and lecture rooms.

Hippodrome

A hippodrome was a building for horse and chariot racing, among the most prestigious of Greek contests. No Greek hippodromes survive, but it is thought that they resembled Roman circuses in being U-shaped. The race would begin from the straight end of the U and move around a central barrier. Here, at the hippodrome in Olympia, a chariot race totalled twelve laps of the course, while a horse race usually totalled one lap.

Palaestra

A *palaestra* was similar to a gymnasium, and the words are often used interchangeably. But it is, properly speaking, a privately owned Greek wrestling school. This *palaestra* at Olympia consists of an open courtyard enclosed by a colonnade, with changing rooms and baths behind.

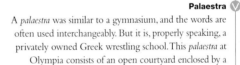

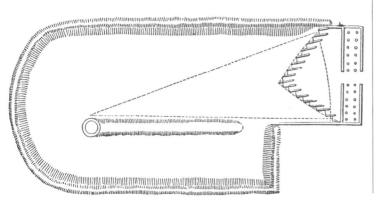

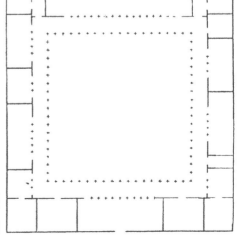

Ancient Rome *C.3rd BC–c.AD 340*

Republican Rome

During the 3rd and 2nd centuries BC Rome was concerned with conquering her enemies and expanding her empire at home and abroad. During the republic, Rome was ruled by an oligarchy of patricians who dominated the Senate and Assembly. The period came to an end with the Civil Wars and the accession of the Emperor Augustus in 27 BC. During the Roman Republic a new form of architecture emerged, building on Etruscan-Italian traditions with the adoption of Greek classical styling and Roman building methods. Very little survives from this period, but what does exist gives a flavour of the innovative search for new building materials, types of building and decorative expression. Through this quest the Romans were able to forge a new architectural style of their own.

Corinthian capital, Temple of Vesta, Rome
Early Roman Corinthian capitals tended to be squatter than later examples, with fleshier acanthus leaves and larger flowers on the abacus. This example is from the Temple of Vesta, Rome, where there were twenty such capitals on fluted columns.

Basilica Aemilia (c. 179 BC)
Little remains of the Basilica Aemilia except fragments such as this. From medals and excavations it is known to have presented its longer side to the forum, but to have been obscured from view by a double-height colonnade housing shops.

Opus incertum
Early republican buildings were often made with cast concrete mixed with an aggregate of small rough stones, sometimes traversed with bricks. This combination (known as *opus incertum*) was used from the 2nd until the early 1st century BC.

Circus Maximus (4th century)
Circuses were used for horse racing and gladiatorial contests. The Circus Maximus in Rome dates from the early 4th century, but was later modified. Built on flat ground, it is 600 m (1,968 ft) long with seating all round, apart from the straight end where there was a set of *caracares* (starting gates). A low wall called a *spina,* with *meta* or turning posts as each end, acted as a turning circle.

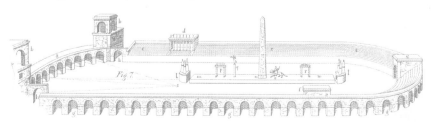

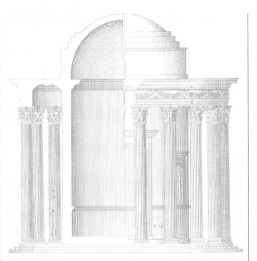

Temple of Fortuna Virilis (1st century BC)

This is an Ionic tetrastyle (four-columned portico) temple. The concrete podium is made of tufa, a local volcanic stone, and faced with travertine, a limestone quarried in nearby Tivoli. The walls are also of tufa, but are faced with stucco.

Temple of Vesta (1st century BC)

This circular temple from the first half of the 1st century BC is descended in plan from Etruscan circular huts. Its elevation, however, is Greek. The columns and walls are made of Pentellic marble brought from Greece. The steps that surround it on all sides, the classical decoration and the materials suggest that the architect may have been Greek. It has lost its entablature, and the dome seen here is purely conjectural.

Plan, Temple of Fortuna Virilis

This plan illustrates the extreme axiality of the temple building, which is an Etruscan inheritance. It is an early pseudoperipteral temple: the columns surround the building, but engage with the wall of the *cella* or sanctuary.

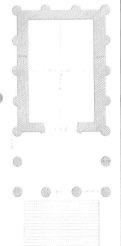

Bucranium frieze, Temple of Fortuna Virilis

This highly decorative and delicate frieze of ox heads, or *bucranium*, garlands and putti comes from the Temple of Fortuna Virilis (1st century BC).

The forum

Roman towns had two main roads, the *decumanus maximus* and the *cardo*. Where these two intersected was the forum, an irregular group of buildings comprising the social, religious, business and political centre of a Roman town. The forum combined the axial market places of the Etruscans with the colonnaded *agoras* of the Greeks.

Ancient Rome

Pompeii

Pompeii, south of Naples and dating from the 3rd century BC on, was first damaged by earthquakes in AD 63 and later preserved under a thick layer of ash after the volcano, Mount Vesuvius, erupted in AD 79. Excavation began in the late 18th century and revealed an early Roman settlement of great architectural richness. The street plan, houses and public monuments were all intact and included many republican-era buildings. Surviving examples are often some of the earliest-known of certain types of Roman building, such as the basilica or bath complexes. The south of Italy had been strongly influenced by earlier Greek settlers, and Pompeii is no exception in revealing a fashion for Greek styling in the homes of the wealthy, which are such a distinctive feature of the city.

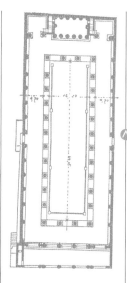

Basilica
Basilicas are probably descended from Greek colonnaded *agoras*, which were gradually covered over. They functioned as a place for business and for the judiciary. This example in Pompeii is entered on the shorter side, with a projecting tribunal or platform for public speaking.

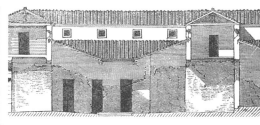

Domus (2nd century BC)
The earliest house, or *domus,* consisted of rooms grouped around a courtyard and was descended from Etruscan models. Greek fashion led the atrium to be extended into a second garden court, or peristyle, around which further rooms were grouped, as in this example, known as the House of Pansa. A second floor might be added and the street frontage leased to businesses.

Atrium tuscanium
In this *atrium tuscanium* (that is, an atrium without columns) one gains a sense of the luxury in which the wealthy owners lived. The walls and ceilings are frescoed, and drapes are hung to divide the *tablinium* from the atrium. Floors were often decorated with mosaic.

Atrium
Atriums were open to the sky (*compluvium*), allowing rainwater to collect in a pool (*impluvium*) below. Gradually Hellenistic columns were introduced in a number of ways. In this example a continuous colonnade surrounds the *impluvium* and is known as an *atrium corinthian*.

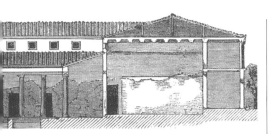

Wall decoration

Early houses were decorated with a dado and plaster patterns. A fashion for painted wall decoration led to the First Pompeiian style (*c.* 200–90 BC) of fresco painting, as seen in this example, which simulates architectural divisions on the wall. The Second Pompeiian style (*c.* 70–15 BC) generally includes colonnades through which an illusionistic landscape beyond is glimpsed.

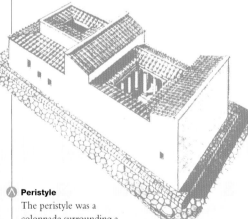

Peristyle

The peristyle was a colonnade surrounding a garden, often decorated with a fountain and statuary. There were few windows on the outsides of houses, and the peristyle and atrium were the only means of allowing light to enter. Gradually peristyles lost one or more sides so that the owner might view the landscape beyond.

House plan

The Roman house was symmetrical in plan. The most important room was the *tablinium*, which stood between the atrium and peristyle and marked the division between public and private areas. To either side were *ala,* or hallways. The *cubicula* (bedrooms) and *triclinia* (dining room) and kitchen lay beyond.

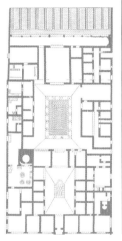

Frescoes and vaulting

This *tepidarium* from the Pompeiian Baths (*c.* 100 BC) indicates the level of internal decoration. The walls are frescoed and the ceiling incorporates an early barrel vault.

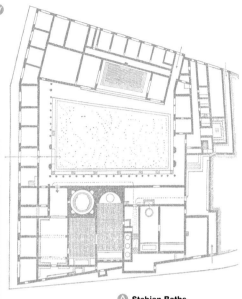

Stabian Baths (2nd century BC)

This is one of the earliest surviving examples of a bath complex. The plan is irregular, but the basic features of later complexes are there, including a *palestra* (exercise yard) and *natatio* (swimming pool). There are separate suites of baths for men and women, each with its own *apodyterium* (changing room), *tepidarium* (warm room) and *caldarium* (hot bath). The baths were heated by means of a brazier. The men's baths are more elaborate and contain one of the earliest-known concrete domes covering the *frigidarium* (cold bath).

Ancient Rome

Buildings Beyond Rome

Republican architecture beyond Rome during the 3rd to 1st centuries BC showed the same trends in building types and materials as the capital. The Romans lacked the extensive quarries of marble that were available to the Greeks and instead exploited their local resources of tufa, travertine and peperino. At this time they also developed and standardised the production of fired brick. The development of extremely durable concrete influenced the construction of both old and new building types. Concrete was never exposed, but was always concealed by an outer layer of brick or painted stucco. Temples in this period beyond Rome fused Etruscan-Italian traditions with the Hellenistic classical orders.

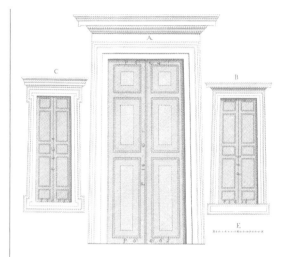

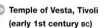 **Temple of Vesta, Tivoli (early 1st century BC)**
The circular Temple of Vesta is perched on a ravine at Tivoli and is dedicated to the goddess of the hearth. Temples in this period are often dramatically sited in the landscape, with panoramic views of the surrounding countryside.

Greek and Roman fusion, Temple of Vesta
The decoration of the Temple of Vesta at Tivoli is essentially Greek with its Corinthian capitals *(above)* and ox-head frieze. Its construction of local tufa, travertine and *opus incertum* is typically Roman, as are its podium, doors and windows *(top)* and axial stair opposite the entrance to the *cella*.

Plan, Temple of Vesta
The plan is derived from the Temple of Vesta in Rome. The main difference is that at Rome the stairs surround the *cella* on all sides, while here they are treated axially.

Sanctuary of Fortuna Primigenia, Praeneste (c. 80 BC)
This temple complex outside Rome was dedicated to the goddess Fortune. Its two parts, a lower forum and an upper sanctuary, are connected by a symmetrical system of stairs and ramps laid out over seven terraces. The site required the use of concrete vaulting for visual effect.

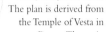

The Roman arch
The Romans developed the stone voussoir arch, with the use of free-standing piers to stabilise it. From this basic form are derived the barrel vault (shown here), the cross-vault and the dome.

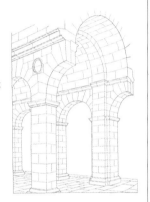

Aqueduct, Segovia (c. AD 10)
Aqueducts were built to transport water from the surrounding countryside to the towns. The water was often contained in an underground channel, but where the terrain necessitated, a monumental bridge was created instead. This example is a detail of the aqueduct at Segovia in Spain, which consists of a double tier of 128 arches 30 m (100 ft) high with rough stonework.

Basilica, Fano (c. 27 BC)
Vitruvius wrote the only surviving ancient Roman architectural treatise, *De Architectura*. His only known building, a basilica, survives at Fano on the Adriatic coast. The plan is rectangular, with the entrance from the forum on the longer side directly opposite the tribunal, where magistrates dispensed justice. He prescribed that basilicas should be built on a warm site for visitors' comfort.

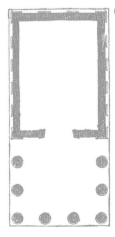

Temple of Hercules, Cori (late 2nd century BC)
This pseudoperipteral (*see page 105*) temple at Cori, south of Rome, has a continuous Doric order around the *cella*, which is engaged with the walls. The deep portico, with its densely positioned columns, deliberately addresses the space in front of the building; the back, by contrast, is unadorned.

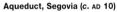

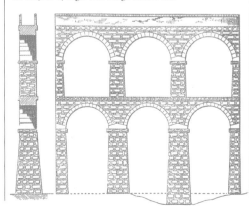

Ancient Rome

Augustan Buildings

When Augustus came to power in 27 BC following a civil war, he ushered in an age of peace and prosperity known as the *pax romana,* which lasted for 200 years. He set about rebuilding the infrastructure of Rome and the empire, building roads, bridges and aqueducts, and encouraged the wealthy to build for the benefit of the city. Sadly, few of these secular buildings survive. Augustus clearly followed the example of his adoptive father, Julius Caesar, in many respects, rebuilding the forum and finishing the Theatre of Marcellus, the earliest and most visible example in Rome of the combination of arch and applied order. There were advances in the use of cement: *pozzolanza*, a volcanic sand, became more widely used and a slower drying process was invented. However, the Augustan age remained essentially conservative in taste.

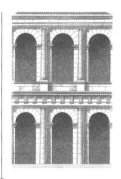

Theatre of Marcellus, Rome
The semi-circular exterior of the Theatre of Marcellus (dedicated in 13 BC to the memory of Augustus's grandson Marcellus) consists of two tiers of arches acting as buttresses to the seating. The combination of the structural arch and the decorative order is quintessentially Roman.

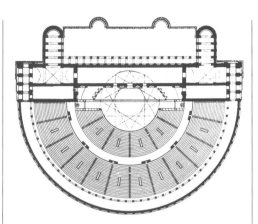

Roman theatre
Roman theatres differed from their Greek antecedents. They were semi-circular, rather than circular, and were enclosed by a wall, the *scaena frons* (see page 133), rather than open to the countryside on their straight side. The *cavea,* or seating, was built on an arcuated sub-structure with radial ramps and corridors for access, so that the theatre could be sited on flat ground rather than on a hillside.

Superimposed orders, Theatre of Marcellus
Only two storeys of the Theatre of Marcellus survive, upon the arches of which are superimposed the Ionic and Doric orders. It is not known whether there was a third Corinthian storey or simply an attic storey. Roman Doric always had a base.

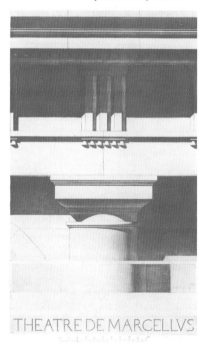

THEATRE DE MARCELLVS

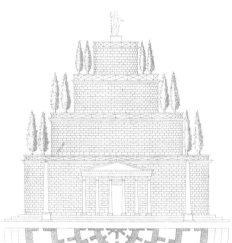

Pyramid of Cestius, Rome (c. 12 BC)

The Pyramid of Cestius represents an older form of burial chamber than the mausoleum of Augustus. Built of cement, it is faced with marble and encloses a painted chamber.

Arch of Tiberius, Orange, France (1st century BC)

The triumphal arch was by nature non-functional and purely symbolic. The earliest to survive are from the reign of Augustus and include the Arch of Tiberius at Orange.

Mausoleum, Rome (28–23 BC)

Augustus built a family tomb within the city walls, breaking the law forbidding burial within Rome. It follows the basic cylindrical form of Etruscan tombs, topped by a mound covered by cypress trees and a large effigy of the emperor.

Bridge of Augustus, Rimini (1st century AD)

The Romans exploited the hydraulic properties of their concrete, which would dry under water, to create bridges of great strength and aesthetic appeal. This bridge at Rimini on the Adriatic is an example, with five arches of varying size and immense piers.

Ancient Rome

Augustan Temples

Augustus claimed to have found Rome a city of brick and to have left it a city of marble. Above all, this is true of the many temples that he built and restored. In his autobiography, *Res Gestae Divi Augusti,* he claimed to have rebuilt eighty-two temples in one year in Rome alone. The temples of this period are conservative, building on republican traditions uniting the Etruscan plan and the Greek classical language. The plans of Augustan temples vary, but overall there is a tendency towards height over length or width. The high podiums that are so often a feature of the temples serve only to emphasise this aspect. The majority of Augustan temples are Corinthian, which accords with a taste for elaborate detail and the opulent use of marble.

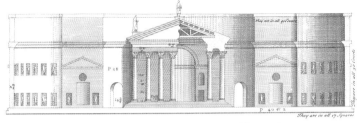

Temple of Mars Ultor, Rome (dedicated AD 2)
The Romans continually exploited architecture in the service of politics. At the Battle of Philippi (42 BC) Augustus swore to avenge the death of Julius Caesar and to build a temple in his memory. The Temple of Mars Ultor (The Avenger) in the Forum of Augustus was given as a gift to the city.

Plan, Mars Ultor
The plan of the Temple of Mars Ultor, with its strong frontal emphasis, symmetry and axial approach, is typically Roman. It is an octastyle temple (having an eight-columned portico) and is almost square. It is set against a 47-m (155-ft)-long rear wall and dominates the colonnaded precinct in front, from a high podium.

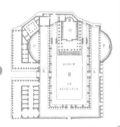

Use of marble, Temple of Concord, Rome (dedicated AD 10)
Until the quarries at Luna were opened in 20 BC, marble remained an expensive building material. Under Augustus, Luna marble was used extensively and its whiteness was exploited, in contrast to imported coloured marble. The Temple of Concord used opulent marbles throughout.

Forum of Augustus, Rome
Augustus extended the forum at right angles to his predecessor Julius Caesar's additions. Like Caesar's forum, the temple is set at the end of a colonnaded courtyard with semi-circular courtyards on a cross-axis. Rather than exploit the asymmetrical site as a Greek architect might have done, the architect chose to disguise it with an axial plan.

Temple of Castor and Pollux, Rome (dedicated AD 6)
Under Augustus the use of the orders was gradually standardised – in particular, the Corinthian order. The Corinthian capital of the Temple of Castor and Pollux became the standard form with its richly moulded architrave and deeply projecting modillion cornice.

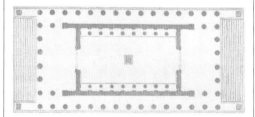

Plan, Temple of Castor and Pollux
The Temple of Castor and Pollux, like many Augustan temples, was built on the site of an older temple, and this may explain its unusual plan. It was peripteral and octastyle, with a double podium. The podium rose sheer from the ground of the forum and was often used by orators.

Detail of architrave, Temple of Castor and Pollux
Greek craftsmen's skills were needed to work with the marble that is such a feature of Augustan architecture. Their mark has been left in the opulent and crisp classical detail of many temples. This architrave may have been carved by Greek craftsmen.

Maison Carrée, Nîmes, France (AD 1–10)
The long walls of the Maison Carrée support the structure. The columns along the walls are mere shadows of the trabeated Greek system: where once they would have supported the roof, they now assume a subordinate, pureley decorative role.

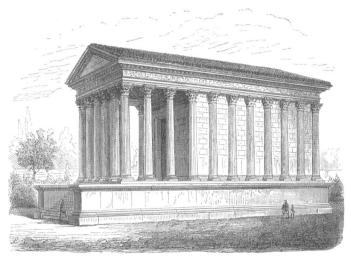

Stairs, Maison Carrée
The steps of temples form a way of controlling an axial approach. At the Maison Carrée, low retaining walls on either side do not allow any other approach, and also provide another surface for sculptural decoration. The altar, or *ara,* was often placed outside the temple at the top or bottom of the stairs.

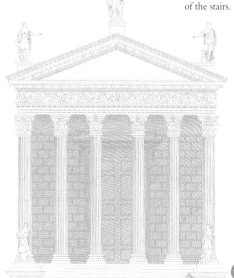

Ancient Rome

The Flavians

The Emperor Vespasian (ruled AD 69–79) founded the only imperial dynasty, the Flavians. Like their predecessors, they rejected the architectural austerity of the republican and Augustan eras. Their legacy is one of extravagance that could only have been produced in an age of peace and plenty. Domestic and palatial architecture produced experimental new room and vault shapes, although it was in the bath complexes that most Romans would have seen this revolution. Mastery of concrete and vaulting allowed for ever greater spans without the need for support, such as the octagonal toplit room in Nero's Domus Aurea. In AD 64 fire destroyed much of the city, and Nero passed legislation regarding its rebuilding; he forbade the use of wood and recommended cement floors and ceilings, with arcading on lower levels.

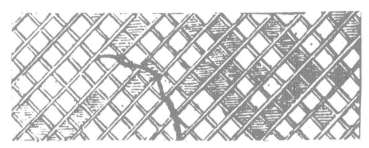

Opus reticulatum

Many concrete buildings from this period were encased in pyramid-shaped tufa laid on the diagonal. At the building stage a casement of *opus reticulatum* would be erected, into which the cement was poured. Once this had set, the *opus reticulatum* served no structural purpose, but instead acted as a smooth surface upon which to lay marble or stucco.

The Tuscan order

The origins of the Tuscan order lie with the Etruscans and are found on their tombs. Although the Romans perceived it as specifically Italianate, the Tuscan order found on Roman monuments is in fact closer to the Greek Doric order than to any Etruscan example. Unlike the Doric order, the Tuscan order has a plain frieze and no mutules in the cornice. Overall, it has a wider intercolumniation and was perceived to be cruder than the other orders.

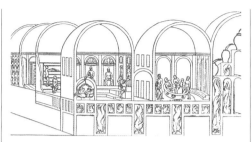

Composite order, Arch of Titus

The Romans invented the Composite order by uniting the Corinthian order with the Ionic capital, possibly as early as Augustus's reign. This example on the Arch of Titus is one of the earliest-known examples on a public building. The order was frequently used and is particularly associated with Rome.

Orchestra

The purpose of the semi-circular flat area of Roman theatres, the orchestra, had changed from its Greek circular prototype. Rather than acting as a stage, it was often used for seating for the most privileged members of society.

Hypocaustum

The Romans developed underfloor heating, whereby heat from a central furnace was conducted under the floor and through flues in the walls. This is most typically found in bath complexes, of which few survive from this period. It is known that the Palace of Domitian had this heating system, known as a *hypocaustum*.

Arch of Titus, Rome (after AD 81)

This was completed in the reign of Domitian. The single arch is surrounded by attached columns, topped with an attic storey with a dedication to the Emperor Titus commemorating the conquest of Jerusalem. It is surmounted by a *quadriga,* or four-horsed chariot sculpture.

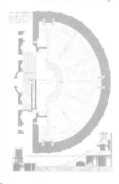

Scaena frons

The enclosing back wall, or *scaena frons,* of Roman theatres is one of their most distinctive features. It would be decorated with statuary and niches. Behind was the *scaenae* or stage building, and in front the *proscaenium* or stage itself.

Emperor Domitian's Palace (inaugurated AD 92)

The hill in Rome known as the Palatine was the site of the Emperor Domitian's palace, which was built by one of the few known Roman architects, Rabirus. The palace remained the official residence of all Roman emperors for the next three centuries. The design combined public and private rooms around garden courtyards, which were arranged symmetrically over the irregular site.

Ancient Rome

The Colosseum, Rome

The Colosseum, or Flavian Amphitheatre, was begun by Vespasian in AD 70, as a gift to the city of Rome. It was inaugurated by his son Titus in AD 80 and was finished by Domitian. It was built on the site of the artificial lake in the ornamental gardens surrounding Nero's Domus Aurea. The clay subsoil formed an ideal base for the immense weight of the building. The nearby *colossus*, a vast statue of Nero, may be the origin of the amphitheatre's name. In contrast to Nero's selfish extravagance, Vespasian shrewdly donated the amphitheatre to the Romans for watching gladiatorial shows, and in so doing created the first permanent amphitheatre in the city. It is essentially conservative in plan and decoration, but its sheer scale, at 188 x 156 m (616 x 512 ft), and the logistics of building on such a scale, make it unique.

Materials

The materials were deliberately chosen to deal with the weight and scale of the design. The foundations are made of concrete, the radial walls of tufa rising to brick-faced concrete at the top, and the exterior is of travertine.

▷ Arcuated sub-structure

To carry the seating, an arcuated sub-structure was used, rising through three storeys. Radiating staircases (*vomitoria*) took people to their seats, each wedge of which was known as a *cuneus*. The outer ring of corridors, apart from facilitating the movement of the crowds, worked to buttress the outward thrust of the building.

△ Velarium

Holes remain on the attic storey, which held brackets that supported an awning called a *velarium*. This stretched across all or part of the amphitheatre to protect spectators from the sun. It was held up by a system of pulleys, which were attached to the ground outside the amphitheatre.

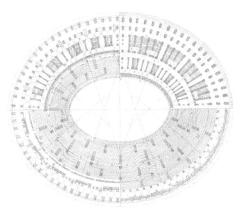

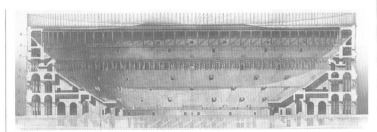

Plan

The essential challenge of the design was how to facilitate the flow of a maximum of 50,000 (possibly unruly) spectators. The Colosseum comprises an ellipse plan, with eighty radiating walls and seventy-six numbered entrances. There were four porticoes for entrance to the imperial box.

Seating

There was marble seating on the first three storeys for the wealthy, rising to wooden seating at the top for the poorer members of society, to minimise the thrust where there was only the attic wall to contain it. Below the floor of the Colosseum was a series of corridors and service passages where the animals, participants and scenery were housed prior to entering the stadium.

Exterior decoration

The combination of arches and superimposed orders on the exterior was inspired by the Theatre of Marcellus. The attic storey has windows in alternate bays to allow light into the top section of seating. Between the windows were bronze shields.

Hierarchy of orders

The three-quarter columns on the exterior rise through the Tuscan, Ionic and Corinthian orders, with a Corinthian pilaster on the attic storey. It was this 'hierarchy' that so influenced Renaissance architects.

Later history

By the 6th century AD gladiatorial combats no longer took place in the arena. During the medieval period the Colosseum was fortified and converted into a castle. Subsequently its fine travertine marble was quarried and used in a number of other buildings in Rome. In the 18th century the Colosseum was dedicated to the Passion of Jesus and was sanctified by the blood of the martyrs who had died there in the pre-Christian era.

Ancient Rome

Trajan

The Spanish soldier Trajan became emperor in AD 98. He is known as one of the great builder emperors, but sadly few of his works survive, the Markets of Trajan being the major exception. These brick and concrete streets of shops rose up the Quirinal Hill above the Forum of Trajan. He built a bath complex on Nero's Domus Aurea, which largely followed the plan of Titus's baths, further developing the subsidiary rooms. He also developed the port of Portus and the wharves at Rome. But it was the Forum Romanum for which he reserved his most extensive projects. In general his buildings were conservative; one could even describe the Forum as retrogressive in decoration, as it imitates the Forum of Augustus.

Libraries, Rome
On either side of Trajan's Column and opposite the Temple of Trajan stood two libraries: one Greek, one Latin. Inside, recesses with cupboards enclosed the scrolls. The choice of brick-faced concrete may have been made to minimise the risk of fire.

Statue, Trajan's Column
The podium of Trajan's Column contains a tomb chamber where the emperor was buried. The gilded bronze statue of Trajan on the top was reached by an interior spiral stair. The statue was later replaced with one of St Peter.

Trajan's Column, Rome (C. AD 112)
Standing 47 m (155 ft) high, this monumental Luna-marble column was built to commemorate Trajan's victories during the Dacian Wars. Other earlier columns exist, but the originality of this example lies in the sculptural frieze that extends from the podium right up to the capital in one long spiral.

Trajan's Arch, Benevento (C. AD 115)
Trajan's Arch at Benevento in central Italy follows the model of the Arch of Titus in Rome. It is a single arch with an applied Composite order and an attic storey above. Its chief characteristic is the multitude of surface sculpture that covers it.

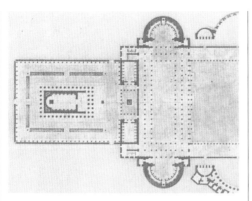

Forum of Trajan, Rome (*c.* AD 100–12)

This final extension to the Forum Romanum was
the grandest addition of all. In detail and decoration it
follows the Forum of Augustus, but in plan it breaks with
tradition. Where one would normally expect a temple
to dominate the forum, here it is the Basilica Ulpia
positioned axially across its full width.

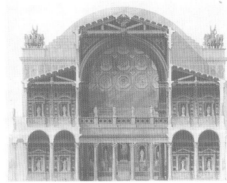

Basilica Ulpia, Rome (*c.* AD 100–12)

This was the monumental side-view that visitors to
the forum would have seen. The small windows that
are situated in the clerestory level allowed light to enter
the body of the building.

**Cross-section,
Basilica Ulpia**

The central nave was
entirely surrounded by a
double colonnade through
which could be seen an apse
at either end. Above the
colonnade were probably
galleries. Even in antiquity
the Basilica was famous for
its scale and beauty and it
may have served as a
model for the first
Christian churches.

Trajan's Temple, Rome

Following Trajan's death, his successor Hadrian
commissioned a temple to the deified emperor
and his wife, which completed the forum
complex at its westerly end.

Sculptural decoration, Trajan's Temple

This sculptural detail is taken from the Temple
of Trajan and is illustrative of the extremely
fine sculptural reliefs that are found on many
of the monuments built at this time.

Ancient Rome

Hadrian

Hadrian's reign from AD 117 to 138 witnessed the culmination of a number of architectural trends in late-imperial Rome, notably the complete mastery of the architecture of concrete and brick, as seen at his villa at Tivoli. There the interplay of curves and countercurves in such spaces as his island retreat, the Teatro Marittimo, is almost baroque in its plasticity and sense of movement. And in the pavilions of the Piazza D'Oro are seen the first expression of these complex interiors on the exterior of the building. Hadrian's deep admiration for Greece is notable in much of the architecture associated with him. Such was his nostalgia for the glory of Greece that he lived in Athens and commissioned a number of buildings there. Not only was he a notable patron, but he designed the Temple of Venus and Rome, among other buildings.

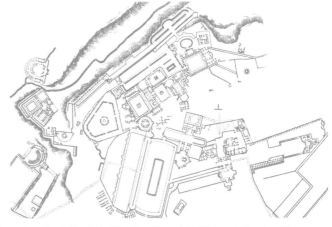

A country retreat: Hadrian's Villa, Tivoli (c. AD 118–34)
The name 'Hadrian's Villa' is misleading for what is effectively a palace. Set in the countryside near Tivoli, it comprises an interconnected series of buildings and spaces where the defining architectural characteristic is the use of the curve and countercurve, easily achieved with concrete and brick as building materials. Throughout the complex there is a delightful mixture of water and sculpture, all set against a backdrop of verdant countryside.

Temple of Venus and Rome, Rome (consecrated AD 135)
This double peripteral temple consists of two enormous decastyle temples sited back-to-back and built of a blue-veined marble from Proconnesus, by workmen from Asia Minor.

Façade, Temple of Venus and Rome
The design is known to be by Hadrian himself. We are told that the architect Apollodorus dared to criticise it (possibly for its ungainly size), for which he lost his life. Sited on a low plinth, like a Greek temple, it has a continuous colonnade around it, including twenty columns on each of the long sides.

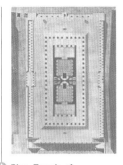

**Plan, Temple of
Venus and Rome**
Along the longer sides of
the Temple of Venus and
Rome ran colonnades. The
short sides were open.

The so-called Temple of
Diana at Nîmes in France
was built entirely of ashlar
(square-hewn) masonry. In
order to carry the weight
of the barrel vault, it has
ribs that carry the thrust
downwards and out on
to the outer walls
of side-passageways.

Lozenge coffering, Temple of Venus and Rome
The Temple of Venus and Rome was rebuilt by
Maxentius following a fire in AD 283, which
burned the roof and *cella* of Hadrian's original
temple. The surviving lozenge-shaped coffering
of the apses of the temples was highly
influential on later
generations.

**Pons Aelius, Rome
(AD 134)**
Hadrian commissioned a
bridge consisting of seven
arches to link the Campus
Martius area of Rome to
his mausoleum.

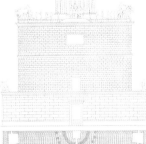

**Hadrian's mausoleum,
Rome (completed AD 140)**
Hadrian's mausoleum
closely follows the model
of Augustus's mausoleum,
which was by then full.
The most significant
difference is its square
podium base and the more
lavish use of statuary and
gilded fittings.

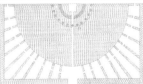

Ancient Rome

The Pantheon, Rome

The Pantheon was built between
c. AD 118 and 128 by Hadrian on the
site of an older temple constructed by
the consul Marcus Agrippa. Ostensibly
it was a temple dedicated to all of the
gods, but Hadrian's motive for building
it and the curious inclusion of an
inscription from Agrippa's temple on
the portico remain an enigma. It is one
of the great surviving buildings of
antiquity, in part due to its very
completeness – thanks to its
preservation and conversion by Pope
Boniface into a church in AD 609.
However, its survival alone does not
explain the powerful influence it has
exerted throughout architectural
history. This lies both in its technically
innovative design
and in its vast
scale and awe-
inspiring interior.

Interior

Inside, there are only two
rather than three layers
before the springing arch
of the dome, which is
surmounted by an opening
to the sky known as an
oculus. This is the only
source of light in
the building.

Exterior

The temple consists of a
drum divided into three
layers surmounted by a
shallow dome, attached to
a portico of eight columns
in width by three in depth.
Originally, the exterior
was probably covered with
stucco, but is now brick-
faced concrete.

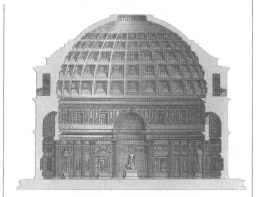

Roman decoration

The Pantheon reflects a
new and distinctly Roman
emphasis on interior space
and decoration. This
was brought about by
the liberation of design
through the use of
decorated concrete,
allowing for a far greater
variety in plan and scale
of building types.

Scale and proportion

The dome of the Pantheon was not surpassed in size until
the Renaissance. Its width of 43 m (141 ft) is equal to its
height from the *oculus* to the floor – in effect it is a sphere
that has been flattened in its lower half to create a cylinder.

Plan

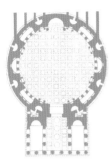

The arrangement of a conventional temple façade with a circular *cella* is uncomfortable. Originally the Pantheon was set in a colonnaded precinct, where the disjunction of the two parts of the building would have been disguised behind a wall of columns.

Coloured marble interior

The walls are lavishly decorated with coloured marbles, reflecting a growing taste for expensive marbles from the empire, in contrast to fresco or mosaic decoration. The classical decoration shown here is structurally irrelevant.

Structure

The core of the building is made of concrete. The aggregate of the concrete varies, from heavy basalt in the foundations through to tufa in the middle of the building, rising to the lightest pumice in the dome. Throughout the structure – both visibly and invisibly – there are voids to lighten the load of the walls and of the dome.

Coffering

The dome consists of five layers, each of twenty-eight coffers. These reduce in scale as they approach the *oculus,* giving the illusion of greater height and lightening the load of the dome.

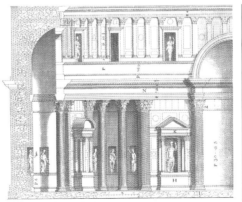

Exedra

Opposite the door and on the only axis in the building is an apse. To either side are *exedrae,* or recesses, which are alternately square and semi-circular. These voids are screened by columns.

Ancient Rome

The Severan Age in Rome

The Severan emperors came to power in AD 193 following a period of civil war. The waning importance of the city of Rome in contrast to the rest of the empire seemed only to inspire them to build ever grander projects. Their major contribution to architecture in Rome were the vast bath complexes, or *thermae*. The essential design roots of late-imperial baths actually lie in the baths of Titus and Trajan of the 1st century AD. The basic symmetry and room sequences were already in place. What was new was the scale upon which the Severans built: the Baths of Caracalla were built on 20 ha (50 acres) and could be used by 1,600 bathers at any one time. The use of concrete domes and vaulting allowed these vast spaces to be spanned without internal support.

The Arch of Septimus Severus (AD 203)
This triumphal arch in the Forum Romanum is fairly conventional in design. Its setting on a series of steps emphasises its ceremonial function. However, the use of detached columns surrounding the triple openings is a new departure in triumphal arch design.

Coffering, Arch of Septimus Severus
The Arch of Septimus Severus has a high level of sculptural decoration. Each barrel vault over the archways is elaborately coffered with flowers surrounded by acanthus leaves and the egg-and-dart motif.

Septizodium (AD 203)
The purpose of the Septizodium tantalised later generations, until it was destroyed in 1588. It consisted of three tiers of free-standing columns arranged hierarchically. It is now thought to have acted merely as a screen to the palatial buildings on the Palatine Hill. This engraving is a later exercise in how it might have looked.

Baths of Diocletian (AD 298–305)

The Baths of Caracalla (AD 216) were the first to enclose a large area of gardens around the central bath complex. Here, at the Baths of Diocletian (AD 298–305), secondary structures such as libraries, theatres and lecture halls are evenly distributed around the perimeter. The baths themselves look out on to the landscaped gardens.

Bath decoration

Late-imperial baths are the embodiment of concrete architecture, with their domed and arched spaces of varied size and shape. The interiors of baths were lavishly decorated with marble, mosaic and fresco and would have dazzled the visitor with their interplay of light and space.

Baths of Caracalla (dedicated AD 216)

The late-imperial bath complexes are notable for their symmetry. The Baths of Caracalla (AD 216) are planned along two axes, one with the swimming pool and baths, and the other with the exercise yards and service rooms duplicated on either side. The concrete and brick building materials allowed for flexible room shapes, such as the circular *caldarium*. This room projects from the central block to catch the afternoon sun.

Corinthian order

The Corinthian order was the most widely used order in Roman architecture. It differed from the Greek Corinthian in its more ornate entablature and capital, but more particularly in the introduction of modillions – horizontal consoles that supported a deeper cornice. Sometimes coffering was introduced between these to create a greater impression from the ground.

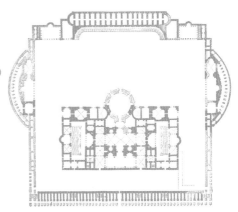

Ancient Rome

The Severan Empire

While Rome was in decline, it was in the broader Severan Empire (AD 193–305) that new building types and styles developed. The Romans exported their architecture to the empire's provinces, but their subjects modified it, depending on local building practices and resources. Beyond Rome, cement was rarely used and this limited what was feasible. The dome of the mausoleum of Diocletian at Split (in present-day Croatia), for instance, is made entirely of brick in a complex fan shape, restricting the overall dimensions. In the provinces, cut stone continued to be used long after its discontinuation in Rome, although the provincials also acquired a taste for foreign marbles. A new freedom in the use of classical orders emerged, in particular manipulation of the entablature to create novel forms.

Interior decoration, Temple of Bacchus
The Temple of Bacchus's interior is one of the richest to survive. Every part of its limestone walls is embellished with classical ornament. It is divided by a giant order rising the full height of the building. Between the columns, the wall is sub-divided into two rows of niches: one pedimented, and the other round.

Temple of Vesta, Baalbek (3rd century AD)
The striking Temple of Vesta has a round *cella* enclosed by a masonry dome. It may have been the need to buttress this that led the designer to surround it with five-sided Corinthian columns with curved architraves, which create a baroque interplay of curve and countercurve.

Niches, sanctuary of Baalbek
Around the courtyard of the Baalbek sanctuary are alternate rectangular and semi-circular *exedrae* (niches). Every part of the wall surface is decorated with pilasters and entablature or with two tiers of niches.

Temple of Bacchus, Baalbek (2nd century AD)
The elevation of the temple, situated close to the sanctuary at Baalbek (in present-day Lebanon), is typically Roman, with a deep porch and large *cella* on a high podium. But its exceptional height is more Hellenic. It is one of the best-preserved temples in the world.

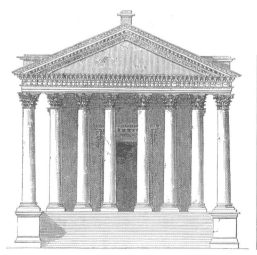

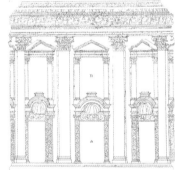

Corbelled columns, Diocletian's Palace, Split (c. AD 300–6)
Above the entrance to Diocletian's Palace are probably
the earliest examples in the West of columns supported by
corbels. Earlier examples can, however, be found in Syria.

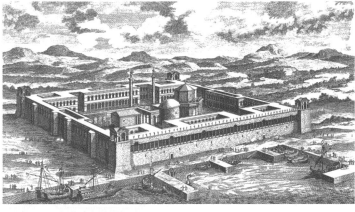

Fortress architecture, Diocletian's Palace
The influence of military architecture on Diocletian's Palace is clear
from its enormously thick walls and square lookout towers on each
corner, from which the complex could be guarded.

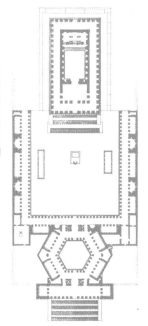

**Plan, sanctuary
of Baalbek**
Built over several
centuries on the site
of an earlier temple,
the sanctuary at
Baalbek centres on
the Temple of Jupiter,
set in a rectangular
courtyard entered
through a hexagonal
forecourt. Nearby
stands the Temple
of Bacchus.

Room plan, Diocletian's Palace
The plan of Diocletian's Palace resembles a
Roman *castrum,* or fortified town. The complex
is intersected by two colonnaded streets. The two
quarters nearest to the sea housed the emperor's
mausoleum, temple and living quarters, while the
other two probably housed the guards.

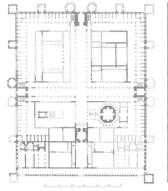

Springing arches, Diocletian's Palace
In the entrance courtyard
to Diocletian's Palace there
is a colonnaded arcade,
where arches spring from
Corinthian capitals. In the
same courtyard is visible
the bending of the
cornice that recurs
on the sea façade, which
became known as a
Diocletian window.

Ancient Rome

The Late Empire

The Emperor Constantine made two significant changes during his reign, which were to have a lasting effect on the architecture of Rome. In AD 313 he recognised the legitimacy of Christianity and became a Christian himself, and in AD 330 he made Constantinople his capital. With the Empire under increasing threat from northern tribes and a politically unstable Rome, older materials were reused and the practice of certain skills, such as stone carving, became less sophisticated. But much building occurred, including construction of the Aurelian walls around Rome. The Emperor Maxentius even built himself a new villa and race track near the Via Appia. The late Empire (AD 306–*c.* 340) was a point of transition between the imperial and the Byzantine world, as buildings such as the Temple of Minerva Medica, with its dome, drum and projecting apses, show.

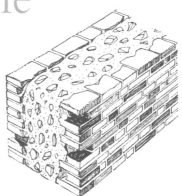

Side-bays, Basilica of Maxentius
The three side-bays on either side of the nave served a structural purpose. They acted to buttress the thrust of the immense concrete vault, and looked forward to Byzantine and medieval architecture.

Cross-vaulting, Basilica of Maxentius
The cross-vaulting here is 35 m (115 ft) high and 25 m (82 ft) wide. To shorten the span the architect used immense Proconnesian marble columns attached to the piers from which the arches spring.

Opus testaceum
Although it had been used since the time of Augustus, *opus testaceum* or brick-faced concrete had become the predominant building material in the late empire – so much so that, apart from in triumphal arches, stone was hardly used at all.

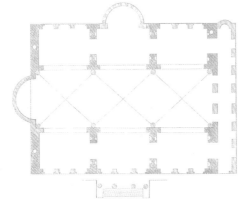

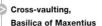

Basilica of Maxentius, Rome (AD 307–12)
The Basilica of Maxentius was in fact finished by Constantine, who changed the axis of the building, adding a new entrance and apse on the longer sides. Its design is derived from the *frigidarium* of imperial baths.

Relief sculpture, Rome (c. AD 312–15)

The relief sculpture on the Arch of Constantine is a mix of old and new taken from monuments of the 1st and 2nd centuries AD. The contemporary sculpture is often crude in comparison to earlier work. This may have been due to a loss of skills, as stone was now less commonly used.

Campo dei Vaccino, Rome

Following Constantine's move of the capital to Constantinople in AD 330, Rome was left to fall into decline. Its glorious monuments were buried beneath the soil, just sticking out for later generations to see while grazing their cows, so it became known as the *Campo dei Vaccino*, or 'Field of Cows'.

Constantinian mausoleum (c. AD 350)

The emperor built a mausoleum in Rome to his daughter Costanza. The dome sits on a drum pierced by windows, supported by double columns and surrounded by an ambulatory.

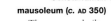

Arch of Constantine: the last triumphal arch

This arch was built to commemorate the emperor's victory over his rival Maxentius at the Milvian Bridge in AD 312. It was the last triumphal arch to be built in Rome, but also the largest. It takes its form from that of Septimus Severus, but articulates the tripartite division more clearly in the attic storey.

Porta Nigra, Trier (early 4th century AD)

The Porta Nigra at Trier in Germany was built as an imposing entrance to the city. Despite its traditional arch and applied order decoration, there is a play on light and shade, and void and mass, that heralds a new age.

Early Christian and Byzantine *c. 313–1453*

The Basilica

In 313 Christianity was officially recognised when Constantine I, Emperor of Rome, issued the Edict of Milan. By 326 it had become the official religion of the Roman Empire. With its new capital based in Byzantium – renamed Constantinople (now Istanbul) – the empire stretched from Milan and Cologne in the west, to Syria in the east, and south to Greece and Egypt. Requiring a new architecture, the emerging religion adopted one of the most characteristic Roman typologies: the basilica – a rectangular assembly hall that could serve as anything from market hall to law court. As an official public architecture with no pagan associations, this was suitably grand to be adapted for Christian use. Throughout the empire, basilicas exhibited great variety, according to local traditions.

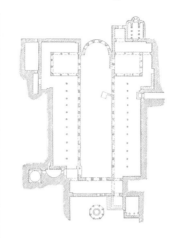

Transept, St Demetrius, Thessalonika (late 5th century)
In some church basilicas, lateral extensions were added between the apse and nave to form a Latin-cross plan. The transept at St Demetrius in Thessalonika is divided into nave and aisles, like the main body of the church – a cross-transept.

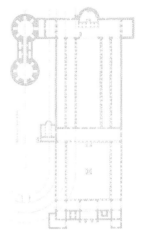

Plan, St Peter's, Rome (319–22)
St Peter's, built by Constantine, had an uninterrupted 'continuous transept', which housed the relics of the apostle. The church was unusual in being occidented (with its apse at the west end), not oriented. At the opposite end a *narthex*, or anteroom, ran across the nave and aisles, leading on to an atrium.

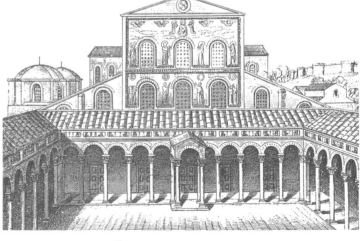

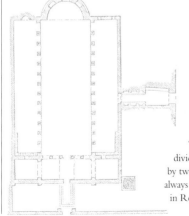

Basilica plan
The basilica was a rectangular hall, its interior divided longitudinally into a central nave, flanked by two or four aisles. At one end of the hall, almost always the east, was a projecting hemispherical apse: in Roman basilicas this housed a tribunal, whereas in Christian churches it held the sanctuary.

Atrium and façade, St Peter's, Rome
The atrium was a forecourt situated in front of the *narthex*, surrounded by colonnaded porticoes. It provided a withdrawing space for catechumens (non-baptised believers), who could participate in the first part of the church service, but not in the Mass of the Faithful.

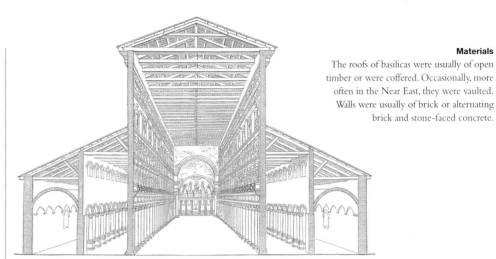

Materials

The roofs of basilicas were usually of open timber or were coffered. Occasionally, more often in the Near East, they were vaulted. Walls were usually of brick or alternating brick and stone-faced concrete.

Exteriors

As the façade of St Peter's *(below left)* shows, the exteriors of Early Christian basilicas were extremely plain. This was equally true in the Near East, where ashlar (cut stone) was the primary building material. This 5th-century church at Turmanin was typical of Syria, having a colonnaded entrance porch or *propylaeum* flanked by two towers.

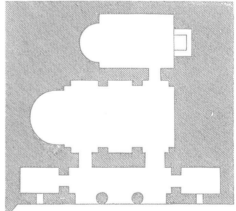

Later basilicas

The basilica form proved to be amazingly durable and flexible for church architecture, and it continued to be used throughout the Early Christian and Byzantine era, for example, in cave-churches in Turkey (this example is from Cappadocia), where simple, aisleless basilicas were carved out of rock.

Early Christian and Byzantine

Early Christian Interiors

In contrast to their plain exteriors, the interiors of Early Christian churches (3rd–5th centuries) were splendid, fusing colour, light and precious materials. Every surface was covered with rich decoration: on the walls were marble revetments and frescoes and mosaics, both decorative and figural; the columns and piers of the arcades were also marble, finished with gilded capitals; roofs (open timber or coffered) were gilded; floors were often covered with marble mosaics; ornate carvings in geometric and foliate patterns also appeared on architraves, entablatures and screens; altars were in gold and silver, encrusted with jewels; and in the apse the half-dome was covered with a vast fresco or mosaic, often of Christ and the prophets. Particularly in the Western Empire, capitals, columns and entablatures were often spoils from Roman buildings.

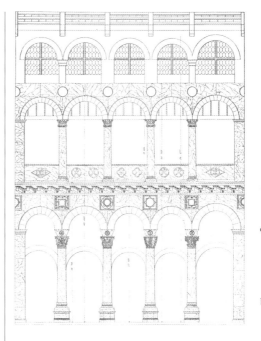

Capital and dosseret
Constructed from spoils, the nave at St Demetrius, Thessalonika, features a variety of capitals. This double-zone *protomai* capital comprises acanthus leaves surmounted by half-figures of eagles. Above, a dosseret or impost block forms the transition from the circular capital to the square arcade base.

Clerestory
The roofs of the aisles were lower than that of the nave, allowing windows in the upper nave walls – the clerestory – to light the interior from high above.

Gallery
The aisles were sometimes surmounted by a second storey, or gallery (often designated for women, thus taking the name *gynaecea*). If no such galleries existed, men and women would sit on opposite sides of the nave.

Arcade
The nave and aisles were divided by rows of columns or piers, surmounted either by arches to form an arcade, or by an entablature – carved horizontal bands of masonry.

Apse
At the end of the arcade, the apse, usually domed and articulated with a triumphal arch, housed the sanctuary and *synthronon* – concentric seating for the clergy. Within or before the apse, the shrine or high altar of the church was sheltered by an elaborate canopy – the *baldacchino* or *ciborium*.

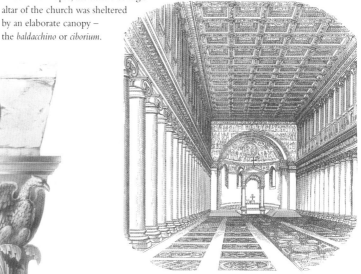

Near Eastern interior

In contrast to interiors in western and central regions, those in the Near East tended to be austere, with heavy, squat arcades of low, widely spaced piers.

Window

The windows of Early Christian basilicas added to their mystique, providing an ethereal, opaque light, either through stone plaques perforated with decorative holes, or through coloured glass (mica) or alabaster. At night, the marble and glass, silver and gold that filled the church would glint in the flickering light of candles.

Liturgical furniture

The sanctuary was sometimes raised on a platform, or *bema*, reserved for the clergy. This was often separated from the nave by a low parapet or high screen – an iconostasis. From here the clergy could proceed along a raised pathway, or *solea*, projecting into the nave, to the pulpit, or *ambo*.

Ambo

The *ambo* was a raised platform from which the Epistle and the Gospel were read. Usually made of stone, it was – like all other liturgical furniture – richly decorated with ornamental panels.

Opus sectile

The walls and floors of many churches featured an ornate surface decoration of *opus sectile* – marble stones cut to form geometric patterns. Other floor coverings included flagstones and marble pavements.

Early Christian and Byzantine

Centralised Plans

Early Christian architecture also drew on Roman buildings with centralised plans, based on a circle, cross or polygon. This form was most prominent in Roman architecture in the building of mausolea, and this tradition strongly influenced Early Christian funerary architecture, particularly monumental tombs built as memorials to the dead. Shrine sites, initially commemorated within congregational churches, as at St Peter's in Rome, gradually became independent, with their own free-standing martyria, usually centrally planned. In turn, centralised plans were gradually absorbed into church architecture, and palatine chapels in particular began to take on circular, octagonal and quatrefoil forms.

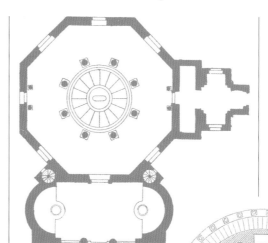

Lateran Baptistery, Rome (c. 315)
The Early Christian era saw the emergence of separate buildings for baptism, often featuring the centralised plans of public baths initially adapted for the purpose. These buildings were often octagonal, eight symbolising regeneration, because the world started on the eighth day after the Creation.

Mausoleum
Early Christian tombs followed directly from the tradition of Roman mausolea, which were also centrally planned. They differed from their Roman models, however, in typically being built near a cemetery basilica. Most had a central area delineated by columns, with a surrounding ambulatory.

Cross-section, S. Costanza, Rome (c. 350)
S. Costanza, built for Constantine's daughter Costanza, comprises a circular domed area supported on an arcade of twelve pairs of columns, forming a sort of *baldacchino*, surrounded by a barrel-vaulted ambulatory. The central area, lit by clerestory windows, is surmounted by a dome beneath a timber roof.

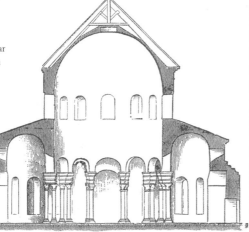

Interior, S. Costanza
The interiors of mausolea were lavishly decorated, as at S. Costanza. Here, mosaic decoration covers the walls in a scheme that starts with geometric patterns, then moves on to vines and putti; it culminates over the sarcophagus opposite the entrance with the golden dome of Heaven, with Old Testament scenes on the dome.

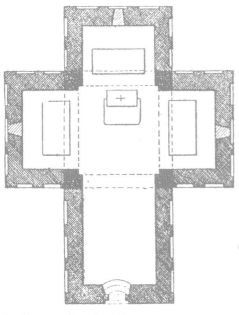

Cruciform plan, Mausoleum of Galla Placidia, Ravenna (c. 425)
The cruciform plan was a popular form for martyria *(see above right)* and mausolea. The mausoleum of Galla Placidia is an early example, one arm being slightly elongated to form a Latin cross.

Martyrium, Qal'at Si'man, Syria (480–90)
Structures created for the veneration of martyrs and holy sites were also centrally planned. At Qal'at Si'man a huge cross martyrium commemorates the pillar on which St Simeon Stylites spent the end of his life. Around this, four basilicas form the arms of a cross. This huge complex was designed to accommodate large numbers of pilgrims.

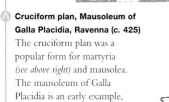

Interior, Mausoleum of Galla Placidia
Within the mausoleum, the cross arms are barrel-vaulted, while the square tower conceals a dome over the centre bay.

Tetraconch, S. Lorenzo, Milan (c. 378)
The tetraconch, or quatrefoil (four-lobed pattern), was also commonly used for martyria. S. Lorenzo is, however, a palace chapel. It is a double-shell design, its domed centre forming an inner core, with *exedrae* (large niches) that penetrate an outer ambulatory and gallery.

153

Early Christian and Byzantine

Ravenna

In 395 the Roman Empire was again divided. While in the East the emerging Byzantine Empire flourished, the West was subject to constant invasion. As a result Ravenna, on Italy's east coast, assumed increasing importance. In 402 the Western capital was moved there from Milan, and at the end of the 5th century the Ostrogoth king, Theodoric (495-526), set up court in Ravenna, keeping close ties with Constantinople. When Italy was reconquered by Justinian in the 6th century, Ravenna became the see of the Byzantine viceroys. Politically and geographically, therefore, it bridged East and West and the many buildings initiated by its rulers show the influence of the nascent Byzantine style.

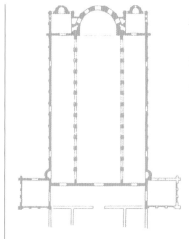

S. Apollinare in Classe (532–49)
Although it is apparently a simple, single-aisled basilica, S. Apollinare in Classe incorporates a number of Eastern elements: the *narthex*, with its two low towers projecting sideways; an apse that is polygonal rather than hemispherical on the exterior; and the projecting side-chambers beside the apse, with their curved absidioles (subsidiary apses).

S. Apollinare Nuovo (c. 490)
The basilica of S. Apollinare Nuovo is most notable for its mosaics, which broke with Western tradition by showing not biblical scenes but processions of figures advancing along the nave: on the north wall, twenty-two female saints and, on the south, twenty-six male martyrs.

Mosaic
Mosaics were formed from small cubes of stone or glass – tesserae. Clear glass was often backed with gold leaf to create a rich, shimmering effect. Increasingly, mosaics were used to cover every surface, replacing mouldings and cornices and flowing uninterrupted over walls, arches and domes. This mosaic shows the Emperor Justinian.

Interior, S. Apollinare in Classe

The interior of S. Apollinare in Classe also shows an Eastern influence: the marble veneers and capitals – in the 'wind-blown' style – were almost certainly provided by the imperial workshops near Constantinople.

Campanile, S. Apollinare in Classe

On the exterior is one of the earliest circular *campanile*, or bell towers, its windows increasing from single to double to triple as they ascend. Rather than the high bricks traditional in Ravenna, the church was constructed from specially made long, thin bricks, typically used in Constantinople.

S. Vitale (526–47)

Comprising two concentric octagons, S. Vitale is a double-shell church. Its core is defined by eight piers with seven *exedrae* between, pushing into the surrounding ambulatory (the roofed passageway of a cloister or round the apse of a church). On the eighth side the core leads directly into a chancel and projecting apse, flanked by circular chapels.

Lacework and basketwork

Many churches from 5th- and 6th-century Ravenna feature Byzantine capitals. Naturalistic Corinthian acanthus leaves gave way to less naturalistic 'lacework' or 'basketwork', with stylised foliage and interlaced straps carved with deep undercutting. Byzantine capitals also took on new shapes, such as the near-hemispherical 'cushion' or 'basket' capital.

Dome, S. Vitale

The dome over the central octagon at S. Vitale is made not of brick or stone but of earthenware pots inserted into each other. This Western technique created a structure so light that no buttresses or arches were required to support the dome. The whole is covered by a timber roof.

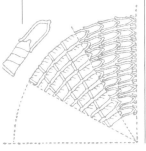

Early Christian and Byzantine

Early Byzantine Architecture

The 6th century was the high point of the Byzantine Empire. The reign of Justinian (527–62) saw a period of unprecedented expansion and prosperity. With the Western Empire under threat, Constantinople dominated as the political and cultural – if not the religious – centre.

A huge, propagandising programme of building works ushered in a period of architectural innovation, which saw the development of Early Christian forms into the Byzantine style. While the basilica remained predominant in the West, in the East there was an increasing tendency towards greater complexity and, above all, towards centralisation, with square domed bays being introduced into rectangular basilical plans. This tendency was partly linked to the Eastern liturgy, which stressed the processional entrances of the clergy during the Mass. The new centralised plans focused attention on the nave, which became a stage for the processions, while the congregation watched from the aisles, the galleries and the *narthex*.

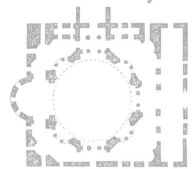

SS. Sergius and Bacchus, Constantinople (527–36)
Built by Justinian, SS. Sergius and Bacchus is similar to S. Vitale, comprising a double shell of central octagon and outer square. However, it shows greater complexity, the niches of the inner core being alternately squared and rounded and finding an echo in the niched outer wall.

Pumpkin dome, SS. Sergius and Bacchus
The dome, measuring 16 m (52 ft) in diameter, is a pumpkin dome, with sixteen sides formed of scooped segments with ridges. Rather than being hidden beneath a timber roof, it is visible externally.

Fold capital, SS. Sergius and Bacchus
On the ground floor of SS. Sergius and Bacchus the capitals are 'folded', with spiky tendrils that are deeply undercut so that they stand out in strong relief from the dark ground.

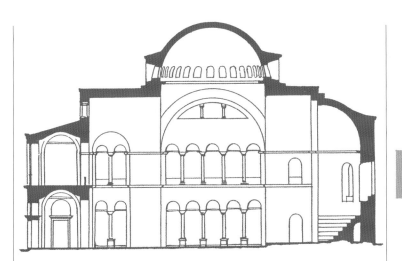

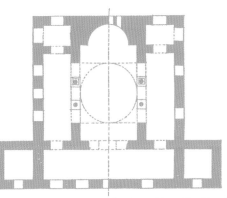

Condensed domed basilica, Qasr Ibn Wardan, Syria (564)

At Qasr Ibn Wardan, the nave around a domed centre bay is reduced to short barrel vaults, surrounded on three sides by a double storey of aisles and galleries linked with a two-tier *narthex*. This condensed domed basilica focuses all attention on the nave.

Domed basilica: St Irene, Constantinople (532)

Square domed bays were introduced into basilical plans to create domed basilicas, as at St Irene in Constantinople, built by Justinian in 532. Here, the dome rested on four arches supported by four huge piers, while the nave to east and west was barrel-vaulted and flanked by vaulted aisles and galleries.

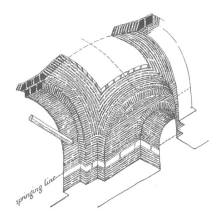

Pendentive

The introduction of the domed centralised plan was made possible by the pendentive – a curved triangle spanning between arches. Whereas the Romans were able to build domes only over circular spaces, the pendentive allowed the Byzantines to build domes over square plans. The form probably originated from Aegean and Syrian architecture.

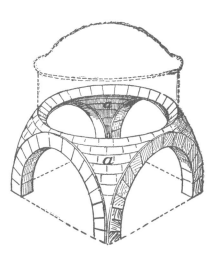

Use of bricks

Another key element in the introduction of domed spaces was the use of brick for construction, with thin bricks laid in thick beds of mortar. Where vaults in concrete and stone could span only small spaces, brick could be used to create thin, light vaults, allowing greater flexibility and larger spans, with fewer, thinner supports.

Early Christian and Byzantine

Hagia Sophia, Constantinople (532–37)

Hagia Sophia – meaning 'divine wisdom' – is considered the greatest monument of Byzantine architecture. It is, however, unique – nothing like it was ever constructed again. Built by the Emperor Justinian on the site of a ruined basilican church of the same name, its creators were not master builders, as was traditional: Anthemius of Tralles and Isidorus of Miletus were more scientists than architects, with expertise in mathematics and physics. The result was a fusion of two types – a double-shell domed church and a domed basilica – as if SS. Sergius and Bacchus had been sliced in half and intercepted by a vast domed bay. This innovative form was made possible by the use of thin brick as the primary building material, with the exception of the eight enormous piers, which were built of ashlar. The dome's collapse in 558, twenty years after completion, suggests the church's daring as a feat of engineering, pushing to their limits the technological boundaries of the time. It was reconstructed in 563.

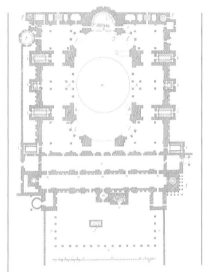

Core
The dome is supported to east and west by two semi-domes, each flanked by two *exedrae*, also with semi-domes. Finally, barrel vaults lead to an apse to the east and a *narthex* to the west. This domed core is surrounded by two storeys of aisles, *narthex* and galleries to form a roughly square plan.

Plan
Hagia Sophia retains the nave and aisles of a basilica, but its inner arcades curve at each end to form an oval. Within this space a 32.6-m (107-ft)-diameter dome rests on four arches, supported in turn by four huge piers, spanning to the outer walls and pierced to accommodate aisles and galleries.

Exterior
Rather than being concealed beneath a timber roof, the various domes and semi-domes were covered with lead. In this way they are clearly expressed on the exterior, their volumes leading the eye upwards to the apex of the central dome. Built in brick, the massive exterior is austere and undecorated.

Arcade

The arcades establish a rhythm of three, five and seven, with the nave arcade comprising five bays at ground level and seven bays in the gallery, with seven windows in the clerestory above, while in the *exedrae* or conchs at each end, three bays at ground level are surmounted by seven in the gallery.

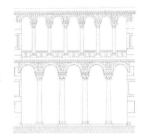

Cross-section

Within, the shell was sheathed with marble slabs in green, red, white, blue, black and yellow. Forty windows in the lower part of the dome brought shafts of light into the interior, with further windows in the semi-domes and *exedrae* and the flanks of nave and aisles.

Interior

The vast interior is a complex interplay of convex and concave volumes. The huge dome soars overhead and the arcades of the nave and *exedrae* form screens on to the surrounding aisles, so that the central core seems to expand outwards and upwards.

Mosaic

Covering the walls, domes, half-domes, vaults and soffits were mosaics in simple non-figurative patterns, including foliage and crosses. The central dome was covered in plain gold mosaic.

Cubiform capital

The capitals in the main arcade are cubiform in shape – a form produced by the interpenetration of a cube and a hemisphere. They have small Ionic angle volutes, combined with deeply undercut stylised foliage.

Early Christian and Byzantine

Post-Justinian Architecture

Early Byzantine architecture never again reached the grandeur or complexity of Hagia Sophia. After Justinian's death in 562, the empire lost much of its territory, including parts of Greece, Syria, Palestine and North Africa. During the 8th century the Franks gained increasing power in the West, forming an alliance with the Pope, who in 800 crowned the Frankish king, Charlemagne, Emperor of the West. Believing the Byzantine Empire's troubles to be the result of divine wrath at the worship of icons, Leo III instituted an iconoclastic movement in 726; figural mosaics within churches were replaced by crosses, foliage and geometric patterns. The austerity of the period was reflected in a move towards smaller, less daring churches. The key buildings of Justinian's age did, however, confirm the tendency towards centralisation, and the domed basilica and cross-domed church predominated.

St Nicholas, Myra (8th century)

Like S. Irene in Constantinople, St Nicholas at Myra is a domed basilica. The longitudinal emphasis of the Roman basilica has been even further reduced, the nave comprising only a central domed bay and deep supporting arches to east and west, with galleried aisles not only to the north and south, but also to the west.

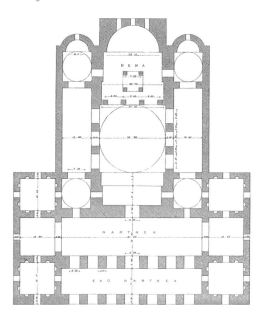

Cross-domed church, S. Sophia, Thessalonika (780s)

In the 250 years following Justinian's death the cross-domed church was highly popular. A domed centre bay was supported on four barrel-vaulted cross-arms of near equal depth. This cross-shaped core was enclosed on three sides by a galleried *narthex* and aisles to form a square outer shell.

Plan, S. Sophia

This is a typical cross-domed church, its cruciform nave being linked by arcades of alternating piers and columns to barrel-vaulted aisles, while aisles, *narthex* and galleries interlink to form a U-shaped two-storey ambulatory. The east arm of the central core forms a chancel, ending in an apse flanked by side-chambers with absidioles.

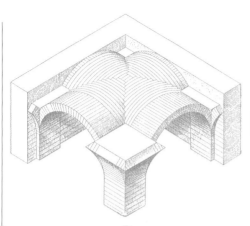

Brick and ashlar
Masonry often consisted not of pure brick but of alternating bands of brick and ashlar, arranged in courses. This technique was employed in Constantinople and the Aegean from the 5th century. Sometimes brick masonry was strengthened with single courses of ashlar.

Groin vaults, S. Sophia
At S. Sophia, Thessalonika, the west piers supporting the dome are pierced to incorporate small groin-vaulted bays. Groin vaults, also known as cross-vaults, were not a Byzantine invention; they were often used to cover square bays, the intersection of two barrel vaults forming a diagonal cross.

Triple sanctuary plan, Dere Agzi, Lycia (8th century)
As the Byzantine liturgy was finalised in the 7th and 8th centuries, church plans increasingly included side-chambers, or *pastophories*, flanking the apse. In the south room, or *diaconicon*, were kept the Gospels, and in the north room, or *prothesis*, the Eucharist was prepared, facilitating the ritual entrances of the Mass.

Post-Justinian interior
In accordance with the austerity of the times, a cross-section of S. Sophia reveals a greater simplicity and solidity of form in comparison to 6th-century churches: walls and piers are heavy; the openings of windows and arcades are small; and clearly defined spaces replace complex, interpenetrating interiors.

Post-Justinian exterior
The exterior of S. Sophia, like those of Justinian churches, is simple, with little decoration, but its proportions are more squat. Above a plain cube, a low drum pierced with windows conceals the dome. The apse, hemispherical within, is polygonal on the exterior, a feature typical of Greece.

Early Christian and Byzantine

Middle Byzantine Architecture

The period from the end of iconoclasm in 843 to the Latin occupation of Constantinople in 1204 is known as the Middle Byzantine period. The first 180 years under the Macedonian dynasty were something of a golden age: territory was recovered in Greece and Italy, new lands acquired to the east and a cultural renaissance saw the emergence of many new typologies in church architecture. Following the decline of the Macedonian dynasty after 1025, the Comnene dynasty seized power in 1057, establishing an era of stability, reflected by a process of consolidation in architecture. This period also saw the formalisation, in the Great Schism of 1054, of the division that had long been emerging between the Eastern Orthodox and Western Catholic Church. At the same time the influence of the Eastern Church expanded to Serbia, Bulgaria and Russia.

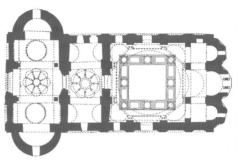

Domed octagon, Nea Moni, Chios (1042–56)
One of the new church types that became popular at this time, particularly in Greece, was the domed octagon, as at Nea Moni in Chios. This form had a square nave with no aisles. Squinches spanning the corners of the nave formed an octagon supporting a circular dome.

Squinch ▼
Squinches had been a feature of Armenian church building since the 7th century and were also widely used in Islamic architecture from the 10th century. They comprised a small arch or niche placed at the corners of a square bay to form a base for a dome.

Ambulatory church, Fetiyeh Carvii/S. Mary Pammakaristos, Constantinople (11th century)
The ambulatory church was similar to the earlier cross-domed church, but its nave was smaller, the cross-arms being reduced to wall arches. The surrounding spaces were also wider and of a uniform width, while the gallery zone was eliminated, creating a simple ambulatory around a domed core.

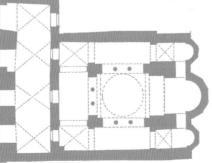

Greek-cross octagon, Church at Daphne (c. 1080)
The Greek-cross octagon was another new form, again found mainly in Greece, that used the squinch. From the centre bay of a domed octagon, four barrel-vaulted arms projected to form a cross. The whole was enclosed within a rectangle, with vaulted bays in groups around each corner.

Cross-in-square, Myrelaion Church, Constantinople (920–21)

The most popular and enduring Mid-Byzantine plan was the cross-in-square or quincunx. A domed square bay with four vaulted arms formed a Greek cross, with a domed bay at each corner. This was articulated on the exterior by the drum of the central dome and the cross-arms rising above the corner bays.

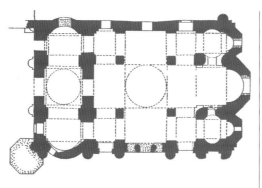

St Mark's, Venice (1063)

Despite the Great Schism, Byzantine influence remained strong in Italy, which maintained close diplomatic and trade ties with Constantinople. As at St Mark's in Venice, elements of the Orthodox Church were absorbed into the Western Church and combined with a revival of Early Christian traditions under Charlemagne in the Romanesque style.

Mid-Byzantine exterior

The Mid-Byzantine period saw greater decoration of the exteriors of churches. Bricks were arranged in patterns – herringbone, chevrons, meander, dog's-tooth – and in Greece thin bricks framed blocks of stone, in a style known as cloisonné. Blind niches, recessed arched windows, colonnettes and pilasters were also introduced.

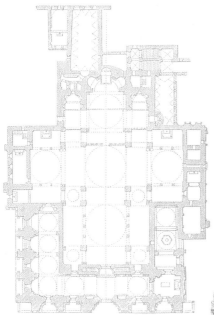

Plan, St Mark's

St Mark's was originally a basilican church, transformed by the addition of transepts to form a cruciform plan with domes over the centre bay and each arm. A U-shaped *narthex* was also extended around the west arm. Within, St Mark's is highly ornate, with marbles and mosaics covering every surface.

Early Christian and Byzantine

Late Byzantine Architecture

In 1204 Constantinople was sacked by the Franks and the empire went into decline, losing territory to surrounding tribes. Byzantine strongholds were maintained in Nicaea, Trebizond, Arta and Thessalonika, and Constantinople was recovered in 1261 by Michael VIII Paleologos, who gave the ensuing era (1261–1453) its name – the Palaiologan Period. But in 1453 Constantinople was captured by the Ottoman Turks and the empire collapsed. Byzantine culture remained strong, however. No new forms emerged, but variations of old typologies featured an even greater elaboration of exteriors and increasingly steep proportions. Most notably, the demand for separate areas for funeral monuments led to the attachment of auxiliary spaces to existing churches to create large, irregular complexes.

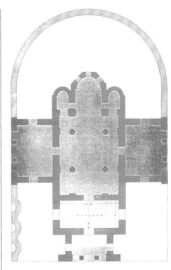

S. Sophia, Trebizond (1238–63)
This quincunx church has projecting porches to the north, south and east, a feature possibly taken from Georgian architecture. Its elongated western corner bays introduce a longitudinal emphasis that reflects a revival of Early Byzantine style at this time, which led to a fusion of central and basilican plans.

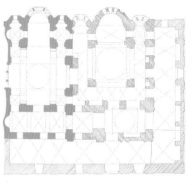

Parakklesion, St Mary Constantine Lips, Constantinople
From 1282 to 1304 a small ambulatory church dedicated to St John the Baptist was added to the south of the tiny quincunx church of St Mary Constantine Lips (907). The two were linked by an *exonarthex* extending along the west ends of both churches, joined to a funeral chapel, or *parakklesion,* to the south.

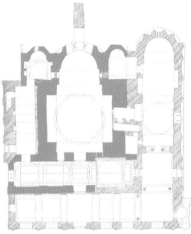

Kariye Camii/S. Saviour in the Chora, Constantinople
This church was restored from 1315 to 1320, its domed core being augmented by an annexe to the north, a domed *narthex* to the west and, across the entire west front, an *exonarthex* continuing into a *parakklesion* to the south. *Parakklesia* became increasingly complex, taking on domed, barrel-vaulted forms, as here, and even quincunx plans.

Kilise Camii/S. Theodore, Constantinople
The 11th-century quincunx church of Kilise Camii was extended *c.* 1320 by a five-bayed *exonarthex* (outer *narthex*) with three domes – a form traditional in Thessalonika. The elaborate façade of the *exonarthex* features tall niches framing triple arcades with parapets, while on the upper floor five semi-circular blind arches are disposed in a different rhythm.

Colourism, Kilise Camii
Kilise Camii shows a new emphasis on colour, as red brick alternates with white ashlar. The adoption in Constantinople of this technique from the provinces, probably Macedonia, indicates the city's weakening position. Elsewhere coloured stones were also introduced.

Holy Apostles, Thessalonika (1310–14)
This quincunx church is framed by a U-shaped *exonarthex* with a dome in each corner. Its exterior is richly decorated, its faceted apse featuring steep recessed niches and elaborate brickwork with bands of double zigzags.

Silhouette, Holy Apostles
The tall, narrow drums of the five domes of the Holy Apostles create a dramatic silhouette, the various parts of the church seeming to climb ever higher. The tiled roofs of the domes flow over the arched windows of the drums to create a rippling eaves line that was particularly popular in Greece.

Onion domes, S. Sophia, Novgorod (1052)
S. Sophia in Novgorod combines the steep proportions of Mid- to Late Byzantine architecture, with the more Eastern feature of onion domes. Long after the Byzantine Empire's decline, its culture was upheld by the Eastern Church beyond its borders in Russia and the Balkans, where its influence continued for centuries.

Islamic *AD 632–1800*

The Middle East: Early Islamic Architecture

Islam, one of the three major world religions, was founded by the Prophet Muhammad, who was born in Mecca (present-day Saudi Arabia) in *c*. AD 570 and died there in 632. Islamic architecture began in the Middle East in the 7th century. It has undergone regional stylistic developments as Islam has spread to neighbouring countries – such as Persia (modern Iran) and Egypt, westwards to North Africa and Spain, and north to Asia – while remaining identifiably Islamic. Its distinctive stylistic features can readily be seen in the principal Islamic building type: the mosque, or Muslim place of worship. This incorporates the pointed arches, domes, minarets, portals, enclosed courtyards and elaborate surface decoration that are associated with the Islamic style.

Pointed arch, Aksah Mosque
The columns of this mosque are connected by beams. All the pier arches are pointed – an early use of the pointed arch – but above is a range of openings with rounded heads.

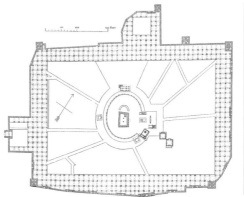

Ka'ba, Mecca
The Prophet Muhammad's own mosque was rebuilt in Mecca after his death as a tent-like pavilion with a flat roof supported by six columns. The principal Islamic shrine, the black-canopied Ka'ba, lies at the heart of the 7th-century walled sacred compound.

Aksah Mosque, Jerusalem (AD 637)
Built by Caliph Omar in 637, the Aksah Mosque was a contemporary of Jerusalem's Dome of the Rock and is one of the earliest Islamic mosques. It comprises a simple, plain-vaulted cell (*hujra*). In 691 it was extended by al-Walid, with a large, square, aisled hall containing marble and stone columns.

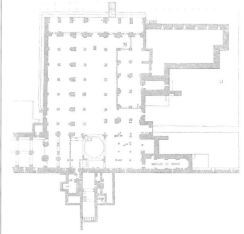

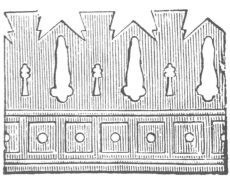

External battlement
This detail of an external battlement forms a geometric design that is more akin to a pierced solid than an assembly of separate elements.

Jali

A perforated screen known as a *jali* filled the external window and served to reduce the glare and dust. Carved marble window grilles with elaborate geometrical patterns were characteristic features of early mosques. Wooden screens or grilles, *masharabiyya*, are also common in houses in Islamic countries.

Early Islamic arch: detail of piers

Early arches curve inwards at their base (the imposts), a wholly Islamic feature. The capitals are carved and the arches are incised with stylised floral motifs. The flat surfaces of the wall are embellished with arabesques: straight or curved lines resembling organic forms.

View into courtyard, Ibn Tulun Mosque, Cairo

One of the most striking features of all Islamic buildings is their focus on the enclosed, interior space (*sahn*), rather than on exteriors and façades. It is rare that the function and inner form of an Islamic building can be readily understood from the exterior, unlike its Western counterparts.

Plan, Ibn Tulun Mosque (AD 876–79)

This early complete mosque in Cairo includes all the features that subsequent mosques were to have: a square court surrounded by arcades, with additional corridors (*ziyadas*) and a covered five-aisled prayer hall, with the sanctuary and pulpit against the external wall. A domed ablution fountain occupied the centre of the court.

Arcades

This cross-section of arcades has the prayer hall on the left. The arcades, with pointed arches, are based on massive piers with engaged columns. These arches are among the earliest pointed arches in the history of architecture and represent a progression from primitive trabeation (post and beam).

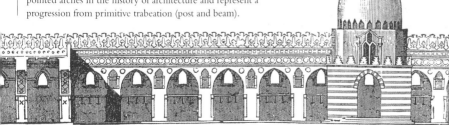

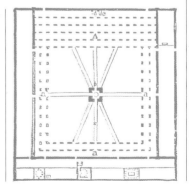

Islamic

The City

While early Islamic buildings had no uniform style, the Fatimid period in Egypt (969–1171) saw the emergence of a common architectural vocabulary for sacred and secular buildings: the dome, the keel arch and stone masonry. Two impressive 11th-century gateways to Cairo demonstrate the skill of the builders of fortifications. Within the city walls were the courtyard houses and palaces; beyond them lay the tombs and cemeteries. The Persian tomb at Sultaniya is a sophisticated form of the domed chamber, while the Mamluk tombs outside the walls of Cairo capture the elegance of the quintessential Islamic silhouette. The Mamluks ruled Egypt from 1250 until the Ottoman conquest of 1516, and built exquisite mosques, *madrasas* (colleges) and tombs.

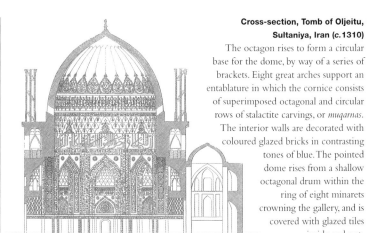

Cross-section, Tomb of Oljeitu, Sultaniya, Iran (c.1310)
The octagon rises to form a circular base for the dome, by way of a series of brackets. Eight great arches support an entablature in which the cornice consists of superimposed octagonal and circular rows of stalactite carvings, or *muqarnas*. The interior walls are decorated with coloured glazed bricks in contrasting tones of blue. The pointed dome rises from a shallow octagonal drum within the ring of eight minarets crowning the gallery, and is covered with glazed tiles inside and out.

Dargah, Tomb of Oljeitu
This view of the tomb shows the remains of the staircases flanking the elegantly arched entrance or *dargah*. This portal feature began to have more architectural prominence from the beginning of the 14th century.

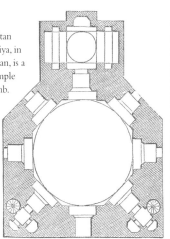

Octagonal plan, Tomb of Oljeitu
The tomb of Sultan Oljeitu at Sultaniya, in north-western Iran, is a magnificent example of an Islamic tomb. It is octagonal in plan, with staircases on either side of the entrance, and a small chapel (shown at the top of the plan) in which the body lay.

Gateway of Bab an-Nasr, Cairo (1087–92)
The splendid monumental fortified gateway of Bab an-Nasr (Gate of Victory), with its square towers, was built by the Fatimid vizier around his palace in Cairo. The original mud-brick fortifications of the city were now replaced with stone. The large blocks of squared stone, and the high vaulted ceiling of the wide passages within the walls, were refined and sophisticated in form.

Gateway of Bab al-Futuh, Cairo (1087)
The gateway of Bab al-Futuh (Gate of Conquests) is another of the gateways in the city walls to the north, separating the palace from the rest of the city. These rounded towers were a more effective form of defence than the square ones. They contained shafts for pouring boiling oil on the enemy, and slits for firing arrows.

Funerary complex of Sultan Inal, Cairo (1451–56)
The Egyptian obsession with death resurfaced in a new guise under the Mamluks. This funerary complex of mosque, mausoleum, *madrasa* and *khanqah* (monastery) was an attempt to ensure the dominance of the Mamluk elite. Mamluk architectural detail is distinguished by its strong sense of colour and by its use of *ablaq* ('piebald'): marble in bands of contrasting colours.

Domes, Mamluk tomb, Cairo (14th century)
The range of dome shapes (oval, spherical and pyramidal) and forms of decoration (zigzag, geometric star patterns and floral designs) are shown on these small Mamluk domes protecting the headstones.

Early Mamluk tomb, Cairo (14th century)
The characteristic domes of the early Mamluk period are these ribbed domes raised on high drums above a tall façade. The minarets had different-shaped storeys with open loggias and belvederes. By contrast the lower walls of the tombs were kept deliberately plain and cliff-like.

Islamic

Middle Eastern Islamic Mosques, Mausolea and Madrasas

In his house at Medina (modern Saudi Arabia) in 624 Muhammad established the direction of prayer (*qibla*) to face Mecca. In mosques built subsequently, a small niche or *mihrab* indicated this direction; it remains a feature of all mosques. Beside it is the pulpit (*mimbar*), with steps leading to the canopied throne, which is left vacant as the seat of absent authority – Muhammad; the prayer leader (*imam*) takes the top step. These features, established from the 7th century, were later extended to include vast courtyards and minarets: the towers from which the *imam* calls Muslims to prayer with the words 'Allah is Great and Muhammad is his Prophet'. The mosque has to provide a courtyard for people to gather in, a place for washing before prayers and a large space for the prayer mats. Prayers at noon on Fridays are congregational, hence the term 'Friday mosque'. The mosque acts as the religious, social and political centre of Islamic life.

Elevation and cross-section, mosque-madrasa of Sultan Hassan
The sultan's mausoleum was a square domed chamber flanked by two tall minarets. The college rooms, housed in nine storeys of the *madrasa*, flank the open courtyard, with the entrance portal on the right. The cross-section shows the tall chamber on the left and the open courtyard in the centre with its domed fountain.

Iwan, mosque-madrasa of Sultan Hassan, Cairo (1356–63)
This plan shows how a mosque could be combined with a mausoleum and a theological college (*madrasa*) to form a complex consisting of vaulted halls open on one side to a courtyard (*iwan*). The *iwan* replaced the hypostyle hall that had been common in mosques. This particular complex exemplifies the Islamic four-*iwan* arrangement.

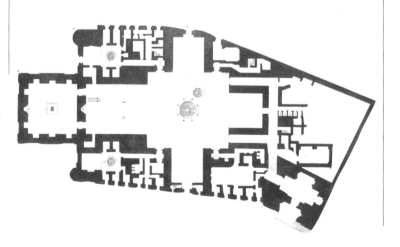

Muqarna

Ostentatious display was characteristic of the royal funerary *madrasas*. The elaborate *muqarna* (stalactite or honeycomb vaulting) inside the entrance portal was part of that display, as were the marbles of contrasting colours surmounted by a frieze of Kufic script (shown on the right).

Cross-section, mosque-madrasa of Sultan Hassan

The central court is open, with one huge niche in each of the enclosing walls – the niche facing Mecca being the largest. Beyond, the founder's tomb is covered by a dome resting on pendentives (*nasta'liq*).

Ablution fountain

The large ablution fountain (*fisqiya; hannifiya; haud*) in the centre of the courtyard is where Muslims wash before entering the prayer hall. Primarily a utilitarian structure, it also echoes the architecture of the mosque.

Islamic

Mosque Complexes of Egypt and Persia

In Egypt, *iwan*-type buildings were established from the late 12th century. This form was particularly suitable for the mosque-*madrasa* groups erected up until the 18th century in Cairo. Persian Islamic architecture, on the other hand, was particularly influenced by the invasion of the Seljuks in the 11th century, who brought with them the cylindrical minaret form, the four-*iwan* plan for mosque-*madrasa* complexes, large domed spaces and complex brick patterning. In the later Safavid period of the 17th century, ornamentation with glazed tile-mosaics was developed particularly at Isfahan (the Safavid capital), with buildings distinguished by blue domes and coloured façades.

Madrasa of Shah Sultan Hussein, Isfahan (1706–15)
The *madrasa* of Sultan Hussein at Isfahan, with its bulb-shaped dome and double arcades on either side of the entrance portal, was similar to the earlier *madrasa* courtyards of the Maidan Shah. These were among the finest public buildings in Persia.

Mosque of Qa'itbay, Cairo (1472–74)
This funerary complex owes its splendour to its high-quality decoration and *ablaq* (striped marble bands), the carved stone dome of the sultan's mausoleum with its intertwining arabesques and star patterns, the decorations of the portal, and the minaret. The mausoleum symbolised the wealth and status of Sultan Qa'itbay.

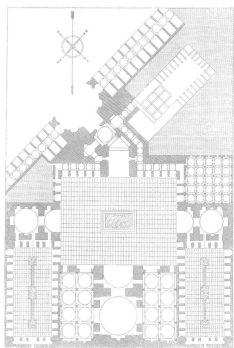

Maidan, Mosque of Isfahan, Persia (1612–37)
This mosque was built with its entrance at an angle, to ensure that the mosque was correctly orientated towards Mecca. The open courtyard (*maidan*) contained fountains and basins of water. The prayer hall was divided by a central compartment surmounted by a dome; the two outer compartments contained the *madrasa*.

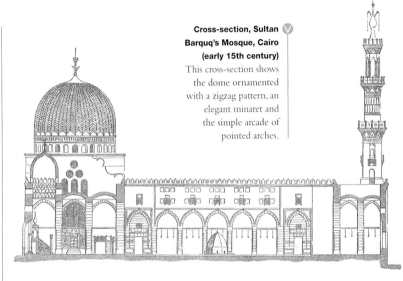

Cross-section, Sultan Barquq's Mosque, Cairo (early 15th century)
This cross-section shows the dome ornamented with a zigzag pattern, an elegant minaret and the simple arcade of pointed arches.

Antler tower, Isfahan (early 17th century)
Hunting was a great sport in Persia, and hunting towers such as this were erected to celebrate successful hunts, with feasts and banquets held at the base. The towers were often adorned with the antlers of slain beasts.

Mosque of Vakil, Persia (1750–79)
This two-*iwan* mosque contains a prayer room resting on five rows of twisted stone columns. The exterior was notable for its *pishtaq* – the monumental portal – and for its tile-mosaic panels and pink walls.

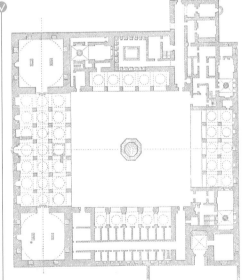

Plan, Sultan Barquq's Mosque
Sultan Barquq's mosque, sepulchral chambers and *khanqah* (monastery) form a monumental funerary complex outside Cairo, dating from the early 15th century. The complex included two mausolea, a monastery, mosque and fountains integrated around a central courtyard. The prayer hall of three naves is flanked by the mausolea, with the monks' cells on the other sides.

Islamic

Islamic Architecture in Spain: The Moorish Mosque

The Iberian peninsula was conquered by the Arabs in 711. In 755 Abd el Rahman founded an independent Arabian empire in Spain, establishing its capital at Cordoba, where he built a large mosque – the first Islamic building in that country. It was begun in 786 and completed by 796, then extended with another court in 965 and finally completed under El Mansar between *c.* 987 and 990. The mosque reflected the growing splendour of Cordoba, which, in the 10th century, was the largest and most prosperous city in Europe and its most sacred place of pilgrimage. Islamic rule continued in the Iberian peninsula until 1492, with architectural influences including north African Islamic (Maghribian) stylistic features, as well as earlier Visigoth and Roman traditions.

Plan, Mosque of Cordoba
The mosque's earliest part comprises the rectangle of eleven aisles. In 965 Al-Hakam II added fourteen extra rows of columns and a new *mihrab*. In the late 10th century a further seven columns were added on the east side.

Wooden rib dome support, Mosque of Cordoba
The sanctuary entrance was in the form of a horseshoe arch. Above this were three domes supported by complex rib systems, made of richly carved and painted wood.

Screen, Villa Viciosa, Cordoba (*c.* 1200)
This screen was built with interlacing arches resting on Roman columns. The arches are rounded, not pointed, demonstrating the enduring influence of the Roman and Byzantine arch.

Mosque of Cordoba
This cross-section of the mosque shows the stone and brick arcades, with marble columns supporting the double arches. The 10th-century extension reveals intersecting lobed arches supporting a domed sanctuary in front of the polygonal chamber containing the *mihrab*.

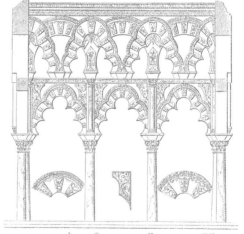

Interior, Mosque of Cordoba
This view shows the intersecting lobed arches in front of the *qibla* wall. The central *mihrab* is a deeply recessed polygonal chamber with floral motifs and inscriptions from the Koran in marble, with gold and glass mosaics on the rectangular *mihrab* frame.

Squinch
A squinch (*sirdab*) is a structure, or small vault, in the corner of two right angles, which builds up to form a different shape: for instance, changing a square to a circle or octagon.

Sectional view, San Christo de la Luz, Toledo (11th century)
This is one of the oldest Moorish monuments in Spain: a small, square building with four stout pillars on the floor, dividing the space into nine equal compartments. The central one is carried up higher and terminates in a dome.

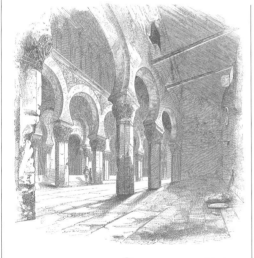

Horseshoe arch, Toledo Synagogue (13th century)
The interior of this synagogue in Toledo looks more like a mosque, with its brick-and-plaster arcades comprising octagonal pillars supporting horseshoe-shaped arches moulded in plaster, and with arabesque decoration in the spandrels.

Horseshoe arch, Mosque of Cordoba
The sanctuary was also rebuilt in 965, and is an excellent example of Islamic architecture in Spain. The columns were reused from Roman buildings and were strong but quite short, so a row of square columns was placed on the apex of the lower ones. For extra strength, a horseshoe arch was placed above the lower pillars. The brick and stone in the arches were alternated creating the distinctive red-and-white striped pattern.

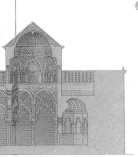

Islamic

Islamic Architecture in Spain: The Alhambra

A citadel was built at Granada in 1248 and was completed by 1300. Within its fortified walls lay the two palaces of the Alhambra – the palaces of the Nasrid rulers – which were built in two major phases in the 14th century. Together they comprise a combination of large halls or state rooms for the sultans, and private apartments of intimate rooms looking out on to courtyards with fountains, pools and gardens. The whole effect represents a brilliant use of light and space, but the architecture is primarily a vehicle for the ornamental and complex plaster decoration of the arcades and ceilings. The interest in light, highly decorated structures was a distinctive characteristic of Islamic architecture in Spain. The decoration in carved stucco and tiles includes intricate geometric and floral designs as well as Koranic inscriptions. The sharp contrasts of dark and light colours create the illusion of different planes, demonstrating that not all Islamic art is restricted to two dimensions.

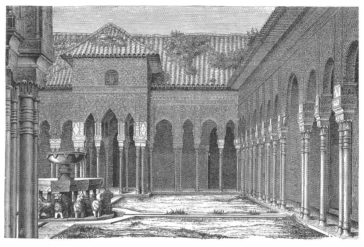

View of the Court of Lions
This open court has a cruciform layout – a symbolic representation of paradise – and shows the projecting pavilions of the palace rooms at each end. The court is an interior garden with shrubs, aromatic herbs and a marble fountain in the centre, ringed with twelve stone–carved statues of lions.

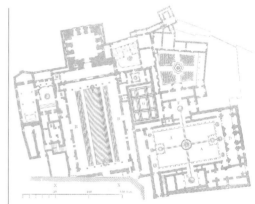

Arcades, Court of Lions
This detail shows the beauty of the arcades, supported on slender columns that are alternately single and coupled. The capitals are in the shape of a cube, with the corners rounded off, and adorned with interlacing representations of plants. The arches are raised (stilted), and the soffits are richly decorated with filigreed plasterwork containing cursive inscriptions, where the letters are elongated to form intricate patterns.

Plan
The Alhambra consists of two palaces, each with an oblong court. The earliest (early 14th century) is the Court of Alberca (B), or Myrtles, with an audience hall (the Hall of Ambassadors) and a banqueting room at the northern end. The other is the Court of Lions (A) (mid- to late 14th century), with its surrounding halls.

Moorish wall decoration

Ornament in Islamic architecture consists of the decoration of flat surfaces, because three-dimensional or representational decoration is forbidden in the Koran. Arabesques, the intricate overall pattern of geometric or stylised plants, could either be incised in plaster or painted.

Ornament

Both Kufic script (squarish in character) and cursive script (more flowing and curving) were also used as ornament. The writing refers to passages from the Koran or to proverbs. A common inscription at the Alhambra is *Wa-la ghaliba illa-Llah* – 'There is no conqueror but God'. The *ataurique* (decorative plasterwork), shown in this detail, is a stylised floral motif derived from the acanthus, but Greek palmettes, pineapples and shells also appear.

Plasterwork

Plaster was used for all wall decoration, arches, stalactite cornices, capitals and honeycomb vaults. Ornament was chiselled into the wet plaster or a mould was used.

View of the Court of Alberca

This court was used by ambassadors and distinguished guests, and formed part of the earliest palace complex. The rooms open out on to the court, which is lined by marble-columned arcades. There is a basin of water in the middle flanked by rows of myrtle bushes down the sides. At the north end is the large, square throne room: the Hall of the Ambassadors. The ceiling is vaulted with *mocarbes* – a Spanish term for *muqarnas* ('honeycombed' work) and, in Spain, painted in a rich variety of colours or gilded.

Islamic

Islamic Architecture in India: Combining Hindu and Islamic Features

From its origins in 7th-century Arabia, Islam spread through Iran, central Asia and Afghanistan, arriving on the Indian subcontinent as early as the 8th century but not reaching northern India until the 12th century. The Muslim invaders brought with them a mature theory of structural mechanics, the pointed arch, vault, squinch and dome, with decorative themes based on calligraphy and geometric patterns. Native Hindu architecture was based on the post-and-beam system used in building stone temples decorated with intricate wooden carving. It was the interaction of the Hindu and Islamic building traditions that resulted in the magnificent buildings of the Delhi sultanates (the Muslim Pathans), and the Mughal mosques and mausolea built between the 16th and 18th centuries.

Minar, Qutb (late 12th century)
This tall minaret was a victory tower. It stood four storeys high, with two rounded upper storeys of white marble surmounted by a pillared kiosk. The lower storeys of red sandstone were fluted, with lateral belts carved with Arabic inscriptions.

Lall Durwaza Mosque, Jaunpore (1400–50)
This mosque has a bold massive gateway, tall enough not to need a minaret. It shows the combination of Islamic forms, such as the pointed arch, with Hindu features, such as short columns.

Patah Tomb, Shepree (mid-16th century)
A mixture of short, broad Jain columns supporting rectangular enclosed walls form the base of an octagonal drum, which supports the dome of this tomb.

Tomb of Khan-I Jihan Tilangani, Delhi (1368–69)
This is an example of a Pathan tomb, showing Islamic features. The octagonal chamber is surrounded by an open verandah, each face of the octagon being pierced by three pointed arches on square piers. This mix of octagonal plan, arcaded verandahs, eave-stones and cupolas was used as a model for future tomb designs.

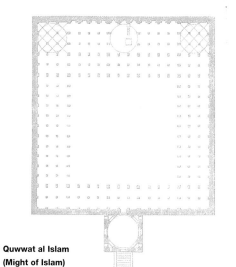

Pathan Mosque, Mandu (1305–1432)

This plan shows a square courtyard, with three aisles on two sides, two aisles on one side and five at the top, facing Mecca. The courtyard is lined with eleven-arched arcades. The three domes are each supported by twelve equally spaced pillars.

Exterior, Pathan Mosque

This view faces in the direction of Mecca. It is distinguished by the smaller domes on the aisles and the three large domes.

Quwwat al Islam (Might of Islam) Mosque, Delhi (1199)

This was the first mosque in India to be constructed inside a captured Hindu citadel. A courtyard was surrounded by arcades of reassembled Hindu and Jain columns, but all the walls were Islamic, with pointed arches and Arabic ornament. This range consisted of three larger and eight smaller arches.

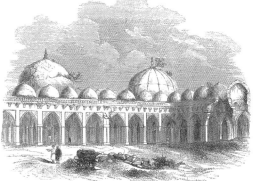

Minar, Ghazni (early 11th century)

This *minar*, or tower, is one of many pillars of victory erected by conquerors on the battlefield to show the supremacy of the new religion of Islam. Made of brick covered with terracotta decoration, its cross-section is star-shaped on the lower part and circular on the upper part.

Squinch, Old Delhi Mosque

This squinch from the mosque at Old Delhi demonstrates the vaulting of Indian-style *muqarnas*, which resembles stalactites or honeycombs. This is a traditional Hindu method of constructing the squinch vaulting.

Islamic

Islamic Architecture in India: Mughal Mosques, Tombs and Palaces

The richest period for Indian Islamic architecture was the Mughal era, lasting from the 16th to the 19th centuries. Perhaps the ultimate achievement of Mughal architecture was the Taj Mahal at Agra, the work of craftsmen from all over the Islamic world, using their skills in construction, carving marble and inlaying precious stones. Bijapur, in south central India, was one of the capitals of the Islamic dynasties in India, and here Muhammad Adil Shah built one of the outstanding monuments of the mid-17th century: an enormous domed tomb, larger than the Pantheon in Rome. Islamic features were also used on imperial palaces in India (at Agra, Mandu, Bijapur, Delhi and Allahabad), together with pavilions, halls, verandahs, courts and gardens.

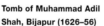

Tomb of Muhammad Adil Shah, Bijapur (1626–56)
A system of intersecting arches transfers the shape of the square chamber to the circular drum of the dome. A circular platform masks the springing of the dome, creating the illusion that it hovers over the chamber. The towers are eight storeys high, with smaller domes; the walls have deeply projecting cornices.

Plan, Tomb of Muhammad Adil Shah
The tomb is a gigantic cube, with octagonal turrets attached at the corners, surmounted by a huge hemispherical dome. The weight of the dome is supported by a mass of masonry, shown in the star-shaped intersections of the pendentives and their arches: a major feat of engineering.

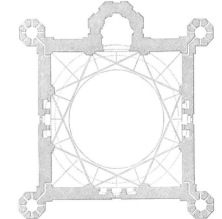

Friday Mosque, New Delhi (1644–58)
The large central gateway has a broad keel arch, three bulbous domes and symmetrical ranges of arcades. The raised prayer hall is flanked by a pair of minarets. The courtyard has open colonnades, with kiosks at the junction. The materials are fine red sandstone with bands of white marble.

Plan, Taj Mahal

This comprises a square plan with a circular centre, covered by a dome above the tombs of the shah and his wife. The four corners are angled, each with a smaller dome above, and are connected to each other and to the centre by means of passages.

Taj Mahal, Agra (1632–54)

This splendid mausoleum, built by the emperor Shah Jahan for his wife, Mumtaz Mahal, lies at the centre of a large enclosure. The white-marble building, decorated with arabesque carving, stands on a raised platform on a terrace; a tall minaret stands sentinel at each corner. The outer court is surrounded by arcades and has four gateways, the central one leading from the court to the gardens.

Palace Hall, Allahabad

The square hall is supported by eight rows of eight columns, and is surrounded by a deep verandah of double columns with richly carved bracket capitals.

Cross-section, Taj Mahal

This shows the vault under the main compartment, where the royal bodies were interred. The dome has an inner and an outer shell, set on a high drum. The inner dome is separated from the tomb chamber by a screen of trelliswork in white marble, which allows the light to filter through. The wall surfaces are also covered with white marble, inlaid with precious stones.

Islamic

Islamic Architecture in Turkey and North Africa

The Muslim Seljuks from Persia established a powerful state in Anatolia in the 11th century, with architecture of brick minarets and colourful tilework. But with the conquest of Constantinople (present-day Istanbul) by the Ottomans in 1453, the Seljuks gave way to the Ottomans, who ruled central Asia until the early 20th century, and their architecture represents the last stage of the Islamic style. Early in the period, the Ottomans converted Christian buildings, such as the church of Hagia Sophia, into mosques. Building on the Byzantine style, Ottoman architects developed the centralised mosque, with its characteristic hemispherical vault built on a cube, smaller domes and a prominent portico framed by tall, slender minarets. Wall surfaces were covered with the varied colours and sophisticated designs of Iznik tiles. In North Africa a style known as Maghribian developed.

Suleymaniye Mosque complex, Istanbul (1550–57)
Built by the architect Sinan, this mosque has a square plan. The forecourt, which contains the fountains, is enclosed on each side by an arcade. The garden-cemetery contains the tombs of Suleymaniye and his wife.

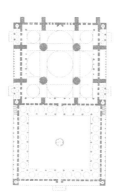

Sultan Ahmed (Blue) Mosque, Istanbul (1609–17)
This complex includes a tomb, *madrasa* and *imaret* (soup kitchen). The plan is square, and the walls support a vast central dome on massive piers. Four semi-domes surround the central one, with four smaller ones at the corners.

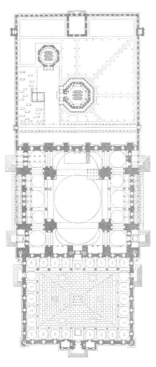

Façade, Sultan Ahmed Mosque
The mosque occupies the central area between the fountain court and gardens. From the main entrance the effect is one of perfect symmetry, with the smaller domes of the fountain court building up to the highest and largest central dome, framed by minarets.

Djama Mosque, Algiers (1660)

This cruciform building demonstrates features that are typical of Algerian mosques during the Ottoman period. The sanctuary is barrel-vaulted and there is a central ovoid dome, supported on Ottoman-type pendentives and semi-circular arches. The drum of the dome is decorated with a frieze of carved stucco niches made by Algerian craftsmen. The square minaret is more typical of the Maghribian than the Ottoman style.

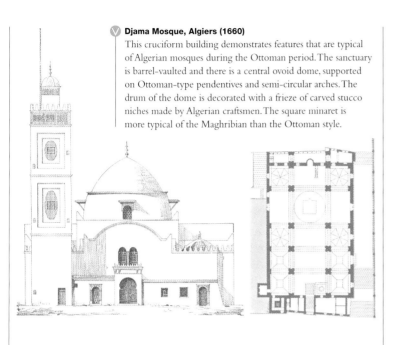

Perspective, Suleymaniye Mosque

This classic Ottoman mosque complex includes seven colleges, a hospital, baths, fountains, a mosque with four tapering minarets and a cemetery. The fountain courtyard has a portico supported by columns of porphyry, marble and pink granite. The semi-domes support the huge central dome, in front of which is a set of three further domes. The wooden doors of the mosque are inlaid with ebony, mother-of-pearl and ivory.

Cross-section, Suleymaniye Mosque

Internally the structure rests on four great piers. The screen of windows on each side is borne by four porphyry columns. The central dome is the largest of 500 domes in the complex (vying with that of Hagia Sophia). To the left are the *mimbar* and *mihrab*. The *mihrab* wall is decorated with stained glass and Iznik tiles.

Minaret, Tunis

This minaret is typical of Maghribian Islamic architecture: plain detailing on a polygonal brick shaft, with just one balcony stage: a monument of simple grandeur.

Romanesque *c. 1000–early C.13th*

French Romanesque: Origins

The early 19th-century term 'Romanesque' was applied to the architecture of the 11th and 12th centuries because it revived classical precedents established by the Romans. Chief among these was the use of Roman-style barrel vaults and the desire to vault ever broader spaces in stone – a skill lost with the Romans. This led to the emergence of the rib vault in England in the early 1200s and its adoption in Normandy and across the Continent by the early 13th century. France was not a unified country at this time, but a series of divided territories. There was therefore not one recognisably 'French' idiom, but a number of regional schools that used the main components of Romanesque – the round arch, vault, exuberant surface decoration and towers – to diverse effect. The four main pilgrimage routes through France to Santiago de Compostela in Spain resulted in a series of pilgrimage churches such as St Sernin, Toulouse.

Ornament, Porch of St Trophime, Arles
Many provincial churches had porches added in the late 11th century. This ornate example shows the mastery of sculptural carving and a rich range of motifs: grotesque masks, fantastical beasts and figures.

Plan, St Sernin, Toulouse (begun 1080)
The expanded plan of this late 11th-century church reflects its location on one of the main pilgrimage routes. Its vast precincts contain five aisles, a wide transept with aisles and four chapels to the east, and an apse with ambulatory and five apsidal chapels.

Radiating chapels, St Sernin
Chapels dedicated to the veneration of saints, radiating out from the apse (the semi-circular or polygonal vaulted termination to a chancel) and transepts, often resulted in striking exterior elevations. The east end of St Sernin (1080–96) is a particularly dramatic architectural composition.

Galleries, St Sernin
Located above the aisles of the nave, galleries gave visual access to events in the nave and choir. They are a common feature of major churches with large congregations and of pilgrimage sites.

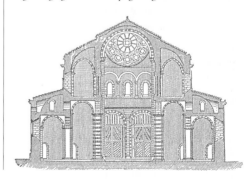

Pilasters, St Menoux
De-based classical decoration was a feature of provincial architecture. In 11th-century Burgundy the reworking of classical models by local masons led to the creation of their own vernacular style. The vaguely classical capitals of the pilasters surrounding the east end of St Menoux exemplify this transitional idiom.

Mosaic decoration, Notre Dame de Puy
Most commonly associated with Italy, isolated examples of mosaic decoration are found in France in areas where local stone is of a particularly decorative nature. Mosaic decoration is usually geometric; it is introduced here in a deep band below eaves level, and in the area of walling bounded by pilasters and the arch of the windows on the chapels.

Greek-cross plan, St Front, Périgueux
Variations on the Greek-cross plan flourished *c.* 1125–50. Each area – nave, choir and transepts – is composed of four equal arms with a domed vault. Semi-circular chapels extending to the east modify the plan to enable the veneration of saints.

West front, Church of the Holy Trinity, Caen
The western façades of 12th-century churches in Normandy were generally symmetrical in elevation. Square towers rising out of the main body served as a symbolic focal point.

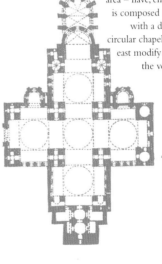

Chevet, St Menoux
Chevet is the French term for the east end of a church when it comprises a circular or polygonal apse, surrounded by an ambulatory with radiating chapels. This view shows the centrally located shrine around which the ambulatory passage runs.

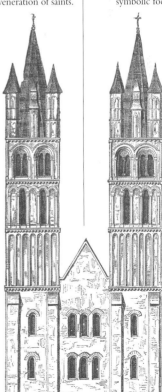

Romanesque

French Romanesque:
The Influence of Pilgrims

Pilgrims journeyed from all over the Continent and aided the promulgation of the emergent architectural styles. They also had an impact on the design of churches, which were adapted to accommodate both the clergy and large crowds of pilgrims following a processional route. In the majority of French churches the planning of the east end was developed to follow either a radiating or staggered (echelon) plan. In the former, an ambulatory (a shaped aisle) was added around the perimeter of the apse to allow access to subsidiary chapels, which extended out from the main body of the church. The staggered plan saw the introduction of chapels to the eastern sides of the transepts. These developments in spatial organisation enabled divisions to be maintained between the worshippers and the clergy; and between the altars of saints and the high altar of the church.

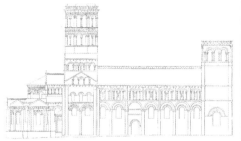

Towers, Issoire
Erected increasingly on western elevations, towers also predominate in central positions at the point of the crossing of the transepts and at their south and north ends. This 12th-century example has an established arrangement of a short, square-headed tower at the west end and a taller tower of similar profile rising out of the crossing.

Barrel (or tunnel) vaults, Issoire
The simplest form of vaulting, these are formed from an uninterrupted semi-circular section. As this cross-section reveals, the central vault over the nave is supported by half-vaults carried over the aisles, which counteract the lateral thrust of the vault.

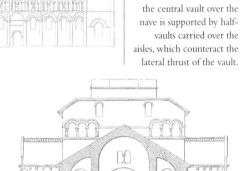

Staggered (or echelon) plan, Issoire (11th century)
The staggered plan, with chapels radiating from both the apse and transepts, was quickly adopted and employed throughout France. It remained a French phenomenon and was not commonly used elsewhere in Europe.

Single-aisle nave, Fontevrault (11th century)
A variation on the increasingly common plan form of a nave and two side-aisles, the single-aisle nave persisted in smaller churches in the 11th and 12th centuries. The internal wall of the nave was articulated by a series of clustered columns standing proud of the wall face. Aisleless naves were a characteristic feature of Aquitanian architecture.

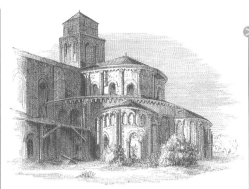

Blind arcading, Fontevrault
Exterior decoration took a variety of
forms. The most universal treatment was the
repetition of rows of round-headed arches and
arched openings, or blind arcading, which
enriched otherwise bare sections of wall.

Exterior ornament, Loupiac
Bold sculptural decoration,
often of a figurative nature,
became a frequently exploited
feature of Romanesque
churches in the 12th century.
Flourishing alongside this
movement was a fashion
for quieter, more restrained
geometric ornament, which
relied on the sense of unity
achieved by repetition
and proportion.

Pointed arch, Fontevrault
Although associated with the later architectural
style of Gothic, and one of the key points of
difference between it and Romanesque, the
pointed arch did occasionally occur during the
Romanesque period. Normally of a shallow
profile, it gave only the merest suggestion of
the architectural idiom to come and always
occurred in buildings alongside traditional
round arches.

**Bay, Church of the
Holy Trinity, Caen**
The mass of the nave is
traditionally broken up by a series
of bay divisions, which follow a
repetitive pattern from west to east
and from ground to vault in order
to accentuate the linearity of the
interior space. Full-height shafts
rise up through the elevation to
give support to the vault; and
compound piers, composed of a
number of shafts, mark the bay
openings. A triforium, or arcaded
wall passage, runs horizontally
above the arches of the bay
and an arcaded clerestory
level lights the nave.

Romanesque

The Romanesque in Germany

German architecture in the 11th and 12th centuries drew on the forms established under Charlemagne and the Ottonian rule and adapted them to create some of the first buildings in a truly Romanesque idiom. In Speyer Cathedral (*c.* 1030–1106), Germany created a turning point in European architecture. Built as the pantheon of the German emperors, it drew its inspiration from the classical past and dwarfed other northern churches, looking back to the colossal early Christian basilicas of the 4th century. When finished, it was the largest church in the West and the first to introduce articulation to the internal wall faces of the nave. Its influence extended to the Rhineland and Cologne, and abroad to France. Germany is also credited with introducing twin towers to the west façade of churches, as at Speyer, Mainz, Worms and Laach.

Carved decoration
Highly stylised scrolling foliage decoration was part of the universal language of the Romanesque and was not confined to Germany – or to any one region or country. As the period progressed, increasing emphasis was placed on naturalistic forms, and their truthful representation in stone was highly prized.

Capital, Speyer Cathedral
Numerous different styles of capital abound in German architecture. Plain block capitals were superseded by more original and ornate forms. This early 12th-century example, of stylised leaves unfurling alongside two intertwined swans' necks, gives confident expression to the carver's art and typifies the increasing richness of the decoration.

Cable moulding
Carved in emulation of twisted rope, cable moulding or ropework is a characteristic form of the period. It is not found on earlier buildings and appears to have been the creation of Romanesque carvers. Its most favoured use was as a means of accentuating door and window openings.

Narrative decoration,
Gelnhausen
Scenes of a didactic nature, which sought to impress upon the congregation biblical teaching, feature on many church surfaces. Doors, west fronts and pulpits are favoured locations for such treatment. This scene, forming part of a sequential narrative surrounding the arcade at Gelnhausen, is beautifully calculated to meet the limitations of the spandrel that it decorates.

**Baptistery, Bonn
(11th century)**
Distinct baptisteries are only occasionally found in Germany. The external façades of the Baptistery at Bonn were articulated with engaged strip pilasters and eaves-level decoration derived from Lombardy in Italy.

Castle of Wartburg (late 12th century)
The castle of Wartburg is one of Europe's few surviving (although heavily altered) Romanesque palaces. As in religious architecture of the period, the dominant decorative idiom on secular structures was the repetitive use of the round-arched arcade, window, doorway and corbel table (*see page 195*).

**Towers, Worms Cathedral
(begun 1171)**
Stair towers at the east and west ends are a dominant feature of church elevations. Worms Cathedral has six towers of varying heights, all with allied decorative treatment, such as open blind arcades.

Plan, Worms Cathedral
This has a traditional arrangement of a very long nave with side-aisles covered by rib vaults and massive piers. Of the two apses, the older east choir appears as a flat elevation outside but rounded within.

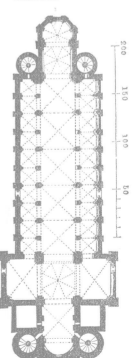

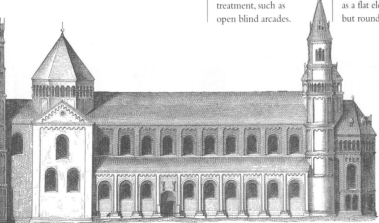

Romanesque

The Romanesque in Spain

Romanesque architecture in Spain was the product of several distinct traditions. Spain's long history of occupation by the Moors had produced highly idiosyncratic Christian-Islamic styles known as Mozarabic and Mudéjar, elements of which were combined in the 11th and 12th centuries with the influential European architectural language spreading from France. This often produced a hybrid style, based on French models but continuing earlier tradition in the use of Islamic decoration. Spanish Romanesque is most associated with churches along the pilgrimage route to Santiago de Compostela – the Cathedral there (c. 1075–1120) standing as the architectural climax. Finely carved, often highly realistic sculpture is also evident in churches throughout Spain.

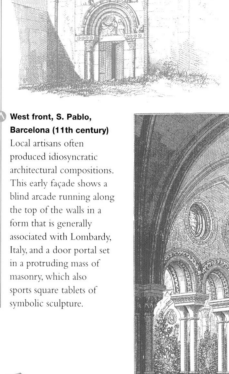

West front, S. Pablo, Barcelona (11th century)
Local artisans often produced idiosyncratic architectural compositions. This early façade shows a blind arcade running along the top of the walls in a form that is generally associated with Lombardy, Italy, and a door portal set in a protruding mass of masonry, which also sports square tablets of symbolic sculpture.

Quadripartite vaulting, Tarragona
This is a ribbed vault where each bay is divided into four compartments by two diagonal ribs. The roundels set into the outer wall of the cloister have interlaced tracery decoration with a decidedly Moorish character.

Covered arcade, S. Millán, Segovia
A feature of provincial Romanesque, found in cities such as Segovia, was the construction of covered arcades, in the form of cloisters, built up against the main body of the church. The raised, open arcade shown on the west elevation of this Segovian church demonstrates this local tradition.

**Decorated shafts,
Santiago de Compostela Cathedral**
Highly sophisticated abstract and narrative decoration sit alongside one another on these door shafts at Santiago de Compostela. One shaft carries a twisted moulding interlaced with a flowing foliate design; the other sets religious figures within a miniature architectural framework of columns supporting highly ornate round-arched niches, which serves to echo the wider architectural composition of the cathedral.

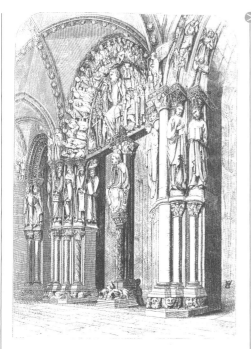

Lantern tower, Salamanca Old Cathedral
The exterior of the *cimborio* at Salamanca Old Cathedral has a strong suggestion of Moorish architecture. The strikingly articulated, eight-sided ribbed dome is covered in fishscale stone slates and supported by two bands of multiple arches. It is stylistically allied to the nearby cathedral at Zamora (*c.* 1174), which sports sixteen branches of ribs and a rounded dome all covered in the same distinctive local material.

Figure sculpture, Santiago de Compostela Cathedral
The Portico de Gloria, the original west front of the cathedral, is celebrated for the life-like quality of its carved figures, which demonstrate the sculptor's great ability to integrate sculptural ornament with the architectural form of the building.

Façade, Church of Santiago, La Coruña
Plain elevations are often combined with bold massing to produce churches with a strong sculptural feel. Wall faces are broken up by powerful vertical lines introduced by buttresses and the occasional engaged column, but decoration is minimal.

Lantern, Salamanca Old Cathedral
A lantern, or *cimborio*, covers the crossing of Salamanca Old Cathedral (late 12th century). The circular lantern is lit by two rows of alternating blind arches and windows, the upper register of which has shaped heads known as rounded trefoils.

Romanesque

English Norman Style: Churches

The Norman style, as Romanesque is known in England, flourished during the 11th and 12th centuries. In 1066, with the victory of William the Conqueror at Hastings, England welcomed a new style of art and architecture. As the Normans sought to impress upon England their military might and religious fervour, two main building types predominated: the castle and the church. In an unparalleled spate of ecclesiastical building, nearly every cathedral and abbey church was rebuilt. The cathedrals of Canterbury, Lincoln, Rochester and Winchester and the abbeys of Bury St Edmunds, Canterbury and St Albans were all subject to building campaigns in the 1070s. They were characterised by their vast scale, which surpassed anything previously seen in England and vied with continental models of the period.

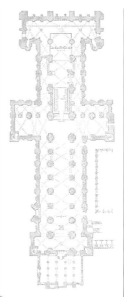

Lady Chapel, Durham Cathedral
This plan shows the unusual feature of a Galilee or lady chapel that was added to the west end of the cathedral in *c.* 1170–75. Lady chapels dedicated to the Virgin Mary are traditionally located at the east end.

Bay decoration, St Peter's Church, Northampton
Zigzag and other geometric ornament was particularly characteristic of Norman interiors. Here, clustered columns with undecorated shafts and foliate capitals support highly decorated arches.

Square tower, St Peter's Church, Northampton (mid-12th century)
Most Norman churches consist of a central space that incorporates the nave, choir and aisles, and a tower at the west end housing the bells. These are mainly square in plan, but regional variants such as round towers exist.

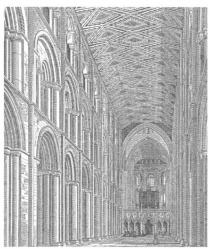

Nave, Peterborough Cathedral
On entering this nave from the west, a sense of rhythm and order was achieved by the regularly spaced round-arched bays and the repetition of detail rising up through the triforium (or wall passage) to the clerestory (the upper level of windows lighting the interior spaces). A flat wooden roof would originally have overlain the nave, pre-dating this canted stone vault of *c.* 1220.

Piers, St Peter's Church
This interior of *c.* 1150 is distinguished by the presence of supports, which alternate between quatrefoils and round piers with broad waistbands (shaft rings). This highly ornate articulation is unusual for a parish church.

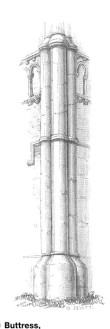

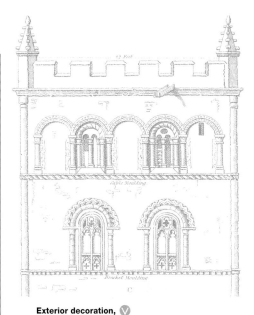

Crossing tower,
St John's Church
This rises up from above
the intersection of the
nave, chancel and transepts.
Parish church towers are
often castellated and
surmounted by pinnacles
decorated with carved
projections called crockets.

Interlaced arches,
St John's Church
Repetitive decoration
enlivening the treatment
of the internal wall faces
is common in Norman
style. In typical fashion,
regularly spaced columns
are shown supporting
intersecting arches,
which are purely
decorative and serve no
functional purpose.

Buttress,
St Peter's Church
A buttress is a mass of
masonry projecting from,
or built up against a wall
to provide additional
support or to counteract
the outward thrust of the
structure. This angle
buttress is composed
of three shafts, all
semi-circular in plan.

Exterior decoration,
St John's Church,
Devizes (12th century)
This is composed of
characteristically Norman
elements, including
buttress supports, a pair of
blind windows with
decorated arches and a
small upper window
with an elaborately
ornamented arch.

Window, St John's Church
Columns rising to scalloped capitals support deeply
recessed rows of sculptural ornament in zigzag form,
known as chevrons. The upper run of moulding is
decorated with a ballflower motif.

Capital,
St John's Church
A variety of different
forms of capital were used,
including cushion and
block capitals. These were
often the focus for
elaborate decoration with
stylised motifs drawn
from nature. Foliage, birds,
beasts, geometric ornament
and narrative scenes are
all depicted.

Romanesque

English Norman Style: Ornament and Innovation

English architecture looked to the Continent, but also drew on its own recent past – both Anglo-Saxon and Viking – most notably for detail of ornament, such as the chevron or zigzag decoration found in the nave of Durham Cathedral (begun 1093). Richly ornamented decoration on both the interior and exterior of buildings is a particular characteristic of the period. At the beginning of the 12th century, England also witnessed a critical moment of technical innovation. Although the walls of churches were of stone, roofs were of wood because the ability to vault the vast expanse of the nave in stone eluded masons. However, by *c.* 1130 the nave of Durham Cathedral was covered by a stone rib vault. The stone interior of walls and vault was visually united for the first time and a sense of soaring space was achieved. Durham is believed to be the first church in Europe to have achieved this technical feat.

Chapter house, Bristol
A chapter house is a building for the use of clergy, attached to the main body of the church and often reached via the cloister. This vaulted example at Bristol has lavish decoration in the form of tiers of blind arcading (horizontal rows of arches) and diaper work (a repetitive surface decoration of lozenge shapes). Diaper work can also take the form of squares, stylised foliage or scales.

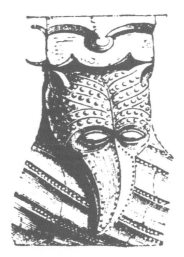

Beakhead
Stylised decoration of bird, animal or occasionally human heads biting a roll moulding is a frequently found 12th-century motif that appears to have originated in Scandinavian architecture.

Plan, Canterbury Cathedral
The plan of cathedrals was dictated by their highly controlled use. The main body of the church is typically composed from west to east of a nave, aisles, choir and choir aisles; and to north and south of transepts and small dedicated chapels for the worship of the Virgin Mary and other saints.

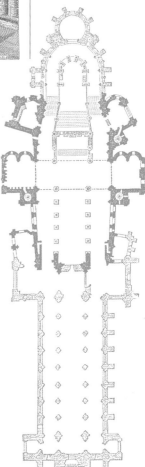

Doorway, Iffley Church (c. 1140)
Exuberant sculptural decoration characterised the late 12th century, when a full complement of motifs was found, including zigzag and sawtooth decoration on the round arch, diaperwork shafts, rosettes, quatrefoils and capitals depicting narrative scenes of both a secular and religious nature: horsemen fighting as well as Samson and the lion.

Groin vault, Gloucester Cathedral
The chamber beneath the main floor of a church is known as the crypt. This example in Gloucester Cathedral has a stone groin vault formed by the intersection of two tunnel vaults at right angles. Double chevron decoration lines the underside of the arches. Crypts are predominantly found below the east end of churches.

Stiff-leaf capital, Bloxham, Oxford
Sculptured foliage capitals were a feature of both Romanesque and Gothic decoration. The circular ring at the top of the shaft is known as a roll moulding. The formalised foliage ornament is derived from the acanthus leaf, a highly popular classical motif.

Corbel table, Romsey Church (12th century)
A projecting course of masonry, often sited just below the eaves and supported by blocks of stone, is known as a corbel table. Found on both the interior and exterior of buildings, corbels are occasionally plain, but tend to be exploited as a point for decoration. Grotesque animals and grimacing human faces are particularly favoured subjects.

Billet moulding
Regularly spaced ornament in the form of short raised squares or cylinders is known as billet moulding.

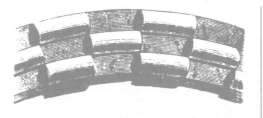

Romanesque

Italian Romanesque: Diversity

At this time, Italy was subject to the ongoing struggle for temporal supremacy waged between the Papal States and the Holy Roman Empire. Like France, it was made up of distinct regions with individual architectural styles, which assimilated the emergent styles of western Europe. Although northern regions like Lombardy saw a spate of new church building, Italy as a whole was relatively conservative and did not witness the scale of activity found in France, England and Spain. Italy's rich stylistic inheritance of antique, Byzantine and Muslim influences was exploited to the full by Romanesque architects, who continued to use diverse features, such as cupolas on raised domes, the basilical plan, separate *campaniles* and baptisteries, and the facing of exterior elevations in marble. Few of these stylistic trends are found elsewhere in Europe, except in occasional isolated examples.

Plan, S. Miniato al Monte
The basilical plan, little altered from its Roman inception, was still favoured in the majority of churches. At S. Miniato the traditional arrangement of a wide central nave with two narrow side-aisles leads to an unusually large choir raised on a platform above a vast crypt.

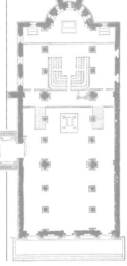

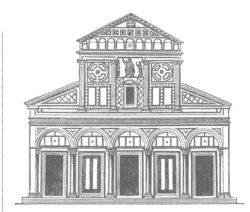

West front, S. Miniato al Monte
One of the chief characteristics of Florentine Romanesque is the use of coloured marbles, to stunning visual effect. Arranged in a coherent geometric pattern that exploits the play of light on the smooth surface of the material, this treatment has a richness and delicacy that are in decided contrast to the sculptural façades evident in northern Europe.

Cross-section, S. Miniato al Monte, Florence (begun c. 1018)
The choir-crypt beneath the main choir at S. Miniato al Monte is a relatively rare feature, occasionally found when the clergy demanded a separate choir from that used by the laity in the conventional proceedings of the Mass.

West front, St Mark's, Venice (c. 1063–96)
This monumental arched west front was erected in the 11th century but not fully decorated until the early 19th century. The third church to be built on this pivotal site, its Romanesque form of cruciform plan drew heavily on the city's Byzantine history for inspiration.

Rib vault, S. Michele

A rib vault is a framework of arched ribs built across the sides and diagonals of the vaulted area to act as a support for the roofing material – a feature of Lombardic churches.

Lombard bands, Piacenza Cathedral

Arched colonnades in the form of blind arcades, following the eaves line of screen façades, became a prominent feature of the Lombardic-Rhenish style.

East end, S. Michele, Pavia

The majority of Italian churches terminate in an apse-ended choir, which is clearly expressed as a curve on the external elevation. Decoration of the east elevation is often quite conservative in comparison to that of the highly ornamented west elevation, which serves both as the public entrance to the church and as a powerful architectural statement in celebration of the deity.

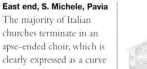

Belfry tower, S. Maria, Cosmedin

Elegant, square belfry towers attached to the church are a common feature in Lombardy. This example (found further south in Rome), does not have the soaring height of many of the Lombardic towers, being little more than 4.5 m (15 ft) square and 34 m (110 ft) high, but its banded decoration of arched niches dividing the tower into stages and its non-tapering form are highly typical.

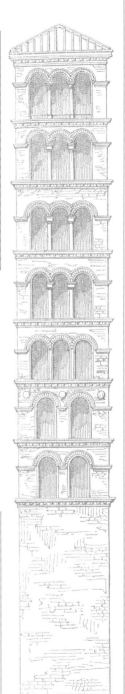

Cross-section, S. Michele (c. 1100–60)

The three-level interior elevation of bays, tribune and clerestory clearly express the strong verticality of this church. Although it features stone vaults, it has a slightly heavy feel and does not achieve the soaring quality of the finest French churches of the same date. It also has a raised choir and choir-crypt, in a similar arrangement to those at S. Miniato.

Wheel window, S. Maria, Toscanella

Circular windows in the form of a wheel are a feature found on the west front of Italian churches in the 12th and early 13th centuries. Highly wrought and decoratively fashioned, they also serve to allow light into the nave. They may exist in addition to a row of clerestory windows or function in their stead.

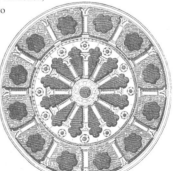

Romanesque

Italian Romanesque: Local Features

Lombardy exhibited the strongest awareness of French and German models. Its churches had broad naves and stone vaults, and often supported tall towers rising out of the main body of the church. Building campaigns in Rome were limited during this period, its conservatism being a product of the stock of extant classical buildings within its precincts. By contrast, the Tuscan cities of Florence, Lucca and Pisa all developed highly idiosyncratic local styles, which incorporated the Byzantine use of mosaics and marble with a plan form little altered from Roman models. This flourishing local Romanesque is exemplified by the ensemble of marble-faced buildings at Pisa, where *duomo*, *campanile* and baptistery sit separately but alongside one another in a grassed setting, bordered by a contemporary *camposanto* (burial ground).

Gateway, Palazzo della Ragione, Mantua
Decorated in the round-arched style, secular and religious buildings used the same stylistic vocabulary, with no clear difference between what was suitable for a church and for public buildings such as gateways.

Screen façade
Screen façades, sited at the west end and composed of huge elevations surmounted by a single broad gable, were a feature of 12th- and early 13th-century north Italian churches. This was one of two main elevational treatments found in this area – the other being the twin-towered west front of Lombardic churches.

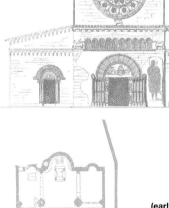

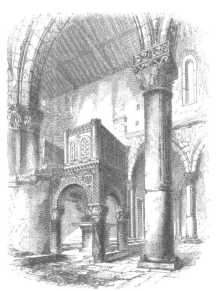

Capital, S. Maria, Toscanella
The archaeological nature of the Romanesque form is demonstrated in key stylistic motifs, often copied or adapted from earlier models. Anthemion (honeysuckle) leaf ornament, as depicted on this early 13th-century sub-Corinthian capital, originated in Greece and was one of the most enduring forms of foliage decoration.

Plan, S. Maria, Toscanella (early 13th century)
This basilica plan shows a *campanile*, or detached bell tower, situated in front of the west end of the church. *Campaniles* come in a variety of different forms. The earliest recorded one in Rome was a square 8th-century one (like this example), but circular *campaniles* such as the one constructed at Pisa (1173 onwards) are also to be found.

Columns, S. Paolo

The influence of Byzantium is seen in twisted, fluted and geometrically patterned shafts as late as the early 13th century. This round-arched cloister screen demonstrates the merging of Byzantine and Romanesque elements to create a highly elaborate and visually exciting feature. The twinned column shafts are encrusted with mosaic and look forward to the flowering of this decorative tradition in Rome, which became known as 'Cosmati work', later in the 13th century.

Cruciform plan, Pisa Cathedral (begun 1063)

The traditional cruciform or cross-shaped plan was occasionally adapted to create original plan forms for Italian churches. At Pisa the strongly projecting transepts terminate in an apse, and both the nave and choir have double aisles. The crossing is surmounted by an oval dome of Islamic origin.

Mosaic decoration, S. Paolo, Rome

Mouldings inlaid with mosaic were a feature of Rome, Venice and the southern Italian states. Geometric patterns were the most common form of decoration, although abstract and naturalistic motifs were also depicted. This early 13th-century example reveals the quality of the craftsmanship and the rich, jewel-like effect created.

Porch, S. Zeno, Verona (begun c. 1123)

Round-arched porches supported by detached columns rising from recumbent carved animals are a feature of 12th-century north Italian churches. One of the finest examples is this magnificent porch, which is exuberantly carved and sports paired lions guarding the entrance and relief sculptures depicting the months on the lintels. Saint Zeno is shown trampling the devil in the didactic sculptural decoration of the tympanum (the segmental or triangular area above a doorway enclosed by the mouldings of a pediment – often highly decorated with sculptural reliefs).

Articulation, Pisa Cathedral

The decorative treatment of the west front of Pisa Cathedral, with its four tiers of variegated colonnades and subtle interplay of dark and light marble, represents the archetypal Pisan Romanesque style. This highly articulate treatment, which has both lightness and rhythm, served as a model for imitators across southern Italy and Europe.

Gothic *mid-C.12th–c. 1530*

France: Early Gothic

The pointed arch, the ribbed vault and the flying buttress, the essential elements of Gothic architecture, had all been used in Romanesque buildings, but not together. It was their combination in France in the mid-12th century that represented the start of the style destined to dominate European architecture for the next 350 years. Increased verticality, a reduction in wall mass and the admittance of light through large windows filled with rich stained glass were the results; they were to be taken to further and further extremes as Gothic developed. Sculptural decoration initially followed late-Romanesque forms, but soon found its own momentum and by the 13th century the Gothic style had truly broken free, in form and decoration.

**West front,
Chartres Cathedral**
Dating from the mid- to late 12th century, Chartres exhibits the flanking towers and central circular (or rose) window first combined at St Denis in the 1140s. It was subsequently a much used formula for the west entrance fronts of French cathedrals.

**Pointed arch,
Abbey of Pontigny**
At the east end (chevet) of the Abbey of Pontigny the pointed arch prevails. It allowed a greater height to be achieved than did a semi-circular arch, and could be used for a rectangular as well as a square bay, thus greatly freeing planning.

**Rib vault,
Auxerre Cathedral**
In rib vaults such as this one (early 13th-century), a wooden form or support is required for the rib alone, rather than for the whole vault, thus speeding up construction and providing extra strength.

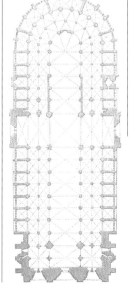

**Cathedral plan,
Notre Dame, Paris**
The plan of Notre Dame shows the patterns of the rib vaults, the diversity of bay shapes supported by them and the relative unity of the whole space.

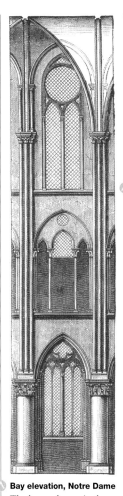

Bay elevation, Notre Dame
The base columns in the nave at Notre Dame are still massy, but are uniformly treated. Above, all is light and vertical, including the slender, elongated shafts.

Buttress niche, Rouen Cathedral
Decoration of buttresses became increasingly extravagant as Gothic developed. The top of this buttress is ornamented with a pinnacled niche containing a sculpted figure.

Flying buttress, Chartres Cathedral
The flying buttress transmits the thrust of the vault to the ground, thereby relieving the wall. As a result, this can be lighter in construction, with a greater proportion of window.

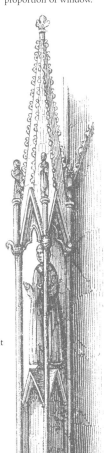

Bar tracery, Bayeux Cathedral
This window is articulated and supported by slender stone mullions (bars), rather than being divided by solid masonry, as previously. There is a profusion of cusping (*see page 211*).

Plate tracery, St Martin, Paris
Early Gothic windows are little ornamented and are pierced through the masonry, without secondary divisions – this being known as plate tracery. The grouping of individual glazed elements, as here, was to develop into bar tracery.

Rose window, Chartres Cathedral
A standard element in the west fronts and transepts of French cathedrals, the rose window is so named because of its flower-like appearance and its circular form.

Capital ornament, Reims Cathedral
This ornament at Reims is not far removed from the classical. However, unlike classical antecedents, each capital is treated differently and the foliage is freer, allowing the mason greater scope for individual expression.

West front, Notre Dame
By the early 13th century, when the west front of Notre Dame was constructed, a greater unity of effect was achieved with the same components (compare with Chartres, *opposite*). There was also richer ornamentation and the development of bar tracery.

Gothic

France: Rayonnant and Flamboyant

Two specific phases followed the Early Gothic in France: the Rayonnant (from the mid-13th century) and the Flamboyant (into the 16th century). Both are named after their distinctive tracery patterns – radiating and flame-like, respectively – and, as this suggests, changes were primarily decorative rather than structural. The Rayonnant did, however, see great heights achieved – 48 m (157 ft) at Beauvais Cathedral – and the proportion of glass to wall expanded to about as far as it could go.

Decorative profusion was added to these traits in the Flamboyant, which developed from the late 14th century and lasted into the early 16th century. Its influence was largely restricted to exteriors, although some interior fittings did break away from the relative simplicity of the Rayonnant.

Flamboyant decoration, Troyes Cathedral
The 16th-century west front of Troyes Cathedral demonstrates the somewhat leaden profusion of Flamboyant decoration, which was heavier in effect than either its French predecessor or its English contemporary – the Perpendicular.

Blind tracery, Beauvais Cathedral
The Flamboyant transept doorway at Beauvais has every element decorated, with much use of blind tracery – this having a stone rather than a glass infill.

Transitional tracery, St Ouen, Rouen
The west window at St Ouen, with its radiating inner tracery and flame-like outer tracery, demonstrates the move from Rayonnant to Flamboyant.

Lantern tower, St Ouen
A development of the Rayonnant period, the lantern tower – here over the crossing at St Ouen – throws light into the inner reaches of the church. What is not window or blind tracery (as in the parapet and pedimental heads) is openwork – that is, tracery without any infill.

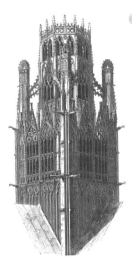

Flamboyant window, St Germain, Pont-Audemer
The flowing lines and attenuated flame-like forms of the Flamboyant are clearly visible here. The result is freedom of effect, but it lacks the cohesion of the Rayonnant and of the curvilinear tracery that had already developed in England. English curvilinear may well have been an influence on French Flamboyant.

Rayonnant window, Chartres Cathedral
The flowing tracery of this window (built later) at Chartres still has an element of control and geometric form; and stone cusping is used in much the same way as previously, albeit more profusely. There is a slenderness and verticality about the treatment of Rayonnant windows and their surrounding masonry.

Radiating tracery, St Ouen
One of the great monuments of the Rayonnant, St Ouen at Rouen (begun 1318) soars skywards. Individual, pyramidal roofs over the east-end chapels allow as much space as possible for glazing, the window heads exhibiting typical, radiating tracery.

Rood loft, Ste Madeleine, Troyes
A rare survival in France, the rood loft (here dating from the Flamboyant period) separates the nave from the chancel and provides a gallery for musicians.

Gothic

France: Domestic and Secular Gothic

Fortified towns and cities, castles, houses and administrative buildings were constructed in profusion during the Gothic period in France, and good examples survive. Form generally followed function, and external ornamentation (as on churches) was concentrated around such features as entrances, windows and buttresses. Unlike churches, however, the greatest prominence in French domestic buildings was given to staircases, which usually protruded from the façade, formed the principal entrance to the building and gave access to the different categories of rooms. The medieval French domestic layout was not, as in England, centred around the great hall.

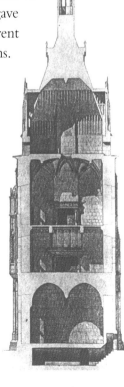

Hierarchical vaulting, Hôtel de Ville, Dreux (begun 1516)
This building is a late example of French Gothic and a particularly sophisticated one. The vault on the second floor is superior to that in the basement, reflecting the relative importance of the spaces.

Window treatment
These 13th-century windows on a house in Beauvais are treated in much the same way as they would have been on a church, but are grouped together to serve the room behind and consequently give a more horizontal effect.

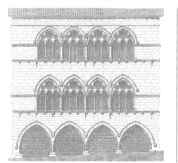

Urban façade
The three floors of this urban house are expressed by two tiers of windows and an open arcade. Further horizontality is added by the sculptural string courses (horizontal bands).

Entrance treatment, Ducal Palace, Nancy (1502–44)
The street entrance to the Ducal Palace at Nancy in Lorraine is heavily ornamented in late Flamboyant Gothic, but as well as cusping and naturalistic foliage there is also evidence of the Renaissance. This is particularly so in the upper level with its shell motif, pilasters and portrait panels.

Manor house: Château de Coulaine (15th century)
As at Jacques Coeur's town house, this manor house near Chinon has a dominant staircase tower. The corner *tourelles*, or round turrets, hark back to defensive architecture, although this was no longer a practical necessity.

Civic building: Palais de Justice, Rouen (begun 1499)
This Flamboyant civic building, like others of the period, does not so clearly express the function of its various parts on the exterior. There is a reliance on multiplication of a standard decorative unit for effect.

Domestic staircase, House of Jacques Coeur, Bourges (15th century)
The importance of the principal staircase is clear at this town house in Bourges: it protrudes into the courtyard in an octagonal tower ornamented at all levels, and is situated opposite the gatehouse.

Castle: Château de Mehun-sur-Yèvre (late 14th century)
This reconstruction of a chateau near Bourges, based on an illustration in *Les Très Riches Heures du Duc de Berry*, shows the multiple round-tower appearance of later French castles, without a separate keep. Ornamentation is concentrated above the defensive walls – in this case in the form of pinnacled, cone-roofed and multi-windowed belvederes.

Gothic

Early English Gothic: Exteriors

The early 19th-century architect Thomas Rickman was responsible for categorising English Gothic into three distinct phases: Early English, Decorated and Perpendicular. Gothic was introduced to England by a French mason, William of Sens, who began the reconstruction of Canterbury Cathedral's east end in 1174, about thirty years after the formation of the style in France. It soon gained momentum and Early English buildings (*c.* 1170–*c.* 1280) are distinct from contemporary French architecture, both in plan and detail. There is generally a more rectilinear approach, a greater division into constituent parts and a consequent lack of spatial unity.

Lancets, Oundle Church
Five lancets, without any cusping to their heads (as is typical of the Early English), are grouped together in this church window at Oundle, Northamptonshire. The masonry between has become so slender that it effectively forms tracery bars, precursing the Decorated. Above is a projecting stone band, or hood moulding, to deflect water.

Exterior elements, Beverley Minster (early 13th century)
Tall slender windows (lancets), a doorway divided by clustered shafts with a quatrefoil (four lobe-shaped curves between the cusps) in the space above, bold buttresses and the use of circular windows are common components of the Early English façade. They are seen together here.

Double transepts, Salisbury Cathedral (begun 1220)
Apart from its 14th-century tower, Salisbury Cathedral, Wiltshire, is completely Early English. Unlike Gothic churches elsewhere in Europe, transepts in England generally protrude substantially from the building and in some cases, as here, are duplicated.

Doorway, Great Milton
Most Early English doorways, like this one in Oxfordshire, are pointed. They are also often deep and can be lined with clusters of shafts – the arch above having mouldings of alternate rounds and deeply cut hollows.

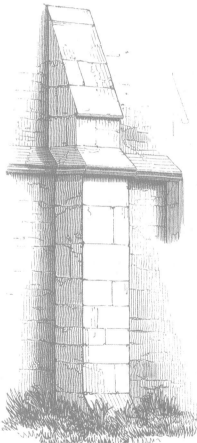

Flying buttress, Westminster Abbey
This example at Westminster Abbey, London, is sparsely ornamented, like most Early English buttresses. It rises above the parapet to a pyramidal termination, thereby forming a primitive pinnacle.

Early English ornamentation, Warmington
Where there is ornamentation, it is restrained, as here at Warmington, Northamptonshire, where a buttress is chamfered and has a simple concave moulding terminating in carved foliage.

Flat buttress, Ensham
This buttress at Ensham, Oxfordshire, which is placed directly against the wall, is as broad as it is deep, with a steeply pitched termination. It is typical of the Early English.

Gothic

Early English Gothic: Interiors

In contrast to contemporary buildings in France, Early English interiors generally have wider aisle bays and a greater tolerance of horizontal lines. The great cathedrals and churches of the period are therefore visually more flowing and actually more elongated than their French counterparts, with the eye being drawn as strongly towards the east end as skywards. Being so spread out, the interior is not treated as a whole, either in plan or in the decoration employed in the individual parts. Ornamentation is bold, relying for richness of effect on a profusion of shafts, often of Purbeck marble or some other fine stone, and on deeply cut mouldings. Decorative use of vault ribs and a concentration on surface texture later in the period was the precursor to English Decorated Gothic.

Horizontality, Lincoln Cathedral
Lincoln Cathedral (begun in 1192) is one of the masterpieces of the Early English style. Its nave, seen here, demonstrates the horizontality created by wider bays, the absence of full-height shafts and the east–west spine rib of the vault.

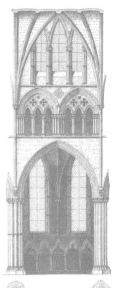

Bay, Lincoln Cathedral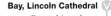
Everything about Lincoln's nave bays is broad. At the bottom is the aisle arcade, in the middle the triforium (an arcaded passage) and at the top the clerestory.

Capital ornament, Lincoln Cathedral
Bold, deeply carved leaf ornament terminates the shafts in the north transept at Lincoln. Only the bell, or main body of the capital, is ornamented, and even that can be left plain, relying for effect upon mouldings alone.

Pier shaft, Lincoln Cathedral
Early English piers, such as this one at Lincoln Cathedral, are usually decorated with a series of slender, cylindrical shafts, often constructed of Purbeck marble. They balance the deeply cut mouldings above.

Dog-tooth ornament
The Early English so-called 'dog-tooth' ornament is actually a four-petalled flower, the centre of which protrudes to form a point.

◁**Blind arcading,
Beverley Minster**
Walls of this period often have blind arcading (with a stone infill), as at Beverley Minster, where the trefoil arcade continues in front of a staircase. The shafts are of Purbeck marble and the ornament in the arches is dog-tooth.

**Nave arch,
Westminster Abbey**
The influence of France has resulted in a narrower bay, which relates to a very high and narrow nave. The shafts are of Purbeck marble and the capitals are undecorated, but the wall surface is covered with diaper work *(see below)*.

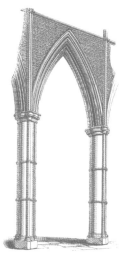

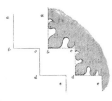

Early English moulding
Such mouldings are usually deeply cut and formed of a series of rounds and hollows. The larger rounds in this example from Shere, Surrey, are known as 'keel' mouldings, being shaped like a boat's keel; the smaller are ogee or S-shaped. They are all cut from a rectangular profile.

Diaper work
During this period, and subsequently, a series of carved, square flowers placed against each other sometimes formed an all-over decoration, known as diaper work.

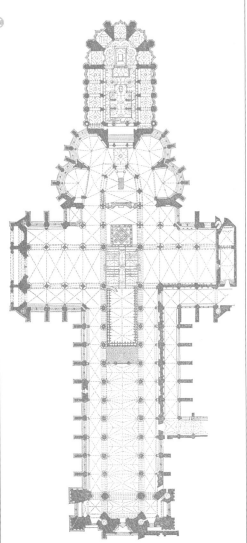

Plan, Westminster Abbey
Westminster Abbey was French-influenced in its height and in the radiating chapels at the east end, the latter being rare in England. However, it also has the typical English features of protruding transepts and a strong west–east emphasis, assisted by the ridge rib of the vault. At the far east end of the church was a projecting Lady Chapel, its site now occupied by the Chapel of Henry VII (built 1503–*c.* 1512). Connected to the church is the abbey cloister and, off the plan, the chapter house and domestic buildings.

Gothic

England: Decorated Gothic Exteriors

Decorated Gothic was dominant in England from *c.* 1290 to *c.* 1350. As its name implies, it is typified by a profusion of decoration and decorative structural forms. There is, however, considerable variety within the buildings of the period, with greater and lesser amounts of ornamentation employed and some buildings tending towards height and large areas of glazing, while others were closer to the Early English in their squat proportions and restraint. Variety is also seen in the tracery, which developed sophisticated geometric, reticulated and flowing patterns, with windows being broken up into an ever larger number of component parts.

Decorated tower, Bloxham
The tower of Bloxham church, Oxfordshire, exhibits numerous features typical of the Decorated, including the acuteness of the spire, the diagonal setting of the corner or angle buttresses and the use of much carved decoration.

Crocketed pinnacle, Bloxham
These buttresses, as was common at the time, rise above the level of most Early English examples and end in spire-like pinnacles decorated with knobbly, carved decoration known as crocketing *(see opposite)*.

Corbel table, Bloxham
When projecting stones, or corbels, supporting the masonry above them are arranged in a row, they are known as a corbel table. In this example they are set among intricate ornamentation, which is distinctly three-dimensional and accentuates the change from tower to spire.

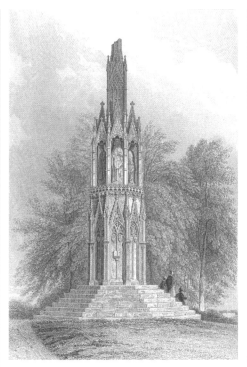

Eleanor Cross, Northampton
Some of the earliest mature Decorated work appears on the series of crosses, including this one at Northampton, erected in the 1290s to commemorate the progress of the body of Edward I's queen, Eleanor of Castile.

Ballflower ornament, Bampton

The ballflower *(above)* is characteristic of the Decorated period and is usually employed in long runs, as on the west door at Bampton *(right)*. Doorways are generally comparatively plain in their treatment and less deep than in the Early English.

Cusp, Lincoln Cathedral

These pointed projections became a common feature during the Decorated period. They are used to form the different shapes within window tracery and in other ornamentation, as here on the screen at Lincoln Cathedral.

Crocket

Projecting leaves or flowers were carved in runs to decorate the angle mouldings of spires, pinnacles and other acutely angled forms. Their use on vertical mouldings is rarer.

Curvilinear tracery, St Mary's, Cheltenham

Flowing tracery is also known as curvilinear tracery, because of its reliance on the curving line for its numerous, multi-cusped shapes, as demonstrated in this beautiful rose window.

Flowing tracery, Irthlingborough

In later Decorated windows, bars are no longer as evident in the upper part, which often reads as reticulation (a net of shapes). Tracery may comprise flowing forms, including the *mouchette* or dagger-shape, as here in Northamptonshire.

Geometrical bar tracery, Raunds

By the late 13th century mullions had become slender bars (hence bar tracery) and rose either to form a mesh in the upper window or to encompass a series of geometrical forms, as in this Northamptonshire window.

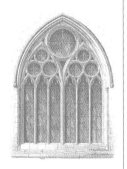

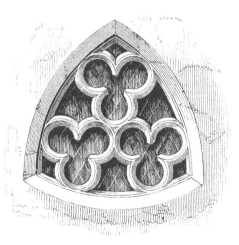

Foils, Dover

Where cusps create a near-circle they are known as foils. In this triangular window at Dover, Kent, three near-circles are conjoined to create a trefoil. Cusped forms in the 14th century were no longer necessarily individually contained within a stone circle, as had formerly been the case.

Gothic

England: Decorated Gothic Interiors

The S-shaped ogee arch is one of the most characteristic developments of the Decorated period. Although it can be seen on both exteriors and interiors, it is in the latter that most use was made of it. Ogee arches were either carved in line with the wall or, in some exuberant cases (including Ely's Lady Chapel), nodding forwards in a three-dimensional way to form a canopy (a roof-like covering). Vaults developed well beyond what was needed structurally, with subsidiary or lierne ribs being introduced for decoration and rib patterns becoming increasingly complex. Carved foliage, as on capitals, was more intricate and less stylised than previously and decoration, where employed, was richer.

Early Decorated style, Lichfield Cathedral
The nave of Lichfield Cathedral (c. 1260–80) has geometric tracery and lozenge-shaped clusters of shafts to its pillars. The stiff leaf carving and profusive use of dog-tooth moulding are conservative.

Chapter House, Wells Cathedral
The polygonal form and particularly lavish treatment of the chapter house (place of assembly for the dean and canons of the cathedral) is peculiar to England. The chapter house at Wells (early 14th century) has a vault with some thirty-six ribs rising from the central pillar.

Four-leafed flower, Ely Cathedral
At Ely Cathedral (early 14th century) there is profuse decoration to the arch and above, including the four-leafed flower ornament that spans the outer mouldings of the arch. This was popular in the Decorated and Perpendicular periods.

Flat east end, Holy Trinity, Hull
The east ends of English churches and cathedrals – unlike their continental counterparts – are usually flat, which allows a great display to be made of the east window. This one has good examples of the curving bars and multitude of cusped shapes of curvilinear tracery.

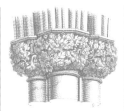

**Foliage carving,
York Minster**
Foliage carving of the
period is frequently based
on actual plants, as in
this example. The stylised,
stiff-leaf forms of the Early
English period, however,
continued in use.

**Easter sepulchre,
Stanton St John's**
A bold ogee arch with
elaborate cusping and
crocketing forms the recess
at this Oxfordshire church,
intended as a representation
of the entombment of
Christ at Easter.

**Tomb decoration,
Gloucester Cathedral**
Altar or table tombs with
recumbent figures, like
this one of Edward II, are
frequently found in the
Decorated period. Like all
significant medieval tombs,
Edward II's follows the style
of the moment and is richly
bedecked with ogees,
cusping, niches, pinnacles
and more besides.

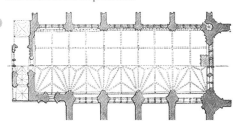

Sedilia, Grafton Underwood
Triple seats, or sedilia, set into the southern walls
of chancels were intended for the priest, his dean and
sub-dean. Sedilia were often grouped, as here, with a
piscina, a stone basin set in a niche and used for the
washing of communion or Mass vessels.

Plan, St Stephen's Chapel, Westminster
Built (1298–1348) in direct competition with the Ste-
Chapelle in Paris, this aisle-less glass box with strong
rectilinearity was the precursor to some of the great
monuments of the Perpendicular.

Timber roof, Polebrook
Where not vaulted, churches
are ceiled with a weighty
timber construction such as
this one in Northamptonshire.
It is a comparatively plain
example, others of the period
incorporating pierced tracery.

Lierne vault, St Stephen's
The crypt of St Stephen's
survives and contains
an early lierne vault, a
development of the
Decorated in which cross-
ribs that do not emanate
from the lowest (or spring)
point of the vault are
incorporated.

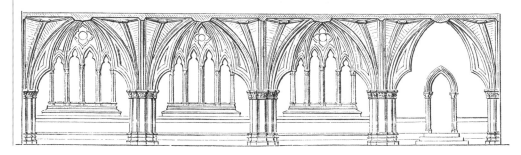

Gothic

England: Perpendicular Gothic Exteriors

The key characteristic of the Perpendicular (*c.* 1340–*c.* 1540) is the stressing of straight lines, both vertical and horizontal. Windows and wall surfaces are often divided by tracery into row upon row of rectangular panels, with vertical ribs rising through all and striking the head of the arch without being deflected (as previously). The Perpendicular is quite unlike anything else in Europe and represents the continued vibrant development of a style that was elsewhere often stale or being displaced by the Renaissance.

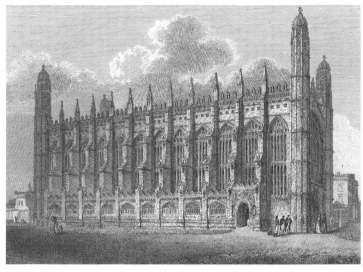

King's College Chapel, Cambridge (1446–1515)
One of the most important buildings of the Perpendicular, King's College Chapel was begun in 1446 but, because of the Wars of the Roses, not completed until 1515. Like St Stephen's Chapel, Westminster, it is in the same vein as the Ste-Chapelle in Paris, with profuse glazing and strong verticality.

Perpendicular finial
Finials are located at the apex of pointed or acutely angled elements of a building and developed at the same time as crockets.

Spandrel
The triangular space above and to either side of an arch is known as a spandrel. It was often richly carved, particularly in the Perpendicular period.

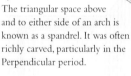

Four-centred arch, Yelvertoft
As well as rectangular panelling of the wall surface and undeflected vertical tracery bars (mullions), the north chancel window at Yelvertoft Church, Northamptonshire, exhibits another key characteristic of the Perpendicular – the four-centred arch. It is known as such because drawing it requires four different circumference centres, enabling it to be depressed in form.

Pierced parapet, Cromer
The Perpendicular saw the introduction of low-pitched roofs with parapets, often pierced, concealing the roof line from below. Such parapets were also much used on towers.

Perpendicular doorway, Kenton
Door mouldings are almost always shallow and formed into a square at the top, as here at Kenton, Devon. This emphasises the spandrels, which are ornately carved. Shafts are reduced to a minimum and there is often only one deep hollow in the jambs, here filled with four-leafed flowers.

Panel tracery, York Minster
This window in the clerestory of the choir (c. 1380–1400) at York has undeflected mullions and horizontal tracery bars (transoms), thereby – to a certain extent – forming panels. Only the central of the five principal lights has a rectangular cusped head, whereas later buildings (such as Henry VII's Chapel at Westminster Abbey and King's College Chapel, Cambridge) were to exhibit such a feature more consistently, thereby stressing the horizontal as well as the vertical.

Perpendicular buttress
There was no significant change in the basic form of buttresses in the Perpendicular period, but from the 15th century they were often panelled, in line with the treatment of other flat wall surfaces.

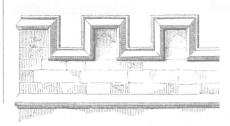

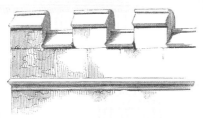

Battlements
A battlement is a notched parapet (of numerous types) at the top of a wall – the two shown here have different capping arrangements. The raised parts are known as merlons, and the indentations as embrasures. Their use as ornamentation on the transoms and bases of windows is peculiar to the English Perpendicular style.

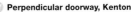

Gothic

England: Perpendicular Gothic Interiors

The earliest consistently Perpendicular interior is the chancel of Gloucester Cathedral, which was begun in 1337 and exhibits overall tracery panelling of windows and wall surfaces, and strongly vertical principal shafts rising without interruption to the complicated vault. This encompasses the main characteristics of Perpendicular interiors, which are seen at their best in the great royal foundations of the 15th and early 16th centuries, but are also evident in many parish churches. The style retained its inventiveness to the end, particularly in the treatment of roof structures.

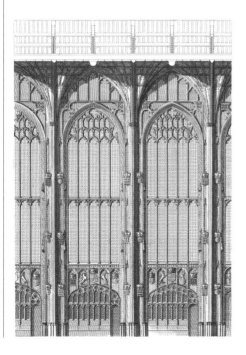

Fan vaults, King's College Chapel, Cambridge
The fan vault developed from the intricate lierne vaults of the 14th century. It is cone-shaped with an applied decoration of cusped panels. At the intersection there is often a protruding boss, and the fans may be divided by strong cross-ribs.

Dynastic architecture, King's College Chapel
The great monuments of the Perpendicular were erected by the opposing royal dynasties of the Wars of the Roses (1455–85), in part as statements of authority and solidity following periods of strife. King's College Chapel was completed by the ultimate victors, the Tudors, and is marked as their dynastic achievement by profuse heraldic carving at the west end, in contrast to the simplicity of line and flatness of the rest of the decoration. The Tudor rose and portcullis are attached to the shafts, and the King's coat of arms is carved beneath the vast windows.

Perpendicular plan, King's College Chapel
Simplicity of plan and concentration on unity of space are typical of the Perpendicular. King's College Chapel is without transepts and aisles, and there is no architectural differentiation between nave, choir and chancel.

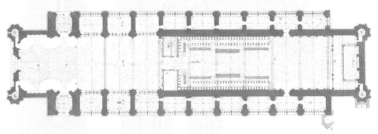

Pendant fan vault, Henry VII's Chapel
Henry VII's Chapel (1503–19) in Westminster Abbey represents the last flowering of Gothic in England and incorporates a late development, the pendant fan vault. The fans have now become complete cones, hanging down as elaborate pendants.

Square label, Rushden
A hood mould, or label, is normally associated with exteriors, to deflect water, but in the Perpendicular was also used internally to accentuate the squaring-off of openings, as in this Northamptonshire church.

Capital ornament, Christ Church, Oxford
Perpendicular capitals are often plain, but where foliage carving has been employed, it is usually stylised like this example at Christ Church, Oxford.

Hammerbeam roof, Trunch
Horizontal or hammer beams support the arching roof structure and are themselves supported by arched braces. Spaces are filled with tracery, and the ends of hammer beams can be carved with angels, as here at Trunch, Norfolk.

Cathedral Perpendicular, Winchester and Canterbury
In most cathedrals, such as Winchester (*above left*) and Canterbury (*above right*), the impact of the Perpendicular was less dramatic than it was in the royal foundations of the time. The same language was employed, but in a far more contained and conventional way, often being bound by existing structures, as well as having to accommodate more complicated liturgical requirements.

Vignette
In the Perpendicular, as in the Decorated, hollow mouldings were often carved with trailing stems and leaves, creating a continuous frieze or vignette. The carving of Perpendicular examples is normally stylised and stiff, more akin to that of the Early English than the Decorated.

Gothic

England: Early Domestic and Secular Gothic

Gothic was adopted in England for secular and domestic architecture at much the same time as it was for ecclesiastical architecture, but there are fewer surviving examples because of the changes in living and administrative requirements over time and the buildings' consequent alteration or replacement. Function governed form in most early cases, and ecclesiastical Gothic was adjusted to fit a secular context. The need for defence, however, often precluded a great display being made of windows and doors and made large areas of glazing at low levels inappropriate. An additional architectural language was needed for elements relating solely to defence or the home, including fireplaces, chimneys, kitchens and living quarters.

Manor house: Stokesay Castle (begun 1285)

The basic form of nearly all medieval English manor houses is the same and is not found elsewhere in Europe: a central great hall (demarcated here by the tall windows) flanked by the lord's rooms at one end and service rooms at the other. At Stokesay, Shropshire, there is also a defensive tower, and it originally had a moat and a curtain wall to the courtyard side.

Defensive house: Markenfield Hall (early 14th century)

At Markenfield, Yorkshire, the great hall is on the first floor to keep the windows away from the ground. Apart from these two large arched, geometric windows, the other openings were small.

Machicolation

The parapets of defensive buildings often overhang the plane of the wall to create a honeycomb of spaces through which missiles could be thrown at assailants below. These are known as machicolations.

Solar, Sutton Courtenay (c. 1330)
Located at first-floor level at the lord's
(or high) end of the great hall, the solar was
a room to which the lord and his family
could withdraw. Consequently it often has
richly treated windows and a fireplace.

Chimneys and louvres
Fires for heating and cooking required
chimneys and, in the case of open hearths,
roof louvres: lanterns open at the sides to
allow the smoke to escape. These were
often ornamented in the style of the day,
as can be seen in the examples below,
dating from the 13th and 14th centuries.

Great hall, Sutton Courtenay
The great hall was the entrance,
assembly point and eating place. At
the far, low end there was usually a
screen, beyond which lay the kitchen.

Fireplace, Aydon Castle
Most early houses had an
open hearth in the hall,
but other chambers had
fireplaces such as this
one at Aydon Castle,
Northumberland.

Spiral staircases
Internal staircases were
mostly spiral and were
located in turrets or set
into the depth of the wall.
Their narrowness assisted
defence and the clockwise
upward direction gave a
right-handed defender
the advantage.

Tower house: Langley Castle (14th century)
Where a building needed to be strongly
defensible at all times, as at Langley Castle,
Northumberland, but was not on a sufficient
scale to have outer defences, sheer walls with
minimal openings resulted.

Gargoyle
Gargoyles, a popular feature of all Gothic
architecture, are water spouts that project
from the roofing of a building. They take
the form of a grotesque figure, human or
animal, the water issuing from the
figure's open mouth.

Gothic

England: Late Domestic and Secular Gothic

From the mid-14th century there was a burgeoning of domestic and secular architecture and it is from this period that most of the Oxford and Cambridge colleges date, as well as a large number of substantial houses and essentially domestic castles. In spite of the Wars of the Roses, which were sporadic and localised, defence was no longer of paramount importance. Life was now sufficiently settled to inspire building on a greater scale and, with no further need to avoid large openings, there was more scope for display and ornamentation. Function still largely dictated external appearance, however, and it was only with the great collegiate buildings that symmetry – or, at least, balance – was achieved.

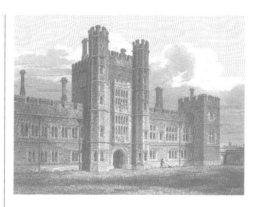

Collegiate buildings, Eton (begun 1451)
Collegiate buildings are planned around courtyards or quadrangles and have many of the essentials of the great house – the gatehouse (by now mainly for show), hall, chapel and lodging ranges. The entrance range of Eton College, Berkshire, incorporates a gatehouse.

Polygonal windows, Windsor Castle
Henry VII's alterations to Windsor Castle, Berkshire, included these complex polygonal windows, corbelled out from turrets. They demonstrate a continued inventiveness in English Gothic and are similar in concept to the contemporary windows of Henry VII's Chapel at Westminster Abbey.

Great house: Compton Wynyates (early 16th century)
The medieval domestic plan still lay at the core of the later great house, which continued to be arranged around a courtyard with a gatehouse, but was now far more outward-looking and the defences had been dropped. Battlements, towers and turrets now formed part of a wider decorative repertoire. A good example is provided by Compton Wynyates, Warwickshire, which exhibits exuberant polygonal and twisted chimneys and the use of fashionable brickwork, with diamonds (or diapers) formed out of geometrically placed, darker-coloured bricks.

Bay window, Compton Wynyates

Windows forming a bay or recess, often at the high end of the great hall and sometimes also lighting the great chamber or a parlour, were introduced during the Perpendicular period. The bay window at Compton Wynyates has typical Perpendicular wall and tracery panelling and a battlemented parapet, like many ecclesiastical examples.

Collegiate room, Divinity School, Oxford (begun 1427)

Large collegiate rooms, such as this one at Oxford, could be treated in a manner approaching that of churches. The vault (*c.* 1480), windows and blind tracery would not be out of place in a church, although the space does not have the height that one might expect in an ecclesiastical context.

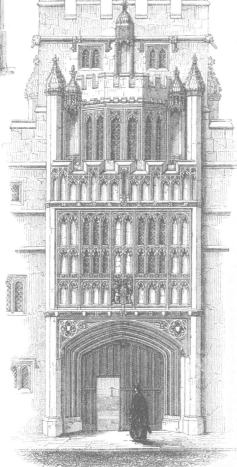

Oriel window, Vicar's Close, Wells

On one of the 14th-century buildings in the Vicar's Close at Wells is this projecting, oriel window. The term is derived from the word for a small place of prayer.

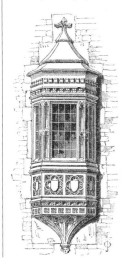

Market cross, Chichester (begun 1501)

Polygonal vaulted structures with open arches were erected in major market places to provide shelter and a meeting place. Chichester's market cross has particularly luxuriant ornamentation.

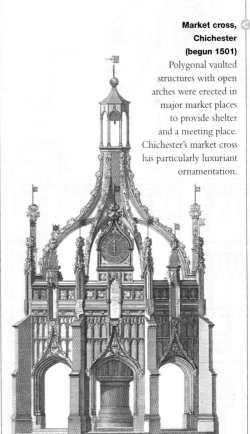

Gatehouse, Brasenose College, Oxford (1512)

The approach to significant domestic and secular buildings is through a gatehouse, which is often highly ornamented. In the case of buildings in an urban setting, as here, the gatehouse is usually formed into a tower, rising above the flanking ranges so that it can be clearly identified.

Gothic

Iberia

Spain saw the arrival of Gothic architecture in the late 12th century. By then the Moors had been driven out of most of the Iberian peninsula, and the strengthened Christian kingdoms were in a good position to devote their energies to building. Considerable French influence is seen in the early Gothic cathedrals of Spain, but a distinctly Spanish approach evolved into a confident national style, often severe and bulky on the outside while spacious and light inside. Spanish Gothic persisted well into the 16th century, invigorated by the incorporation of Islamic elements and increasingly encrusted with ornamentation – a characteristic that it shared with the late-Gothic Manueline style in Portugal.

West front, Burgos Cathedral (begun 1221)
The west front of Burgos Cathedral shows the strong influence of French Gothic, with its three doorways, rose window and flanking towers. The upper stages of the towers, including the openwork spires, are, however, 15th-century and much more distinctly Spanish. The agglomerative development of churches is a particular feature of Spanish Gothic.

Cloisters, Las Huelgas, Burgos
Arcaded and covered walks surrounding a courtyard garden constitute the cloister, which was an essential element of every monastic establishment.

Manueline style, Belém Monastery (begun 1502)
Portuguese Gothic progressed along similar lines to Spanish Gothic, until the development of an even more uncontrolled mass of ornamentation than that associated with the Isabelline style *(see opposite)*. This occurred under the patronage of King Manuel I in the late 15th and early 16th centuries and is shown on the monastery at Belém. It was an expression of the riches pouring into the Iberian peninsula from overseas.

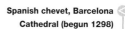

Spanish chevet, Barcelona Cathedral (begun 1298)
The chevet, or radiating east end, of the French church was developed in Spain into something far more severe. Here, chapels have been constructed between the massy buttresses needed to support the vault.

Battered walls, Medina del Campo (15th century)
The 15th century saw a series of starkly defensive castles constructed in Spain. Medina del Campo has battered or sloping curtain walls to provide greater strength, while still being difficult to scale.

Aisleless nave, Gerona Cathedral
In the 14th and 15th centuries, particularly in Catalonia, huge unimpeded ecclesiastical spaces were being created. The nave at Gerona Cathedral (begun in 1416) has a vault span that exceeded anything else in Europe at the time.

Isabelline style
The purity of early Gothic interiors was often obscured by the encrustations of ornament associated with the 15th-century Isabelline style (named after Queen Isabella). This illustration shows the east end of Toledo Cathedral.

Mudéjar style, Guadalajara Palace
This late 15th-century palace exhibits elements of the Islamic-based Mudéjar style, which formed part of the Isabelline exuberance. There are multiple-cusped arches, overall surface decoration and an intricate patterned balustrade.

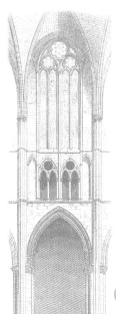

Spanish tracery, Bishop's Palace, Alcalá
The mix of European and Islamic influences created some particularly imaginative forms, such as this window tracery in the Bishop's Palace at Alcalá. The individual components are comparable to mainstream Gothic elsewhere in Europe, but their arrangement is distinctly eastern.

French influence, León Cathedral (begun 13th century)
Early Spanish Gothic buildings are hardly distinguishable from their French counterparts – this cathedral bay being close in detail to those of Reims and Amiens. In the extensive windows at León much use was made of stained glass.

Gothic

Northern and Central Europe

In the Middle Ages much of northern and central Europe lay within the bounds of the Holy Roman Empire, or (in the case of the Low Countries) under the control of the Germanic archdiocese of Cologne. There was initially a reluctance in these lands to allow Gothic to displace the Romanesque, and the first true examples of Gothic there are not to be found until the mid-13th century, long after the wholehearted adoption of the style in France, England and Spain. Thereafter, however, it quickly took a hold, developing a vibrancy and individualism of form that resulted in some of the finest examples of late-Gothic work in Europe.

Double quatrefoil, Cologne Cathedral
The Rayonnant is clearly evident in the tracery at Cologne, but already there are signs of individualism, as in this window, whose complicated cusping creates a double quatrefoil out of three conjoined trefoils. This gives a less rigid effect than is found in contemporary French tracery.

West front, Cologne Cathedral
Constructed in the 19th century, but to late 13th-century designs, the west front is – like the rest of the cathedral and much early Germanic Gothic – predominantly French Rayonnant in form.

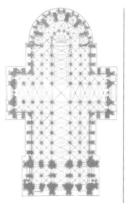

Early Gothic plan, Cologne Cathedral
With its radiating east-end chapels, modestly protruding transepts and simplicity of vault patterns, the plan of Cologne Cathedral – like the façade – differs little from contemporary French models.

Vineleaf capital, Cologne Cathedral
The early Gothic of northern and central Europe saw some particularly fine naturalistic carving, as in this example from Cologne Cathedral.

Late Gothic capital, Frauenkirche, Esslingen
This capital is typical of late-Gothic fluidity, both in terms of its foliage carving and in the extraordinary twisting star vaults of the late 15th century.

Scandinavian Gothic, Sandeo

Although much influenced by Germany, France and England, Scandinavian Gothic had its own identity, as shown in the imaginative ogee and circular cusping on this doorway at Sandeo, Sweden.

Cloth Hall, Ypres (14th century)

The cloth hall at Ypres is one of a number of such buildings in the Low Countries associated with the prosperous trading status of the area at the time. Corner towers or turrets and a central belfry tower are common components.

Sondergotik, St Barbara, Kutna Hora (begun 1388)

The late-Gothic style of south Germany and Bohemia – known as the *Sondergotik* – owed much to the Parler family of mason-architects. They were involved in numerous major commissions of the 14th to 16th centuries, including St Barbara at Kutna Hora, Bohemia, with its mass of pinnacled flying buttresses.

Domestic architecture, Bruck-am-Mur

Inventiveness and fluidity of form in *Sondergotik* can be seen in this 16th-century Austrian house at Bruck-am-Mur. The balustrade is, in part, carved to appear as if made of wood.

Secular architecture, Marienburg Castle

Buttresses, square-headed windows, fin-like machicolations (projecting parapets – *see page 218*), and battlements with panel decoration make up the façade of Marienburg Castle's knight-hall, one of the most impressive secular buildings of the Middle Ages in Germany.

Gothic

Italy

As well as being the most short-lived of all the Gothic styles of Europe (lasting for just 200 years from the mid-13th century), Italian Gothic was also the most hesitant. The attenuated verticality of France and elsewhere was only rarely achieved and does not seem to have been particularly desired; and Romanesque forms lingered in combination with the Gothic. The flying buttress was generally eschewed and the artist, as much as the mason, was responsible for the overall impact of façades and interiors. For secular buildings, the Gothic language was more enthusiastically embraced, particularly for the numerous balconies and arcades so suited to the benign Mediterranean climate.

West front, Orvieto Cathedral (14th century)
Whereas the west fronts of most Gothic cathedrals are a riot of sculpted and structural masonry, the pinnacles, pointed arches and mouldings of Italian examples are often merely a frame for the artist. At Orvieto Cathedral the generous pediments and spandrels are filled with colourful mosaics, and the overall impression is of a giant painted altarpiece, rather than a rockface of sculpture.

Italian tracery
There is less emphasis on glazing in Italian churches, both because of the climate and due to a desire to preserve as much internal wall space as possible for fresco-painting. This 13th-century example has comparatively little glazing in the upper part.

Survival of Romanesque forms, Cremona Cathedral
Domes remained popular throughout the Gothic period in Italy and the round arch was never entirely displaced by the pointed, as shown by this window at Cremona Cathedral. There is also evidence here of the influence of the East, resulting from Italy's exposure to the Islamic world through trade links.

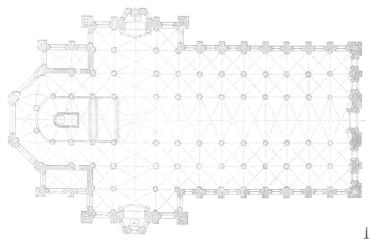

Italian Gothic plan, Milan Cathedral (begun 1386)
Even where side-aisles exist, as here, the body of the Italian church is usually treated as one area, with broadly spaced arcades and a wide central aisle. Milan Cathedral was built on a vast scale and is closer than any other church in Italy to fully embracing the Gothic.

Dentil moulding
One particular development of Venetian Gothic is a curious form of staggered dentil moulding, which is commonly employed around openings. Here, the incongruous juxtaposition of a near-classical column with Gothic tracery is tied together by the moulding.

Striation, S. Anastasia, Verona
Bands of alternating coloured stone or marble, creating a striation, are common in Italian Gothic, as here at S. Anastasia, Verona. Striation is one of a number of features that keep the architecture more horizontal than it was elsewhere in Europe at the time.

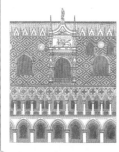

Balconies, Doge's Palace, Venice
Tracery patterns were much used for the balconies and arcades of secular buildings including the most famous of them all, the Doge's Palace in Venice.

Campanile, Verona
Detached bell towers – *campanili* – are a particular feature of Italian architecture. They continued to be built in much the same square, untapering form as previously. It is only in their detailing that they are distinguishable as Gothic, as is this example in Verona.

Capital
Italian Gothic capitals are usually ornamented with foliage carving, rather than being left plain, and are associated with single shafts or columns rather than with clusters. They thus lack the variety of other European examples and have more in common with foliate classical forms.

Renaissance *early C.15th–c. 1630*

Early Renaissance Architecture in Florence

Renaissance architecture in Italy is characterised by harmony, clarity and strength. It features the use of classical motifs and the architectural orders, or column styles, of antiquity. Yet the reappearance of classically inspired architecture in 15th-century Italy, and most particularly in Florence, where it had its first flowering, did not signal a sudden break with Gothic or indeed earlier Romanesque styles. New architecture sometimes included design elements from significant local buildings, linking old and new with ideas of continuity and civic pride. The new style was fully bound up with Renaissance interest in aspects of antiquity, such as literature, philosophy and mathematics. Rulers and patrons realised the importance of both architecture and urban planning as means of promoting notions of an ordered society.

Florence Cathedral Dome (15th century)

This huge dome (*duomo*) has become symbolic not only of Renaissance Florence but also, in broader terms, of the revival of structural and engineering skills, which some contemporary authors compared to the achievements of the ancients. When built in the early 15th century, it was the largest dome to have been built since antiquity.

Lantern, Florence Cathedral

The polyhedral cupola (small dome surmounted by a lantern) of Florence Cathedral has a Gothic profile, but elegant classical forms appear in the lantern, or windowed superstructure, which provides the dome's massive balancing force. The *all'antica* vocabulary of fluted Corinthian pilasters, bold volutes (scrolls) and shell niches, and the use of stone, makes the lantern one of the first examples of classically inspired Renaissance architecture.

Arcade, Piazza S. Maria Novella, Florence (1490s)

Filippo Brunelleschi, architect of the cathedral's dome, used rhythmic arcades of Corinthian columns and semi-circular arches in several buildings. They were much emulated by other architects, as here in Piazza S. Maria Novella. The clarity and symmetry of these early arcades were in striking contrast to the city's medieval fabric.

Revival and quotation

Revival of forms and the quotation of earlier motifs were important ideas in Italian Renaissance architecture. These are exemplified in Leon Battista Alberti's chapel for a wealthy Florentine family. As a local reference, the exterior is decorated with inlaid marble work, a skilled Tuscan technique.

Inscribed frieze

In the Rucellai chapel in Florence there is reference to a Roman precedent, as the commemorative frieze is inscribed in antique Roman lettering based on forms found on an Early Christian tomb. By making such direct citations, both patron and architect associated themselves with Renaissance ideas and erudition of the time.

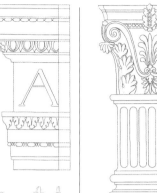

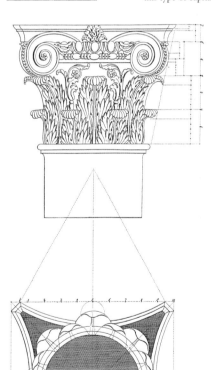

Variation of forms

The Early Renaissance use of the architectural orders was not a slavish copying of antique examples. Renaissance architects' knowledge of the Greek Corinthian order came mainly from its form as developed in Roman buildings. Innovative use of the defining elements of acanthus leaves and corner volutes produced numerous Renaissance variations of this type of capital.

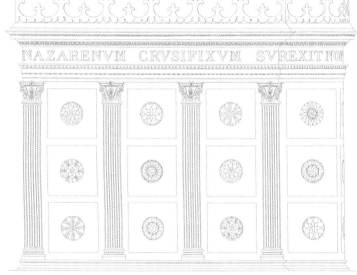

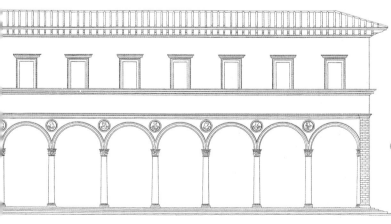

Composite capital

In his architectural treatise, *De re aedificatoria*, Alberti made the first mention in literature of a separate Italian architectural order, which he called 'italic'. It was subsequently known as the Composite order, as it included Corinthian acanthus leaves and Ionic volutes.

Renaissance

Ecclesiastical Architecture of the Early Italian Renaissance

Two major types of church building were developed in the Early Renaissance and both traced their evolution from ancient building forms and through Early Christian models. These types were the basilican form and a number of variations on a regular centrally planned church or chapel. The central plan tended to be used for small spaces and was particularly associated, from antiquity, with mausolea and martyria. The basilica plan was based on the Constantinian longitudinal churches, which in turn had developed from Roman meeting halls. Two major architects of the early Renaissance were commissioned to build both types of church, and their use of the revived classical language makes informative comparison.

Interior
Basilica-type churches typically have one or two aisles on either side of the nave, and these are usually lower in height than the central space. Brunelleschi separated the nave and aisles in his churches with tall Corinthian arcades supporting round-headed arches, with clerestory windows lighting the nave.

Modular basilica plan
Filippo Brunelleschi developed a basilica design with an underlying modular plan in which the square of the crossing was the module repeated to make a Latin cross. From the crossing, four modules create the nave, one creates the chancel, and one on either side of the crossing form the transepts. A quarter division of the module forms the aisle bays. It was an innovation to have such a rational and strictly measured design.

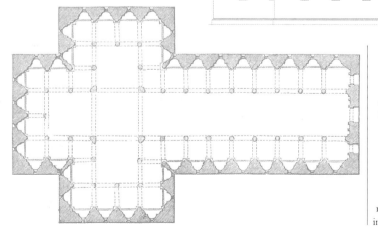

Rational planning
The innovation of Brunelleschi's architecture was not solely linked to his revival of classical motifs and his pared-down simplicity of form. It was also due to the highly rational nature of his architecture, in which interior and exterior forms were closely related, and to his attention to strict measurement and proportion in plan, elevation and volume.

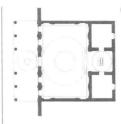

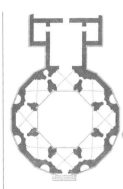

**S. Andrea, Mantua
(begun 1470)**
The architect and theorist
Leon Battista Alberti
designed this basilican
church, although much of
it was built after his death.
His basilica plan replaces
side-aisles with large
chapels off the nave and
smaller chapels within the
giant nave piers.

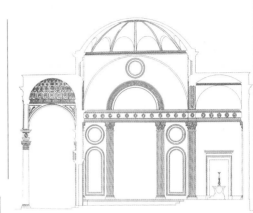

Centrally planned chapel
Centrally planned
structures were normally
based on regular-sided
polygons, circles or
squares. These geometrical
forms carry underlying
connotations of
perfection and were later
recommended by Alberti
as ideal temple forms.

Polygonal plan
Brunelleschi experimented
with centrally planned
designs, such as this oratory
chapel where he interlocked
two complex polygons.

Roman form
By contrast with Brunelleschi's elegant
interpretation of classical motifs,
Alberti translated his considerable
first-hand knowledge of
ancient Rome through
more monumental forms.
S. Andrea's vast coffered
barrel vault supported
by huge piers is
reminiscent of massive
Roman bath structures.

Pazzi Chapel, Florence
A feature of Brunelleschi's work, which was
emulated by a number of Florentine and
Tuscan architects, was his decorative restraint,
here exemplified by a section through the
Pazzi Chapel, Florence. He favoured white
stucco, with the classical architectural detailing
(columns, pilasters, roundels, brackets) carved
in local grey stone, *pietra serena*.

Temple façade, Mantua
At S. Andrea, Alberti sought a fitting solution
to front a Renaissance church. He chose four giant
pilasters supporting a triangular pediment, which
gives the effect of a portico, while elements of
a triumphal arch are introduced by the deep barrel-
vaulted entrance. In his writing on the ideal town,
Alberti stated that the temple should be the
most beautiful building, something he aims
for in Mantua with this striking façade.

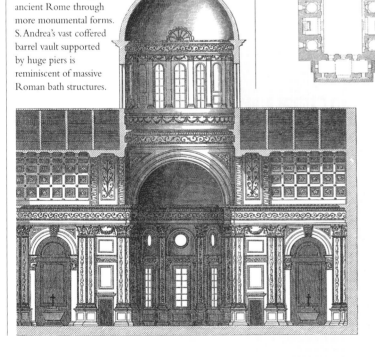

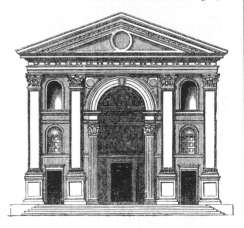

Renaissance

Florentine Renaissance Palaces

Italian medieval palaces presented defensible and rugged exteriors, but within the political and cultural climate of 15th-century Florence a new form of domestic architecture was required to complement the perceived elegance of Renaissance life. The Renaissance palace developed from influential early examples, particularly Michelozzo di Bartolommeo's Florentine palace for the powerful Medici family. Usually on three well-defined storeys, and often built round an inner courtyard, these buildings became the power bases of important dynasties, in which families supported their ambitions within the readable architecture of power and wealth.

Courtyard, Palazzo Medici

Enclosed courtyards were both functional and elegant, providing light to inner facing windows. Typically, a courtyard (cortile) was surrounded with arcades of vaulted bays, supported on colonnades and brackets. They could also be used to display sculpture and for taking the air under shaded walkways. Ground-floor rooms off courtyards were used mainly for business or for service rooms and storage. Many early Florentine palaces included the *bifora* (two-leaf) window (*left*), which was derived from local medieval buildings.

Façade, Palazzo Medici, Florence (begun 1444)

Wealthy merchants and princes sought significant and prominent sites for their palaces. In the manner of the Palazzo Medici, palaces characteristically consisted of three storeys of expensively dressed stone, built on island sites or bold corner plots. Italian Renaissance palaces featured a far greater number of windows than medieval palaces, giving much lighter rooms, especially on the top two storeys. Although harmonious and regular in exterior disposition, this façade features few classical motifs, apart from the huge overhanging cornice.

Interior arrangement ◁

The main living areas of palaces were on the first floor or *piano nobile*, while the upper storey was often for the use of minor family members and children. The hierarchy of each floor's use was signalled from the palace exterior, where the rough blocks of rustication of the lower level gave way to the smoothly dressed stone of the upper levels.

Use of the orders,
Palazzo Rucellai, Florence ▽

The use of pilaster orders to articulate a palace façade was first used by Alberti on the Palazzo Rucellai. A Doric order at ground level, and two Corinthian orders above, each support an entablature separating the storeys.

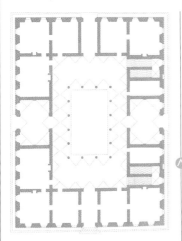

Plan, Palazzo Strozzi (designed 1489/90)

The Palazzo Strozzi was constructed on a vast island site around a rectangular courtyard. As shown on its ground plan, stairways were usually wide and practical, but they did not constitute a major design feature in early Renaissance palaces.

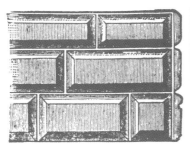

Rustication

The use of large, stone blocks on the ground floor of palaces visually anchors the buildings and gives an impression of great strength and solidity. Sometimes formed into cushioned blocks and sometimes rough-hewn, the stone can be prominently jointed to enhance its texture further. An extremely costly feature, the use of stone rustication emphasised the patron's wealth and status.

Renaissance

Variations on the Classical Vocabulary

In any language there are regional variations, and this is true of the architectural language of Renaissance Italy. Architectural styles are major factors in defining a region's autonomy and, in cities like Venice, new buildings still reflected strong local traditions although the classical vocabulary was introduced as well. Brick was widely used as a building material in northern Italy and many buildings continued to be covered by tiles, marble and sculptural panels, which made the underlying classical forms less easy to read. Nonetheless, by the 16th century there were examples of classically inspired High Renaissance buildings in many parts of Italy.

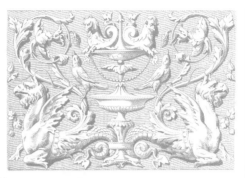

Relief ornamentation
Rich and highly decorated sculptural reliefs are a long-established form of decoration, particularly in Lombardy and Tuscany. Such ornamental work, much used for internal decoration, characteristically includes consciously classicising motifs of fantastic beasts, swirling foliage and urns, in emulation of Roman relief sculpture.

Pilaster
Pilasters, shallow piers with rectangular profiles, are decorative and have no structural purpose. Decoration could be achieved in marble, stucco or paint.

Inlaid marble
Venice's reflective waters enhance the visual effects of its traditionally lavish and colourful façades. The late 15th-century church of Sta Maria dei Miracoli exemplifies the use of the classical with the local style. The two-storeyed exterior is precisely articulated by Corinthian and Ionic pilaster orders, while the walls are encrusted with costly coloured marble decoration.

Venetian palace
Typically L-shaped in plan, Venetian palaces usually had quite narrow façades fronting a deep building. The Palazzo Loredan of the early 16th century, in common with other Venetian Renaissance palaces, has a strong classical framework with added Venetian exuberance. Its three storeys topped by a heavy cornice all feature the decorative Corinthian order, encasing *bifora* windows featuring large amounts of glazing, manufactured by the local glass-making industry.

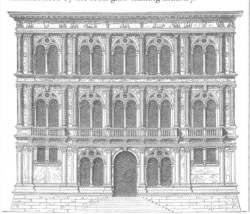

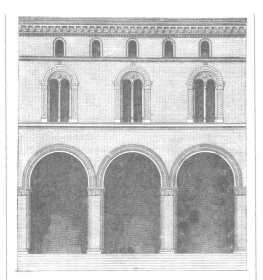

Brick and terracotta

Several northern Italian provinces had a long history of brick-making, and classical forms were adapted to the possibilities of this material. Renaissance palaces such as the Palazzo Fava (1480s) in Bologna blend local features like street arcading and a narrow upper storey, with bold round-headed piers, string courses (continuous moulded horizontal bands) and a large cornice. Delicate terracotta decoration around windows and cornices was a local feature.

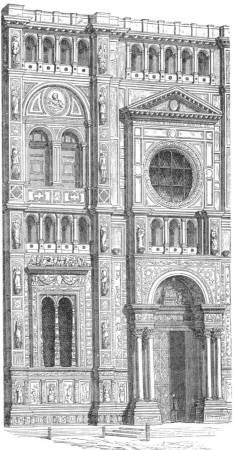

Architectural allusions

Many buildings of the Renaissance include specific references to important earlier buildings. In Venice, for instance, Gothic tracery from the Doge's Palace was replicated in a Renaissance palace; and here, in the Scuola Grande di San Marco (1480s/90s), the domed roof of St Mark's Basilica is alluded to in the arched tympanums of the skyline.

Use of colour

It is not just the amount of decoration that was a feature of much northern Italian architecture, but also the colour that was achieved through the use of different materials. Buildings such as the Certosa (1429–73) in Pavia were literally encrusted with decoration in black, green and white marble, and in red porphyry – materials with strong antique associations.

Overall decoration

Although some individual classical elements can be read clearly in isolation, details like niches, capitals and brackets tend to become subsumed in the overall decoration of some northern Italian architecture.

Renaissance

Ecclesiastical Architecture in 16th-century Italy

From the early 16th century the main centre for architectural innovation in Italy was Rome. The re-establishment of the papal court there, and the urgent need to restructure the dilapidated city, provided the stimulus for commissions from popes, cardinals and new religious orders. Architecture was a powerful tool with which the Catholic Church could emphasise confidence following the Catholic Reformation, and important examples of the main church types, both longitudinal and centrally planned, were built in the 16th century. These designs responded to changing liturgical and functional requirements. With architects studying the antiquities of Rome at first hand, and new buildings by Donato Bramante and others, the architectural language of the High Renaissance became more monumental and considered.

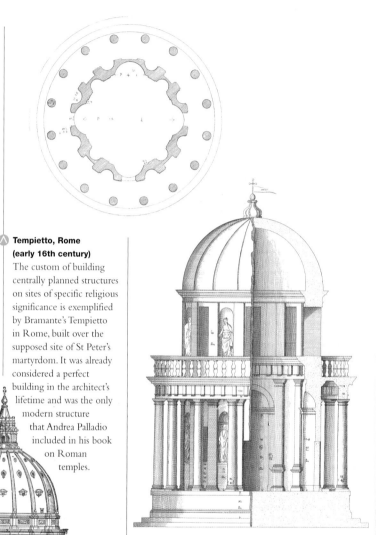

Tempietto, Rome (early 16th century)
The custom of building centrally planned structures on sites of specific religious significance is exemplified by Bramante's Tempietto in Rome, built over the supposed site of St Peter's martyrdom. It was already considered a perfect building in the architect's lifetime and was the only modern structure that Andrea Palladio included in his book on Roman temples.

St Peter's Basilica, Rome
Rebuilding St Peter's spanned the 16th and part of the 17th century. Bramante's crossing piers set the scale of the church, although the final decision to make it longitudinal was not taken until 1605. The articulation of the liturgical east end was by Michelangelo, who built a giant order of Corinthian pilasters supporting a massive attic storey.

Temple form
Bramante chose to reinterpret the circular temple form for the Tempietto, constructing a peristyle, or colonnade, around a central *cella,* or sanctuary. A hemispherical dome covers the interior, as in the Pantheon, but here it is raised on a tall drum. Apart from choosing the masculine Doric order as appropriate for a building dedicated to St Peter, Bramante also included emblems of the papacy on the metopes, or square panels, of the frieze.

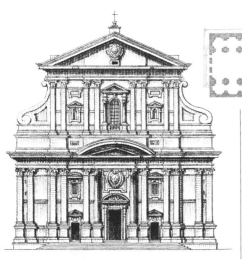

Redentore, Venice (begun 1577)

Andrea Palladio's contribution to ecclesiastical architecture was characteristically impressive. His efforts to find an appropriate solution for a church façade resulted in designs with interlocking pedimented temple fronts with engaged columns and pilasters. The interiors of his Venetian churches, lit by large 'thermal' (Diocletian) windows, feature columnar screens behind the high altar, which separate the monastic choir from the main body of the church.

The Gesù, Rome (begun 1568)

Recently formed religious orders were major architectural patrons, as they required a new type of church for reformed religious practice. The Jesuits' mother church of the Gesù proved an influential model since it seemed to embody the architectural requirements codified after the Council of Trent (this included a wide nave and side chapels). Its two-storeyed pedimented façade was much emulated.

S. Andrea in Via Flaminia, Rome (1550–53)

Renaissance buildings inspired by celebrated precedents sometimes proved highly innovative in their own right. For example, the small commemorative church of S. Andrea in Via Flaminia clearly alludes visually to the Pantheon, but the architect Giacomo Barozzi da Vignola experimented with the design, placing an oval dome carried on pendentives above the rectangular interior space.

S. Maria della Consolazione, Todi (begun 1508)

The search for an ideal centralised design exercised architects throughout the Renaissance. The pilgrimage church at Todi embodies several features of Alberti's theoretical ideal. It stands prominently on an open site and incorporates a circle, square and semi-circle within a regular centralised form.

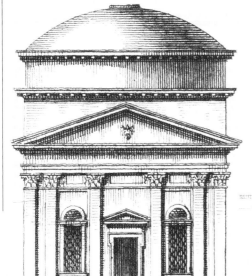

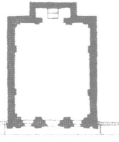

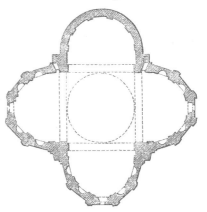

Renaissance

Architectural Expressions of Power and Prestige

During the 16th century, architects used the classical vocabulary with greater assurance and clarity. Authors had codified the use of the orders and expounded on architectural theory. There was much more attention to urban planning and cities were embellished with majestic civic and private buildings. Cities and individuals projected their power through the grandeur of new buildings, and the classical language they used carried within its forms connotations of civilisation, order and authority.

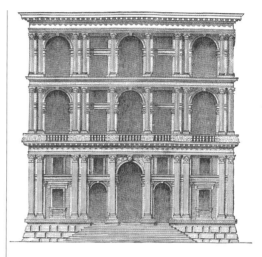

Palazzo Farnese, Rome (16th century)
Impressive palace architecture in many cities was often still based on the Florentine model of the three-storeyed block with a central courtyard. The Palazzo Farnese exemplifies 16th-century developments of this building type. Here, pedimented tabernacle windows replace the medieval *bifora* style, walls are treated uniformly and the main entrance is emphasised with massive stone voussoirs, or wedge-shaped stones.

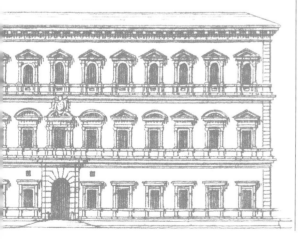

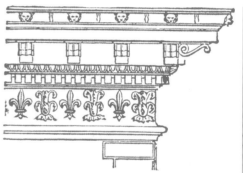

Entablature, Palazzo Farnese
Individuals sought not only to embellish their cities, but also to express their own status through architecture. Ownership and patronage were proclaimed through prominent display of coats of arms and family devices. On this huge entablature, the Farnese emblems are used to decorate the frieze below the dentils – the band of square, tooth-like blocks.

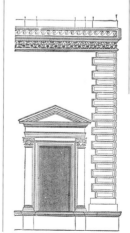

Venetian palace
The fundamental design of Venetian palaces changed little during the 16th century, but architects embraced a confident classical idiom for façades, which reflected the Venetian love of exuberance and texture. This could be achieved using the decorative Corinthian order, fluted shafts and paired columns.

Library, Venice (begun 1537)
The remodelling of St Mark's Square in Venice by Jacopo Sansovino was one of the most significant Renaissance urban-planning projects. The Library is a model in the controlled, sophisticated use of classical vocabulary.

Quoins, Palazzo Farnese
Stone quoins dress and frame the corners of buildings. They can also provide a prominent design feature, as here at the Palazzo Farnese, where they contrast with the planar walls and boldly delimit the vast free-standing block.

Palazzo Chiericati, Vicenza (begun 1554)

Grandeur of design sometimes belies the size of a building. The symmetrical and compact plan of buildings like the Palazzo Chiericati in Vicenza maximised available space. Here, conspicuous trabeation with clearly defined classical elements creates an elegant façade.

Basilica, Vicenza (begun 1549)

The city of Vicenza, although under the dominion of the Venetian Republic, exerted its communal pride through the building of impressive civic architecture. Andrea Palladio literally encased the old medieval town hall with a double loggia, with balconies on the upper level. Palladio himself called the building the 'Basilica', consciously linking it with public buildings of antiquity.

Palladian motif, Basilica, Vicenza

The Palladian motif refers to the use of arches and columns to provide an opening where the entablature can form a lintel to create further side-openings. Although visually the arches at the Basilica look regularly spaced, in fact Palladio was able to vary the width of the side-openings to accommodate the medieval building behind.

Palladian domestic architecture

Palladio made use of long vistas and space in his villa designs, but the restricted views and narrow streets of town architecture required bolder solutions. Massive rustication, paired columns with projecting entablatures and sculptural skylines all demanded attention from the viewer.

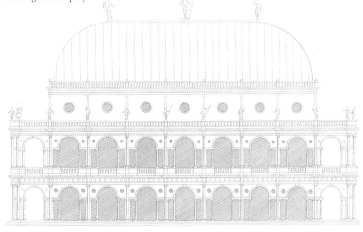

Renaissance

Villas and Gardens

Villas, landscapes and gardens have connotations of pleasure and leisure, and these ideas were important in the Renaissance when the pursuit of contemplative tranquillity in the countryside was seen as a counter-balance to the heat and bustle of an active town life. Many important families, princes and cardinals sought to create idyllic retreats. These ranged from large villas, sometimes set in productive farming estates, to the smaller *villa suburbana,* often located in vineyards and gardens a short distance from the city. Renaissance scholars and patrons gained most of their knowledge of antique villas from ancient texts and literary sources, and in 16th-century Rome there was great interest in trying to establish how ancient houses were planned and how they had functioned.

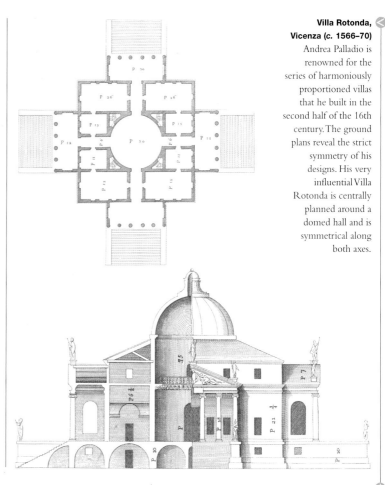

Villa Rotonda, Vicenza (c. 1566–70)
Andrea Palladio is renowned for the series of harmoniously proportioned villas that he built in the second half of the 16th century. The ground plans reveal the strict symmetry of his designs. His very influential Villa Rotonda is centrally planned around a domed hall and is symmetrical along both axes.

The villa suburbana
Suburban villas, like the Villa Rotonda, were not generally used for long summer sojourns, but for dining and entertainments. Most rooms were multi-functional and their use was varied to take account of the weather and season. Service rooms were typically on ground level, which served also to raise the main rooms to take advantage of the views. The main floor of the Villa Rotonda is reached via four identical pedimented porticoes.

Siting of villas
The choice of site for a villa was important for both practical and aesthetic reasons. A hillside or raised site was preferred, and views of rivers and lakes were particularly sought-after. Natural springs, such as the one at Palladio's Villa Barbaro at Maser (1577–78), could serve both garden and household use.

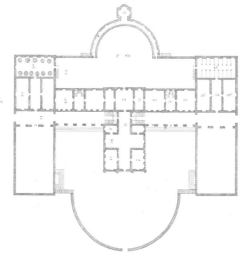

Villa Giulia, Rome (mid-16th century)

Water in Renaissance gardens was important for its aural and visual qualities. The gushing, trickling and splashing of water features added to the notion of delight and surprise. At the Villa Giulia, for example, a nymphaeum and grotto, with river gods, had to be sought like a hidden garden, via curving staircases.

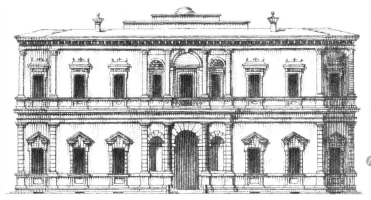

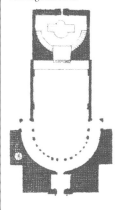

Façade, Villa Giulia

Several popes chose to locate their villas in the cool hillside sites beyond the walls of Rome. Pope Julius III's Villa Giulia has a palace-like external façade. Two-storeyed, with a Tuscan and Composite order, this more formal architectural language contrasts with the frescoed portico and delicate stucco of the garden side.

Gateway and entrance

Conspicuous gateways delimited important gardens and estates. Bold, well-defined stonework, rustication and fantastic forms all found a setting in garden architecture.

Entertainment space

Terraces and gardens of villas and palaces supplied the stage setting for spectacular entertainments. The perfume of fragrant shrubs, the sound of water and the visual effects of vistas and sculpture all added to their appeal.

Villa Barbaro, Maser

Palladio built several villas in the Veneto as the focus of large agricultural estates and they broadly conform to a design that features a main central block fronted by a columnar pedimented portico and flanked by wings of farm buildings. Bold classical elements, like giant orders and temple fronts, are used to define the family domain, while simple piers form the arcaded wings.

Terrace, balcony and belvedere

Raised balconies and terraces were built to take advantage of the finest views. Towers or belvederes, which had open aspects on all sides, were also characteristic of many villas.

Renaissance

Royal Chateaux of 16th-century France

The language and style of Italian Renaissance architecture were quite slow to spread outside the Italian city states. Gothic architecture continued to be common in France, Spain and Northern Europe throughout the 15th century. Knowledge and interest in classically inspired Italian buildings began to be disseminated by travellers returning from Italy, and by Italian architects and craftsmen working outside their own country. François I and his son, Henri II, were acutely aware of the inherent power of cultural, as well as political domination and both monarchs engaged in ambitious and spectacular building programmes.

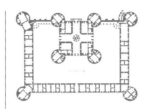

Plan, Chambord
While the ground plan of Chambord displays strict Renaissance symmetry, the corner towers are reminiscent of the defensive architecture of medieval castles.

Appartement, Chambord
An increasingly important feature of French palace architecture, the suite of rooms, or *appartement*, featured probably for the first time at Chambord, where corridors lead to them from the central staircase.

Château de Chambord, Loire (begun 1519)
The architecture of Renaissance France did not simply replicate Italian examples for, although an Italianate classical language was often employed, a distinctively French style evolved. Many buildings display mixtures of forms. At Chambord the lower storeys are articulated by pilasters and superimposed arcuated loggias. Above the large cornice and balustrade, however, is a lively skyline of turrets and high-pitched roofs, associated with the earlier French building tradition.

Central staircase, Chambord

The famous double-corkscrew staircase at Chambord was possibly based on the drawings by Leonardo da Vinci. Palladio was impressed by its novelty, beauty and practicality and included it in his chapter on stairs in Book I of *I quattro libri dell'architettura*.

Staircase, Château de Blois, Loire

Staircases were given more importance in French architecture of the 16th century than was usually the case in Italian palaces of the same period. There was a tradition of spiral staircases in France from the 15th century, and the large, open stone staircase built at the Château de Blois (1515–24) for François I continues this tradition, albeit with elements of classical decorative language.

Classical decoration

Tall chimneys appear in many French buildings and were often given applied ornamentation and features that would not conventionally be used high on buildings or roofs. These two chimneys terminate in sarcophagus-like elements, with scrolls, pilasters and egg-and-dart decoration.

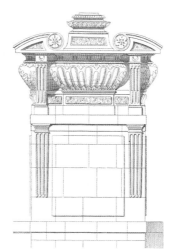

Renaissance

Architectural Language in France

France responded to the Italian classical style in a more direct and thorough manner than other European countries, although at times classical forms still featured only as decorative motifs. Not only was France's proximity to Italy a significant factor in the transmission of knowledge of new buildings, but information also spread in France through architectural engravings, drawings and treatises. Sebastiano Serlio, an Italian architect with first-hand knowledge of the architectural environment of Bramante and Raphael in Rome, was among several Italian artists and humanists whom François I called to his court. Serlio's *L'architettura*, the first modern treatise to include illustrations, proved highly significant in disseminating knowledge of Italian High Renaissance forms.

▲ Interior decoration, Fontainebleau
François I called many Italian artists to France and several were responsible for the sumptuous interiors of Fontainebleau. The distinctive style that evolved used painting, stucco and sculptural effects within an architectural framework of orders, lunettes and friezes.

▼ Tomb sculpture
The architectural structure of many large-scale Renaissance tombs employed a distinctly classical vocabulary, although sometimes the placing and carving of effigies reflected the medieval tradition. Several French royal tombs were made by Italian sculptors, such as the tomb built for Louis XII, which features an arcuated canopy with richly decorated Corinthian pilasters, a wide frieze and a projecting cornice.

▼ Design ingredients, Fontainebleau
Colour, texture and opulence were major design elements in the Fontainebleau interiors. Marquetry ceilings, wood-panelled walls, gilded frames and mirrors all contributed to the splendour of this style of decoration, which was emulated not only in France but elsewhere in Europe.

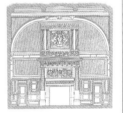

The orders, Fontainebleau

Serlio deals with the architectural orders and their ornamentation in Book IV of his treatise and shows a progression from the simple Tuscan to the richly decorated Composite. At Fontainebleau refined rustication gives an elegant, but unmistakably solid, ground-floor base.

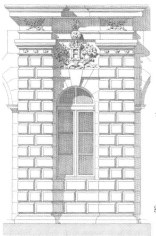

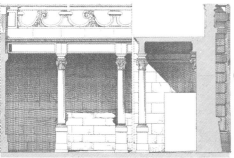

Portico, Fontainebleau

A trabeated, post-and-lintel system is employed for this portico at Fontainebleau. A Corinthian order, with high pedestals, supports the straight beams above.

Perron, Fontainebleau

A *perron* is a platform, frequently at first-floor level and usually reached by steps, on to which the main doors of a building open. The term is now generally used to describe the outer flight of steps or the staircase itself. An impressive example at Fontainebleau has two curved arms with steps rising in two flights.

French innovation

Even though architectural treatises codified the use of the orders and their decoration, many architects chose to invent their own variants rather than adhere to strict precedents. Fantastic winged figures here replace volutes, although the more conventional acanthus leaf decoration is also included.

The 'French' order

French architects, such as Philibert Delorme, visited Italy to study not only modern 16th-century architecture but also the classical remains. Delorme proposed a distinctively 'French' order, which included a banded shaft with alternating thicknesses of stone, fluting and decorated rings.

Originality

Part of Delorme's argument for a French order had a purely practical aspect. As most French building was in stone, a banded structure hid unsightly joins and added strength. The decorative possibilities were also numerous, as this example from the Louvre illustrates.

Renaissance

Civic Architecture in Northern Europe

Renaissance architectural language is generally perceived in terms of classical forms based on antique Greek and Roman precedents. It was not the only architectural language of the 16th century, nor – given its Catholic associations – was it appropriate for much of northern Europe. One strong architectural feature, without any Italian connections, which developed throughout much of northern Europe was the decorated gable. This was widely used on civic and domestic buildings. The power of architecture to convey civic pride and national identity was often exploited in northern cities in large-scale public buildings. Several of these 16th-century Town and Guild Halls combine local architectural traits with the idiosyncratic use of classical motifs, to achieve powerful and monumental public buildings.

Town Hall façade, Leiden (1595)
In times of particular prosperity many cities sought to modernise their civic buildings by remodelling or enlarging them. One such example is at Leiden, a city with a flourishing textile trade in the late 16th century, where Lieven de Key designed a lively façade to front the existing Town Hall building. Here all manner of classical motifs (fluted columns and pilasters, triangular pediments, banded shafts and rusticated stone) vie for attention with an exuberant gabled skyline.

Town Hall, Antwerp (1561–65)
Knowledge of Italian architecture was transmitted to northern Europe by architectural treatises, some translated into Dutch and other languages, and by northern architects who had worked in Italy. Cornelis Floris, who had spent many years in Italy, built the vast Town Hall in Antwerp, in which he displays his knowledge of Bramante and Serlio. The grave and monumental classicism of the building is given a gabled frontispiece, added more for decoration than for functional purpose. One of the first Italianate buildings in the region, it was hugely influential on Town Hall design throughout the Low Countries.

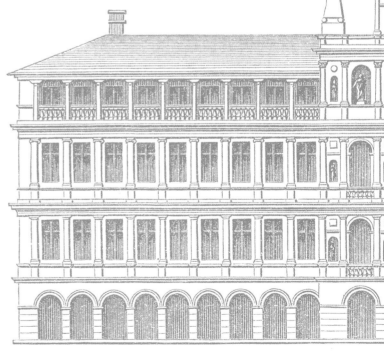

Cloth Hall, Brunswick

The proceeds of trade and commerce were responsible for the impressive architecture that dominates numerous main squares in northern European cities. Brunswick in Lower Saxony, for example, has an imposing many-storeyed Cloth Hall, which includes superimposed architectural orders on its first four levels, in the accepted sequence. Northern features of strapwork and scrolled gables also appear on its lofty façade.

Armoury, Gdansk

Many northern European countries had a tradition of finely constructed brick buildings and this continued during the Renaissance period. The Armoury in Gdansk is in this tradition, with stone mullions and transoms, and bold stonework around the massive portals. Ornate curved gables with obelisk-type finials surmount the upper storey.

Renaissance

Decorated and Unadorned Styles in Spain

Renaissance motifs began to be incorporated in secular buildings in Spain from the early 16th century, but the rich, decorated style of the Spanish Gothic persisted in many areas, particularly for ecclesiastical buildings. Although some architects used a more Italianate vocabulary, this was often employed as applied decoration to structures that were still fundamentally Gothic. As knowledge of Italian architecture and architectural theory became more widespread, buildings were constructed with greater regard to the rules of proportion and harmony. In the second half of the 16th century Philip II's architect, Juan de Herrera, built in a very severe and pared-down classical style, which became known as *estilo desornamentado*, or austere style.

Alcazar façade, Toledo (1537)
The main façade of the Alcazar, designed by Alonso de Covarrubias, brings together elements of both palace and castle architecture and is a good example of the less conventional use of classical motifs. While rustication and bracketed projections are usually found at ground level, here they appear on the top storey, used almost as ornament between the strong corner projections of the building.

Fountain, Royal Hospital
Courtyards and patios are important features of Spanish architecture. The Royal Hospital in Santiago features a rectangular courtyard surrounded by square-sectioned pillars supporting semi-circular arches. The central fountain incorporates classicising motifs of fantastic creatures and acanthus leaves.

Royal Hospital, Santiago de Compostela (1501–11)
The term *plateresque* (silversmith-like) refers to Spanish architecture that uses lavish ornamentation, often unrelated to the structure of the building. The Royal Hospital has a rich portal featuring four superimposed pilaster orders and a wide arched tympanum. Overlaying this, niches are filled with high-relief figure sculpture, while low reliefs cover pilasters and other surfaces.

Golden Staircase, Burgos Cathedral (1524)
The Golden Staircase features architectural orders, including pedestals and entablatures, but the level of surface decoration masks these classical forms. Sculptural exuberance is typical of much Spanish ornamentation and often uses such *all'antica* motifs as shells, foliage, medallions and urns.

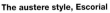

The austere style, Escorial
Contrasting strongly with earlier Spanish styles, the austere classicism of the Escorial became very influential in Spain from the late 16th century. The Escorial is constructed of granite and is almost devoid of ornament, and the severity of its monumental presence can be read as an architectural statement equated with the ideology of the Catholic Reformation.

Use of the orders
Architectural orders were often used in courtyards, although their exuberant decorative capitals were unrelated to classical norms or proportions. The arcading of the patio in the early 16th-century Mendoza Palace in Guadalajara uses stone for the shafts, bases and capitals of both its lower and upper orders, while the lintels and brackets are of wood.

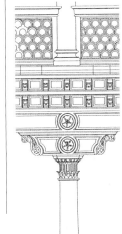

Escorial, Madrid (1563–84)
The ground plan reveals the symmetry and complexity of the Escorial, which was built for Philip II as a mausoleum for his father Charles V. The domed cruciform church, probably based on Italian centrally planned models, provides both the physical and symbolic focus of this vast royal project. The Escorial also incorporates a monastery, cloisters, royal apartments and a library.

Bracket capital
Bracket capitals, found in many Spanish buildings, include a wide bracket above the capital. Here the wooden bracket is carved with scrolls and its carved roundel (small circular panel) links decoratively with the frieze above.

Renaissance

Elizabethan Prodigy Houses

England, in common with much of northern Europe, continued to favour the Gothic style well into the 16th century. Knowledge of classical architecture was received through the filter of other European countries (not directly from Italy) and was influenced by French and Flemish traits. There were few ecclesiastical or royal commissions in Reformation England. By contrast, a number of great houses were built by high-ranking members of Elizabeth I's court. The architectural historian Sir John Summerson labelled these buildings 'prodigy houses' and several were specifically built, or remodelled, to provide a suitably splendid setting in which to entertain Elizabeth I, and her entourage, on her annual Royal Progress. Many of their most significant characteristics feature in Longleat and Wollaton Hall.

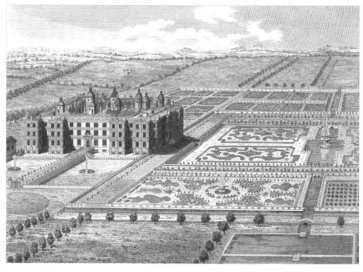

Longleat, Wiltshire (1570s)
Incorporating an earlier house, Longleat was rebuilt in the 1570s. Part of its originality lies in the symmetrical and harmonious façades, which incorporate large mullioned windows and lavish quantities of glass.

Façade, Longleat
Longleat's façades combine the classical restraint and order of Renaissance architecture with the adaptation of an English motif, the bay-window. Here, the slightly projecting bay systems enliven the façade without breaking up the harmony of its grave monumentality.

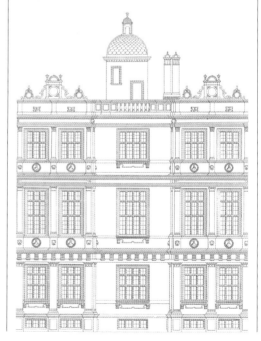

Plan, Longleat
A house suitable to accommodate the court needed not only a long gallery and great halls for splendid entertainments, but also well-planned kitchens and service rooms to facilitate the smooth running of the household. Suites of rooms were also required. These features are included at Longleat within a ground plan that is symmetrical along both axes.

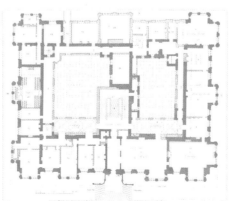

Wollaton Hall, Nottinghamshire (1580s)
Knowledge of Italian and other European architecture came to England by various means, including architectural treatises. At Wollaton Hall, built in the 1580s by Robert Smythson, there is evidence of the influences of both Serlio and Hans Vredeman de Vries in its design and decoration.

Tower, Wollaton Hall
The four corner towers add to the dramatic skyline of the building and feature distinctive strapwork (interlaced bands of relief ornamentation) gables deriving from the designs of de Vries. As on the façades, the pilasters are banded and frame the large mullioned windows.

Plan, Wollaton Hall
The symmetrical plan shows the four towers, formed at the corners of the rectangular block. There is no internal courtyard space, but instead a central great hall. This plan probably derives from a design by Sebastiano Serlio.

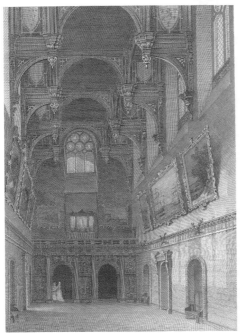

Great hall, Wollaton Hall
Great halls continued to appear in Tudor architecture. This one has no windows at the lower level, and is lit by clerestory windows in a Gothic design. Details of the strapwork screen derive from 16th-century Dutch designs.

Renaissance

Jacobean Architecture

Although no major shift in architectural style took place during the reign of James I, England's first Stuart monarch, a Jacobean style emerged nonetheless in the early 17th century, partly due to the use of many overseas carvers and craftsmen, particularly from the Low Countries. Interior decoration included much stucco work and wood carving, as well as ornate fireplaces and doorways. Decorated 'Dutch' gables featured in many new buildings, and this trait continued particularly in domestic architecture in the east of England, where links with the Low Countries were strong. As in the Tudor period, little church architecture was built, but several important Jacobean prodigy houses were constructed. While they were similar in many ways to earlier examples, changes occurred in their ground plans, which tended to be either H- or U-shaped. There was an interest in giving houses bold and impressive silhouettes and in obtaining striking vistas of them.

Audley End, Essex
A fine example of a Jacobean prodigy house, Audley End was begun in 1603. Embodying the characteristics of harmony and monumentality, it achieved added visual interest by varying the height of the side-wings in contrast to the lower central block.

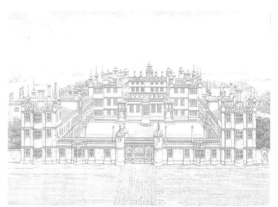

Porch, Audley End
Projecting entrance porches were often the part of a building on which classical architectural orders were used. At Audley End the double-tiered porches have arched openings framed by clustered columns, but the porches are headed by deep balustrades with fretwork decoration.

Fenestration
Many of the great Elizabeth and Jacobean houses used large amounts of glass, and sometimes fake windows were included. Typically windows were tall and mullioned, and divided into lights by bold transoms.

Blickling Hall, Norfolk (1616–27)
Building materials not only play a vital structural role, but perform a significant aesthetic role. Towards the east coast of England, brick was widely used and, combined with motifs such as curving gables, the Jacobean architecture produced in that region had strong affinities stylistically with the Low Countries. A fine example, Blickling Hall has its rich red brick finely offset by stone quoins and the heavy mullions and transoms of its windows.

Entrance, Browsholme Hall, Lancashire (1603)
The entrance here features superimposed orders on three storeys. The Doric order signifies strength on the ground floor, while the elegant Ionic order is used on the upper levels.

Gables
Gable decoration was an important element of Jacobean architecture, and a preference developed for curved and scrolled lines rather than stepped designs. Striking and dramatic skylines were achieved with curving gables, turrets and towers.

Renaissance

The Architecture of Inigo Jones

The harmonious classical architecture of Inigo Jones (1573–1652) was very different from the filtered Renaissance style that appeared (mainly as decoration) on 16th-century English buildings. Jones visited Italy and undertook detailed study of ancient monuments and Renaissance architecture, particularly the buildings of Andrea Palladio. Jones's copy of Palladio's *Four Books of Architecture* (1570), with his marginal notes, still exists. He was concerned with the fundamental architectural truth of his buildings, which involved the function, harmony and proportion of the whole, and not simply with the addition of classical motifs as applied decoration. He chose to emulate a High Renaissance style which, in Italy, was already giving way to the baroque.

Plan, Banqueting House
The Renaissance notion of the visual and psychological satisfaction inherent in perfect forms is exemplified in the single-volume double-cube interior of the Banqueting House.

Banqueting House, London (1619–22)
Jones's embracing of Italian Renaissance architecture is epitomised by this solid, harmonious building, whose two-tier classical façade shows a complete understanding of the High Renaissance.

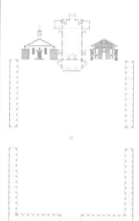

Covent Garden, London
At Covent Garden, Jones designed the first regular and symmetrical London square, modelled after urban spaces he had seen in Italy. A unified urban plan is achieved, which includes rows of dignified and unadorned houses, with open galleries at ground level.

St Paul's Church, London (1631)
The redevelopment of Covent Garden included the first new post-Reformation church to be built in England. The church is a simple rectangular shape with a bold Tuscan portico at the east end. Although not the main entrance to the church, the portico provides the striking focal point of the whole urban plan.

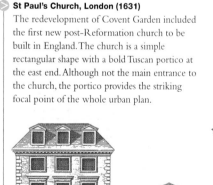

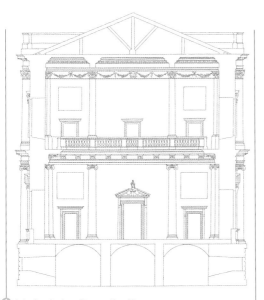

Interior design, Banqueting House

The Banqueting House provides a fine example of Jones's concern for the integrity of a whole building. The articulation of the façade is reflected internally with the use of similar superimposed orders, which in the interior space are separated by a gallery.

Texture and form

Architectural drawings for fireplaces, portals and gates reveal Jones's fascination with texture and form. Here, a rusticated gate combines great variety of finish, with rough, banded columns, bold voussoirs and a Doric frieze.

Winchester Cathedral Screen (c. 1638)

Jones's choir screen for Winchester Cathedral typifies the clarity and order of his architectural forms. His inventive and innovative architecture was developed within the discipline of codified Renaissance architectural rules and practice.

Baroque and Rococo *C.17th–late C.18th*

Roman Baroque

Baroque architecture originated in 17th-century Rome, where it developed as an expression of the newly triumphant Catholic Church. The Counter-Reformation stated that architecture, painting and sculpture would play an important role in transforming Rome into a truly Catholic city. The streets radiating from St Peter's Cathedral were soon dotted with reminders of the victorious faith. Breaking with the somewhat static intellectual formulas of the Renaissance, baroque architecture was first and foremost an art of persuasion. The act of stepping into a church became an experience in which symbolic and illusionist schemes appealed as much to the emotions as to the intellect of the faithful. A new dynamic architectural vocabulary emerged, often based on the repetition, breaking-up and distortion of Renaissance classical motifs. Broken pediments, giant orders, convex and concave walls were all used relatively freely by baroque architects, leading to very personal styles.

Church decoration: The Gesù, Rome (1568–84)
The Gesù, mother church of the Jesuit order, was redecorated following the Counter-Reformatory principles of dramatic emphasis, for an immediate strengthening of the belief of the faithful. Painted stucco, three-dimensional sculpture and fragmented architectural features are combined to frame large fresco panels depicting the lives and miracles of the saints.

Broken pediment
One of the chief leitmotifs of baroque architecture, broken pediments are round or triangular pediments 'broken' at their apex or in the middle of their base (broken-based). The gap was sometimes filled with a cresting ornament. Broken pediments brought dynamism to the façade, allowing for the vertical interaction of its architectural elements.

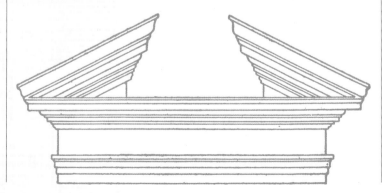

Plan, St Peter's piazza, Rome (begun 1656)

For the plan of the piazza at St Peter's, Gian Lorenzo Bernini used two major tricks of perspective. Carlo Maderno's long, unfinished church façade was given new baroque dynamism with the construction of a trapezoidal square in front, giving the illusion of a narrower entrance façade. Bernini chose a transverse oval plan for the second piazza, creating yet another spatial distortion.

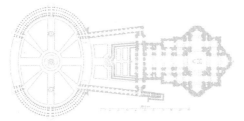

Colonnades, St Peter's piazza

Bernini framed the oval piazza of St Peter's with colonnades (1656) forming the required covered ambulatory for processions. It is four columns deep with two rows of paired columns giving the illusion of a massive precinct wall while still interacting with the city beyond. Bernini himself described the colonnade as 'maternal arms' stretching out to receive and reunite the faithful.

S. Carlo alle Quattro Fontane, Rome (1665–67)

Francesco Borromini's façade of S. Carlo alle Quattro is entirely articulated by concave and convex planes. Four concave bays frame two superimposed central ones, rendered convex by a balcony and projecting aedicule (small pedimented structure) on the upper storey, and a convex entablature and steps below.

Entrance, S. Andrea al Quirinale, Rome (1658–70)

The façade of Bernini's small church of S. Andrea is a monumental aedicule (using a pediment and column as a framing device) entrance. A semi-circular porch and steps project outwards, counterbalancing short concave arms to either side. Inside, the oval plan creates an immediate relationship with the climactic altar.

Baldacchino, St Peter's (1624–33)

The monument known as the Baldacchino sits over the crypt leading to the tomb of St Peter, symbolic foundation stone of the Catholic Church. It is a giant bronze altar consisting of an ogee-shaped canopy supported by four salomonic or twisted columns, referring to those used in Early Christian antiquity. An orb sits on its apex, symbolic of the propagation of Christianity.

Baroque and Rococo

Roman Baroque

Pope Sixtus V and his successors had succeeded in making a systemised religious capital out of Rome. Soon high-ranking Roman families demanded that their own private worlds be transformed in the persuasive baroque style. Bernini, Borromini and others were commissioned to remodel older palaces using unifying devices such as open loggias, grand staircases and an emphasis on entrances. Painters and sculptors then adorned the architecture with great symbolic fresco cycles. By the mid-17th century, the baroque style had reached a maturity known as 'High Baroque' and its influence spread north of Rome. High Baroque churches were characterised by centralised plans, illusionist grand altars and ceilings, and heavily ornamented, muscular façades. One of the masters of this style was Guarino Guarini, who settled in Turin and contributed to its propagation across Europe in the early 18th century.

Loggia, Palazzo Borghese, Rome (1607)
The use of open loggias (covered galleries open on both sides) became increasingly widespread in the 17th century. An early example is the Palazzo Borghese, where the three-storey wings of the building are connected by an open two-storey loggia. The Renaissance courtyard format is preserved, but a baroque longitudinal axis is created from the courtyard to the garden.

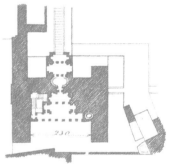

Longitudinal axis, Palazzo Barberini
The passage in depth through the palace into the garden becomes the central focus from which the rest of the palace unfolds. The three-bay-deep arcaded portico leads to a grand four-flight open staircase and an oval *salone*, from which the garden is accessed at a higher level.

Palazzo Barberini, Rome (1628–33)
Carlo Maderno, Borromini and Bernini were responsible for the new Palazzo Barberini, which departed from the traditional courtyard city *palazzo* in having an H-plan. Set at the end of an open courtyard, the entrance façade is one long portico of three superimposed arcades, suggesting a baroque open loggia.

Cartouche

A characteristically baroque form of ornamentation, the cartouche is an oval panel with crested or scrolled borders, used on palace and church façades as a framing device for a cresting or coat of arms, but also as a purely decorative infill motif. It usually features inside a broken pediment, over an entrance or in the axis from the one to the other.

Spatial unity

Italian baroque spatial unity reaches its climax in the northern churches of Guarini. With a skeleton of Gothic-like ribs, a juxtaposition of domes, semi-domes and diagonally orientated spaces, Guarini's churches succeeded in making the Counter-Reformatory 'experience' more strictly spatial and architectonic.

Giant order

The giant order is a single column or pilaster rising up at least two storeys of a façade in a unifying vertical movement. Its proportions in width and height, reminiscent of the columns of antique temples, gave both dramatic emphasis and authority to 17th-century elevations.

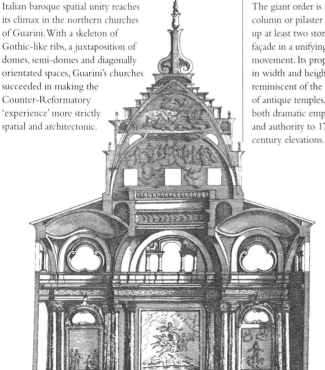

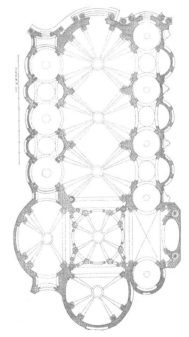

Undulating wall

Both the exterior and interior profiles of Guarini's churches show a continuously broken or undulating wall. Juxtaposed convex, straight and concave walls are the result of a plan that successfully merges ovals and circles for purposes of dynamism.

Baroque and Rococo

French Baroque

French architecture in the 17th century developed as a more natural consequence of the Renaissance than Counter-Reformatory Roman architecture did. Nevertheless, Henri IV returned to Paris after the Civil War with the desire to reaffirm the monarchy's presence by creating a network of *places*, or squares, with statues of the sovereign and housing for the aristocracy. The resulting sober, uniform style was soon adopted for countryside chateaux of the aristocracy as well as for city houses and palaces. Architects such as François Mansart, Jules Hardouin-Mansart and Louis Le Vau were commissioned to build long façades with repetitive motifs, producing insistent baroque effects.

Château de Maisons, Paris (1642–46)

This is the work of François Mansart, who succeeded in unifying three clearly defined pavilions with the use of a climactic frontispiece in which the paired columns and pediments of the side-blocks are repeated with variations. The frontispiece overlaps the high-pitched roof and its mass recedes in several layers in the centre.

Palais du Luxembourg, Paris

The palace was begun in 1615 for Marie de' Medici by the architect Salomon de Brosse on a traditional courtyard plan. The elevations were treated with a continuous system of rusticated coupled pilasters and columns. Traditional French dormer windows are set behind a balustrade.

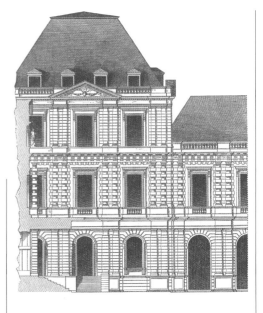

Place Royale, Paris (1605–12)

Henri IV's major town-planning project in Paris was the creation of the first *places royales* with housing for the nobility. Place des Vosges (Place Royale) consists of two storeys above a continuous arcade, with steep mansard roofs defining the pavilions. The brick façades are treated with a surface decoration of vertical strips, or *chaînes*, of dressed stone.

Paired columns

Characteristic of 17th-century French architecture, coupled or paired columns and pilasters conveyed rhythm to otherwise long, repetitive palace façades. Often fluted or rusticated, they represented an elegant and sober form of decoration. The wide intercolumniations also allowed for larger palace windows and entrances.

East front of the Louvre, Paris (1667–70)

After ordering and later rejecting designs from Bernini and other Italian architects, Louis XIV set up a commission of French architects to build the east front of the Louvre. The result was a sober, majestic colonnade of giant paired columns on a high plinth.

Church at Les Invalides, Paris (1680–1707)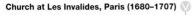
The façade of this church is governed by a strong vertical movement, starting from the columns of the portico and continuing up the ribs of the dome. The dome's height is increased by the introduction of an attic between the drum and the dome. Diagonally projecting consoles and gilt relief panels around the dome add to the baroque dynamism of the royal church.

Console
Large ornamental brackets or consoles, often in the shape of a scroll or volute, appear frequently in exaggerated form in late 17th-century French architecture. They regularly feature in a decorative rather than a supportive role.

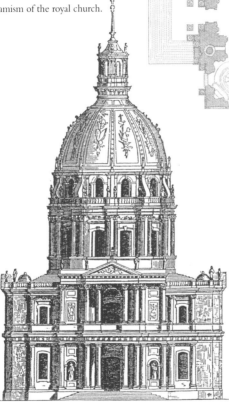

Plan, Church at Les Invalides
Jules Hardouin-Mansart was commissioned by Louis XIV to build a domed church between the two wings of the Hôtel des Invalides. His ingenious solution was a centralised plan to which he gave a longitudinal axis by connecting it to the older church by means of a baroque oval sanctuary housing the altar. The corner chapels are placed on a diagonal, hidden behind large piers to preserve the unity of the central domed space.

Bull's eye aperture
Round or oval *oeil de boeuf*, or bull's eye apertures, ornate the top of French baroque buildings, particularly mansard roofs and domes. They sometimes function as dormer windows, but are more often used as decorative piercings in the wall.

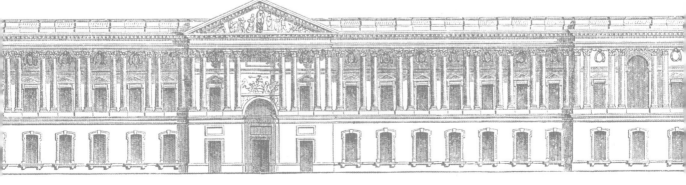

Baroque and Rococo

French Baroque (Versailles)

In 1664 Louis XIV commissioned the architect Le Vau to rebuild the Château de Versailles. The monarch wanted a palace that would surpass those of his ministers in size and magnificence. The palace and gardens at Versailles were developed in several phases during the 17th and 18th centuries and constituted the major building activity of that period, influencing the whole course of French architecture. In the strategic layout of the chateau and the gardens, Louis XIV created for himself a self-contained centralised baroque system or universe. All the major sculptors and painters of the day were employed on ambitious decorative schemes on the theme of 'the monarch triumphant'. In Paris, the reaction of the aristocracy was the development of the *hôtel*, or private urban villa, whose interiors relied heavily on the decorative style at Versailles.

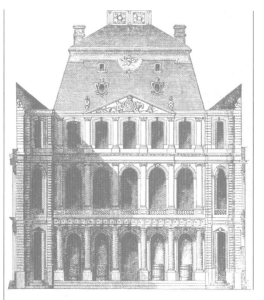

Hôtel window-head

Hôtel exterior decoration, particularly on the street front, was often limited to windows, doors and balconies against expanses of bare wall. These, however, could be extremely ornate, influenced by the decorative style of Versailles, with console brackets, broken pediments, intricate mouldings, sculptural relief panels and caryatids.

Parisian hôtel

The façade of this new type of nobleman's city residence was set behind a forecourt, or *cour d'honneur*, with an entrance wall to the street and a garden behind. Plans were necessarily cramped and two *hôtels* often shared one courtyard, with the classical façade acting as a screen.

Plan, Château de Versailles

The chateau was planned in several stages as the projection of Louis XIV's ideals of absolute power. His *appartement* at the end of the great courtyard is the focus of the plan, from which great *enfilade* (with doors in line) rooms extend in the side pavilions and wings. The monarch's bedroom is on an axis, with Le Notre's garden layouts to one side and with the great avenue leading to the towns of Versailles and Paris on the other.

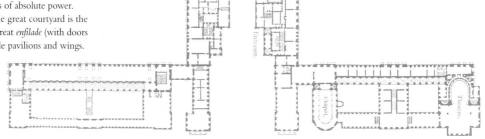

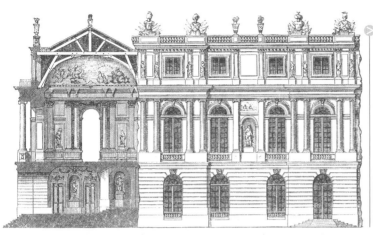

Door panel, Versailles
Most of the decoration at Versailles is in the form of gilt relief arabesques, scrolled foliage and swags. These are set in classical, rectilinear panels of wood or coloured marble.

Galerie des Glaces (Hall of Mirrors), Versailles, 1678
The gallery was added by Hardouin-Mansart in 1678 and was decorated by Charles Le Brun. The long hall has large windows looking down on to the gardens on one side, echoed by large Venetian mirrors on the other, reflecting the light, gold, coloured marbles, and Le Brun's fresco cycle depicting the life of the monarch. The style of the gallery became the model for 18th-century European palace decoration.

Decoration of a salon, Versailles
The rooms that served as salons (reception rooms) at Versailles were themed. At either end of the Galerie des Glaces were the salons of War and Peace. The seven rooms of the King's apartment were named after seven planets and were decorated with related allegories praising the virtues of the monarch. Each salon was then decorated with relief panels relating to the iconography employed in the illusionist ceiling fresco.

Decorative capital, Versailles
A particular unorthodox decorative style was developed in the interiors at Versailles, due in part to the scale of the building whose impact depended on the whole rather than on its parts. Some of the interior capitals are gilded and sculpted with swags, acanthus leaves, animals and small chimeric figures (fantastic assemblages of animal forms).

Baroque and Rococo

Early English Baroque

The course of 17th-century English architecture was precipitated by the Great Fire of London in 1666, which destroyed an important part of the city, including eighty-seven parish churches. Soon afterwards a series of Acts were passed for Rebuilding the City of London, with particular reference to its churches and cathedral. The Office of Sir Christopher Wren, then Surveyor-General, was made responsible for the design and erection of the new churches. Scientifically trained, Wren excelled at overcoming structural difficulties with inventive 'baroque' solutions involving distortions and adaptations. The rebuilding of St Paul's Cathedral was his greatest challenge, for which he produced a quantity of drawings. In the final design, however, Wren was confronted with an English reluctance to adopt the continental baroque style.

St James's, Piccadilly (1683)
As Wren stated in a later Memorandum (*c.* 1711), his city churches were built as 'auditories' or small theatres, with pews in galleries running around three sides of the church enabling the congregation to hear the preaching, a particular emphasis in Protestant worship. At St James's, Piccadilly, the pulpit is characteristically placed between the pews in the middle of the church, with the altar set back on the east-end wall.

St Bride, London (1701–03)
The city churches were built on constrained sites with cheap materials. The elegant and often ingenious steeples, rising above the neighbouring houses, constituted their principal form of exterior decoration. At St Bride, Fleet Street, the steeple is four storeys high with a stone staircase running through its core. Each storey is octagonal, pierced with arched openings and corner pilasters.

Trinity College Library, Cambridge (1676–84)
Wren was commissioned to build this library at Trinity College between two existing blocks in Neville's Court. He adopted an illusionary design for the façade in which he disguised the discrepancy between the necessarily low level of the library floor and the height of his Doric order by filling in the ground-floor arches with carved lunettes.

Church of St Bennet, London (1683)
Large round-headed windows recur often in Wren's architecture, particularly his city churches. Heavy swags (ornamental garlands or festoons) on otherwise plain brick elevations are a Wrensian characteristic, as is the juxtaposition of brick and stone for polychromatic effects.

The Great Model for St Paul's Cathedral, London (1673)
The preparatory designs for St Paul's Cathedral culminated in the Great Model design. In plan it was a centralised structure with concave exterior walls, a large central domed area surrounded by an ambulatory ring of chapels and a second smaller dome near the entrance portico. The design was reminiscent of the great baroque churches of the Continent and did not meet the approval of the clergy, who thought it broke with tradition and was impractical.

Round-headed window, St Paul's Cathedral
On the exterior of St Paul's, Wren used a particular ornamental window surround, in which shallow mouldings curve around the head of the opening and end abruptly at the level of the springing, framing the window with decorative 'ears' resembling broken architraves.

Double-shelled dome, St Paul's Cathedral
The idea of a high dome rising above the city of London had been a part of Wren's conception from the start. The final solution is a highly complex feat of engineering, involving an inner dome with an oculus looking up to a second outer dome and lantern, with the intermediate buttressing support of a hidden brick cone.

West front, St Paul's Cathedral (1675–1710)
Wren originally planned a giant order for the west-front portico of St Paul's, but was forced to compromise when the Portland quarries declared that they could not find blocks of stone large enough for the entablature. Wren's façade is nonetheless strongly baroque, with its coupled Corinthian columns and pilasters and its richly decorated towers echoing the colonnade of the central drum.

Baroque and Rococo

Later English Baroque

The second phase of the English baroque started in the early 18th century with a new generation of architects, some of whom had worked in Wren's Office. The two principal masters of the style were Nicholas Hawksmoor and John Vanbrugh. Hawksmoor had assisted Wren in a number of royal works, including Greenwich Hospital, finished long after Wren's death. With a double courtyard and wings opening up in stages from Inigo Jones's Queen's House to the river bank, the Royal Hospital was the precursor of the type of English baroque palace developed by Hawksmoor and Vanbrugh. As partners, they built country houses with engaging concave and convex wings. Their interest in mass and in the intrinsic movement of the walls was reflected at an ornamental level in the play with scales and the humorous dismantling of classical vocabulary.

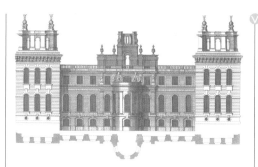

Blenheim Palace, near Oxford (1705–24)
The Duke of Marlborough commissioned Vanbrugh to build a palace that would also serve as a monument to British military success. Vanbrugh, with Hawksmoor, exploited this opportunity for a triumphal architecture, resulting in massive fortress-like pavilions of differing height tied together by colonnades and by a playful use of classical motifs.

Castle Howard, Yorkshire (1699–1712)
Vanbrugh's plan of Castle Howard is based on the Greenwich approach scheme of two merging forecourts. The service buildings forming the sides of the first open court are attached to the climactic domed body of the building by means of short, curved colonnaded arms forming a second court.

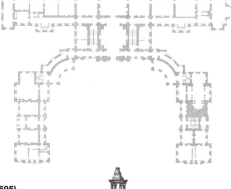

Greenwich Hospital, London (1695)
A commission was set up in 1695 for the building of a Royal Naval Hospital in Greenwich. Wren devised a double open courtyard plan, incorporating a view of the Queen's House on the main axis. The elevations were finished by Wren's successors and included such motifs as the towering arch with broken-based pediment.

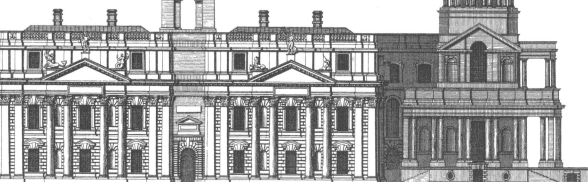

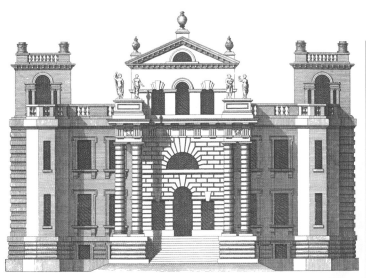

Seaton Delaval, Northumberland (1720–29)

Vanbrugh's fortress-like approach to mass is most evident in tighter compositions such as Seaton Delaval, where different types of wall banding and pairs of giant ringed Doric columns serve to enhance the masses of the different units. Two balustraded towers and a central smooth-walled block emerge above the defensive front.

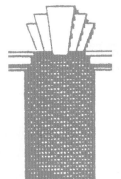

Giant keystone

Giant keystones were frequently used by English baroque architects as an emphatic ornament on doors and windows. While some architects favoured a group of five stones to create the effect of breadth, Hawksmoor often used a single isolated giant keystone overlapping the opening by half its length and conveying strong vertical accents to the front.

Ringed column, Seaton Delaval

Ringed columns are a striking feature of Seaton Delaval and most of Vanbrugh's other country houses. Usually in the form of a giant Doric order, the shafts are carved with precise and regular grooves. Already a common feature of Italian and French Renaissance architecture, they are used with new effect by Vanbrugh to provide an emphatic measure of horizontality to a mass of wall.

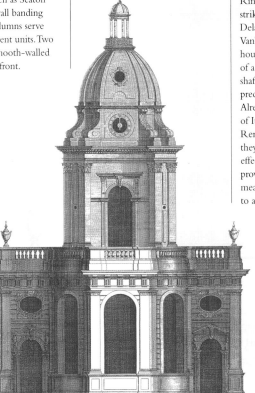

St Philip, Birmingham (1709–15)

Thomas Archer was one of the Commissioners in the 1711 Act for church building. His church of St Philip, Birmingham is strongly reminiscent of Italian and French baroque churches with its convex walls, domed tower, diagonally projecting console buttresses and bull's eye openings. The church nevertheless has an English box plan derived from Wren's churches.

Baroque and Rococo

Northern and Central European Baroque

The baroque style spread across northern and central Europe in the late 17th century, in a meeting of Roman Catholic baroque on the one hand and secular French court classicism on the other. European Catholic cities emulated Rome, while the great European monarchs planned their own Versailles. The palaces of Prague, Vienna and Stockholm have strong resonances of French palaces in their plan, but their façade articulations display a rich sculptural plasticity reminiscent of Roman baroque. In the 18th century, Counter-Reformatory southern Germany and Austria took Italian High Baroque churches as their prototypes. The publications of Guarino Guarini were highly influential. The tendency was for rich sculptural façades with literal antique Roman quotations, recalling the authority of Rome as the Christian capital. By the 1800s Vienna and Prague were leading cities in what had become the international baroque style.

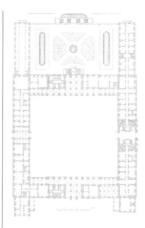

Royal Palace, Stockholm (1697–1771)
Built by Nicodemus Tessin for Charles XII of Sweden, the Royal Palace in Stockholm exemplifies the type of European palace that became so popular in the early 18th century. The large courtyard with entrances on four sides, the garden-terrace between two projecting wings and the unified block shape of the exterior are reminiscent of the palaces of the Luxembourg, the Louvre and Versailles.

Atlantes
A leitmotif of baroque architecture in Central Europe, atlantes – giant muscular figures in contorted positions – struggle to hold up the arches of portals in the palaces by Fischer von Erlach and his contemporaries. The giant figures are often paired.

Palace of Clam Gallas, Prague (1791)
Count Jan Vaclav Gallas commissioned the Viennese court architect Fischer von Erlach to design his palace in Prague in the fashionable continental style. Inventive alternating pediments on the second-storey windows climax in a concave central pediment crowned by an overlapping cartouche. The heavily ornate portals display a richness halfway between Roman baroque plasticity and the Versailles decorative style.

Historical façade, S. Carlo Borromeo

The eclectic style of S. Carlo Borromeo results from Fischer's attempt to give antique authority to the Christian votive church by creating an 'historical' architecture. The front is adorned by two giant columns reminiscent of Trajan's column in Rome and by a monumental temple portico. The arms of the church front recall those of St Peter's, while the effect of units of differing height crowned by a giant oval dome are inspired by Guarini. The total composition seeks to re-create the Bible's Temple of Solomon.

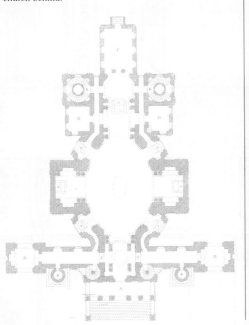

Plan, S. Carlo Borromeo, Vienna (1715–37)

The plan of the church shows a central domed area of oval shape, with a strong longitudinal axis. It is preceded by a majestic porticoed front in the form of two extensive arms or wings disguising the truth about the size of the church behind.

Kollengienkirche, Salzburg (1696–1707)

The Benedictine Order required a church which would differ in style from the Jesuit churches of southern Germany. Fischer's unusual curvilinear design relies on the Baroque 'oval' shape in elevation as well as in plan. The façade is a convex oval volume flanked by slender Borrominesque towers. The verticality is furthered by a giant order of pilasters, the tall dome, and oval windows.

Baroque and Rococo

Rococo

The rococo style was essentially a decorative movement that developed in the early 18th century in the town houses and *hôtels* of the Parisian nobility. Although the style originated in the rich decoration at Versailles, it was also a reaction to the formality of the royal palace. Juste-Aurèle Meissonnier, Gilles-Marie Openordt, Nicolas Pineau and Germain Boffrand were among the designers who succeeded in reflecting the more intimate scale and comfortable arrangement of rooms by decorating them with light, frivolous and colourful schemes in which panels and door-frames dissolved and walls merged with the ceiling. The repertoire of motifs, including rocaille arabesques and chinoiseries, was infinitely varied. While few rococo exteriors were built in France, a number of rococo churches are found in southern Germany.

Overlapping mouldings
In reaction to the formal panelling and framing at Versailles, rococo decoration merges panels, mirrors, doors and ceilings by overlapping the mouldings. At the Hôtel de Soubise (1738–39) all the room angles are curved and the corners disappear into the ceiling.

Rocaille patterns
Characteristic of the rococo style were rocaille motifs derived from the shells, icicles and rockwork of grotto decoration. Rocaille arabesques were mostly abstract forms, laid out symmetrically over and around architectural frames.

Scallop shell
A favourite motif was the scallop shell, whose top scrolls echoed the basic S and C framework scrolls of the arabesques and whose sinuous ridges echoed the general curvilinearity of the room decoration.

Church of St Paul and St Louis, Paris
The Jesuit church of St Paul and St Louis is baroque, but is an early example of a façade in rococo character, with multiple cartouches, arabesques, monograms, volutes, scrolls, cherubs and three sculptures in niches.

Hôtel balcony

The sober, classical façades of 18th-century French *hôtels* contrasted with the rococo style of the interiors. Yet window balconies became an opportunity for rococo expression on the exterior. The classical stone balustraded balcony was sometimes substituted by an ironwork balcony of interlacing scrolls supported on ornate console brackets.

Pure decoration

The motifs of rococo decoration were neither historical nor symbolic. The rocaille, scrolls and foliage were often arranged around exotic figures, masks, herms, sphinxes and imaginary coats of arms. A common figure was the *tête en espagnolette*, a female mask with a ruff around her head.

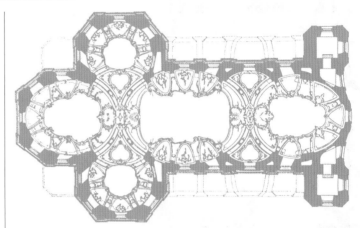

Pilgrimage church of Vierzehnheiligen, southern Germany (consecrated 1772)

J. B. Neumann planned this church using linked ovals of varying size, the central one resembling a rectangle with curved corners. The ambiguous shape of the basic units, as well as their scalloped inner profile, strengthens the effect of the later rococo decoration of the interior.

Rococo church decoration, Vierzehnheiligen

The structural elements of the interior are kept under the level of the cornice, leaving the vaults clear for rococo decoration, emphasising the continuity of the surface. Scalloped panels, frescoes, cartouches and arabesques overlap a network of shallow ribs. At the centre of the nave is the free-standing Shrine of the Fourteen (1764), in rocaille style.

Palladianism *early C.18th–early C.19th*

The Legacy of Inigo Jones

English Palladianism was essentially an early 18th-century movement in reaction to the personal and extravagant 'deformities' of baroque architects, and sought to establish foundations for a 'national taste' of strictly classical architecture based on Palladio and Inigo Jones (1573–1652). Indeed, a century earlier, Jones had revolutionised English architectural thought by coming to a deep understanding of Palladio's theories as laid out in his treatise, the famous *Four Books of Architecture* (1570). He challenged the lessons in Palladio's work with his own observations of antique ruins and the study of other treatises, including those of Sebastiano Serlio and Vincenzo Scamozzi. He brought back to England an intellectual attitude rather than a style, in which Palladio's ideas were used profoundly rather than superficially.

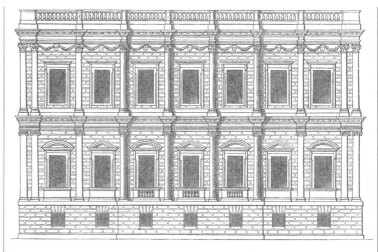

The Four Books of Architecture (1570)
Part of the popularity and appeal of Palladio's treatise lay in its clear presentation of a proportional system of the orders, based on careful study of antique ruins. The clarity of the woodcut illustrations of private, public and antique buildings and the concise text had a universal appeal.

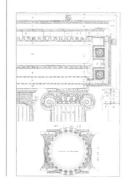

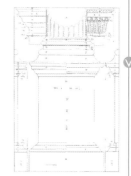

Banqueting House, Whitehall (1619–22)
Jones's Banqueting House is the original result of a calculated combination of Palladio's reconstruction of a Roman basilica after Vitruvius, in plan, and Palladio's two-storey palaces in Vicenza, in elevation.

Rustication
Rustication consists of courses of cut stone whose edges are chamfered (bevelled), often at a 45-degree angle, and whose projecting faces are smooth or roughly textured and suggest solidity and mass.

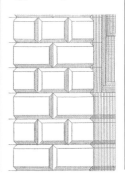

Queen's House, Greenwich (1616–35)
Inigo Jones's profound understanding of Palladian theory is evident in the proportions of the design of the Queen's House in Greenwich. The ornamentation of the façade is restrained and dependent for its effect on the proportional relationship of the windows to the loggia, and of the loggia to the whole. Jones thought that outward ornaments should be 'proportionable according to the rules, masculine and unaffected'.

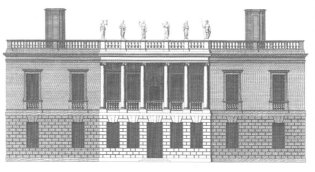

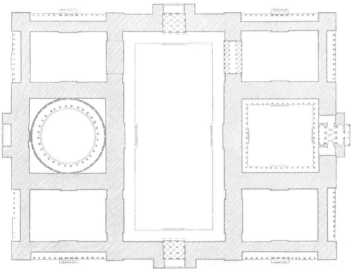

Amesbury House, Wiltshire (c. 1661)

Amesbury House, built by Jones's pupil and assistant John Webb, only survives as an engraving by Colen Campbell in *Vitruvius Britannicus*. Webb's domestic architecture, which was, until recently, attributed to Jones, is important to the story of Palladianism since Jones designed very few, if any, country houses.

Project for a palace at Whitehall, London (c. 1647)

A number of drawings by Jones and Webb survive for a vast Palladian palace at Whitehall incorporating the existing Banqueting House. This plan shows a circular court to one side and a proportionate square one on the other.

Palladian window

The Venetian or 'Palladian' window consists of a central arched opening with two smaller rectangular openings on either side, whose height is determined by straight architraves at the level of the springing of the arch.

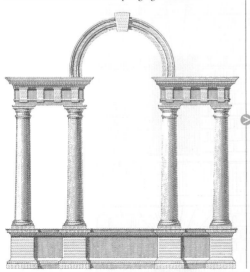

Quoins

Quoins are rusticated blocks of stone of alternating size, which run in strips up the corners of a building, often marking the sides of different pavilions. They are a Renaissance motif that appealed to Palladian architects because of their astylar nature.

Palladianism

18th-century English Palladianism

In the early decades of the 18th century there was a strong desire in England among members of the Whig aristocracy to reintroduce architectural standards, not in isolated instances, but as part of a national movement substituting the individual and fanciful values of the baroque for true and absolute values found in antiquity. The Earl of Shaftesbury suggested in a famous letter of 1712 the creation of an academy to ensure the formation of a national taste. But the foundations of the new style were established, instead, through the publication of treatises. Colen Campbell's *Vitruvius Britannicus* (1715) and Giacomo Leoni's edition of Palladio's *Four Books* (1715–20) determined that the 18th-century architect should find his references in the works and ideas of Palladio and Jones.

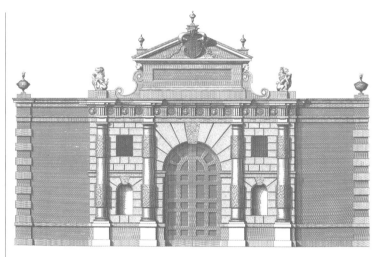

Great Gate, Burlington House
Inigo Jones had set the precedent for Palladian gateways with a number of carefully proportioned designs. Campbell's Great Gate (1718) at Burlington House, London was a particularly imposing showpiece, with a full Doric entablature that was supported on four widely spaced banded columns.

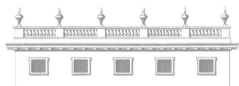

Balustrade
The classical balustrade is a motif inherited from the Renaissance, when it was used essentially for balconies and staircases. With the Palladians, however, a long balustrade was used almost systematically to define the horizontal roofline, sometimes interrupted by statues and urns.

Burlington House, London (1715)
On his return from Italy in 1715, Lord Burlington employed Campbell to remodel his house in London in the new Palladian style, which Campbell had promoted with the recent publication of *Vitruvius Britannicus*. The design, based on Palladio's Palazzo Porto-Colleoni in Vicenza, included two large Palladian windows on the side-pavilions.

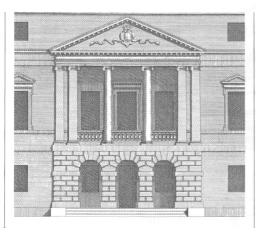

Lord Herbert's House, London (c. 1723–24)
A portico or loggia, sometimes surmounted by a
pediment and raised on a small Serlian arcade, became
the standard formula for the frontispiece of Palladian
town and country houses. It appears in Campbell's
house for Lord Herbert in Whitehall and is based on
Inigo Jones's design for the Gallery at Somerset House.

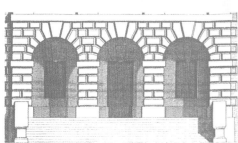

Serlian arcade
A rusticated arcade, often
limited to three arches, is
characteristic of Palladian
houses. It heightens the
importance of the first
floor and central block.
Rusticated arcades appeared
in Serlio's treatise, but Inigo
Jones had also used them
in the piazza at Covent
Garden, thereby entering
the motif in the 18th-
century Palladian repertory.

**St Martin-in-the-Fields,
London (1726)**
James Gibbs never fully
espoused Palladianism.
Yet through his *Book of
Architecture* he contributed
to the propagation of
important Palladian motifs
such as the Venetian window
and the blocked surround.

General Wade's House, London (1723)
General Wade's House in London was Lord Burlington's
first town house. It was an almost exact replica of a
design by Palladio that Burlington had in his collection.
At the centre of the façade is a Palladian window in a
relieving arch (an arch built into a wall over a window,
doorway or arch to discharge the weight of the wall
above), a leitmotif of Burlington's later designs.

**Palladian window in a
relieving arch**
Much favoured by Lord
Burlington, recessed
Palladian windows set
within relieving arches
represented an advantage
over simple Palladian
windows by tightening the
composition. The relieving
arch repeats the arch of the
entrance, while the smaller
arch of the window
corresponds to the height
of the other windows of
the elevation.

Palladianism

Vitruvius Britannicus

Colen Campbell's *Vitruvius Britannicus* (1715) was perhaps the most important architectural publication of 18th-century England. Most owners of country houses subscribed to the volumes, thereby participating in an intellectual movement that reached far beyond the scope of the book. In the first pages of each volume, Campbell included as much Jonesian material as he could. Inigo Jones was dubbed the 'British Vitruvius' who had brought antique Rome to England through Palladio. Campbell's own works occupied a prominent position in the book, promoting him as leader of the Palladian movement. In his designs, he slavishly imitated his sources, which later earned him the criticism of his contemporaries. However, large houses such as Wanstead and Houghton were highly influential and contributed greatly to the definition of Palladianism.

Design 'in the style of Inigo Jones'
Among the designs in *Vitruvius Britannicus* that Campbell claimed as his 'own invention' was one of a country house said to be 'in the style of Inigo Jones'. It was indeed based on Jones's Gallery at Somerset House, which also had a Corinthian order over a rusticated arcade.

Voussoirs
In the relieving arches of the rusticated ground floor of some Palladian country houses, the decorative effect of voussoir stones of gradually diminishing length surrounding the arch was heightened by the repetition of keystones over a square window inside the arch.

Mereworth Castle, Kent (c. 1723)
The most slavish imitation of an actual building by Palladio was Campbell's Mereworth Castle, based both in plan and elevation on Palladio's Villa Rotonda in Vicenza. Both buildings are compact centralised plans with four identical porticoed fronts. Horace Walpole described Campbell's villa as 'perfect in the Palladian taste'.

Wanstead, Essex (1715–20)
Some country houses, such as Wanstead House, were built on a grand scale. All three designs that Campbell produced for this house included the monumental hexastyle portico, proportionate to the size of the house.

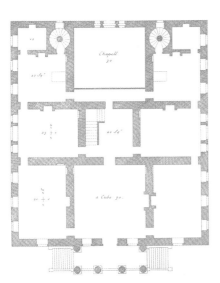

Great Hall at Houghton, Norfolk (1722)
Campbell's Great Hall at Houghton is a typical 1720s Palladian interior, with archaeologically and mathematically accurate architectural elements, such as chimneypieces, entablatures, pedimented doorways and windows, and a bracketed, balustraded balcony.

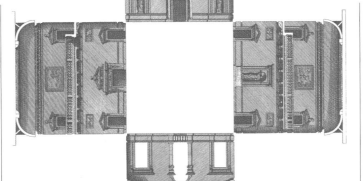

Stourhead, Wiltshire (c. 1721)
Campbell's first plan for Stourhead was derived from Palladio's Villa Emo at Fanzolo. But the typically Palladian plan of simple proportional relationships did not satisfy Campbell's patron, Henry Hoare, who thought it impractical because it did not include service stairs while it had two useless symmetrical newel staircases leading to the bedrooms. The built plan was a compromise between symmetry and practicality.

Blocked surround
Sometimes referred to as a 'Gibbsian surround', because of its frequent appearance in buildings by John Gibbs, this motif consists of a simple architrave surround interrupted at regular intervals by square blocks of stone. The blocked surround either continues around the head of the opening or is surmounted by keystones in a pediment. The motif was repeatedly used by Campbell to emphasise entrances and the windows of the *piano nobile*.

Palladianism

Chiswick House, London

Chiswick House (begun in 1725) was Lord Burlington's architectural show-piece, one in which he could delight in practice of the knowledge he had acquired through study of his personal collection of original drawings by Palladio and Jones. The result was an unusual, over-articulated building in which architectural quotations abounded. In both interior and exterior, the proportions were generally based on Palladio, while the detailing was an academic juxtaposition of motifs from Palladio, Scamozzi, Jones, Vitruvius and others. But the amount of detail was not to the detriment of the quality of each individual feature, which was crisp and correct and revealed Burlington's more profound understanding of the old masters. While Chiswick House was based on Palladio's Villa Rotonda at Vicenza, it was not an imitation of it, but an original Palladian interpretation.

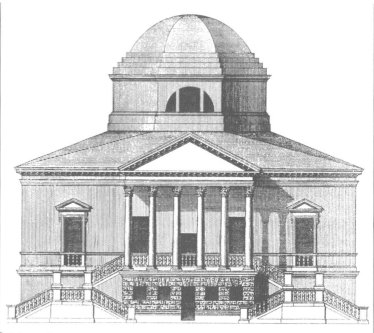

Entrance front

A podium of vermiculated rustication supports a rich Corinthian portico (for which every detail is taken from Palladio) with two double balustraded staircases. The balustrade continues between the columns of the portico and below the side-windows, as at Jones's Queen's House.

Vermiculation

Vermiculation is a type of emphatic rustication in which the face of each stone is carved with curvilinear formations resembling patterns left by worms. The vermiculation on the front of Chiswick House contributes to its sculptural richness.

Plan

In plan, Burlington's villa was a miniature version of Villa Rotonda. The new house consisted entirely of state rooms. Practical matters (relegated to the old house) did not interfere with the purity of the design, based on a contrasting sequence of proportional rooms: round, octagonal, rectangular and apsidal.

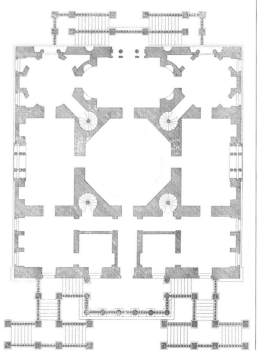

Garden front

This is composed of three Palladian windows set within relieving arches. The niches, the round-headed doorway under the central window and the Diocletian window reiterate the arched theme.

Gate pier

Two Palladian gate piers frame the entrance front of Chiswick House, repeating the vermiculation under the portico. The decorative piers, with festive swags above alternating vermiculated and smooth stones, support large classical sphinxes.

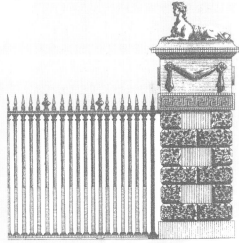

Section of hall

The central octagonal hall, or tribunal, is lit from the top by four Diocletian windows. The richly ornamented pedimented doorways are adapted from Jones, while the decoration follows Palladio's guidelines for Corinthian rooms.

Orange Tree Garden temple (c. 1725)

Burlington also designed a number of garden buildings at Chiswick. As with the house, he was meticulously and archaeologically close to his sources. This garden temple is a circular *cella* fronted by a proportionate replica of the portico of the antique temple of Fortuna Virilis, Rome.

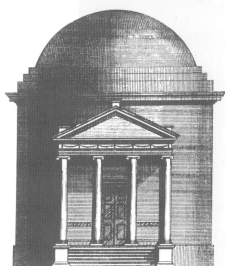

Diocletian windows

Diocletian or 'thermal' windows appear on several of Palladio's drawings and buildings and derive ultimately from antique Roman baths, such as the Baths of Diocletian. They are a recurring feature in Burlington's designs. On the garden front at Chiswick, the two dividing mullions of the segmental opening are aligned with the columns of the central Palladian window.

Palladianism

Lord Burlington and William Kent

Burlington and Kent's partnership
culminated at Chiswick, where Kent
contributed greatly to the definition
of the Palladian villa by designing the
garden. He later turned to architecture
and worked for the Office of Works
where, in partnership with Burlington,
he produced designs for a palace at
Whitehall, almost none of which was
executed. However, he published Inigo
Jones's designs for Whitehall, which
exerted great influence on 18th-century
public building. Beyond the private
sphere, the Palladian style produced
some important public buildings.
Burlington's Assembly Rooms in York,
for instance, demonstrate a tendency
for an antique Roman monumentality
reaching beyond Palladio and Jones.

**Gardens, Chiswick ◀
House, London**
Kent was largely
responsible for the
development of a classical
garden around Burlington's
Palladian villa, in which
miniature architecture
was a major component.
A gateway, cascade, pond,
obelisk and other
architectural 'incidents' – as
well as small temples based
on antique, Palladian or
Jonesian prototypes – are
found at the end of every
path. The garden was
designed on geometrical
principles, but with a
conscious effort to
appear 'natural'.

▶ Treasury, London (1734)
The Treasury was the
only executed building in
Kent's plans for Whitehall
Palace. It relies on Jones's
and Webb's designs for
Whitehall, which Kent
had published: it features
an applied pedimented
portico marking the
centre of a long rusticated
façade with a Venetian
window in the central
bay. The square corner
pavilions with single
Venetian windows,
however, are typical of
18th-century Palladian
country houses.

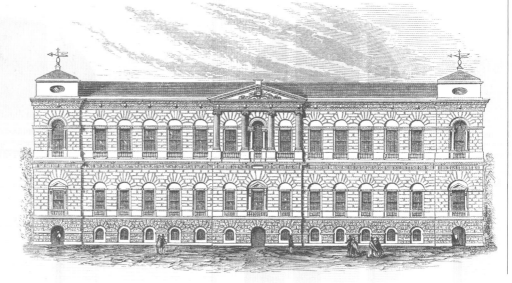

Assembly Rooms, York (1730)

This plan shows an arrangement of en-suite rooms of varied shapes, as at Chiswick House, including an apsidal room. This was also a feature of some reconstruction drawings by Palladio of Roman baths, which Burlington owned and published in 1730.

Front elevation, Assembly Rooms

While Burlington relied heavily on Palladio's design for the interiors of the hall, the design of the entrance front came from his own imagination, inspired by the theme of the imperial Roman baths.

Palladio's 'Egyptian hall', Assembly Rooms

For the design of the requisite grand dancing hall, Burlington used a design in Palladio's *Four Books*, which was described as 'suitable for festivals and entertainments' and was itself based, according to Palladio, on a description of Egyptian halls in Vitruvius. By imitating Palladio's design, Burlington thought he was conscientiously following Roman antique recommendations.

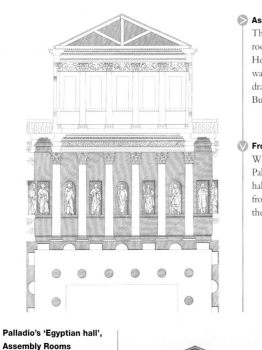

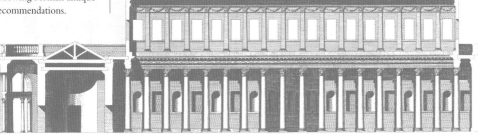

Cross-section, Assembly Rooms

Palladio recommended that the length of the hall should be that of ancient basilicas, and Burlington duly used a length of eighteen columns. But the plan was criticised for being impractical for its function, the aisles and intercolumniations being too narrow for the dancers.

Palladianism

American Palladianism

In America, the first appearance of Palladian motifs dates from the mid-18th century or Georgian period. The designing of buildings was largely the affair of gentlemen amateurs and carpenters, who relied on the architectural treatises of 18th-century England, primarily the Palladian ones. The treatises were used as pattern books for the finishing details of the elevation, and only towards the end of the century did Palladianism take on a new meaning, with more deliberate and self-conscious plans. Thomas Jefferson (later to become the third President of the United States) was an amateur architect who owned a library of architectural treatises and used the Palladian style in institutional buildings to support his republican and democratic ideals.

Georgian house
Towards the middle of the 18th century, a type of house prevailed in North America consisting of a rectangular box plan with a hipped (upward-sloping) roof and pedimented dormer windows. Doors, windows and chimneys were symmetrically arranged and designed according to classical motifs and proportion, as found in Batty Langley's *Treasury of Designs* (1740) and James Gibbs's *Book of Architecture* (1728).

Palladian dormer window
The hipped roofs of new houses were not as steep as earlier colonial ones, their gable-ends often interpreted as classical pediments. Dormer windows were occasionally given the form of a Palladian window, of which multiple examples appeared in the circulating English treatises.

Projecting entrance pavilion
Projecting entrance pavilions with pediments were a recurring feature. A heavy modillioned cornice, much favoured in America and often continued inside the pediment, is supported by two free-standing columns. The projecting entrance pavilion was a practical and climactic adaptation of the applied aedicule entrance and had resonances of the temple-front portico.

Mount Vernon, Fairfax County (1757–87)
Mount Vernon was remodelled and extended in several stages by its owner, following a Palladian villa plan. The asymmetrical arrangement of the windows caused by the first remodelling was disguised by strong symmetrical and Palladian accents elsewhere, such as projecting quadrant arcades forming a forecourt and a large octagonal cupola on the roof ridge, above a broad central pediment.

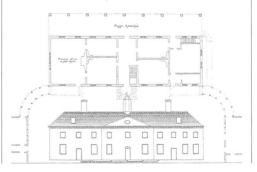

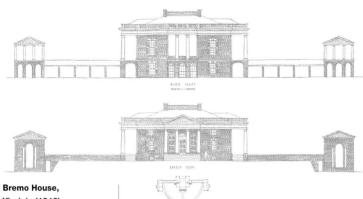

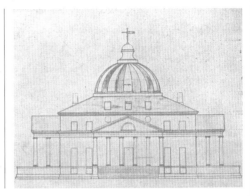

Bremo House, Virginia (1818)

Bremo House is a Late Georgian example, typically broken up into blocks. The design is reminiscent of English Palladian houses, with Palladian windows isolated in side-pavilions framing a temple-front portico on the main block.

Poplar House, Virginia (1820)

Jefferson's plan for Poplar House was based on an octagonal design by Jones. Jefferson introduced practical divisions without breaking the symmetry.

Monticello, Virginia

The first design of Jefferson's own house at Monticello had a two-storey central portico with details taken from Palladio's plates of the Doric and Ionic orders. Upon his return from France in 1796, Jefferson remodelled the house completely, with French 'republican' rather than Palladian details. The siting of the house on a hill was still romantically resonant of Palladio's Villa Rotonda, as were the domed cupola and the free-standing portico.

Competition design for the President's House, Washington (1792)

In his unexecuted design for the President's House in Washington, Jefferson shows himself truly Palladian in the sense of Lord Burlington and Colen Campbell. His design of a centralised villa with identical temple-front porticoes on four sides is closely based on Palladio's Villa Rotonda, Vicenza.

University of Virginia, Charlottesville (1823–27)

Jefferson designed this university following a Palladian villa plan, with a central Pantheon-inspired rotunda at the end of a long forecourt. The characteristic Palladian 'service wings' (the students' and professors' dormitories) were in pavilions to either side.

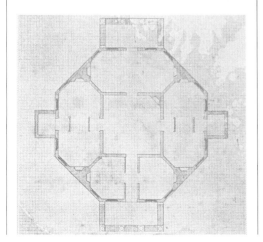

Neo-classical *mid-C.18th–mid-C.19th*

The Origins of Neo-classicism

Neo-classicism is a complex and varied style. In part a reaction to the excesses of baroque and rococo, it was an attempt to return to a purity and nobility of architecture perceived to have been lost. Though the term 'neo-classicism' was not coined until the late 19th century, the style itself was widely adopted from the mid-18th century onwards. With its roots in intellectual enquiry, neo-classicism developed out of four main strands: archaeology, printed sources, romanticism and structural purity. Ancient Greek and Roman buildings were studied with archaeological rigour; volumes of engravings depicted them as romantic ruins; and the simplicity of Greek structures suggested designs in which ornament was removed or pared back.

Arch of Constantine, Rome
Giovanni Battista Piranesi, an 18th-century painter and architect, brought many Roman buildings to the attention of a wider public through his volumes of engravings. This depicts the Arch of Constantine, shown in semi-ruinous state.

Fragments of Roman capitals
These fragments of capitals are a typical example of the eclecticism of Roman architecture. Though they are based on the Corinthian form, they use the language playfully: the left-hand capital shows women and armour supporting the top, while the right-hand one depicts a horse galloping out of an acanthus leaf.

Trophy of Octavius Augustus
A combination of arms and armour, decoratively arranged, the Trophy of Octavius Augustus was a motif in Roman decoration. It was seized on by 18th-century architects and was used to enliven entrance halls. In this context it refers back to the medieval idea of keeping arms in the hall for defence.

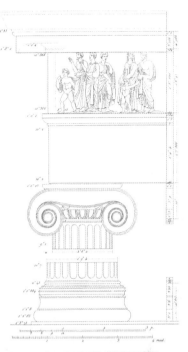

Ionic order, Temple on the Ilissus
This shows the base, capital, frieze and entablature of the Ionic order as used at Ilissus. The publication of such detail meant that individual elements could be picked out and reused in new buildings, providing a glossary of architectural forms and references.

Temple at Baalbek, Syria
This cross-section shows the typical combination of romanticism and accuracy that accompanied the archaeological investigations. The detail is perfectly recorded, but plants are drawn growing over the section to lend a romantic note.

Temple on the Ilissus, Athens
This Ionic temple on the Illisus is one of many Greek buildings used as inspiration in the 18th and 19th centuries. The simple temple façade, using four columns, would reappear on numerous churches throughout Europe.

Frieze, temple at Palmyra, Syria
The leaping horse motif here emerges from the centre of a flower, on a frieze instead of a capital. Archaeologists discovered much variation in built examples, rather than a single form existing for each order.

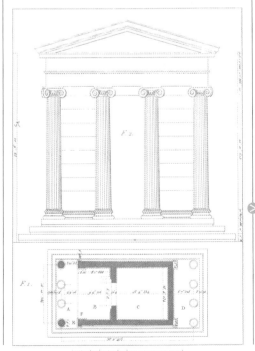

Reconstruction of the primitive hut
In this reconstruction of a primitive hut, the French theorist Marc Antoine Laugier took the notion of structural purity to its extreme, showing how the forms of the orders derive from the post-and-lintel construction of the 'first' hut.

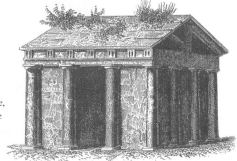

Neo-classical

A New Look at the Orders

The five orders are the building blocks of classical architecture and many writers had recorded their interpretation of the orders throughout the ages. Archaeology in new sites and a careful re-examination of known buildings brought a fresh understanding of the diversity of detail that could be embraced. It was now possible to choose to copy a baseless Greek Doric column or a Roman version with a base. Both were well documented and could be put forward as suitable prototypes. A few architects wanted to extend the traditional canon of the five orders and create their own – sometimes choosing part from one example and part from another; or even, in certain instances, creating a completely new type to embody a particular idea.

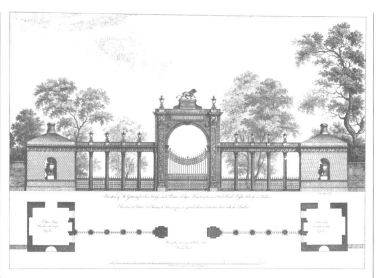

Doric order on the gateway, Syon House, Middlesex
Doric was seen as a masculine order and was therefore particularly appropriate for use on either a gateway or an entrance. Liberties have been taken here with the elements of the order, providing a playful interpretation.

Base of pilaster on the gateway, Syon House
The base of this pilaster is allowed a flight of fancy, with the addition of four lion's claws. There is no precedent for this and it should be considered as a joke, possibly intended to warn off unwanted visitors.

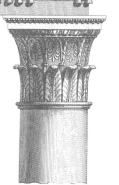

Capital of the Doric order, Syon House
This capital of the Doric order is more highly decorated than its classical antecedents, with leaves and honeysuckle (anthemion) woven together. The frieze is more restrained, though traditional *bucrania* (ox skulls) alternate with a sculpted ram's head.

Doric order, Shelburne House, London
The elaborate treatment of the Syon House Doric order contrasts with the simple base, capital and entablature used at Shelburne House (*c.* 1762–67). In the frieze, centaurs replace the more traditional *bucrania*, alternating in the metopes with *paterae* (medallions in bas-relief).

Corinthian order, Williams Wynn House, London
This variation of the usual Corinthian form incorporates small rams' heads in place of volutes and has a frieze composed of rosettes within circular wreaths of flowers. The traditional form of the entablature is retained.

Ionic order, anteroom, Syon House
This example of the Ionic order shows how highly decorated the orders could be. The volutes of the Ionic have been adorned with a scrolling pattern of leaves, and the abacus has been wrapped in palm leaves.

Design for the Britannic order
This design for a new order boasts a capital composed of a lion and unicorn, flanking the British crown, borrowed from the royal coat of arms. The frieze continues the patriotic theme, alternating the lion and unicorn, and is reminiscent of the Palmyra horse frieze.

Ionic order, Shelburne House
This is a much simpler version of the Ionic order, but just as recognisable. The volutes are plain, as is the abacus; the frieze has an alternating rhythm of honeysuckle motifs.

Neo-classical

Neo-classicism in France

France was one of the first countries to react against the baroque and rococo styles. From the mid-18th century architects were designing buildings steeped in the classical language of architecture, but restrained in their detailing and decoration. French theorists approached classicism in a spirit of rational enquiry and constructed theories of the origins of the orders. When these were put into practice, the resulting buildings had a character of their own, which distinguished them from their predecessors. The French were also pioneers of the new archaeological approach to antique buildings. In 1758 Jean-Dénis Leroy was the first to publish a record of the buildings of ancient Greece, romantically entitled *Ruines des plus beaux monuments de la Grèce*.

The primitive hut

French theorists were the first to propose the development of the orders from the principles of construction of the primitive hut. Works published in the mid-18th century suggested that logs could be equated to columns and that decoration on friezes was derived from joints in the timber.

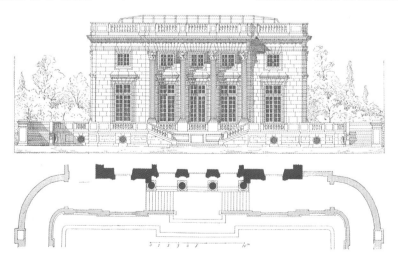

Façade, Petit Trianon, Versailles (1761–64)

This façade perfectly expresses the new desire for simplicity and restraint. It is articulated by a controlled Corinthian order, spanning the central bays, and the windows are adorned with the simplest possible mouldings. The whole is surmounted by a plain balustrade, with no statuary.

Portico roof, Comédie-Française, Paris

The roof of this portico also doubles as a balcony. There is no precedent for this in Greek and Roman architecture and it is an example of French rationalism, adapting a normally redundant space to a new use.

Thermal-window detail, Comédie-Française

Thermal windows, already features of the English Palladian movement, were also adopted in French neo-classical designs – here on the main and side-elevations.

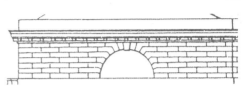

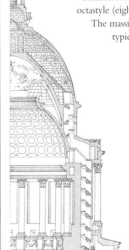

Plan, Pantheon, Paris (begun 1757)

This plan is in the form of a Greek cross, with four arms of equal length. Many 18th-century architects considered the symmetry of the Greek cross a particularly perfect shape and an improvement on the Gothic tradition of a long nave and short choir.

Cross-section, Pantheon

In this cross-section through the Pantheon, rows of free-standing structural columns articulate the nave. The piers supporting the crossing are reduced to a minimal size and the entablature is unbroken. The effect is one of light and space, similar to the feel of a Gothic church.

Elevation, Comédie-Française (1787–90)

The exterior of the theatre is covered in rusticated masonry and articulated by an octastyle (eight-columned) Doric portico. The massive simplicity of the design is typical of the pared-back style of French neo-classicism.

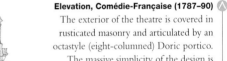

Dome cross-section, Pantheon

This section through the dome shows its unique construction. It is made of three shells, of which the outermost forms the shape of the exterior dome. The middle shell is completely invisible to the viewer, but is important structurally, as it supports the cupola.

Neo-classical

English Neo-classicism: the Vocabulary of the Neo-classical House

Neo-classicism was less a style of invention and more a new interpretation of the old. Invention in form was replaced by invention in composition, massing and the ordering of various elements. The vocabulary of classical architecture, as recorded in the buildings of ancient Greece and Rome, was reinterpreted to create new building types. Few small-scale domestic buildings survived in Greece and Rome. Instead, elements from temples, arches, baths and other public buildings were plundered and put together to form domestic settings, suitable for life in English towns and countryside. Scale, proportion and symmetry were key elements, but the wealth of published sources available at the time meant that each house could have different and varied detailing.

Design for the principal façade of a villa
This design shows a rigorous symmetry in the elevation and the inclusion of many motifs – such as the Ionic portico and the use of statuary and bas-reliefs – that are inspired by temple designs.

Cross-section through a villa
This section shows how the use of symmetry extended to the plan, as well as the exterior, as far as was practicable. Here rooms are disposed around a central hall and staircase, though the raised ceiling of the saloon on the right necessitates the introduction of a mezzanine floor on the left.

Detail of an arabesque
Based on flowing natural forms arranged in a geometrical pattern, arabesques were applied in plaster or painted directly on to the wall. This motif was widely used in the English neo-classical movement.

Design for a ceiling
Designs for ceilings were often inspired by those that remained in ancient buildings, and geometry was a key feature. This design shows a compartmented ceiling, formed of squares, octagons and hexagons.

Design for a sphinx
A mythical creature with the body of a lion and head of a woman, the sphinx was a recurring neo-classical motif, used on ceilings, friezes and chimneypieces.

Design for a door
Doors were usually divided visually into six sections by 'fielded' or raised panels. There was often a line in the centre of doors, though they rarely opened in the middle. Elaborate door furniture, using motifs such as acanthus leaves, urns and sphinxes, was employed.

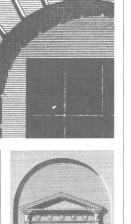

Rustication
Rustication is the use of large blocks of rough-cut masonry, separated by deep joins. It was used mainly to emphasise the lower storeys and tie the building visually to the ground.

Design for a niche
Niches or recesses in the wall were found in many domestic settings and were always arranged symmetrically in the plan of the room. They could be used to contain a piece of furniture or a sculpture.

Design for a chimneypiece
The controlled composition of this chimneypiece is typical of English neo-classical design. It has various recurring motifs, including a Greek key pattern in the frieze and caryatid heads supporting the mantel shelf.

Blind arch
Blind arches were a device used to articulate wall surfaces. They are shallow arch-shaped depressions, most commonly used on the exteriors of buildings and often set around windows. They were also used by themselves in order to break up large expanses of blank wall.

Design for a pilaster
Pilasters were used to articulate both internal and external walls. They could be plain, fluted or enlivened with decoration, such as these interlinked anthemion.

Neo-classical

Robert Adam and the Detail of Design

The architect Robert Adam (1728–92) is inextricably linked with the English neo-classical movement and gave his name to a style of interior decoration. Adam style combines an understanding of proportion with a keen eye for the smallest detail, such as a door handle or vase. Often commissioned to remodel existing buildings rather than build afresh, his genius lay in his ability to create sequences of well-proportioned and interestingly shaped rooms that delight the eye and draw the visitor forward. He referred to this concept as 'movement' and described it as 'the rise and fall, advance and recess with other diversity of form, in the different parts of a building, so as to add greatly to the picturesque of the composition'. These details from Syon House, Middlesex, which was altered between 1761 and 1771, show how he arrived at his style.

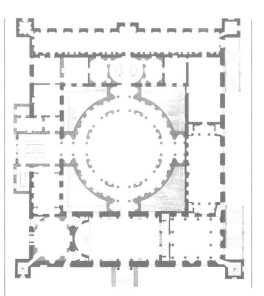

Floor plan, Syon House
Adam reworked the existing Jacobean plan of Syon House to create an interesting sequence of rooms, each with a contrasting shape. The enormous central circular space occupied the courtyard of the original house. Intended as a ballroom, it was never actually built.

Doric screen, entrance hall
This Doric screen partitions the end of the entrance hall and cleverly disguises the change of level in the original hall. The figure of the *Dying Gladiator*, positioned between the columns, further deflects attention from the levels and reinforces the temple ambience of the room.

Statue pedestal, entrance hall
Each element in a room designed by Adam was carefully thought about. This pedestal is decorated with a variety of motifs, including an anthemion frieze and *paterae* suspended by ribbons, below which appears a garland held up by lion masks. All these elements were well known, but had never before appeared in this combination.

Design for an overmantel

An overmantel is a decorative panel set into the chimneybreast above the mantel shelf. In this instance, Adam copied the form of a Roman bas-relief (a sculpture modelled flat against the wall), depicting a woman having her feet washed by her maid.

Design for an oil lamp

The oil lamp, used as an *acroterion*, is an example of practicality combined with decoration. A pair at each end of the screen guided visitors to the gate.

**Design for
a trophy**

This form of decoration, which had been used on triumphal arches in Roman architecture, found a new use, providing decorative panels for entrance halls. In this example, the panel has been symmetrically composed around the central piece of armour, though the varying shapes of the shields prevent it from becoming repetitive.

**Design for the
Long Gallery**

Adam was faced with the challenge of turning a Jacobean form into a classical interior. His solution was brilliant: he used bookcases to articulate bays, punctuating the monotony of the long gallery space with fireplaces, mirrors and doors.

**Design for a
scagliola floor**

Adam usually provided designs for carpets: this floor is unusual in being designed in *scagliola*, a mixture of plaster, pigment and size (a type of glue), mixed into a dough and laid in patterns. When dry, the surface could be polished and varnished.

Design for a vase

The external screen was enlivened with ornamental vases set in niches. Classical motifs included rams' and lions' heads and a laurel wreath around the base.

Neo-classical

The Greek Revival in England

The Greek Revival style is more of a veneer than a full-blown imitation: buildings were not copied wholesale, but elements were borrowed to create new types. The buildings of Greece had become widely known in the later 18th century following the publication of archaeological surveys. In England a key work was *The Antiquities of Athens* (1762) by James Stuart and Nicholas Revett. In the early 19th century a growing belief in the supremacy of the Greek orders provoked architects to copy them slavishly, particularly on public buildings, where they imparted a monumental air and implicitly linked British and ancient Grecian politics. Robert Smirke's Covent Garden Theatre was the first Greek Doric building to appear in London, but his British Museum is perhaps one of the best-known English buildings to encapsulate the Greek Revival style.

Caryatid portico, Erechtheum, Athens
The exterior of the north and south projections of St Pancras Church are copied directly from the caryatid tribune (female figures used as supports for an entablature) at the Erechtheum in Athens. The projections of the church actually contain twin vestries.

Choragic Monument of Lysicrates, Athens
The basic form of the Choragic Monument is combined on St. Pancras Church with that of the Tower of the Winds in Athens, and is lifted above the church to create a lofty English steeple that dominates the roofline.

West elevation, St Pancras Church, London (1819–22)
The west elevation of St Pancras church is a typical example of the Greek Revival style. The basic form of the early 18th-century church is reused, combining a temple form with a Gothic steeple. However, the orders and parts of the building are exact copies of Greek originals.

**Earl Tilney's temple,
Wanstead, Essex (c. 1765)**
This small garden temple was influenced by the floor plan of the Tower of the Winds, with paired columns set at angles, though it differed in its elevation and use of the orders.

Greek key pattern
This pattern is a well-known classical motif and has many variants. It is composed of horizontal and vertical lines, joined at right angles to form a continuous band of decoration, and was used to decorate architraves or friezes.

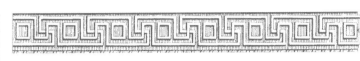

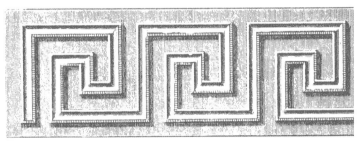

**Greek key pattern,
Kenwood House, London**
This simple example of a Greek key pattern was used as a string course on the exterior of Kenwood House, visually separating the storeys of the building and helping to prevent the stone or brick from weathering.

Façade, The Grange, Hampshire (1804–09)
This is a typical example of a Greek Revival country house. A Greek Doric hexastyle (six-columned) portico has been grafted on to an existing building to give a monumental temple feel, somewhat at odds with its rural setting. Inside, the original floor plan was retained.

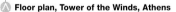

Floor plan, Tower of the Winds, Athens
The same building inspired two very different designs: on the one hand, a small garden building *(top)* and, on the other, the bottom half of the church steeple of St Pancras Church *(opposite)*.

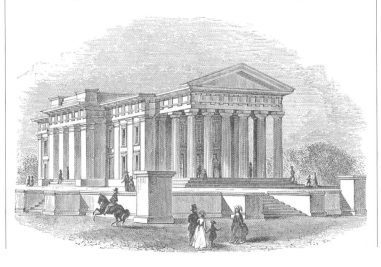

Neo-classical

New Types of Public Buildings

Britain's growing economic strength in the late 18th and 19th centuries led to a need for many new public buildings, as symbols of national pride and achievement. The classical style was a perfect model, combining the right elements of dignity and grandeur with monumental and impressive scale. Individual elements of ancient Greek and Roman public buildings could be freely adapted for use in Britain, and so town halls, museums and universities came to resemble externally Greek and Roman baths and temples. Using such buildings as inspiration also implied a link between the achievements of the ancient empires and those of modern-day Britain. These examples of public building types, erected in the neo-classical style between 1770 and 1850, show the range and versatility that were possible.

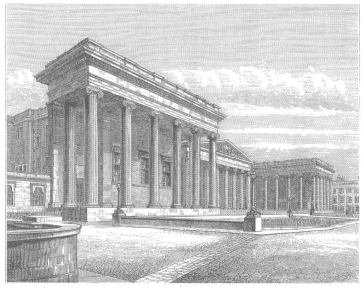

National museums: façade, British Museum, London (1823–47)
The concept of national museums as repositories of a country's acquisitions and, by extension, of its civilisation developed in the mid-18th century. The façade of the British Museum is a continuous Ionic colonnade, built on a huge scale and modelled on the temple of Athene Polias at Priene, Greece.

National museums: model for the door to the British Museum
The entrance door to the inner temple at the Erechtheum, Athens, is similar in detail to the main door at the British Museum. On a monumental scale, it dwarfs the visitor and intentionally creates an awe-inspiring mood.

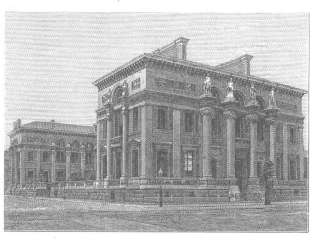

Academic institutions: façade, Taylorian Institute, Oxford (1841–45)
The prominent attic storey, articulated with thermal windows and finished with a deep cornice, disguised an internal gallery fitted with reading desks. The capitals of the projecting columns are based on the Temple of Apollo at Bassae and carry sculpture above the entablature.

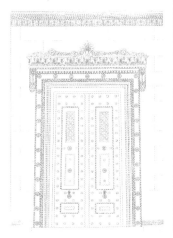

Town halls: elevation, St George's Hall, Liverpool (1841–56)
Built as an assembly room, concert hall and law courts all under one roof, St George's Hall has a restrained and severe façade, crowned by a plain attic storey. The building reflected Liverpool's importance as one of the wealthiest cities in Britain.

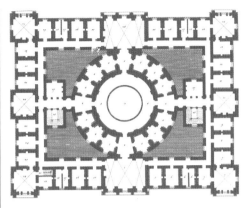

Record offices: plan, Register Office, Edinburgh
This unusual plan shows a circular central space or reading room, surrounded by a ring of wedge-shaped rooms. The staircases are arranged in pairs on each side of the central space, achieving a perfect symmetry along both axes.

Town halls: plan, St George's Hall
Inside, the monumental central meeting room is articulated by a giant order, built in red granite, and is reminiscent of Roman basilica interiors. The pair of court rooms at either end is similarly articulated on a smaller scale.

Record offices: elevation, Register Office, Edinburgh (1771–92)
The main elevation clearly has debts to the Palladian movement, though the detail on the Register Office – including the blind arches, sunken panels of decoration on the portico and the roundel in the pediment – mark it out as belonging to the neo-classical movement.

Government buildings: Admiralty Screen, Whitehall (1759–61)
The screen was designed to provide a monumental entrance and shelter the open courtyard of the Admiralty buildings in Whitehall. The very plain Doric order, using paired columns and blind niches, gives a sombre and imposing impression.

Government buildings: details of the decoration, Admiralty Screen
Built during the period of Britain's naval supremacy, the screen incorporates appropriately themed decoration, with classical references. Mythological winged seahorses sit above the gateway, and the pediments of the pavilions are enlivened with prows of ships in a Greek style.

Neo-classical

Neo-classicism in America

The neo-classical movement in America (1780–1860) was closely linked to its political status as a new republic. This was underlined by the fact that one of America's most influential presidents, Thomas Jefferson (1743–1826), was largely responsible for the introduction of neo-classicism as a Federal style. An accomplished amateur architect, Jefferson's early designs of the 1770s are rooted in scholarly research and show a marked Palladian influence. After travelling widely in Europe, and being struck by the writings of the French rationalists, who advocated a return to structural purity, he recognised that the buildings of Greece and Rome provided perfect models for state and federal buildings. His design for the Virginia State Capitol in Richmond, modelled on the Maison Carrée at Nîmes, was the first public building to imitate the temple form in America.

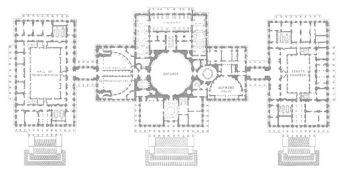

Plan, Capitol, Washington
The floor plan of the Capitol, though altered when built, shows that the central block has arms of equal length, in which are housed a variety of ingeniously shaped spaces, including semi-circular chambers for the Senate and House of Representatives.

Main elevation, Capitol, Washington (1792–1817)
The Capitol building in Washington, home of the Legislative Branch of the government, was the most significant American architectural commission of its time. The basic form consists of a central rotunda, crowned with an imposing dome added at a later date and flanked by two pedimented wings, articulated with a giant order.

Cross-section through the central rotunda, Capitol, Washington
After the fire of 1814, the Capitol had to be rebuilt. The opportunity was taken to create two new 'orders' to reflect important American products on which the country's wealth depended. The columns at the entrance to the Senate were given capitals in the form of tobacco leaves and, elsewhere, a corn cob and maize-leaf capital was introduced.

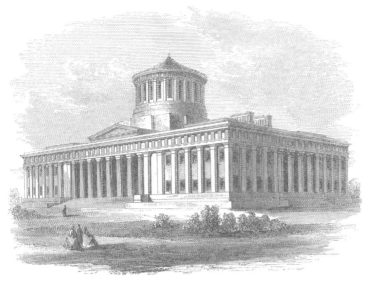

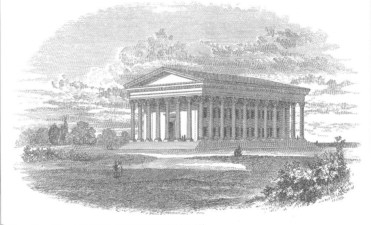

Design for the Rotunda, University of Virginia, Charlottesville (1821)

One of a series of buildings designed for the University of Virginia by Thomas Jefferson (*see also page 283*), the Rotunda was the central feature on the campus and housed the main library. Its form is derived from the Roman Pantheon and the drawing shows that a circle lies behind the form of the elevation, as well as the plan.

Elevation, State Capitol, Ohio (1830–61)

This Greek Revival building uses a baseless Doric order, chosen for its solemnity. The plan is a simple rectangle with an octastyle portico set *in antis*. The order, as pilasters, wraps around the building.

Elevation, Ezekiel Hersey Derby House, Salem, Massachusetts (*c.* 1800)

This four-bay elevation is reminiscent of town houses designed by Robert Adam thirty years earlier. It copies motifs such as the ground-floor blind arches and upper-storey pilasters.

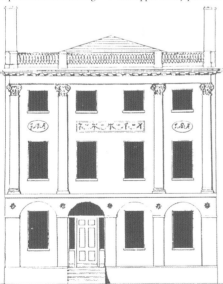

Elevation, Girard College, Philadelphia (1833–47)

Based on the Roman Maison Carrée at Nîmes, France, the imposing exterior of Girard College is articulated by a giant Corinthian order, 17 m (55 ft) high, enclosing a two-storey college building. The form has been copied so completely that the fenestration (arrangement and design of windows) is placed behind the rows of columns, making the interior rather dark.

Neo-classical

German Neo-classicism

Germany did not exist as a nation until 1871, but was a collection of independent states and principalities, united by a common language. The development of the neo-classical style in Germany (1785–1850) is closely linked to the search for a national identity – a movement that had its roots in Prussia, the most powerful state in the German-speaking world. A new generation of architects, influenced by French theorists, seized eagerly on the style of the Greek Revival, as it seemed to combine a beautiful aesthetic with a serious civic purpose; as elsewhere, they considered the Greek style particularly suited to public buildings. Appropriately, the earliest Greek Revival design was for a monument to Frederick the Great, who had laid the seeds of a German nation. The first Greek Revival building to be constructed was the Brandenburg Gate, gateway to Berlin, the capital of Prussia and seat of the court.

Brandenburg Gate, Berlin (1789–94)
Built to frame the western approach to the city, the gate is modelled on the Propylaea on the Acropolis, Athens, which formed the gateway to the sanctuary. The Brandenburg Gate borrows the hexastyle (six-columned) portico with its double row of Doric columns and the flanking pavilions.

Detail of the base of the order, Brandenburg Gate
A significant difference of detail between the two buildings is the use of a base on the Doric order of the Brandenburg Gate. This gives the gateway a lighter, more delicate feel than its Greek predecessor.

Detail of the base of the order, Propylaea
The absence of a base in the Greek Doric order gives an air of massive solemnity and permanence and was therefore particularly suited to the entrance to a sacred space.

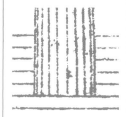

Propylaea, Athens
The Propylaea – source for the Brandenburg Gate – was more than a simple screen of columns: beyond the portico, the visitor would have entered a wide passageway, flanked by rooms on either side, before emerging into the Acropolis.

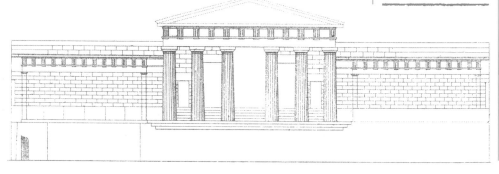

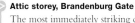

Attic storey, Brandenburg Gate

The most immediately striking distinction between the two buildings is the replacement of the Propylaea's pediment with an attic storey surmounted by a *quadriga*: a sculptural group of a chariot drawn by four horses, often used above façades or memorial arches. The winged figure represents Victory.

Façade, Glyptothek, Munich (1816–30)

Glyptothek is the Greek word for a sculpture gallery. The centrepiece of this elevation is an octastyle (eight-columned) portico with Ionic capitals based on the order at the Erechtheum, Athens, though the columns are not fluted. The projecting wings are more reminiscent of Italian Renaissance architecture.

Façade, Ruhmes-Halle, Munich (1843–54)

Built to honour important Bavarians, the Hall of Fame has an elevation that consists of a continuous colonnade of forty-eight Greek Doric columns, arranged in a U-shape and elevated on a platform, raising the occupants above the spectators. The sculpture in the pediments depicts Bavarian cultural and political achievements.

Neo-classical

German Neo-classicism: Karl Schinkel

One of Germany's most famous architects, Karl Friedrich Schinkel (1781–1841), became a leading figure in the project to establish a national identity. Influenced by the Romantic movement, he travelled in Italy, and admired Gothic as much as classical architecture, believing that they shared qualities of structural purity that had been lost during the Renaissance and baroque periods. But he maintained that architecture could play a bigger role – it could encapsulate political beliefs and express the aspirations of a nation. Schinkel's New Theatre and New Museum were both built in Berlin, a city that was beginning to dominate the German political scene, and were intended to deepen the region's growing cultural awareness.

Pediment, New Theatre
This is the façade's lower pediment, carved with scenes from the Greek tragedies. Contrast the use of this pediment, over an entrance, with that of the upper pediment, which is not structurally necessary.

Detail of acroterion, New Theatre
The *acroterion* on the pediment of the entrance is in the form of a muse holding a mask – an allusion to Greek theatre. This is an example of an architect combining two classical motifs to new effect.

Façade, New Theatre, Berlin (1818–26)
This shows the massive block of the New Theatre, with the grid-style fenestration that came to be characteristic of Schinkel's style. The three main areas of the building are defined externally: the central auditorium, flanked by a concert hall and by rehearsal and dressing rooms.

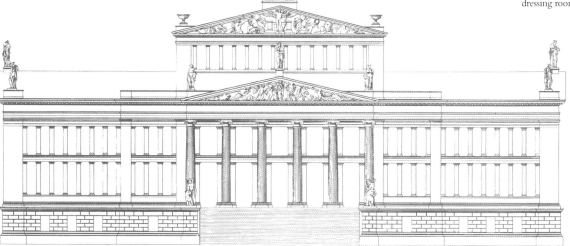

Plan of the ground floor, New Theatre
The plan of the ground floor of the New Theatre shows the three parts of the building that are articulated by the façade. The disposition of the rooms is planned according to need, with numerous small dressing rooms on one side balancing the concert hall on the other.

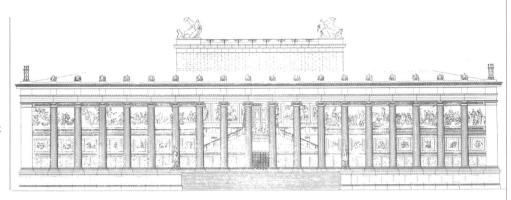

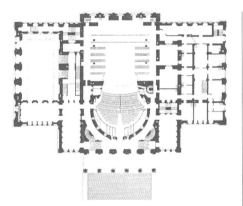

Elevation, New Museum, Berlin (begun 1823)
The row of eighteen Ionic columns forming the façade of the building is truly monumental in scale. Each column is 12 m (40 ft) high and the whole façade is 81 m (266 ft) long. Recalling a Greek colonnade, the façade has no central emphasis and the dome is concealed behind an attic storey.

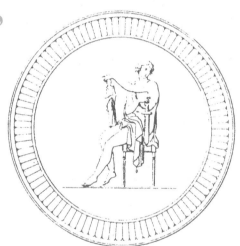

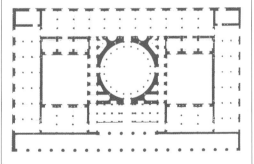

Plan, New Museum
This plan contrasts with that of the theatre *(top)*, as perfect symmetry of planning has been achieved. This is possible because the galleries could be designed to be of equal size: symmetry of planning is retained on each floor, though the exact disposition of the rooms changes.

Roundel, New Museum
The decorative medallion with a Greek figure was part of a larger scheme to articulate the walls. Schinkel enclosed it in a grid pattern of applied decoration.

Rotunda, New Museum
Surrounded by a colonnade of Corinthian columns, this room is the centrepiece of the museum. Designed for the display of sculpture, its circular form and coffered ceiling recall the Pantheon in Rome.

Picturesque *late C.18th–early C.19th*

Fundamentals

The Picturesque movement in architecture stems from the Romanticism of the 18th century and is sometimes known as the late Georgian or Regency style. The term was initially used to describe any building or landscape resembling the compositions of 17th-century painters such as Claude Lorraine, Nicolas Poussin and Salvator Rosa. Then, in around 1795, it was defined as an aesthetic category by the landscape gardening theorist Uvedale Price and the gentleman-scholar Richard Payne Knight. Downton Castle in Herefordshire (begun in 1772 by Knight) – with its irregularity, variety, contrasts, asymmetrical arrangement of forms, castellated exterior and up-to-date neo-classical interior – heralded the beginning of the Picturesque movement in architecture. In order to create a Picturesque effect, these characteristics were adopted alongside every conceivable style and, often, in an eclectic arrangement of two or more styles. There are many aspects to the Picturesque, and the architect John Nash embraced them all – from grand country houses set within informal landscapes to smaller cottage architecture and ingenious town planning.

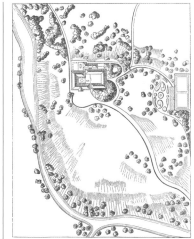

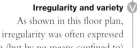

Irregularity and variety
As shown in this floor plan, irregularity was often expressed through (but by no means confined to) the arrangement of rooms. Variety is provided in the size of the rooms, and both qualities are reflected in the exterior of the building, when seen as a silhouette against the skyline.

The villa
A villa is a detached house, often with outbuildings pictorially positioned within an informal landscape. The villa and its surroundings were intended to form a coherent whole, or a Picturesque vision. A dramatic approach to the house was typical, as was the placing of trees around the house to create a pastoral scene.

Gothic style
Architecture of the Gothic period was often thought to intensify the Picturesque or Romantic effect of a building's silhouette. Gothic details included pointed lancet and hood-moulded windows.

Castellated style
The castellated style,
characterised by
battlements, towers and
an irregular massing of
forms, was one of the
most popular styles
used to express the
Picturesque movement
in architecture.

Italianate style
Many Picturesque
buildings were in the
Italianate style, often
characterised by a tower
(square in this example,
but generally round
with a conical roof),
wings at right angles
to the tower, loggias,
balustrades and
arched windows.

The Picturesque in town
Picturesque qualities are created in the town
using scenographic effects. Buildings are cleverly
positioned so that together they change the
direction of a street; a few buildings in a terrace are
set back while others are not; scenic archways are
used to link terraces; and, as shown here, trees and
bushes are used to soften architectural arrangements.

The sham castle
Culzean Castle, Ayrshire (*below right*), and Seton Castle, East
Lothian (*below*) were both designed by Robert Adam *c.* 1779
and built in Scotland. Bold massing of geometrical forms, a
dramatic setting, a sense of movement and an underlying
romantic appeal characterise these buildings, sometimes
known as 'sham castles'. Although not always associated with
Picturesque qualities, these features represent a vision – a
fantasy – that was in itself an essential part of the Picturesque.

Picturesque

Cottage Architecture

The deliberate irregularity and eclectic use of motifs employed in the first Picturesque buildings of the late 18th century remain discernible in the Picturesque cottage architecture of the early 19th century. Between 1790 and 1810 a flurry of publications appeared on the subject of cottage architecture. This craze can be explained, in part, by the notion of 'improvement' that was prevalent at the time; it was believed that landowners would benefit if their labourers were accommodated in comfortable housing. The remodelling of cottages would also enhance the scenery and the Picturesque effect of their estates. A significant source for Picturesque cottage architecture was the neo-classical idea of the 'primitive hut', advocated by the theorist Marc-Antoine Laugier in his *Essai sur l'architecture* of 1753, in which he argued for a return to first principles or natural roots, and stripped architecture of superfluous details, taking it back to a simple structure of four growing tree trunks, lintels of sawn logs and branches that create a basic roof, thus forming a 'primitive hut'.

Cottage orné

Cottages ornés are small houses usually situated in the countryside or a park. They are deeply rustic in character and display many Picturesque qualities: thatched roofs, leaded windows, bargeboards, ornamental chimneys and verandahs. John Nash was responsible for producing a whole hamlet composed of such gems at St Blaise, near Bristol, in around 1811.

Bargeboard

A bargeboard is an inclined and projecting wooden board that sits at the gable end of a building. It covers the horizontal timbers of the roof and is often ornamented.

Creeping plants

It was widely believed that creeping plants, particularly ivy, added greatly to the Picturesque character of a rural cottage. They were trained to grow around features such as a verandah.

Dormer

A dormer is a structure set into a sloping roof. It has a roof of its own – either pitched or flat – sides, and a window set into the front. As shown here, a dormer often has a small gable over the window.

Thatch

Thatch is a dense roof covering of reed, rushes or straw, used most frequently in vernacular buildings. A thatched roof was an essential feature of any Picturesque cottage and was fundamental in creating its rustic charm.

Half-timbered cottages and Cyclopean stonework

Timbers were often applied to the upper storeys of a building, or sometimes just to part of them, while the lower storeys were constructed of stone or brick. The lower storeys were often dressed in Cyclopean stonework: irregular, undressed courses of stone that create a varied texture. These rough pieces of stone, almost in their natural state, provide a reference to the notion of the 'primitive hut' and the return to natural roots.

Porch

A porch is the covered entrance to a building. In Picturesque cottages, porches were often made of timber and, as in this example, were fairly decorative. A porch was considered to add interest and variety to the exterior of a cottage by punctuating the regularity of an otherwise plain elevation.

Verandah

A verandah is an open gallery or balcony with a roof supported by light metal posts or, sometimes, by twisted wooden posts – again referring to a return to natural roots. The verandah became closely associated with the Picturesque and is thought to have originated from sources in India.

Picturesque

Garden and Estate Buildings

Through a very successful but short-lived partnership, Humphry Repton, the landscape gardener, and John Nash remodelled and improved various great estates at the latter end of the 18th century and beginning of the 19th: Repton improved the landscape, while Nash remodelled and added to the estate buildings. Landscape gardening was a brand-new profession at the time and their partnership catered for the wealthy landowner – both long-established and new. The romantic siting of ornamental buildings by lakes or in groves can be seen in the work of earlier generations – as at Rousham, Oxfordshire, of around 1730 by William Kent. However, Repton and Nash, as products of the Picturesque, produced landscapes in which the pictorial positioning of the house was of the greatest importance, and the smooth artificiality of Lancelot Brown's landscapes was replaced with a greater respect for the wild ruggedness of nature, increasing the Picturesque effect and romantic appeal of a landscape.

Dairy
The dairy was essentially a functional building where the cows were milked and the machinery for milking was stored. It could be richly embellished with Picturesque ornament, its functional purpose clearly expressed in this plan with four compartments, including a passage filled with fragrant plants and the servant's room for cleaning the milking equipment.

Stables
Stables were built to accommodate a household's horses and were designed to correspond with the main house, in terms of construction, style and ornament.

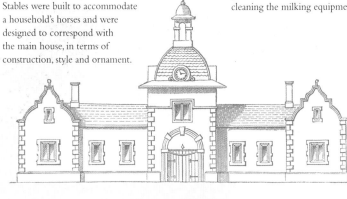

Lodge

A lodge is a small residential building situated on an estate. It is generally well planned, with a convenient arrangement of rooms. The Picturesque character of the building derives from the elevation, which (as shown here) is given variety and interest through the asymmetrical disposition of its external components: the porch, chimneys and windows.

Gatehouse
A gatehouse is essentially a lodge that incorporates part of the gate. Illustrated here in the castellated style, it combines symmetry with variety to create a pleasing architectural and Picturesque composition.

Fountains
Such ornamental water structures were used in Picturesque landscapes in order to enhance their Picturesque effect.

Ornamental bridge
This is a bridge that is given greater decorative effect, so that it can be used to enhance the Picturesque quality of the scenery. It provides variety and a point of focus within the landscape, and presents an opportunity for different styles to be used. Here, for example, in the middle of the bridge stands a Chinese temple.

Conservatory
A conservatory is a more ornamental version of a glasshouse, constructed of iron and glass, with very large windows. It is either an independent structure or is attached to the main house.

Gazebo (belvedere) and treillage
A gazebo is a garden house (often ornamental), usually positioned at a vantage point within the landscape, with windows or openings that command great views. The sides might be of treillage, a decorative form of ironwork that was often combined with a verandah to create a lightly constructed panel, as an alternative to a solid partition.

Elements of Architecture

Domes

A dome is essentially a form of vault, and can be constructed on a circular, polygonal or elliptical plan, and to various profiles. The form probably had its origins in round huts built from bowed saplings joined at the centre and covered with thatch, and came to represent the vault of heaven and to denote authority. The development of concrete by the Romans made the construction of large hemispherical domes possible, and the dome became a major feature of the Byzantine style, in which classical and Eastern influences intermixed. While the Romans only used domes over circular or polygonal spaces, Byzantine builders were able to place them over square or rectangular compartments by the use of pendentives (*see page 157*), a result also achieved in Islamic architecture (*see pages 175 and 179*).

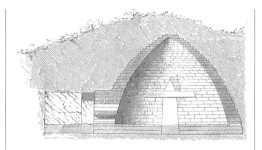

Corbelled dome
Measuring nearly 15 m (49 ft) in diameter, the tholos (main tomb chamber) of the Mycenaean Treasury of Atreus (*c.* 1220 BC) is topped by a pointed corbelled dome, resembling an old-fashioned beehive. Corbelling, used not only in Greece, but also in India and South America, involves the building of tiers of masonry, each projecting over the one below.

Roman dome
The concrete dome of the Pantheon, Rome (AD 126), measuring 44 m (144 ft) in diameter, is typically Roman. Internally, the dome is a hemisphere (half a sphere), its great weight reduced by the use of coffering and an open crown (oculus). Externally, stability is provided by an extra tier and by steps, creating a saucer-shaped dome.

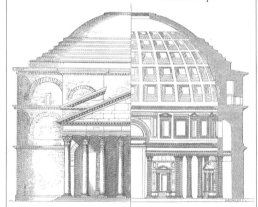

Pointed dome
Islamic architecture is characterised by the use of domes. One particularly common form is the pointed dome, which has a sharply pronounced peak. Here, at the Tomb of Oljeitu, Sultaniya, Iran (*c.* 1310), the dome rises from an octagonal drum, and is ornamented with glazed tiles.

Compound dome
The term compound dome is given to a group of multiple domes and vaults, a feature which became common in Byzantine architecture. At Hagia Sophia, Constantinople (AD 532–37), the main dome is supported on four huge arches, buttressed by semi-domes (half domes). Pendentives allow the circular dome to rest on a square plan.

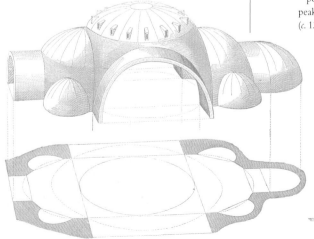

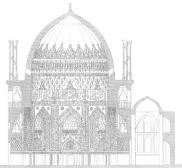

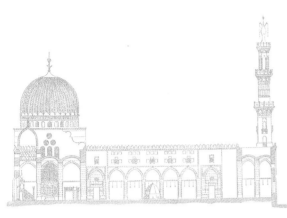

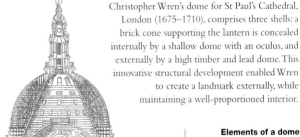

Triple-shell dome

Christopher Wren's dome for St Paul's Cathedral, London (1675–1710), comprises three shells: a brick cone supporting the lantern is concealed internally by a shallow dome with an oculus, and externally by a high timber and lead dome. This innovative structural development enabled Wren to create a landmark externally, while maintaining a well-proportioned interior.

Elements of a dome

The dome of the Parisian Church at Les Invalides (1680–1707) is composed of three major elements: drum, dome and lantern. The drum is the vertical wall that carries the dome, and is often set with windows or decorated with columns. It adds height to the dome, aiding visibility and prominence. The curved dome itself is commonly crowned by a structure known as a lantern. Where this is domical in form, it is termed a cupola.

Stilted dome

The word stilted is most commonly applied to arches, but can also refer to domes. A stilted dome is one in which the curve begins above impost level (the area on which the dome rests, and from whence it appears to spring); the sides continue vertically for some distance, before curving to a point.

Double-shell dome

Designed by Michelangelo, the dome of St Peter's, Rome (1585–90), looks back to Brunelleschi's Florence Duomo in being of brick double-shell construction. The dome has ribs linked by horizontal iron chains and, although hemispherical internally, is slightly pointed on its exterior. The heavy masonry cupola holds the ribs in place and stops them from opening out.

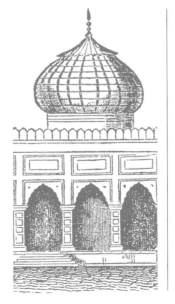

Bulbous dome

Another form of dome common in Islamic architecture is that shown here, at the Taj Mahal, Agra, India (1632–54). This is pointed, but also bulbous, its sides curving out to present a rounded profile. A related form is the onion dome, much used in Russia and eastern Europe, but the latter is structurally not a true dome (it is not vaulted).

Columns

A column is a vertical support made up of a base, shaft and capital. In the vocabulary of classical architecture, the Greeks paired the column with an entablature, which when combined supported the roofs of their buildings. The Romans, however, used columns decoratively rather than structurally, preferring an arcuated (arched) system to the Greek trabeated (beamed) system. The result was a number of new variants, such as engaged columns, half-columns and pilasters. Columns can be paired (Roman), clustered (Norman) or free-standing (like an Indian *lath*). The shaft can be as simple as the plain Tuscan order (*top right*) or highly decorated; the capital ranges from the simple medieval to the ornate Egyptian.

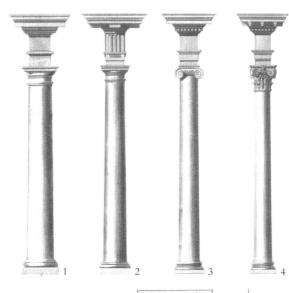

1   2   3   4   5

The five Orders

The five classical Orders are structural systems for the organisation, proportioning and decoration of parts consisting of column with capital and (usually) base, and horizontal entablature. the Doric (2), Ionic (3), and Corinthian (5) were developed in Greece, and Tuscan (1) and Composite (4) in Rome. After an abeyance of nearly one thousand years, the Orders were revived in the Renaissance, and were standardised by architects such as Sebastiano Serlio, Andrea Palladio and Sir William Chambers.

Twisted column

During the Romanesque period, builders continued to reuse and imitate ancient Roman columns wherever possible. Where new, the emphasis was on elegance and beauty, as illustrated by this twisted column. Often these were decorated with mosaic work.

Compound pier

A pier has a much greater load-bearing capacity than a column, and is usually sturdy and massive. In Romanesque and Gothic architecture, the faces of piers were often set with half-columns or shafts, either attached or detached, creating a unified architectural element. These are known as compound or clustered piers.

Persian
The stylistic origins of Persian columns lie in their wooden construction. However, this column from the Hall of 100 Columns, Persepolis (5th century BC), is elegantly carved in stone, with a fluted column surmounted by volutes and a twin bull's head capital.

Egyptian
Egyptian columns often resemble the local flora: columns can resemble papyrus leaves; and capitals, lotus leaves. This example from the Temple of Hathor in Upper Egypt (110 BC–AD 68) is decorated with hieroglyphics and is topped by a Hathoric capital, showing the goddess Hathor on each side.

Chinese
Chinese columns were made of wood and, instead of capitals, were often topped with brackets, which supported the roof. Unusually, the Chinese framed the roof and superstructure of a building before raising the columns. Columns were often painted red as a decorative feature.

Indian
This column from a Dravidian temple imitates the wooden construction of earlier Indian architecture. The entire surface is highly decorated. Single free-standing pillars known as *laths*, used for ceremonial purposes, were common.

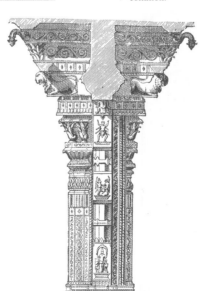

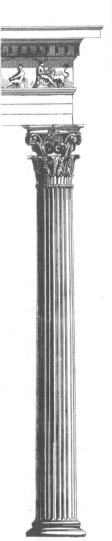

Divisions of a column
A column, whatever its location or age, is divided into three separate components: the base, the shaft and the capital. In this instance the shaft is fluted or grooved and the capital is Corinthian.

315

Towers

Towers, distinguished by their height, are common to the architecture of a wide range of countries and periods. Many forms – such as Italian *campanili*, Islamic minarets and Indian *sikharas* – are associated with religious buildings, though they may not be physically attached to them. Bells in the upper stage (belfry) of a tower call people to worship, while the tower itself serves as a prominent marker of a sacred site. Towers of the Gothic period are particularly rich, and are usually placed at the centre (crossing) or west end of churches. Towers are often topped by a spire, an acutely pointed terminal built in a number of forms. In the unsettled medieval climate, towers became an important measure of defence and were incorporated into castle fortifications, often strengthening the curtain walls. In Scotland, Ireland and northern England, compact, defensible residences were built, known as tower-houses.

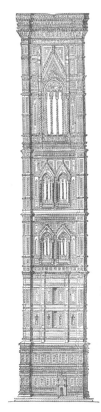

Needle spire
This church near Northampton, England, bears a needle spire, an elongated, slender form that rises from behind a parapet.

Campanile
Italian bell towers – most often free-standing – are known as *campanili* (from *campana*, meaning 'bell'). As in this 14th-century example, they are usually simple in design, and either square or circular in plan.

Bell tower
Bell towers provided a focus for religious and civic life and served as watchtowers. The upper stage of a tower holds the bells and is properly known as the belfry, although this word is sometimes applied to the tower as a whole.

Defensive tower
The largest and most impenetrable tower of a castle is known as a keep or donjon. It is often set apart from the outer defences, and was used as a final measure of refuge. This, the mid-fifteenth-century keep of Tattershall Castle, Lincolnshire, England, is typical in bearing battlements, machicolation and a parapet walk.

Round tower
Simple, unornamented towers built on a circular plan and attached directly to a building. Particularly common among the Norman churches of East Anglia, England.

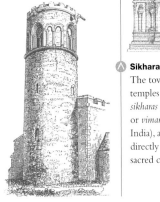

Sikhara
The towers of Indian temples are known as *sikharas* (northern India) ` or *vimanas* (southern India), and are placed directly above a building's sacred centre.

Leaning tower
This exceptional and world-famous example of a tower is the circular *campanile* at Pisa, Italy (begun 1173). Designed to be vertical, the tower began to lean during construction, and now inclines towards the south at an angle of around five and a half degrees.

Irish round tower
In Ireland a number of distinctive round towers exist, having been built on monastic sites dating from the 10th to 12th centuries. They are free-standing, taper slightly towards the top and bear conical stone roofs. The doorways of round towers were placed high above the ground and were reached via a ladder, reflecting their use as refuges in times of danger.

Minaret
The towers of Islamic architecture, usually connected with mosques, are known as minarets, and are very slender in form. They have projecting balconies from which Muslims are called to prayer.

Tower of diminishing stages
The levels of towers are usually known as stages, rather than storeys. The stages of some towers lessen in size as the building grows in height, producing a telescopic effect, as in this example from the Italian Renaissance.

Splay-foot spire
This German church tower is crowned by a splay-foot spire, a form that (like a broach spire) is octagonal for most of its height, but square at its base. Its four main faces open out at their bases to form eaves.

Arches and Arcades

An arch is a construction that spans an opening. The top, or head, is usually curved, but arches vary in shape from the horizontal flat arch through semi-circular and semi-elliptical arches to acutely pointed arches. A curved arch consists of wedge-shaped blocks, or voussoirs, arranged to support each other and be capable of supporting a load. In classical Western architecture, the last stone to be dropped into place in the centre of the arch is the keystone. In pointed Gothic arches there is no keystone, because the thrust is spread outwards and then downwards, with the arch supported at the sides and ends. Arches may also be used to support large expanses of wall, and for foundations. An arcade is a series of arches supported on columns or piers that form an open entrance, or a covered walkway that is open on one side. A 'blind arcade' is a series of arches applied to the surface of a wall, a common form of decoration in medieval churches.

Persian arch

The great arch of Tak Kesra, Ctesiphan (AD 550), formed the opening to the vaulted entrance hall of a palace. The arch is neither pointed nor semi-circular, but rather semi-elliptical. The flanking walls are articulated by blind arcades: a series of round-headed and pointed arches.

Superimposed arcades

The arcades on the façade of the Colosseum, Rome (begun AD 70), are arranged in tiers known as superimposed arcades. The columns are placed one above the other in the conventional order: Doric, Ionic and Corinthian. The arches are typically Roman in having semi-circular heads.

Ogee arch

A common feature of the Gothic style, the ogee arch is a pointed form composed of two double curves in which one part is convex and the other concave, meeting at the apex.

Terminology for the classical arch

This drawing features the terms used for the various structural components and features of the classical arch. The impost is a block or band on which the arch rests, and the intrados is the inner curve or underside of the arch, also known as a soffit.

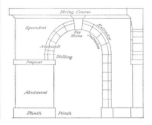

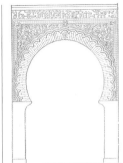

Horseshoe arch

The curves of the arch head continue down and round, past the impost of the arch. This is a common feature in Islamic architecture. Horseshoe arches of semi-circular and pointed form are found in Egypt, Syria and Arabia, (the latter being more common).

Tudor arch

This form of shallow, double-curved arch was much used in the Tudor period, hence its name. In form, it is pointed and four-centred, meaning that the lower curves or arcs are drawn from two centres on the springing line (where the arch begins to curve), and the upper pair from centres below the springing line.

Pointed arch

A Gothic pointed arch of the Early English period (c. 1230) in the nave of Lincoln Cathedral shows how the simplicity of the form could be enriched by multiple mouldings and by decorated piercing – the origin of window tracery.

Renaissance arch

These arches on the Old Library of St Mark, Venice (begun 1537), follow the Roman model, with semi-circular arch heads, keystones, spandrels, frieze and cornice set above each other within the frame of the classical orders.

Round-headed arch

These 12th-century French arches are round-headed, with 'billet' mouldings on the outer arch and 'roll' mouldings on the inner. The inset columns appear to carry the downward thrust, but the weight is borne by the stone piers.

Norman nave arcade

These 12th-century triforium arches on the south side of the nave of Waltham Abbey church, Essex, are the same span and rise as the nave arches below, but rest on shorter columns. The standard Norman arch form was semi-circular or round, but variants included the horseshoe, the segmental and the pointed (shown in the two end bays).

Doorways

Doorways constitute one of the most significant aspects of exterior architecture, generally occupying a central position in the elevation and defining the character and function of the building – whether public or private. Doorways are also the architectural focus of the exterior, and the ornamentation of the doorcase often determines the style of the whole façade. In some examples the entrance extends to a portal involving the balcony above or an entire vertical section of the elevation. Doorways represent the passage from exterior to interior, and the themes and purposes of the interior are usually introduced on the outside through the articulation and sculptural decoration of the doorcase. Being the most vulnerable part of the elevation, doorways are often protected, both practically by means of mouldings, cornices, roofs and porticoes to divert rain, and symbolically by the use of heavy, defensive masonry or sculptures standing guard.

Door jambs
A doorcase, or the frame surrounding the entrance opening, is composed of door jambs or vertical side-members. In their most basic form, jambs are simple architectural mouldings offering opportunities for sculptural decoration. Even the early trapezoidal doorcases of ancient Greek structures, such as the Erechtheum in Athens, were elaborately carved.

Entrance guard
In a number of civilisations, including the Assyrian, important doorways and gateways are symbolically guarded by stone sculptures of mythical beasts, sphinxes, lions or even human figures. These are either integrated into the doorcase (as in Assyrian examples) or are free-standing sculptures on each side of the entrance.

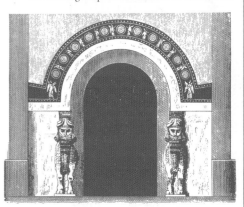

 Defensive doorway
Characteristic of Norman architecture, arched doorways of heavy masonry dress the elevation with a fortress-like monumentality. Such doorways, whose chief decorative features are heavy projecting imposts over monolithic vertical stones, are representative of the largely defensive and protective role of Norman buildings.

Pedimented porch
Gabled porches provide shelter over the doors of Georgian and neo-classical houses. They often became the focus of classical ornamentation featuring columns, entablatures and pediments.

Cathedral portal
Romanesque cathedral entrances are high, wide portals occupying one-third or more of the west front, the actual access into the cathedral being limited to a small hinged panel in the portal.

Moorish entrance
The doorway of Moorish and Islamic buildings is often inserted in a decorated panel, including latticework, mosaics, tiles, stucco work, stones, marbles and a black-and-white band of voussoir stones forming the arch.

Caryatids and atlantes
The baroque period produced heavily decorated entrances, particularly in France and Central Europe, involving muscular atlantes or caryatids supporting an ornate balcony sheltering the doorway.

Elizabethan doorway
Elizabethan doorways often displayed the architectural knowledge of their patrons – the strapwork, herms, and classicising detail were inspired by Flemish and Italian pattern books.

Blocked surrounds
Blocked surrounds, with projecting stones interrupting the architrave moulding, were used in the early 18th century to emphasise the entrance of a sober classical front.

Neo-classical door
Typical neo-classical interiors have panelled double-doors with fine antique Roman decoration, involving imitations of Roman medallions, plaster busts or graceful caryatids.

Windows

The earliest windows were unglazed openings in walls, which let in light and ventilated interior spaces. Glazed windows, at once functional and decorative, were introduced by the Romans in *c*. AD 65, but glass was not widely used until the 13th century in churches and the 16th century in houses. The important aesthetic contribution of windows is reflected in the range of styles that developed. Throughout history the design of glazed windows has been dictated by advances in the production of glass. Early windows, with small panes held together by leadwork, were replaced in the 17th and 18th centuries by wooden-framed windows known as sashes. By the 1840s technological developments meant that sheet glass (thinner, cheaper and larger than earlier glass) could be employed to allow views – uninterrupted by glazing bars – both into and out of buildings.

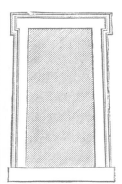

Draughtsman's window
In the majority of architectural drawings and engravings of the 18th century, window openings are delineated as dark voids, with no articulation or indication of the pattern of glazing. The moulded frame around the window is a shouldered architrave.

Circular window
Rose or wheel windows are elaborate confections designed to resemble the petals of a flower or the spokes of a wheel.

Lancet
A tall, narrow arched window characteristic of Gothic and Byzantine architecture, the lancet is predominantly pointed, although round-headed versions also occur, often in pairs or groups of three.

Leadwork
The size of the panes of glass in leaded windows is governed by the strength of the lead strips, known as cames, which hold the glazing in place. Early windows had diagonal leadwork forming a lattice pattern, which gave way to a fashion for rectangular panes in the 17th century.

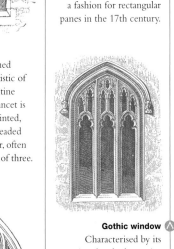

Gothic window
Characterised by its pointed arch, decorative tracery and stained glass, the Gothic window was prevalent from the 12th to early 16th centuries. It was revived in a consciously antiquarian form in the late 18th century and was much used by Victorian architects.

Ogee window
The pointed ogee arch (a combination of a concave and convex line) originated in Islamic architecture. The form is also found in Gothic architecture and was favoured in the 18th century as a decorative statement reminiscent of the East and of antiquity.

Casement window
This is a side-hinged window, fixed to open either inwards or outwards. Casements were the most common form of domestic window before the introduction of the sash, and usually contain leaded lights (panes of glass).

French window
This is a variation on the casement, with windows extended to the height of the doors and carried right down to the floor. French windows may be inward- or outward-opening.

Sash window
A sash window is a glazed wooden-framed window that slides up and down on pulleys. Used throughout the 18th and 19th centuries, sash windows are especially associated with Georgian architecture. There are often regional variations, such as the Yorkshire sash, which slides horizontally.

Diocletian (or thermal) window
This is a semi-circular window divided into three lights by two uprights known as mullions. Particularly associated with Palladian architecture, such windows are based on a model found at the Baths of Diocletian in Rome.

Projecting window
Bay and oriel windows project from the elevations of buildings. Often highly decorative, they let in more light than windows that lie flush with the wall face. Oriels are always sited on upper floors, while bays of the square and canted (angled) type shown here occur at all levels.

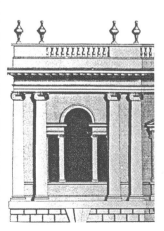

Venetian window
A tripartite window, this has a central arched opening and two flat-headed, narrower side-openings. It is also known as a Palladian or Serlian window after the two Italian architects who popularised its use: Andrea Palladio and Sebastiano Serlio.

Pediments and Gables

Pediments – distinctive features of much classical and classically inspired architecture – are the low-pitched gable ends of buildings, usually located above a portico. They are often decorated with high-relief sculpture, the significance of which can add specific meaning to a building. Pediments are also used as architectural motifs in window and door framings, as well as on tombs and monuments. Gables are formed by the upper part of a wall at the end of a pitched roof, and in their simplest form are triangular and straight-edged, although they may also be curved, bell-shaped or stepped. Gable decoration was a particularly important element of northern European domestic architecture during the 16th and 17th centuries, when very ornate and inventive treatments proliferated.

Doorway pediment
Classical architectural forms were frequently employed during the Renaissance as elements of exterior and interior decoration. Doorways and windows were enhanced with columns, pilasters and pediments. This ornate 16th-century Spanish portal has a high-pitched triangular pediment, framed by egg-and-dart moulding (*see page 100*).

Broken pediment
The shape of a pediment can range from the triangular to the curved segmental. Broken pediments have their line interrupted either at the apex or at the base. Baroque architecture is particularly rich in inventive forms of pediment, as exemplified by this broken-apex pediment topped by an urn.

Temple pediment
In a classical temple the pediment is formed by continuing the horizontal cornice of the order along the gable edges. These sloping edges are called raking cornices. The tympanum thus formed provides an ideal space for bold sculpture, and this decorative possibility was exploited in many classical temples.

Acroteria

Acroteria are strictly the plinths on which statues stand at the end or apex of a classical pediment, but the term is now more generally used for the statuary itself.

Bargeboard

Wooden bargeboards or gableboards are placed along the sloping edges of a gable, sometimes to mask the ends of roof timbers. They range from plain to elaborately decorated, as in this carved example.

Crow-stepped gable

A gable with stepped sides is called crow-stepped or corbie-stepped. As with much gable decoration, the true profile of the roof end is masked by the shape of the gable that fronts it.

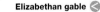

Gable decoration

A major feature of Dutch and northern European secular buildings in the 16th and 17th centuries, gable decoration became very expressive and ornate. Architectural motifs were taken from both Gothic and Renaissance styles, achieving great variety of profile and decorative richness.

Elizabethan gable

Gable decoration seems to have reached England during the 16th century and was taken up with some enthusiasm, with the curved type being most widely adopted. The decorated gable also features in Jacobean architecture of the early 17th century.

Roofs

A roof is the covering of a building, which serves to protect the inhabitants and the internal fabric from the weather. Roofs are often made from timber and clad with tiles – marble or terracotta in classical examples – but may be covered with thatch, slate, stone, wood, lead, copper, turf or other materials. Forms vary with country, region, period and style, but the most basic are pitched and flat roofs. The supporting structure is also termed the roof (properly the roof frame) and can often be viewed from the interior of the building. In early times roof frames were of simple design, but gradually grew more complex in form, culminating in English architecture of the late medieval period. The rigid, triangular framework of timbers spanning a building, and dividing it into bay units, is called a truss, and at its most basic was composed of rafters and a tie beam – the main transverse member.

Pitched roof
The most common roof form is known as pitched or gabled. Roofs of this type have two slopes meeting at a central ridge, and gables at both ends.

Conical roof
Some buildings, such as this church in Sweden, carry cone-shaped (conical) roofs, known as revolved roofs.

Hipped roof
This medieval aisled hall at Nurstead in Kent, England, has a roof in which all four sides slope upwards. Such a construction has four hips (the external angles formed by the meeting of two sloping surfaces) and is thus termed a hipped or hip roof.

Helm roof
The two main towers of this Gothic church are crowned by helm roofs, each composed of four inclined faces rising from the gables. The smaller towers bear pyramidal roofs.

Flat roof

In many buildings of the Italian Renaissance, roofs were flat or low-pitched. Their structure was commonly hidden behind balustrading, great cornices or parapets (low walls placed above the roof-line, and often decorated).

Mansard roof

A mansard roof – named after French architect François Mansart – has a double slope on each of its four sides, the lower section being steeper and longer than the upper. The lower slope is often punctuated with dormer windows.

King-post roof

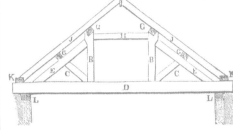

The distinctive feature of this common roof form is the king post, a vertical timber that rises to meet a longitudinal ridge-piece running along the roof's ridge and rests centrally on a transverse (tie) beam. Inclining members (raking struts) are usually placed to either side.

Queen-post roof

Another basic form of roof, this has two vertical members known as queen posts, placed symmetrically on a tie beam and commonly connected by a horizontal collar.

Waggon roof

Waggon, barrel or cradle roofs have closely set rafters supported by curved braces, and may be ceiled, panelled or left open. Viewed from the inside, the roof resembles a waggon, with a covering of canvas stretched over hoops.

Hammerbeam roof

This form of roof was used in England from the 14th century, and is most famously displayed at Westminster Hall, London (1399). It is supported by hammerbeams: short, horizontal brackets that project inwards and are often decoratively carved.

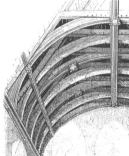

Crown-post roof

A crown-post roof, such as this one at Charney Bassett in Oxfordshire, England, has a vertical post standing centrally on a tie beam. Unlike a king post, it does not rise to the ridge of the roof, but stops short to support a longitudinal collar plate or purlin.

Vaulting

Arched roofs of stone, or vaults, have been a key element in architecture since pre-Roman times. In their simplest form they are constructed on two parallel walls, which, through the way the stones are shaped and laid, gradually slope in towards each other as they rise, eventually meeting and being conjoined by a central keystone. For a vault to support itself, when built above ground, its weight (which thrusts out as well as down) must be transferred to the ground through the structure of the walls and, if necessary, through buttresses. Vaulting was essential in creating the great basilican spaces of classical architecture and reached its zenith and greatest variety in the seemingly gravity-defying cathedrals of the Middle Ages.

Barrel vault
This is a concave vault (also known as a tunnel vault) that is uniform throughout its length. It is the earliest and most basic kind, with examples existing from the 9th century BC.

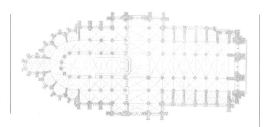

Cathedral vaulting
The vast area of a Gothic cathedral is covered by a complicated web of vaults, in contrast to the single barrel vault of a basilica.

Barrel-vault construction
A barrel vault is constructed over a timber skeleton or form, which is dismantled once the stones have created a full and self-supporting arch.

Buttressing
The buttress was developed to transfer the load of the vault to the ground, without massively thick walls. In Gothic architecture, its most refined form, it could even be detached from the building so that the light-weight glazed walls were unimpeded. Such 'flying buttresses' are seen in this illustration of Cologne Cathedral, Germany.

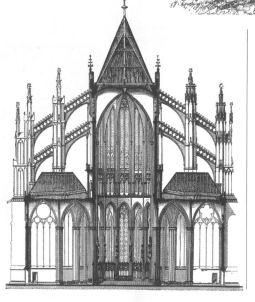

Groining

Where two tunnel vaults intersect at right angles they create ridges, or groins, as shown in this 11th-century church in Sweden. Where these groins are constructed on retained stone forms, rather than on timber ones that are removed, a rib vault is the result.

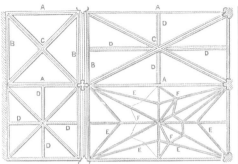

Rib-vault patterns

These range from a simple cross or groin *(top left)* to a complicated system of primary or ridge ribs, secondary or tierceron ribs, and tertiary or lierne ribs *(bottom right)*.

Lierne vault

One of the most sophisticated of Gothic vaults is found at Melrose Abbey, Scotland. Liernes – primarily decorative ribs – are employed, in addition to structural ribs, to create a web-like pattern across the vault.

Pendant vault

One of the last developments of Gothic vaulting was the pendant vault, in which a seemingly unsupported pendant (P) is in fact an extension of the keystone.

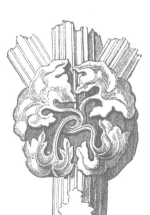

Boss

These projecting stones, often ornately carved, are employed at the intersection of the vault ribs, particularly where it occurs at the centre of a vaulted unit.

Rib decoration

Stone ribs were introduced to support the masonry between them and provided a means of creating sculptural decoration over the surface of the vault.

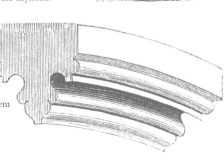

Stairways

Multiple combinations exist to achieve the characteristic role of stairways as an indispensable means of access between two levels or floors. Circular, L-shaped, U-shaped and even straight stairway plans, using varying numbers of flights and landings, are generally adapted to the cylindrical or cubic space that is available for the ascent. Steps, composed of treads (the top surface) and risers (the vertical sections in between), are sometimes painted or carved, but staircases commonly depend on ornamental handrails, banisters (vertical support for a handrail) and balustrades for their decoration. Stairways are also used symbolically and processionally to mark the importance of ascents, relying on breadth, steepness and height for their effect. The layouts of gardens and terraces often depend on the vistas and spatial opportunities offered by sequential flights of stairs.

Newel staircase

A newel staircase (spiral staircase or *caracole*) is a flight of stairs built on a circular plan supported by a central newel, or post. It is ideally suited to towers and spires.

Maya stairway

Stairways (often carved with hieroglyphs) were the most important feature of Maya pyramids. Climbing them constituted the apex of ritualistic life.

Rampant vault

Barrel-vaulted staircases in which the two abutments are set on an inclined plan, required careful engineering to ensure a safe distribution of the weight of the vault.

Stylobate

Antique temples were characteristically raised on platforms, or *stylobates*, partly or entirely composed of a flight of steps. The columns of the temple usually rested directly on the uppermost step.

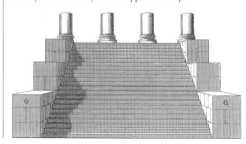

Tribune stairs

Interior tribune stairs in the eastern apses of churches are a form inherited from ancient Roman basilicas, where magistrates sat on high chairs. The speaker's chair or altar is symbolically raised above the masses in later basilicas and churches by means of a flight of stairs, often extending around the whole apse.

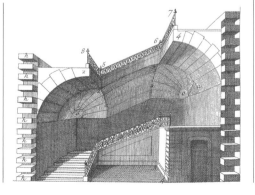

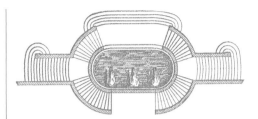

Garden steps

Flights of steps constituted the framework for the design of classical gardens. The flights were built in symmetrical patterns (often circular), with several landings allowing for views and pauses in the ascent.

Open-newel staircase

An open-newel staircase is built around a well, allowing a view down the core of the building, and is sometimes supported on columns. This design offers opportunities for elaborate balustrades, as well as interesting perspectives.

Open string

The sloping board that supports the end of the risers and treads of a staircase is known as the string or stringer. In an open string, as shown here, the top edge of the string follows the profile of the steps. In a closed string, the treads and risers of the staircase are concealed.

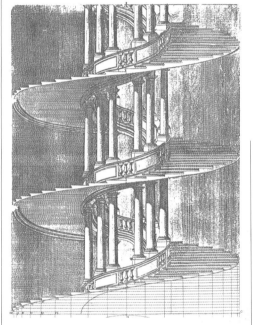

Balustrade

The classical stone balustrade was popular from the Renaissance onwards. Its composing balusters were short stems with an abacus (square slab), a base and either one or two bulbs with rings, *ovolo* (convex) and *cavetto* (concave) mouldings in between.

Stairwell

A stairwell is the vertical space in which a staircase turns. Neo-classical stairwells, in which the first flight faces a wall and continues in two curved flights to either side, were often the climax of the entrance hall and were dramatically lit by an oculus in the ceiling above.

Double-flight staircase

Double-flight staircases rising to a portico allowed for varied views of the house and gardens. In Palladian houses such flights were short, symmetrical and carefully proportionate to the rest of the frontage.

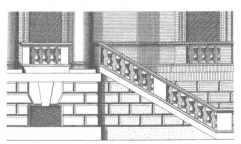

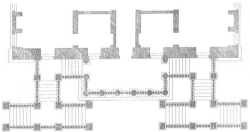

Glossary

Words in **bold** refer to other entries in the Glossary.

ABACUS In classical architecture, a flat square slab placed on top of a column's **capital**. In Roman **Doric** it has some **moulding**.

ACANTHUS A plant whose leaves form the basis for decoration of **Corinthian** and **Composite capitals**.

ACROPOLIS A citadel or fortress of a Greek city, containing temples and other public buildings, as in Athens.

ACROTERION (pl. **ACROTERIA**) A **pedestal** or base for an ornament or statue positioned on the angle or apex of a roof or **pediment**. Also the ornament or statue itself.

ADHISTHANA In Indian architecture, a high basement or **plinth** on which a temple was built.

ADOBE A sun-dried mud-brick used for buildings in Spain, Africa, New Mexico and Latin America.

ADYTUM The space in a Greek temple in which the statue of a god was placed. Also known as a naiskos or sekos.

AEDICULE A **shrine** within a temple, containing a statue and framed by two columns and a **pediment**. Sometimes refers to the framing with columns of an opening such as a door or window.

AEOLIC CAPITAL In classical architecture, a **capital** with an oblong top under which are two **volutes** or spiral **scrolls**.

AGORA An open space used as a market or meeting place in a Greek town. The equivalent of the Roman **forum**, it was usually surrounded by **colonnades** and public buildings.

AISLE In a church, hall or other building, the part that serves as a corridor, usually with an **arcade** of columns on one side.

ALL'ANTICA Refers to features built in imitation of the classical Greek and Roman styles.

ALMSHOUSE A building erected as a home for the old and poor, and financed by a private charity.

ALTAR A raised structure, often a table or stone slab, on which offerings are made to a god and religious rites are performed. Used in many ancient cultures for making sacrifices. In Christian churches it may be adorned with sculptures and other decoration.

AMBO A **pulpit** used for reading the Gospels or the Epistles, commonly found in Early Christian churches.

AMBULATORY The roofed passageway of a **cloister** or round the **apse** of a church.

AMPHIPROSTYLE Refers to a temple that has columns in **porticoes** at the front and back, but not along the sides.

AMPHITHEATRE A circular or elliptical auditorium surrounded by rising tiers of seats. Common throughout the Roman Empire, where they were used for gladiatorial contests and other entertainments.

ANDA A hemispherical dome that is the essential feature of a Buddhist **stupa**.

ANNULET A **moulding** that consisted of a ring around the **shaft** of a column. Also called a shaft-ring.

ANTA (pl. **ANTAE**) A **pier** or rectangular column whose base and **capital** are different from those associated with the **order** used elsewhere in the building. Antae are often found in temple **porticoes**, where they project out beyond the end walls.

ANTARALA A short **vestibule** between the **mandapa** and **garbhagriha** in an Indian temple.

ANTEFIXAE Decorated blocks used to hide the ends of tiles along the edge of a roof.

ANTEPAGMENTA In classical Greek architecture, a **moulding** around a doorway in the form of an **architrave**.

ANTHEMION Ornamentation based on the honeysuckle flower, commonly used in Greek and Roman architecture.

APADANA In ancient Persia, a columned hall used as an audience room. An apadana built in Persepolis in the 6th century BC had 100 columns.

APOPHYGE The concave curve in a column, either at the base where the **shaft** joins the base or at the top where the shaft joins the **capital.**

APPLIED Refers to a column that is attached to, or projects from a wall or **pier**. Also called an engaged column.

APRON A raised **panel** below a windowsill, sometimes decorated.

APSE The semi-circular or polygonal termination to part of a building, such as the **aisles** or **choir** of a church.

AQUEDUCT An artificial channel made for carrying water, either above or underground, which relies on a slight gradient to make the water flow. Invented by the Romans, aqueducts are often brick structures that include arches.

ARABESQUE Intricate decoration based on geometrical patterns and the stems, tendrils, flowers and foliage of plants and trees. It adorns the surfaces of buildings constructed by Muslims, who were forbidden the representation of animals by their religion. It was particularly popular among the Arabs and the Saracens or Moors in Spain.

ARCADE A series of arches supported by columns or **piers**. It may be free-standing or used to decorate the wall of a building, such as a church.

ARCH Construction of stones, bricks or other materials that spans an opening and does not employ a **lintel**. There are numerous different types.

ARCHITRAVE Lintel that spans the space between two columns or **piers**. May also be the moulded frame that surrounds a window, door or other opening.

ARCHIVOLT A form of **architrave** around a curved opening. May also be the ornamental **moulding** around the top of an arch.

ARCUATED Refers to a building whose structure depends on the employment of arches, as opposed to the beamed or **trabeated** form.

ASTRAGAL A small semi-circular **moulding** used in a variety of situations, such as around a column. Also called a bead-and-reel.

ASTYLAR Refers to a **façade** that has no **pilasters** or columns.

ATLANTES Supports in the shape of male figures used in place of columns. They were particularly popular in German **Baroque** architecture.

ATRIUM In Roman architecture, an inner court that was sometimes entirely covered, but usually left open in the middle. In Early Christian architecture it was an open court in front of a church, surrounded by **colonnaded porticoes**.

ATTACHED COLUMN A column attached to, or protruding from, a **pier** or wall. Also known as an engaged column.

ATTIC A space or room within the roof of a house. Also a low wall or storey above the **entablature** of a classical **façade**, as in a Roman **triumphal arch**.

AVANT-CORPS A section of a building that projects from the main part.

AZTEC A culture that flourished in the Valley of Mexico from the 15th century to the 1520s, and at its peak stretched from the Pacific to the Gulf coast. The architecture included many **pyramids** and temples.

BALCONY A platform projecting from the wall of a building. It has a **balustrade** or railing around its outer edge and access to it is usually through a door or window.

BALDACCHINO A **canopy** over, for example, a doorway, **altar** or throne. It may be supported by columns, attached to a wall, or suspended from a ceiling.

BALL-COURT In **Mesoamerican** civilisations, a court surrounded by high walls, with seating for spectators, in which the sacred game of ball was played. Each team attempted to pass a hard ball through one of two large sculpted stone rings attached to the sides of the court.

BALLFLOWER A decoration used in the 14th century, which consisted of a three-petalled flower around a small ball.

BALUSTRADE A series of short posts or pillars, called balusters, that support a rail.

BAND A **string course**, or any horizontal flat, or slightly projecting, strip of **moulding** on an exterior wall.

BANDED COLUMN A column whose **shaft** consists of alternately larger and smaller, decorated and less decorated, stone cylinders (drums).

BAPTISTERY A building or part of a building, such as a church, in which baptisms take place.

BAR TRACERY A form of **tracery** that originated at Reims in France and was first used in Britain around 1240, in which the lines of the window's slender stone **mullions** are extended upwards to form an outline for the decoration at the top.

BARBICAN A tower that protects the gate or drawbridge of a castle.

BARGEBOARD A board that hides the end of a horizontal roof timber. It may be decorated. Also called a **gableboard**.

BAROQUE A style of architecture dating from the 17th to the early 18th centuries. Originating in Rome, it is generally ornate and exuberant with an emphasis on balance between parts to create the perfect whole.

BARREL VAULT A concave **vault** that is uniform throughout its length. It is the simplest and earliest form of vault, with examples dating from the 9th century BC.

BARTIZAN A small **turret** attached to a corner on the top of a tower or **parapet**.

BASILICA An ancient Roman rectangular building that served as a hall of justice or market hall. It had a central **nave** and two side-**aisles**, and often galleries. The term also applies

to churches, such as the Early Christian churches, which have a nave and two or more aisles.

BAS-RELIEF A low-relief carving that protrudes slightly from the background.

BASTION A projecting part of a fortification that is used as a lookout.

BATTLEMENT A **parapet** or wall, often round a castle, with indentations or embrasures through which defending forces shot at their attackers. The raised sections are known as **merlons**.

BAY A vertical division of a building that is not denoted by a wall, but by some other means, such as a window, column or **buttress**.

BAY WINDOW A window within a curved or angular projection of a building.

BEAD-AND-REEL See **astragal**.

BEEHIVE TOMB A circular structure that has a dome and is built from rough stones. The earliest examples are prehistoric. See **tholos**.

BELFRY Usually the upper storey of a tower in which one or more bells are hung. The term may also refer to the whole bell tower, or to the area within a church **steeple** where the bells hang.

BELL GABLE A structure on a roof from which bells are hung. Also called a bellcote.

BELL TOWER A tower, either separate from or attached to a building such as a town hall, in which one or more bells are hung.

BELVEDERE A small lookout tower on the roof of a house. It is a form of gazebo, which may also be a summerhouse with a view of a park or garden.

BEMA A platform used by the clergy in Early Christian churches. It may also refer to a raised **pulpit** in a synagogue.

BIFORA A window in which two arched openings are separated by a vertical column.

BILLET A **Romanesque moulding** in which there are two or more rows of raised square or cylindrical blocks positioned at equal intervals.

BLIND ARCADE An **arcade** that is attached to a wall.

BLIND BALUSTRADE A **balustrade** that is attached to a wall.

BLIND WINDOW A decorative device on a wall that is made up of the parts of a window, but without any opening. It was first used in the medieval period.

BLOCKED COLUMN A column whose **shaft** includes square **rusticated** blocks. Also called a rusticated column.

BOSS An ornamental projection, usually at the intersection of **ribs** or beams in a ceiling or **vault**.

BRACKET A small supporting piece of stone, wood, metal or other material that projects from a wall.

BRACKET MOULDING A type of **moulding** dating from the late **Gothic** period, which consists of two **ogees** (each in the shape of an S or inverted S), with the convex parts touching each other.

BROACH SPIRE A **spire** with an octagonal plan on top of a square tower. Masonry or broach is built up over the base where it does not coincide with the octagonal plan.

BROKEN PEDIMENT A **pediment** that has its line interrupted either at the apex or base.

BUCRANIUM (pl. BUCRANIA) A sculptured ox-head, often garlanded, that appears in classical buildings.

BULL'S-EYE APERTURE See oeil-de-boeuf.

BUTTRESS A mass of stonework or brickwork built against, or projecting from a wall to give it additional strength. There are many different types of buttress, including the **flying buttress**.

BYZANTINE The architecture of the Byzantine Empire from AD 330 to 1453. The architecture that remains is largely ecclesiastical and includes numerous **basilicas**.

CAIHUA In Chinese architecture, polychrome painting applied to all the exterior and interior wooden parts of a building.

CALDARIUM In ancient Roman baths, a room for taking hot baths.

CAMPANILE An Italian **bell tower**, usually free-standing.

CANEPHORA A sculpture of a female figure carrying a basket on her head.

CANOPY A roof-like covering over, for example, an **altar**, door, window, tomb, **pulpit**, **niche** or statue.

CANTILEVER A horizontal projection from a wall, such as a balcony, step or beam, that is supported at one end only.

CAPITAL The top section of a column. Its shape and decoration generally denote the architectural **order** to which it belongs, such as **Doric** or **Ionic**.

CARTOUCHE An oval **panel**, typical of **Baroque** architecture, with crested or **scrolled** borders, used on **façades** as a framing device, but also as a purely decorative motif.

CARYATID A statue of a female figure, which is used in place of a column.

CASEMENT The part of a window that is attached to the upright window-frame by hinges.

CAVETTO Refers to a **moulding** that in section is about one quarter of a circle.

CEJIAO In Chinese architecture, the slight leaning of columns towards the centre of a building.

CELLA The main part of a classical temple, often containing a statue of the god to whom the temple is dedicated. Also called **naos**.

CENOTAPH A monument to one or more people who are buried elsewhere.

CHACMOOL A statue of a reclining human figure.

CHAÎNES A form of decoration that was particularly popular in 17th-century French domestic

Glossary

architecture, consisting of vertical **bands** of **rusticated** masonry, which divide a **façade** into **bays** or **panels**.

CHAITYA HALL An early Indian Buddhist hall that served as a temple and was cut out of rock. The main space was divided by two rows of columns into a **nave** and **aisles**.

CHAMFER The surface created when an edge or corner of a block of stone or wood is cut away, usually at an angle of forty-five degrees. The surface can be concave.

CHANCEL The eastern end of a church, beyond the point where the **nave** and **transept** intersect, which holds the main **altar** and the **choir** stalls. The term sometimes refers just to the area around the altar.

CHANTRY CHAPEL A chapel usually built inside a church and containing an **altar** and the tombs of a chantry's founder and his family. A chantry was a religious foundation endowed with money and lands by individuals, or sometimes guilds, who wished to have prayers and daily masses said for their souls.

CHAPEL A place inside – though sometimes outside – a church with a separate **altar**, often for worship in honour of a particular saint. Also a place for worship in a large house or institution, such as a prison or hospital.

CHAPTER HOUSE The room in a **monastery** where monks gathered on a daily basis to hear a 'chapter' from the Rule of their Order being read, and to discuss business affairs.

CHATEAU A country or manor house, or castle, most commonly found in France.

CHATRI A pillared **pavilion** on top of which is a dome. It is typical of Mughal architecture in 16th- and 17th-century India.

CHAULTRI A pillared hall built as part of an Indian temple complex.

CHENG In Chinese architecture, a city wall or 'to wall a city'. Also city.

CHEVRON A **Romanesque moulding** in the shape of a zigzag.

CHIGI Scissor-like decoration on the roof of a Japanese Shinto temple.

CHINOISERIE refers to European imitations of the style of Chinese art and architecture, which reached their height of popularity in the 18th century. They included numerous **pagodas**.

CHIWEN In Chinese architecture, a **finial** that stands at each of the two ends of a roof's ridgepole to cover the joint of the roof slopes.

CHOIR The section of a church, usually within the **chancel**, used by singers and clergy.

CHORTEN A Tibetan **stupa**.

CHUANDOU In Chinese architecture, the column-and-tie structure, in which the weight of a building's roof is borne directly by columns rising towards the ridge and receiving the **purlins**. A set of horizontal, transversal **tie beams** penetrates the bodies of the columns, knitting them together into a framework.

CHULLPA In pre-Columbian architecture, a sepulchral tower built to bury the dead with their possessions.

CIBORIUM A **canopy** over the high **altar** in a church, usually consisting of a dome supported on columns.

CINQUEFOIL See **foils**.

CIRCUS In Roman architecture, a roofless oblong building with tiers of seats on two sides and on one rounded end. It was most often used for horse or chariot racing.

CLERESTORY The upper section of a church above the **aisle**, which consists of a range of windows.

CLOISTER An enclosed space, usually a **quadrangle**, around which is a roofed walkway with a **colonnade** or **arcade** on the inside. It connects the domestic parts of a **monastery** with the church.

COFFERING Sunken **panels** used to decorate a ceiling, dome or **vault**.

COLONNADE A line of columns bearing arches or an **entablature**.

COLOSSAL ORDER See **giant order**.

COLUMN A free-standing vertical round pillar made up of a base, **shaft** and **capital**. It is normally a form of support, but may be erected on its own as a monument.

COMPOSITE ORDER The last and most elaborate of the **orders** in classical architecture. It was created by the Romans and combined elements of the **Ionic** and **Corinthian orders**.

COMPOUND PIER A **pier** with several **shafts**. Also called a clustered pier.

CONCH A semi-circular **niche** over which is a half-dome.

CONSOLE An ornamental **bracket** with a curved outline.

CORBEL A projecting **bracket**, usually made of stone, that supports a beam and is often decorated.

CORBEL TABLE A projecting layer of stones or bricks supported by a line of **corbels** and creating a **parapet**.

CORINTHIAN ORDER An **order** in classical architecture invented by the Athenians in the 5th century BC and later developed by the Romans. It is distinguished from the **Ionic** order mainly by the column's **capital**, which includes rows of **acanthus** leaves.

CORNICE In classical architecture the top section of an **entablature**. It is also the decorative **moulding** along the top of a building or a part of it, such as a wall, arch or **pedestal**.

CORONA The vertical upper part of a **cornice**.

COTTAGE ORNÉ A rustic building constructed for its **picturesque** qualities, such as a thatched roof and wooden beams. Such buildings were popular in England in the late 18th and early 19th centuries.

COUNTER-REFORMATORY DECORATION A form of decoration based on principles of dramatic emphasis, in which painted **stucco**, three-dimensional sculpture and fragmented architectural features are combined to frame large fresco **panels**.

COUR D'HONNEUR The forecourt of a French **hôtel** or private urban **villa**.

CREPIDOMA The stone platform of a Greek temple, usually with three steps.

CREST An ornamental ridge along the top of a wall or building.

CRESTERIA See **roof comb**.

CROCKET In **Gothic** architecture, an ornamental hook-like spur of stone that projects from the sides of a **gable**, **pinnacle** or **spire**. It may also decorate the **capital** of a column.

CROSS-DOMED Applied to a church built in the shape of a cross, with a dome over the centre. Such churches are associated with Early Christian and **Byzantine** architecture.

CROSSING The place in a church where the **nave**, **chancel** and **transept** intersect.

CROSS-IN-SQUARE The most widespread plan for **Byzantine** churches. It is composed of a central bay with four surrounding large rectangular bays and four smaller bays at the angles of the cross. The bays are either **domed** or **vaulted**.

CROSS-VAULT Another name for a groin **vault**, formed by two **barrel vaults** of identical size intersecting at right angles.

CROW STEPS Also known as corbie steps, used to decorate a **gable**.

CROWN-POST ROOF A roof with a vertical post standing centrally on a **tie beam**. Instead of rising to the ridge of the roof, the crown post supports a longitudinal **purlin**.

CRYPT A vaulted area beneath the main floor of a church, often housing tombs or relics.

CUBIFORM CAPITAL A **capital** whose shape is produced by the interpenetration of a cube and a hemisphere.

CUPOLA A **dome**, especially a miniature one crowning a **turret**, on a **drum** surmounted by a **lantern**.

CUSP A point where **foils** or **tracery** arcs meet in **Gothic** window tracery.

CYCLOPEAN In pre-classical Greek architecture, a term that refers to masonry constructed with very large irregular blocks of stone. Also refers to any masonry constructed from large, rough-hewn stone blocks.

CYMA REVERSA A double-curved **moulding**, convex in the upper part and concave below.

CYMATIUM In a classical **entablature**, the uppermost section of **moulding**.

DADO In classical architecture, the portion of a **pedestal** or **plinth** between the **cornice** and base.

DAGABA See **stupa**.

DAIS A raised platform at one end of a medieval hall.

DARGAH In Islamic architecture, an impressive entrance, gateway or doorway.

DECASTYLE Refers to a **portico** with ten columns across the front.

DECORATED The second of three phases in English **Gothic** architecture, dating from around 1250 to 1340. It was characterised by ornate **mouldings**, multiple **ribs**, and **ogees** in arches and in the **tracery** of windows.

DENTIL A small square block used in series in the **corona** of a classical **cornice**.

DIACONICON In **Byzantine** architecture, a room within or attached to a church.

DIAPER WORK Decoration consisting of a small repeated pattern, such as squares, that completely covers a surface.

DIAPHRAGM ARCH An arch across the **nave** of a church, which partitions the roof into sections.

DIOCLETIAN WINDOW See **thermal window**.

DIPTERAL A term that refers to a building with two rows of columns on each side.

DOME A curved **vault** on a circular or square base. In section it can be semi-circular, bulbous or pointed. When the base is square, **pendentives** or **squinches** are inserted at the corners to change it into a near-circle.

DORIC ORDER An **order** in classical architecture that is divided into Greek Doric and Roman Doric. The Greek Doric column was fluted, had no base and a **capital** with simple **moulding** and an **abacus**. The Roman Doric column was slimmer and non-fluted, and had a low base and smaller capital.

DORMER WINDOW A vertical window in a sloping roof, which has its own roof and **gable**.

DOSSERET In **Byzantine** and **Romanesque** architecture, a block or slab placed on top of an **abacus**.

DOUGONG In Chinese architecture, a **bracket** set (*dou* – bearing block, *gong* – bracket arm).

DRIP STONE A projecting **moulding** above a door, window or arch to provide protection from the rain. Also known as a hood mould.

DROP TRACERY A border of **pendant tracery** on the underside of a **Gothic** arch.

DRUM The vertical wall on which a **dome** or **cupola** sits. Also one of the cylindrical blocks that comprise the **shaft** of a column.

EARLY ENGLISH The first of three phases in English **Gothic** architecture, dating from the late 12th century to around 1250. During this time churches in England began to be built with pointed arches and **rib vaults**.

EAVES The lower edge of a sloping roof.

ECHINUS A convex **moulding** found between the **shaft** and **abacus** of a **Doric** column, and below the **volutes** of the **capital** in an **Ionic** column.

EFFIGY A portrait of a person, usually sculpted.

EGG–AND–DART A decorative **moulding** in which egg-shaped and arrowhead forms alternate.

ELEVATION The flat side or external face of a building. Also a drawing projected on a vertical plane showing the face of a building.

ENCEINTE The main area of a fortress, which is surrounded by a wall or ditch.

ENFILADE An arrangement of doors employed by the French that reveals a view when all the doors in a series of rooms are open.

ENTABLATURE In classical architecture, the section of a building that is supported by columns and consists of an **architrave**, **frieze** and **cornice**.

ENTASIS The slight swelling outwards used on classical columns to counteract the optical illusion of concavity in a straight-sided column.

ESPAGNOLETTE A long, hinged fastening on double French windows and doors, first used in the 17th century.

ESTIPITE A **pilaster** that gets narrower towards the base.

ETRUSCAN A civilisation that flourished in Italy *c.* 780–100 BC.

EXEDRA A large **apse**. Also a semi-circular or rectangular recess or **niche**.

FAÇADE An exterior face of a building, usually the front.

FANLIGHT A window over a door, often semi-circular in shape. Also the upper part of a window with hinges that allow it to be opened separately.

FASCIA A horizontal **band**, usually in an **architrave**. It may be in a series of two or three, each of which juts out slightly further than the one above.

FESTOON A form of decoration, often used in a **frieze** or **panel**, that consists of a garland of flowers and fruit, or length of cloth, perhaps tied with ribbons.

FILLET A narrow, slightly raised **band** between flutes in a column or round an arch. Also the top part of a **cornice**.

FINIAL An ornament, often knob-like and with a leafy pattern, on the top of a **pinnacle**, **gable**, **spire** or **canopy**.

FLAMBOYANT The late French **Gothic** style of the 15th and 16th centuries, characterised by flame-like **tracery** and elaborate carving.

FLÈCHE A slender **spire**, usually made of wood.

FLUTING Shallow concave channels that run vertically down the **shaft** of a **column** or **pilaster**. The channels may be separated by **fillets**.

FLYING BUTTRESS An arch or half-arch that gives extra support to the upper part of a wall by transmitting the thrust of a **vault** or roof to a support that stands outside.

FOILS The lobe-shaped curves between **cusps**, or projecting points, in **Gothic** window **tracery**. A prefix indicates the number of foils, as in cinquefoil (five foils).

FOLIATE BAND A **band** decorated with leaf-like patterns.

FOLLY A decorative building, usually in the form of a classical or **Gothic** ruin or a tower, built to add interest to the landscape.

FORUM An open space used as a market or meeting place in a Roman town. The equivalent of the Greek **agora**, it was usually surrounded by **colonnades** and public buildings.

FRETWORK Decorative geometrical carving or metalwork, sometimes with holes.

FRIEZE A horizontal **band** that may be painted or decorated with sculpture or **mouldings**. It may run along the upper part of a wall, or form the middle section of an **entablature**, between the **architrave** and **cornice**.

FRIGIDARIUM In ancient Roman baths, a room for taking a cold bath.

FRONTISPIECE The main **façade** of a building. Also a **pediment** over a door or window.

GABLE A triangular feature, often the upper section of a wall at the end of a **pitched roof**. It may also be used as a form of decoration above the **portal** of a **Gothic** building. The sides are usually straight, but some are curved, stepped or shaped in some other way.

Glossary

GABLEBOARD A wooden board placed along the sloping edges of a gable, sometimes to mask the ends of roof timbers. Also called a **bargeboard**, it can be plain or decorated.

GALILEE A **vestibule**, or sometimes a chapel, at the west end of a church.

GALLERY An upper storey on the interior wall of a secular building or a church, where it projects over an **aisle**. Also a long room in a large house or palace, used for recreation and sometimes to display paintings.

GARBHAGRIHA The most sacred part of an Indian temple, a small dark room in which the deity was placed.

GARGOYLE A water spout in the shape of a **grotesque** figure, which projects from a roof or wall.

GEORGIAN A style of English architecture between the early 18th and early 19th centuries, characterised by classical features.

GEKU In Japanese Shinto architecture, an outer **shrine** for a local god.

GIANT ORDER An **order** whose columns are several storeys high. Also called the colossal order.

GOPURAM A monumental towered gateway at the entrance to an Indian Hindu temple complex.

GOTHIC A general term for medieval architecture whose chief features were pointed stone arches, **rib vaults**, **flying buttresses** and windows with delicate **tracery** and coloured glass. First appearing in France in the mid-12th century, the style dominated European architecture for the next 350 years.

GREEK CROSS A cross with four arms of equal length.

GREEK REVIVAL A fashion in Europe and the USA, between the 1780s and 1830s, for imitating elements of ancient Greek architecture.

GROIN VAULT See **cross vault**.

GROTESQUE Painted or low-relief decoration based on ancient Roman decoration; it consisted of **arabesque**-like motifs with human figures and animals. It was first used, known as *grotte,* in 16th-century Italy after examples were discovered in underground Roman ruins.

GUILLOCHE A pattern of plaited bands used on a **moulding**.

HAMMERBEAM ROOF A roof in which short horizontal **brackets**, called hammerbeams, project inwards from opposite walls and support vertical beams called hammer-posts.

HARMONIC PROPORTIONS A system used by the Romans, and later developed by Italian **Renaissance** architects and subsequently by Andrea Palladio, under which proportions in buildings were related to music.

HELM ROOF A roof with four inclined faces that rise from **gables** and join at the top.

HEPTASTYLE Refers to a **portico** with seven columns across the front.

HEXASTYLE Refers to a **portico** with six columns across the front.

HIPPED ROOF A roof with four sides that slope upwards. Four 'hips' are formed by the meeting of two sloping surfaces.

HIPPODROME In ancient Greece and Rome a construction, usually without masonry, where horse and chariot races were held.

HONDO In Japanese architecture, originally an image hall in a Buddhist temple. From the 12th century, a temple to enter and pray in.

HOOD MOULD See **drip stone**.

HORSESHOE ARCH An arch in the shape of a round or pointed horseshoe, often a feature of Islamic buildings.

HÔTEL A French private urban **villa** built to a design established in the 16th century, in which the main part of the house and two wings surround a courtyard separated from the street by a wall or a stable and kitchen block.

HYPAETHRAL A construction with its central space wholly or partially open to the sky.

HYPOSTYLE A building, usually a large hall, in which the roof is supported by several rows of columns.

HYPOTRACHELIUM In a **Doric** column, the groove at the top of the shaft, below the **capital**.

ICONOSTASIS In a **Byzantine** church, a **screen** with three doors, placed across the **nave** and in front of the **altar**. From the 14th century it developed into a stone or wooden wall with icons.

IMPOST BLOCK A block between the **capital** and **abacus** of a column, which has splayed sides.

IN ANTIS A term that refers to the columns between the **antae**.

INCA A South American civilisation centred on Cuzco in Peru, dating from the 14th century to the 1530s. At its height, the Inca empire extended 4,200 km (2,600 miles) down the western coast.

INFILL Material used to fill a cavity, or a gap in something such as a row of buildings.

INTERCOLUMNIATION The space between adjacent columns, whose width is frequently a multiple of the diameter of the columns.

IONIC ORDER An **order** in classical architecture that originated in Asia Minor in the mid 6th-century BC. It is characterised by **scroll**-shaped **volutes** on the column's **capital**, **dentils** in the **cornice**, and a **frieze** that may bear continuous low-relief decoration.

IWAN In Islamic architecture, a large vaulted hall open on one side to a courtyard.

JALI In Islamic architecture, a perforated **screen** that fills an external window.

JAMB The vertical side-section of a door or window frame. Also the vertical inside face of an opening in a wall, such as an archway.

JETTY In a timber-framed building, the overhang of an upper storey created by making the beams and joists of the lower storey extend beyond the external wall.

JIAN In Chinese architecture, a **bay** or interval between columns.

JUANSHA In Chinese architecture, the equivalent of **entasis**.

KEY PATTERN An example of a fret, a repeated geometrical pattern made up of straight horizontal and vertical lines, used to decorate a **band**.

KEYSTONE The central stone of a semi-circular arch.

KHANQAH An Islamic **monastery**.

KING-POST ROOF A roof in which a vertical timber, known as the king post, rises from the centre of a transverse (**tie**) beam to meet a ridge-piece that runs along the roof's ridge.

KIOSK An open **pavilion** or summerhouse usually supported by pillars. Most often found in Turkey and Iran, a typical European adaptation is the bandstand.

KUMBHA In Indian architecture, a curved, cushion **capital**.

LABEL STOP An ornamental **boss** at each end of a **drip stone**.

LADY CHAPEL A chapel dedicated to the Virgin Mary.

LANCET WINDOW A tall, slender window with a pointed arch, typical of early **Gothic** architecture.

LANTERN A small circular or polygonal structure that crowns a dome, usually with windows and an open base to allow light to enter the space below.

LATH See **stambha**.

LESENE A rectangular column without a base or **capital**, which is built into a wall and projects slightly from it. It may be either a structural or a decorative feature.

LINTEL A wooden or stone beam across the top of an opening such as a window or door.

LOGGIA A **gallery** or room that is open on at least one side. It may be part of a building or separate, and it may have **piers** or columns.

LOUVRE An opening in the roof of a room to let out smoke from a centrally placed fire. Also one of a series of overlapping parallel slats in a window or door, which slope outwards and let in air while providing protection from rain.

LUCARNE A **dormer window** or a small opening in an **attic** or **spire**.

LUNETTE WINDOW A semi-circular window.

LYCH GATE A roofed gate to a churchyard, traditionally used as a place where a coffin could be temporarily placed – *lych* being a Saxon word for corpse.

MACHICOLATION A defensive construction that projects from a castle wall or tower and is supported by **corbels**. Openings in the floor between the corbels allowed boiling oil and missiles to be dropped on to attackers.

MADRASA An Islamic theological college.

MANASTAMBHA In Indian architecture, the Jain form of a **stambha** or column, which carries a small **pavilion** on its **capital**.

MANDALA In Indian architecture, a geometric diagram used as a plan for a Hindu or Jain temple.

MANDAPA In Indian architecture, an assembly hall for worshippers in a Hindu or Jain temple complex.

MANNERISM A term applied to the art and architecture of Italy, France and Spain between the High **Renaissance** and the **Baroque**, which is characterised by the use of motifs in a way that was not originally intended.

MANSARD ROOF A roof – named after the French architect François Mansart – with a double slope on each of its four sides. The lower sections are steeper and longer than the upper sections.

MARTYRIUM A structure erected on a site sacred to Christianity or symbolising an act of martyrdom. In Early Christian architecture a martyrium was often a circular structure, unless it was a church.

MASHARABIYYA A wooden **screen** or grille, common in houses in Islamic countries.

MASTABA An ancient Egyptian tomb that simulated the plan of a residence. A mound with a rectangular base, sloping sides and flat top covered a broad underground burial chamber.

MAUSOLEUM A large stately tomb.

MAYA A Native American civilisation composed of city-states, which developed in Mexico and north Central America from around 1500 BC and particularly flourished in the period AD 300-800. It went into decline from the 9th century and the Maya people were finally conquered by the Spanish in the 16th century.

MEGARON The central complex of a **Mycenaean** palace and the main domestic unit. It was a long, narrow suite composed of a columned **porch**, an antechamber and the megaron proper.

MERLON The raised section in a **battlement**.

MESOAMERICA A term that refers to Central America and the part of Mexico within which civilisations flourished from about 1000 BC until the Spanish conquest in the 16th century.

METOPE In a **frieze** of the **Doric order**, the rectangular area between two **triglyphs**. It may be left plain or decorated.

MIHRAB A **niche** in the wall of a **mosque** oriented towards Mecca.

MIMBAR The **pulpit** in a **mosque**.

MINARET A tall, usually slender tower with projecting balconies, which is connected to a **mosque**. It is used by the muezzin to call people to prayer.

MINOAN A Bronze Age civilisation that flourished in Crete around 2000–1450 BC.

MODILLION CORNICE A **cornice** whose protruding upper section rests on a series of small, paired **brackets** or **consoles**.

MODULE A unit of measurement used to determine proportions in the design of buildings. In classical

architecture it was commonly half the diameter of a column immediately above the base.

MONASTERY A group of buildings in which a religious community, usually of monks, lives in seclusion from the outside world.

MONOLITHIC Created from a single stone.

MORTICE AND TENON JOINT A joint consisting of a socket (mortice) into which a projecting piece (**tenon**) fits.

MOSAIC An area of surface decoration for a floor or wall composed of small pieces of stone, glass or marble set into cement, mortar (a mixture of cement or lime with sand and water) or mastic (putty-like adhesive).

MOSQUE An Islamic place of worship, usually with one or more **minarets**.

MOUCHETTE A curved, lancet-shaped motif with a round or pointed head, used in **tracery** of the **Decorated** style.

MOULDING A sculpted **band** with a distinctive profile, used to decorate a wide range of protruding surfaces, including column bases and **capitals**, door and window **jambs**, and the edges of **panels**.

MUDÉJAR A Spanish style of architecture that includes Islamic elements in the design of Christian buildings. The most notable examples date from the 13th and 14th centuries.

MULLION AND TRANSOM A mullion is an upright that divides an opening, usually a window, into two or more sections. A transom is a horizontal bar across the window.

MUQARNAS In Islamic architecture, ceiling decoration that resembles stalactites.

MUTULE In the **Doric order**, a rectangular slab that projects from under the **corona** of the **entablature**.

MYCENAEAN A civilisation that flourished in Greece around 1600–1200 BC.

NAIKU In Japanese Shinto architecture, an inner **shrine** for the ancestral god of the imperial family.

NAISKOS See **adytum**.

NAOS The principal enclosed area of a Greek temple, which contained the statue of a god or goddess.

NARTHEX An enclosed **porch** in front of the entrance of some Early Christian churches.

NAVE The central part of a church that runs from the main entrance to the **transept** or apse.

NEEDLE SPIRE A thin **spire** whose base is on a tower roof and is surrounded by a narrow walkway and **parapet**.

NEO-CLASSICISM The last phase of European classicism, dating from the late 18th century. It placed great emphasis on geometrical forms and the sparing use of ornamentation.

NEWEL The central pillar of a winding staircase. Also a post at the top or bottom of a staircase, to which the handrail is attached.

NICHE A concave recess in a wall, usually arched and housing statuary, an urn or other forms of decoration.

NORMAN In architecture, the **Romanesque** style in England dating from the Norman conquest of 1066 to around 1180, when the first buildings in the **Early English** style were constructed.

NYMPHAEUM A Roman building dedicated to nymphs and containing columns, statues and fountains, where people could relax.

OBELISK A tall stone **shaft**, usually granite, **monolithic** and tapering, originally a feature of ancient Egyptian architecture.

OCTASTYLE Refers to a **portico** with eight columns across the front.

OCULUS A round window or an opening at the apex of a dome.

ODEON (pl. **ODEA**) In ancient Greece and Rome, a hall for music that closely resembled a theatre, but was smaller and either partly or wholly roofed over.

Glossary

OEIL-DE-BOEUF A small round or oval window.

OGEE An S-shaped double curve often used in the design of **moulding** or of pointed **Early English** arches.

OLMEC A **Mesoamerican** culture that flourished around 1200–300 BC.

ONION DOME A pointed bulbous dome used on the top of churches and church towers, and common in Russia and eastern Europe.

OPENWORK Work, often decorative, that contains perforations.

OPISTHODOMOS The room within a Greek temple that is situated at the back, behind the **naos**.

OPUS RETICULATUM In Roman architecture, a construction consisting of **pyramid**-shaped stones laid on the diagonal into which concrete was poured.

OPUS SECTILE A covering on a wall or floor made up of tiles or slabs of marble cut to form geometric patterns.

ORATORY A small private chapel in a church or house that contained an **altar**.

ORDER A style of column and **entablature** in classical architecture. There were five orders: the **Doric**, **Ionic** and **Corinthian** were developed by the Greeks; and the **Tuscan** and **Composite** were developed by the Romans. May also refer to any arrangement of columns and **entablature**, as in the **giant order**.

ORIEL A **bay window** projecting from a wall.

PAGODA A tower that is several storeys high, often associated with Buddhism and most common in China, Japan and Nepal. Each storey may be slightly smaller than the one below and have its own roof and **balcony**.

PALAESTRA A privately owned Greek wrestling school, similar to a gymnasium.

PALAZZO An Italian palace or any impressive public building or private residence.

PALISADE A series of strong, thick poles forming a protective fence.

PALLADIANISM A style of building based on the publications of the Italian 16th-century architect Andrea Palladio, and particularly popular in England in the 18th century. It followed classical Roman conventions.

PALMETTE A fan-shaped decoration on the **capital** of a column, which resembles the leaves of a palm tree.

PANEL A flat-surfaced portion that is sunk below, or raised above, the surrounding area, and may be edged with **moulding**.

PARAKKLESION A **Byzantine** chapel that may be attached to another building or be free-standing.

PARAPET A low wall running the length of any feature, such as a balcony, **terrace** or bridge, immediately below which is a sudden drop. May also be a defensive wall, perhaps with **battlements**.

PASTOPHORY In an **Early English** or **Byzantine** church, a side-chamber flanking the **apse**.

PATERA In classical architecture, a small, flat circular or oval piece of decoration, often featuring **acanthus** leaves.

PAVILION A summerhouse or decorative building in a garden or park. May also be an addition to a larger building, in which case it will have a distinctive feature such as a domed roof. In Britain it may be a building at a sports ground, in which players can get changed.

PEDESTAL A support underneath a column, statue, urn or other feature. In classical architecture it consists of a **plinth** or base, on top of which is narrower but taller **dado** surmounted by a **cornice**.

PEDIMENT A low-pitched **gable** end of a building, usually above a **portico**. A distinctive feature of classical and classically inspired architecture, it is often decorated with high-relief sculpture.

PENDANT An elongated **boss** that hangs down from a vaulted roof or ceiling.

PENDENTIVE A concave, inverted triangular piece of masonry that helps to support a circular dome over a square or polygonal base.

PERIPTERAL A term that refers to a building surrounded by a single row of columns.

PERISTYLE A **colonnade** around a courtyard or the exterior of a building.

PERPENDICULAR The third of three phases in English **Gothic** architecture, dating from around 1340 to 1530. It places great emphasis on straight horizontal and vertical lines, with windows and wall surfaces often divided by **tracery** into numerous rows of rectangular **panels** with vertical **ribs**.

PERRON A platform or **terrace** on to which the door of a house, church or other building opens. It may also be a flight of steps leading to a terrace or doorway.

PEW A long bench-like seat in a church.

PIANO NOBILE The main floor in an Italian palace, where the reception rooms are located.

PICTURESQUE A term applied in 18th- and 19th-century England to landscapes and buildings that strike the imagination with the force of a painting. Examples included the **cottage orné** and the castellated **Gothic** house of the type designed by John Nash.

PIER A solid vertical support, often rectangular in shape and sometimes with a **capital** and base.

PILASTER A shallow **pier** that stands out slightly from a wall and in classical buildings has the features of one of the **orders**.

PILLAR See **pier**.

PINNACLE A small **turret**-like, usually ornamental construction at the top of a **spire**, **buttress** or some other part of a building.

PISCINA A shallow stone basin, usually within a **niche**. Also a pool or basin in Roman baths.

PISHTAQ In Islamic architecture, a large gateway.

PITCHED ROOF The most common type of roof, which has two slopes meeting at a central ridge and **gables** at both ends.

PLACE ROYALE A square in France, most commonly dating from the 17th century, with housing for the nobility.

PLATERESQUE Literally 'silversmith-like', a style of highly decorative architecture associated with 16th-century Spain.

PLAZA An open space or square.

PLINTH A block, usually square, that is the bottommost section of a column base. Also refers to a projecting bottom section of a wall.

PODIUM A large platform. More specifically, it may be a platform on which an ancient building was constructed, or a platform encircling the arena in an **amphitheatre** or **circus**.

PORCH A low structure, usually roofed, at the entrance to a building.

PORTAL An impressive entrance, gateway or doorway, often decorated.

PORTICO An open space with a roof supported by columns, at the entrance to a building such as a house, temple or church.

PRAKARA A courtyard surrounding an Indian Hindu temple and containing **shrines** and other structures.

PRASTARA The **entablature** in an Indian building.

PRECINCT An area with a fixed boundary, often in the form of a wall.

PRESBYTERY The area in a church that lies east of the **choir** and contains the high **altar**.

PRIORY A religious house governed by a prior or prioress.

PRONAOS A **portico** in front of the **cella** or **naos** in a classical temple, formed by the projection of the cella's side-walls. It has a row of columns along the front.

PROPYLAEUM (pl. **PROPYLAEA**) A monumental gateway, usually to the area around a classical temple.

PROPYLON In ancient architecture, a monumental gateway.

PROSTYLE A term that refers to a building that has a **portico** with columns only at the front.

PROTHESIS A room in a **Byzantine** church for storing the bread and wine used during Mass.

PSEUDODIPTERAL A term that refers to a temple with one row of columns on all sides.

PTEROMA A passageway in a Greek temple between a wall and a row of columns.

PTERON An external **colonnade**.

PULPIT A raised platform in a church where a preacher or reader stands.

PULPITUM A **screen** in a church that separates the **nave** from the **choir**.

PUMPKIN DOME A dome made up of concave sections with ridges, often found in Islamic architecture. Also called a melon or umbrella dome.

PURLIN A horizontal beam that runs the length of a roof and supports the common **rafters** on which the covering is laid.

PUTTI A decorative sculpture or painting that depicts naked infants.

PYLON In ancient Egyptian architecture, a structure consisting of sloping tower-like walls on either side of the entrance to a temple.

PYRAMID In ancient architecture, a huge stone structure with a square base and four triangular sloping sides that meet in a point at the top.

QIBLA In Islam, the direction of Mecca, to which all must turn when praying. The qibla wall in a **mosque** contains the **mihrab niche**.

QUADRANGLE A rectangular courtyard, often with buildings on all four sides.

QUADRATURA In **Baroque** buildings, the painted architecture found on walls and ceilings. It was often a continuation of three-dimensional architectural features.

QUADRIGA In classical architecture, a sculpture of a chariot drawn by four horses.

QUATREFOIL See **foils**.

QUBBA A dome in a **mosque** or over a Muslim tomb.

QUEEN-POST ROOF A roof with two vertical members, known as queen posts, which are placed symmetrically on a transverse **tie beam** and are commonly connected by a horizontal collar.

QUINCUNX A term that refers to a church, usually **Byzantine**, built on a **cross-in-square** plan.

QUOIN A large dressed stone at the corner of a building, used either for reinforcement or for decoration. Quoins are often placed above each other so that there are alternating large and small faces.

RADIATING CHAPELS Chapels that project radially from an **ambulatory**.

RAFTER One of a number of sloping beams that form the framework of a roof.

RAKING CORNICE A **cornice** that follows the slope of a roof, **gable** or **pediment**.

RATH/RATHA An Indian temple cut from a block of granite. The most notable examples date from the 7th century.

RAYONNANT The mid-French **Gothic** style of the 13th and 14th centuries, characterised by radiating lines of **tracery**.

REEDING Decoration made up of adjacent, parallel convex **mouldings** known as reeds.

RELIEF CARVING A carving that protrudes from a flat background.

RELIEVING ARCH An arch built into a wall over an arch, doorway or window to discharge the weight of the wall above.

RENAISSANCE The period in European history and culture, between the 14th and 16th centuries, when there were dramatic advances in the arts and learning as a result of a 'rebirth' of knowledge about classical Greece and Rome. The architecture was a revival of the classical style of ancient Rome.

REREDOS An ornamental **screen** behind an **altar**.

RETROCHOIR The space behind the high **altar** in a church.

REVETMENT A facing, usually of stone, that is intended to be more attractive or durable than the wall it covers.

RIB A slender, projecting arched **band** on a **vault** or ceiling, which has a structural or decorative purpose.

RIWAQ A hall in a **mosque** with a **colonnade** or **arcade**.

ROCAILLE Ornamentation associated with the 18th-century **rococo** style, which is based on the shapes of water-worn rocks and shells.

ROCOCO The last phase of the **Baroque** style, which originated in France in the mid-18th century. It is characterised by rich decoration – with an infinitely varied repertoire of motifs – and light, colourful interiors.

ROMANESQUE A style of architecture that developed in the 6th century from an interest in Roman imperial culture. It is characterised by use of the round arch and **basilica** plan.

ROOD TOWER A tower built above the **crossing** in a church.

ROOF COMB Generally a wall along the ridge of a roof. In Classic **Maya** architecture, a feature on the summit of a **pyramid** that consisted of two pierced framework walls leaning against each other with attached **stucco** relief sculpture. Also called a cresteria.

ROSE WINDOW A large circular window with **tracery** arranged like the spokes of a wheel. Common in **Gothic** buildings.

ROSETTE A small, flat, circular or oval piece of decoration with a floral motif, made from stone or wood and often attached to a wall.

ROTUNDA A circular building or room, usually domed.

ROUNDEL A small circular and ornamental window or **panel**.

RUSTICATED/RUSTICATION Refers to masonry consisting of large cut stone blocks that are smooth or roughly hewn.

SACRISTY A room in a church where **altar** vessels and the clergy's vestments are kept.

SALOMÓNICA Spanish term for a spirally fluted, or 'solomonic' column.

SANCTUARY The area in a church around the main **altar**.

SANCTUM The most sacred place of a temple. Also an especially private place.

SANGHARAMA A residential court in an early Buddhist **vihara** or **monastery**.

SARCOPHAGUS A stone coffin, often elaborately decorated with sculpture and bearing inscriptions.

SAUCER DOME A **dome** that is not supported by a vertical wall and is **segmental**.

SCAGLIOLA A material that imitates marble and is used to cover the surfaces of columns, **pilasters** and other interior features.

SCALLOP ORNAMENT A piece of decoration in the shape of a shell.

SCOTIA A concave **moulding** such as that on the base of a classical column.

SCREEN A partition, usually of stone or wood, that divides one part of a building or room from another.

SCREENS PASSAGE In a medieval hall, the space between a screen and any doors to the kitchen, buttery and pantry.

SCROLL An ornament or **moulding** in the shape of a partly rolled scroll of paper. An example is

Glossary

the **volutes** found on the **capitals** of some classical columns.

SEDILIA Seats for the clergy (usually three), which are built into the **chancel** wall to the south of the **altar**.

SEGMENTAL Refers to an arch or any other curved feature whose shape is less than a semi-circle.

SEKOS See **adytum**.

SEMI-DOME A **dome** that covers a semi-circular area such as an **apse**.

SEPULCHRE A burial **vault** or tomb.

SERLIAN ARCADE A **rusticated arcade**, often limited to three arches, that is characteristic of Palladian houses and heightens the importance of the first floor and central block.

SHAFT The main vertical part of a column, between the base and **capital**.

SHENGQI In Chinese architecture, the gradual increase in the length of the columns from the centre to the sides of a building.

SHOJI A sliding **screen** that partitions the **vestibule** from the inside rooms in a Japanese house.

SHRINE A container or building in which sacred relics have been placed. Also a site associated with a sacred person, which may contain the person's tomb and be a place of worship.

SIKHARA A beehive-shaped tower in a north Indian temple.

SOFFIT The underside of an architectural feature such as an arch, balcony or **vault**.

SOLAR A room on an upper floor in a medieval house.

SOLEA A raised walkway in an **Early English** or **Byzantine** church that runs between the **ambo** and **bema**.

SPANDREL A roughly triangular area next to the curve of an arch on the left-hand and right-hand sides, or between two arches or the adjacent **ribs** of a **vault**. It is often decorated.

SPHINX In ancient Egyptian architecture, a figure with the body of a lion and a human head.

SPIRE A tall, slender structure that tapers to a point and rises from a roof or tower.

SPLAY-FOOT SPIRE A **spire** that is square at its base but octagonal for most of its height.

SQUINCH A small arch, or sometimes a **lintel**, positioned across the angle of a square or polygon structure to make it more round.

SQUINT An obliquely cut small opening in the wall of a church that allows the high **altar** to be viewed from places where it cannot otherwise be seen.

STADIUM In ancient Greece, a running track. Generally, a sports ground that is usually oval in shape.

STAMBHA In Indian architecture, a free-standing monumental column constructed close to a **stupa** or in front of a temple. Also called a lath.

STEEPLE A tower with a **spire** on top, as in a church.

STELA An upright stone slab decorated with an inscription and possibly a figure, often marking a grave. Also a vertical surface, with a commemorative inscription, on the wall of a building.

STEREOBATE A base constructed from solid masonry for a building, particularly one that includes a row of columns.

STIFF-LEAF A form of sculpted foliage in medieval buildings, usually on **capitals** and **bosses**.

STOA A long, narrow building with an open **colonnade** in place of one or two of the long walls.

STOMION The deep entrance, fronted by a doorway, of a **Mycenaean tholos** or tomb.

STRAPWORK A form of ornamentation in which a number of bands are interlaced.

STRING COURSE A continuous horizontal course of masonry that is either flush with, or projects from

the surface of the surrounding wall. It is usually narrower than other courses and moulded.

STRUT A subsidiary timber that helps to provide support to a principal member of a roof.

STUCCO A durable plaster made of gypsum, lime and sand, for external work. Also a fine plaster used for internal decorative work.

STUPA A Buddhist **shrine** in the form of a hemispherical **dome** (**anda**), built to commemorate Buddha and his teachings or to honour a sacred site or event.

STUPIKA A diminutive **stupa** that sometimes tops a gateway (**gopuram**) to an Indian Hindu temple complex.

STYLOBATE The top step of three comprising a **crepidoma**. More generally, a continuous platform of masonry that supports a **colonnade**.

SUKIYA STYLE A style of Japanese domestic architecture that was informed by the architecture of the tea-house from the late 16th century onwards.

SUN DISC A disc that represents the sun and has wings, and is usually associated with ancient Egyptian architecture.

SUTRADHARA The chief architect of a classical Indian temple, who helped to oversee the temple's construction.

SWAG A **festoon** in the form of a length of draped fabric.

SYNTHRONON The seating for the clergy in a **Byzantine** or Early Christian church, usually within the **apse**.

TABERNACLE A recess or **niche**, with a **canopy**, whose function is to contain a statue. Also a small decorated box on the **altar** of a church, which contains the sacrament of the Eucharist.

TABLINIUM A room in a Roman house that marked the division between public and private areas, and stood between the **atrium** and **peristyle**.

TAILIANG In Chinese architecture, a column-beam-and-**strut** structure in which columns rise up to a roof supported by beams placed vertically over one another and separated by struts.

TALA One of a series of stepped tiers in the tower of a **rath**.

TALAR A tank in an Indian temple complex, used for bathing and sacred purposes.

TALUD-TABLERO In **Mesoamerican** architecture, a feature associated with stepped temple **pyramids**, in which an outward sloping section (*talud*) supports a rectangular, vertical **panel** (*tablero*) that is treated as a **frieze**.

TAMAGAKI In a Japanese Shinto **shrine**, a wooden fence of horizontal boards attached to upright posts.

TATAMI A straw mat in a Japanese house, which has a standard size and is used as a unit of area in measuring and planning the size of rooms.

TEE A **finial**, often in the form of an umbrella, at the top of a **stupa** or **pagoda**.

TEMENOS The sacred **precinct** of a Greek temple.

TEMPIETTO A small, usually ornamental temple dating from the 16th century onwards.

TENON See **mortice and tenon joint**.

TEPIDARIUM The warm room in Roman baths.

TERRACE A platform in front of a building or flat-topped embankment. Also a row of buildings, which are attached to each other on both sides.

TESSERA A small piece of glass or marble used in the construction of a **mosaic**.

TETRACONCH A shape consisting of four lobe-shaped curves that join in points.

TETRASTYLE Refers to a **portico** with four columns across the front.

THEATRE A building for viewing dramas and other types of performance, which in ancient Greece and Rome was entirely open-air.

THERMAE In ancient Rome, public baths.

THERMAL WINDOW A semi-circular window that is divided into three lights by **mullions** running from the outer curve to the straight base. Also known as a Diocletian window.

THOLOS A beehive-shaped tomb dating from the **Mycenaean** period, or any beehive-shaped building.

TIE BEAM The main horizontal transverse beam in a roof.

TITHE BARN A barn used for storing a parish's agricultural tithe, a tax – often in the form of produce – paid for the support of the clergy.

TOLTEC Ancient Native American civilisation that dominated central Mexico from AD 900 to 1200. Among the main features of Toltec architecture are multiple rows of columns and narrative relief **panel**.

TOOTH ORNAMENT A form of ornamentation in **Gothic moulding**, made up of four-petalled flowers with projecting central points.

TOPE See **stupa**.

TORANA In Indian architecture, a gateway, particularly to the area around a Buddhist **stupa**.

TORII In Japanese architecture, a gateway to a Shinto **shrine**.

TORUS A convex **moulding** that generally forms the bottom section of a column's base.

TOURELLE A **turret**.

TRABEATED Refers to a form of construction that uses a horizontal beam over supports, as opposed to the arched or **arcuated** form.

TRACERY The ornamental intersecting stonework in **Gothic** windows, **panels** and **screens** and on the surface of Gothic **vaults**.

TRANSEPT The arm that crosses the **nave** of a church at right angles to produce a cross-shaped plan.

TRANSITIONAL Refers to the period of transition from the **Romanesque** or **Norman** to the **Gothic** style.

TRANSOM See **mullion and transom**.

TRAPEZOIDAL Refers to a quadrilateral in which two parallel sides are of unequal length.

TRAVERTINE A variety of limestone.

TREFOIL See **foils**.

TRIBUNE In classical architecture, a raised platform. Also the **apse** of a **basilica**.

TRIFORIUM An arcaded wall passage that runs parallel to the **nave** in a medieval church. In a three-storey building, it is between the ground-level **arcade** and the **clerestory**; in a four-storey building it is between the **gallery** and the clerestory.

TRIGLYPH A form of decoration in a **Doric frieze**, which consists of three vertical blocks separated by V-shaped grooves or glyphs.

TRIUMPHAL ARCH A free-standing monumental arch or gateway commemorating a great victory in battle. The triumphal arch originated in Rome during the second century BC.

TROPHY A sculptured composition of arms and armour commemorating a victory.

TSUI-TATE In Japan, a low free-standing **screen**.

TUDOR ARCH An arch whose sides start as curves but then straighten out to meet in a point at the apex. It was a common feature of Tudor architecture in England, a form of **Perpendicular Gothic** that developed between 1485 and 1547, during the reigns of Henry VII and Henry VIII.

TUMULUS A mound constructed over a tomb chamber or grave.

TURRET A small tower, often projecting from the corner of a building or wall.

TUSCAN ORDER The simplest of the Roman **orders**. Closest in style to the Greek **Doric**, one of its most notable characteristics is a plain **frieze**.

TYMPANUM The triangular space enclosed by the **mouldings** of a **pediment**. Also the delineated space, often semi-circular, between the **lintel** of a door and the arch situated above it.

TZOMPANTLI In **Mesoamerican** civilisations, a skull rack on which the heads of sacrificed people were deposited.

UNDERCROFT A vaulted room, sometimes partly or totally below ground, often under a church.

UPASTHANASALA In Indian architecture, a meeting hall in a Buddhist or Jain **monastery**.

URUSRINGA In Indian architecture, a small representation of a **sikhara** or tower of a temple used to decorate the sikhara itself.

USHNU In **Inca** architecture, a sacred table.

VAULT An arched roof or ceiling of stone or brick.

VEDIKA A railing that encloses a paved pathway around a **stupa**.

VENETIAN WINDOW A large window divided by columns or **piers** into three lights. The central light is larger than the other two and is often arched. Also called a Palladian or Serlian window.

VERANDAH A covered **porch** or balcony that extends along one or more walls of a building and is open on the outer side.

VERMICULATION A form of decoration on stonework that consists of wavy lines resembling worm tracks.

VESTIBULE An anteroom or entrance area.

VESTRY A room in a church in which sacred vessels and the robes of the clergy and **choir** are kept.

VIHARA In Indian architecture, a Buddhist or Jain **monastery**.

VILLA In Roman and **Renaissance** architecture, a house on a country estate.

VIMANA The multistorey, pyramidal tower of a Dravidian temple.

VITRUVIAN SCROLL A classical form of decoration, often used in **friezes**, in which a wave-like band connects a series of **scrolls**. Also called a running dog.

VOLUTE A spiral **scroll**, the principal feature of an **Ionic** column.

VOUSSOIR A wedge-shaped stone or brick used in the construction of an arch or **vault**.

WAGGON ROOF A roof with closely set **rafters** supported by curved braces, which may be left open, giving the effect of being inside a waggon with a covering of canvas stretched over hoops.

WAVE MOULDING A form of **moulding** typical of the **Decorated** style, in which interlocking convex and concave curves represent the breaking of waves.

WHEEL WINDOW See **rose window**.

XIAOSHOU In Chinese architecture, **acroteria**, each in the form of a fantastic animal, which are placed in line on the sloping ridge at the corner of a roof.

XOANON In ancient Greece, a crude wooden statue of a deity that was housed in a primitive hut.

YASTI The pole above the **tee** on the **pinnacle** of an Indian Buddhist **stupa**.

ZIGGURAT A form of religious monument built in Sumer, Babylon and other Middle Eastern civilisations between 3000 and 600 BC. It had a rectangular or square base and was constructed as a truncated, stepped **pyramid** with rectangular or square tiers. A series of ramps led to a **shrine** at the top.

Bibliography

ANCIENT EGYPT

ALDRED, C., *Egyptian Art*, London, 1988

BADAWY, A., *A History of Egyptian Architecture*, Giza, 1954–68, 3 vols

EDWARDS, I. E. S., *The Pyramids of Egypt,* Harmondsworth, 1985

GORRINGE, H. H., *Egyptian Obelisks*, New York, 1882

MEHLING, M. (ed.), *Egypt*, Oxford, 1990

PETRIE, W. M. FLINDERS, *Egyptian Architecture*, London, 1938

SETON-WILLIAMS, V., *Egypt*, London, 1993 (3rd edn)

SMITH, W. STEVENSON, *The Art and Architecture of Ancient Egypt*, Harmondsworth, 1958 (revised edn 1981)

UPHILL, E. P., *The Temples of Per Ramesses*, Warminster, 1984

WILKINSON, SIR JOHN GARDNER, *The Architecture of Ancient Egypt*, London, 1850

BABYLON, ASSYRIA AND PERSIA

FERGUSSON, J., *The Palaces of Nineveh and Persepolis Restored*, London, 1851

FRANKFORT, H., *The Art and Architecture of the Ancient Orient*, Harmondsworth, 1954 (revised edn 1970)

LAYARD, A. H., *Monuments of Nineveh*, London, 1849, 2 vols

LAYARD, A. H., *Nineveh and Its Palaces*, London, 1849, 2 vols

LEICK, G., *A Dictionary of Ancient Near Eastern Architecture*, London, 1988

MALLOWAN, M. E. L., *Nimrud and Its Remains*, London, 1966, 2 vols

O'KANE, B., *Studies in Persian Art and Architecture*, Cairo, 1995

POPE, A. U., *Persian Architecture*, London, 1965

POPE, A. U. and ACKERMAN, P., *A Survey of Persian Art*, Oxford, 1939

EARLY AND CLASSICAL INDIA

ALLEN, MARGARET PROSSER, *Ornament in Indian Architecture*, London, Newark and Toronto, 1991

BROWN, PERCY, *Indian Architecture: Buddhist and Hindu Periods*, Bombay, 1971 (6th edn)

BURGESS, JAMES, *The Ancient Monuments, Temples and Sculptures of India*, London, 1911

FERGUSSON, J., *History of Indian and Eastern Architecture*, London, 1910 (revised edn), 2 vols

HARLE, J. C., *The Art and Architecture of the Indian Subcontinent*, London and New Haven, 1994

HAVELL, E. B., *The Ancient and Medieval Architecture of India: A Study of Indo-Aryan Civilisation*, London, 1915

MEISTER, MICHAEL W. (ed.), *Encylopaedia of Indian Temple Architecture: Foundations of North Indian Style c. 250 BC–AD 1100*, Delhi, 1988

MEISTER, MICHAEL W. (ed.), *Encyclopaedia of Indian Temple Architecture: North India, Period of Early Maturity c. AD 700–900*, Delhi, 1991, 2 vols

MEISTER, MICHAEL W. (ed.), *Encylopaedia of Indian Temple Architecture: South India, Lower Dravidadosa 200 BC–AD 1324*, Delhi, 1983

MICHELL, GEORGE, *The Penguin Guide to the Monuments of India, Volume One: Buddhist, Jain, Hindu*, London, 1990

MURTY, K. SATYA, *Handbook of Indian Architecture*, New Delhi, 1991

EARLY AND DYNASTIC CHINA

BOYD, ANDREW, *Chinese Architecture and Town Planning, 1500 BC–AD 1911*, London, 1962

KESWICK, MAGGIE, *The Chinese Garden: History, Art and Architecture*, New York, 1986 (2nd edn)

LIANG SSU-CH'ENG, *A Pictorial History of Chinese Architecture: A Study of the Development of its Structural System and the Evolution of its Types*, ed. Wilma Fairbank, Cambridge, MA, 1984

LIU DUNZHEN (ed.), *Zhongguo Gudai Jianzhu Shi (A History of Ancient Chinese Architecture)*, Beijing, 1980

LIU DUNZHEN, *Suzhou Gudian Yuanlin (Classical Gardens of Suzhou)*, Beijing, 1979

MORRIS, EDWIN T., *The Gardens of China: History, Art and Meanings*, New York, 1983

SICKMAN, LAURENCE and SOPER, ALEXANDER, *The Art and Architecture of China*, Harmondsworth, 1971 (3rd edn)

STEINHARDT, NANCY SHATZMAN, *Chinese Imperial City Planning*, Honolulu, 1990

STEINHARDT, NANCY SHATZMAN (ed.), *Chinese Traditional Architecture*, New York, 1984

TITLEY, NORAH and WOOD, FRANCES, *Oriental Gardens*, London, 1991

XU YINONG, *The Chinese City in Space and Time: The Development of Urban Form in Suzhou*, Honolulu, 2000

ZHANG YUHUAN (ed.), *Zhongguo Gudai Jianzhu Jishu Shi (A History of Ancient Chinese Architectural Technology)*, Beijing, 1985

CLASSICAL JAPAN

BALTZER, FRANZ, *Die Architektur der Kultbauten Japans*, Berlin, 1907

DRESSER, CHRISTOPHER, *Japan: Its Architecture, Art and Art Manufactures*, London, 1882

FUJIOKA, M., *Shiro to Shoin*, Tokyo, 1973

INAGAKI, E., *Jinja to Reibyo*, Tokyo, 1968

KAWAKAMI, M. and NAKAMURA, M., *Katsura Rikyu to Shashitsu*, Tokyo, 1967

MASUDA, T., *Living Architecture: Japanese*, London, 1971

MORSE, EDWARD S., *Japanese Homes and Their Surroundings*, London, 1888

NAKANO, G., *Byodoin Hoodo (The Pavilion of the Phoenix at Byodoin)*, Tokyo, 1978

OTA, H., *Japanese Architecture and Gardens*, Tokyo, 1966

PAINE, R. and SOPER, A., *The Art and Architecture of Japan*, Harmondsworth, 1974

SANSOM, G. B., *A Short History of Japanese Architecture*, Rutland, VT, 1957

STANLEY-BAKER, JOAN, *Japanese Art*, London, 1984 and 2000

PRE-COLUMBIAN

COE, MICHAEL D., *The Maya*, London, 1995 (5th edn)

COE, MICHAEL D., *Mexico from the Olmecs to the Aztecs*, London, 1995

HEYDEN, DORIS and GENDROP, PAUL, *Pre-Columbian Architecture of Mesoamerica*, London, 1988

HYSLOP, JOHN, *Inka Settlement Planning*, Austin, 1990

KOWALSKI, JEFF KARL (ed.), *Mesoamerican Architecture as a Cultural Symbol*, Oxford and New York, 1999

KUBLER, GEORGE, *The Art and Architecture of Ancient America*, London and New Haven, 1993

MILLER, MARY ELLEN, *The Art of Mesoamerica from Olmec to Aztec*, London, 1986

PASZATORY, ESTHER, *Pre-Columbian Art*, London, 1998

RUTH, KAREN, *Kingdom of the Sun, the Inca: Empire Builders of the Americas*, New York, 1975

STIERLIN, HENRI, *The Maya, Palaces and Pyramids of the Rainforest*, Cologne, 2001

PRE-CLASSICAL

BOËTHIUS, AXEL., *Etruscan and Early Roman Architecture*, Harmondsworth, 1978

HAYNES, SYBILLE, *Etruscan Civilisation*, London, 2000

LAWRENCE, A. W., *Greek Architecture*, London and New Haven, 1996 (5th edn)

MARTIN, ROLAND, *Greek Architecture: Architecture of Crete, Greece, and the Greek World*, London, 1980

MATZ, FRIEDRICH, *Crete and Early Greece: The Prelude to Greek Art*, London, 1962

MYLONAS, GEORGE E., *Mycenae and the Mycenaean Age*, Princeton, 1966

STIERLIN, HENRI, *Greece: From Mycenae to the Parthenon*, London and Cologne, 2001

TAYLOUR, LORD WILLIAM, *The Mycenaeans*, London, 1964

ANCIENT GREECE

LAWRENCE, A. W., *Greek Architecture*, London and New Haven, 1996 (5th edn)

MARTIN, ROLAND, *Greek Architecture: Architecture of Crete, Greece, and the Greek World*, London, 1980

SCRANTON, ROBERT L., *Greek Architecture*, London, 1962

STIERLIN, HENRI, *Greece: From Mycenae to the Parthenon*, London and Cologne, 2001

TAYLOR, WILLIAM, *Greek Architecture*, London, 1971

TOMLINSON, R. A., *Greek Architecture*, Bristol, 1989

ANCIENT ROME

BOËTHIUS, AXEL, *Etruscan and Early Roman Architecture*, New Haven and London, 1994

BROWN, F. E., *Roman Architecture*, New York, 1961

MACDONALD, W. L., *The Architecture of the Roman Empire*, New Haven, 1965–86 (revised edn 1982), 2 vols

MACKAY, A. G., *Houses, Villas and Palaces in the Roman World*, London, 1975

NASH, E., *Pictorial Dictionary of Ancient Rome*, London, 1961–2 (2nd edn 1968), 2 vols

PLATNER, A. B. and ASHBY, T., *A Topographical Dictionary of Ancient Rome*, London, 1929

SEAR, F. B., *Roman Architecture*, London, 1982

SUMMERSON, J., *The Classical Language of Architecture*, London, 1980

VITRUVIUS, *On Architecture*, London and New York, 1931 (Bks I–V), 1934 (Bks VI–X)

WARD-PERKINS, J. B., *Roman Imperial Architecture*, London and New Haven, 1994

WHEELER, M., *Roman Art & Architecture*, London, 1964

EARLY CHRISTIAN AND BYZANTINE

KRAUTHEIMER, RICHARD, *Early Christian and Byzantine Architecture*, Harmondsworth, 1981

LASSUS, JEAN, *The Early Christian and Byzantine World*, London, 1967

MAINSTONE, ROWLAND J., *Hagia Sophia: Architecture, Structure and Liturgy of Justinian's Great Church*, London, 1988

MANGO, CYRIL, *Byzantine Architecture*, New York, 1976

MATHEWS, THOMAS F., *The Byzantine Churches of Istanbul: A Photographic Survey*, Pennsylvania, 1976

MILBURN, ROBERT, *Early Christian Art and Architecture*, Aldershot, 1988

RODLEY, LYN, *Byzantine Art and Architecture: An Introduction*, Cambridge, 1994

WHARTON, ANNABEL JANE, *Art of Empire: Painting and Architecture of the Byzantine Periphery, A Comparative Study of Four Provinces*, Pennsylvania, 1988

ISLAMIC

BLAIR, S. S. and BLOOM, J. M., *The Architecture of Islam 1250–1800*, London and New Haven, 1994

BLOOM, J. M., *Minaret: Symbol of Islam*, Oxford, 1994

COSTA, P. M., *Studies in Arabian Architecture*, Aldershot, 1994

CRESWELL, K. A. C., *A Bibliography of the Architecture, Arts and Crafts of Islam*, Cairo, 1962 and 1973

DAVIES, PHILIP, *The Penguin Guide to the Monuments of India, Volume Two: Islamic, Rajput and European*, London, 1989

ETTINGHAUSEN, R. and GRABAR, O., *The Art and Architecture of Islam 650–1250*, London and New Haven, 1987

FRISHMAN, M. and KAHN, H. U. (eds.), *The Mosque: History, Architectural Development and Regional Diversity*, London, 1994

GRABAR, O., *The Great Mosque of Isfahan*, London, 1987

HARLE, J. C., *The Art and Architecture of the Indian Subcontinent*, London and New Haven, 1994

HILL, D. and GRABAR, O., *Islamic Architecture and its Decoration*, London, 1964

HILLENBRAND, R., *Islamic Architecture*, Edinburgh, 1994

HOAG, JOHN D, *Islamic Architecture*, New York, 1997

KUHNEL, E., *Islamic Art and Architecture*, London, 1966

MAYER, L. A., *Islamic Architects and Their Works*, Geneva, 1956

MICHELL, GEORGE (ed.), *Architecture of the Islamic World: Its History and Social Meaning*, London, 1978 (2000 edn)

ROMANESQUE

ARCHER, L., *Architecture in Britain & Ireland: 600–1500*, London, 1999

BROOKE, C. N. L., *The Twelfth Century Renaissance*, London, 1969

BUSCH, H. and LOHSE, B. (eds.), *Romanesque Europe*, London, 1960

CONANT, KENNETH J., *Carolingian and Romanesque Architecture 800 to 1200*, Harmondsworth, 1973

DUBY, G., *The Europe of the Cathedrals, 1140–1280*, Geneva, 1966

EVANS, J. (ed.), *The Flowering of the Middle Ages*, London, 1966

FERNIE, ERIC, *The Architecture of Norman England*, Oxford, 2000

HOOKER, D. (ed.), *Art of the Western World*, London, 1989

KUBACH, HANS ERICH, *Romanesque Architecture*, London, 1988

OURSEL, R., *Living Architecture: Romanesque*, London, 1967

SWARZENSKI, H., *Monuments of Romanesque Art*, London, 1974

WATKIN, D., *A History of Western Architecture*, London, 1986

GOTHIC

ARCHER, L., *Architecture in Britain & Ireland: 600–1500*, London, 1999

ARSLAN, E., *Gothic Architecture in Venice*, New York, 1971

BONY, J., *French Gothic Architecture Twelfth to Thirteenth Century*, London and Berkeley, 1983

BRANNER, R., *St Louis and the Court Style in Gothic Architecture*, London, 1964

FRANKL, P., *Gothic Architecture*, Harmondsworth, 1962

GRODECKI, LOUIS, *Gothic Architecture*, London, 1986

HARVEY, J. H., *The Gothic World 1100–1600*, London, 1950

HENDERSON, G., *Gothic*, Harmondsworth, 1967

PUGIN, A. and A. W., *Examples of Gothic Architecture*, London, 1838–40, 3 vols

WHITE, JOHN, *Art and Architecture in Italy 1250 to 1400*, Harmondsworth, 1966

WOOD, MARGARET, *The English Mediaeval House*, London, 1965

Bibliography

RENAISSANCE

ACKERMAN, J. S., *The Villa: Form and Ideology of Country Houses*, London, 1995

ALBERTI, LEON BATTISTA, *On the Art of Building in Ten Books*, translated by J. R. Rykwert *et al.*, Cambridge, MA, 1988

BLUNT, ANTHONY, *Art and Architecture in France 1500–1700*, London and New Haven, 1999 (5th edn)

BLUNT, ANTHONY, *Artistic Theory in Italy 1450–1600*, Oxford and New York, 1978

HEYDENREICH, L. H. (revised by P. Davies), *Architecture in Italy 1400–1500*, London and New Haven, 1996

LOTZ, W. (revised by D. Howard), *Architecture in Italy 1500–1600*, London and New Haven, 1995

MILLON, H. and LAMPUGNANI, V. M. (eds.), *The Renaissance from Brunelleschi to Michelangelo: The Representation of Architecture*, Milan, 1994

MURRAY, PETER, *Architecture of the Renaissance*, New York, 1971

PALLADIO, ANDREA, *Four Books of Architecture*, English translation, New York, 1965

SUMMERSON, JOHN, *Architecture in Britain, 1530–1830*, London and New Haven, 1993

THOMSON, D., *Renaissance Architecture: Critics, Patrons, Luxury*, Manchester, 1993

WATKIN, D., *English Architecture*, London, 1979 (reprinted 1990)

WITTKOWER, R., *Architectural Principles in the Age of Humanism*, London and New York, 1988

BAROQUE AND ROCOCO

BLUNT, ANTHONY, *Art and Architecture in France 1500–1700*, London and New Haven, 1999 (5th edn)

BLUNT, ANTHONY, *Baroque and Rococo, Architecture and Decoration*, London, 1978

BOTTINEAU, YVES, *Iberian–American Baroque*, ed. Henri Stierlin, Cologne, 1995

DOWNES, KERRY, *English Baroque Architecture*, London, 1966

HEMPEL, EBERHARD, *Baroque Art and Architecture in Central Europe*, Harmondsworth, 1965

MARTIN, JOHN RUPERT, *Baroque*, London, 1989

MILLON, HENRY A. (ed.), *The Triumph of the Baroque, Architecture in Europe 1600–1750*, London, 1999

MINOR, VERNON HYDE, *Baroque and Rococo, Art and Culture*, London, 1999

NORBERG-SCHULZ, CHRISTIAN, *Baroque Architecture*, London, 1986

NORBERG-SCHULZ, CHRISTIAN, *Late Baroque and Rococo Architecture*, London, 1986

SUMMERSON, JOHN, *Architecture in Britain, 1530–1830*, London and New Haven, 1993

VARRIANO, JOHN, *Italian Baroque and Rococo Architecture*, Oxford and New York, 1986

WITTKOWER, RUDOLF, *Art and Architecture in Italy 1600–1750*, London and New Haven, 1999 (6th edn)

PALLADIANISM

BARNARD, TOBY and CLARK, JANE (eds), *Lord Burlington, Architecture, Art and Life*, London, 1995

BOLD, JOHN, with REEVES, JOHN, *Wilton House and English Palladianism*, London, 1988

CAMPBELL, COLEN, *Vitruvius Britannicus*, London, vol. I 1715, vol. II 1717, vol. III 1725

HARRIS, JOHN, *The Palladian Revival, Lord Burlington, His Villa and Garden at Chiswick*, London and New Haven, 1994

HARRIS, JOHN, *The Palladians*, London, 1981

PARISSIEN, STEVEN, *Palladian Style*, London, 1994

SUMMERSON, JOHN, *Architecture in Britain, 1530–1830*, London and New Haven, 1993

SUMMERSON, JOHN, *Inigo Jones*, London and New Haven, 2000

TAVERNOR, ROBERT, *Palladio and Palladianism*, London, 1991

WITTKOWER, RUDOLF, *Palladio and English Palladianism*, London, 1983

WORSLEY, GILES, *Classical Architecture in England, The Heroic Age*, London and New Haven, 1995

NEO-CLASSICAL

ADAM, ROBERT and JAMES, *Works in Architecture*, London, 1778

The Age of Neo-classicism, Arts Council exhibition catalogue, London, 1972

CROOK, J. M., *The Greek Revival*, London, 1972

HAMILTON, G. H., *The Art and Architecture of Russia*, Harmondsworth, 1983

HONOUR, HUGH, *Greek Revival Architecture in America*, Oxford, 1944

KALNEIN, W. G. and LEVEY, M., *Art and Architecture of the Eighteenth Century in France*, Harmondsworth, 1972

MIDDLETON, R. D. and WATKIN, D., *Neo-classical and Nineteenth-century Architecture*, London, 1977

PIERSON, W. H., *American Buildings and Their Architects: The Colonial and Neo-classical Styles*, New York, 1970

STILLMAN, D., *English Neo-classical Architecture*, London, 1988

SUMMERSON, JOHN, *Architecture in Britain, 1530–1830*, London and New Haven, 1993

WATKIN, D. and MELLINGHOFF, T., *German Architecture and the Classical Ideal, 1740–1840*, London, 1986

WIEBENSON, DORA, *Sources of Greek Revival Architecture*, London, 1969

WORSLEY, GILES, *Classical Architecture in Britain, The Heroic Age*, London and New Haven, 1995

PICTURESQUE

ARNOLD, D. (ed.), *The Georgian Villa*, Stroud, 1996

BALLANTYNE, A., *Architecture, Landscape and Liberty: Richard Payne Knight and the Picturesque*, Cambridge, 1977

DANIELS, S., *Humphry Repton: Landscape Gardening and the Geography of Georgian England*, London and New Haven, 1999

HARRIS, J., *The Architect and the British Country House*, Washington, 1985

HUSSEY, CHRISTOPHER, *The Picturesque: Studies in a Point of View*, London, 1983

LINDSTRUM, D. (ed.), *The Wyatt Family*, RIBA catalogue, Farnborough, 1974

LOUDON, J. C., *The Encyclopedia of Cottage, Farm and Villa Architecture*, London, 1833

LOUDON, J. C., *The Landscape Gardening and Landscape Architecture of the Late Humphry Repton*, London, 1840

MACDOUGALL, E. (ed.), *John Claudius Loudon and the Early Nineteenth Century in Great Britain*, Dumbarton, 1980

MANSBRIDGE, M., *John Nash: A Complete Catalogue*, London and New York, 1991

ROWAN, A., *Robert and James Adam: Designs for Castles and Country Villas*, Oxford, 1985

STAMP, G., *The Great Perspectivists*, London, 1982

SUMMERSON, JOHN, *Architecture in Britain, 1530–1830*, London and New Haven, 1993

TEMPLE, N., *John Nash and the Village Picturesque*, Gloucester, 1979

WATKIN, D., *The Buildings of Britain: Regency*, London, 1982

WATKIN, D., *The English Vision: The Picturesque in Architecture, Landscape and Garden Design*, London, 1982

Index

Index

Index

Index

Index

ACKNOWLEDGEMENTS
The publisher would like to thank
Steve Parissien and Neil Burton for
their help and advice.